BUILT IN MILWAUKEE
AN ARCHITECTURAL VIEW OF THE CITY

BUILT IN MILWAUKEE
AN ARCHITECTURAL VIEW OF THE CITY

Prepared for

The City of Milwaukee, Wisconsin

Henry W. Maier, Mayor

William Ryan Drew, Commissioner, Department of City Development

by

Landscape Research

Built in Milwaukee is published by the City of Milwaukee, Henry W. Maier, Mayor, and the Department of City Development, William Ryan Drew, Commissioner.

Landscape Research Project Staff

Gail Hunton

Lance Neckar

Carole Zellie

Editor
Randy Garber

Department of City Development

John Bechler, Deputy Commissioner
Michael Holloway, Project Director
Jenann Olsen, Director of Planning
Beverly Johnson, Staff

Research Assistance

Robin Wenger

State Historical Society of Wisconsin
Historic Preservation Division

Jeffrey M. Dean, Head, Historic Preservation Division
Barbara M. Wyatt, Chief of Survey and Planning
Diane Filipowicz, Architectural Historian
Robbie Regner, Grants Coordinator

Acknowledgements

Many people have assisted the project staff during the preparation of **Built in Milwaukee,** and their help is gratefully acknowledged:

George Johnson and Chuck Cooney, Milwaukee County Historical Society

Christine Schelshorn, George Talbot, Myrna Williamson and Jack Holzhueter, State Historical Society of Wisconsin

John Steiner, Bay View Historical Society

Stanley Mallach and Wilbur Stolt, Special Collections, UWM Library

Orvil Liljequist and Paul Woehrmann, Milwaukee Public Library

James Boerner, Bureau of Bridges and Public Buildings

Ted Rozumalski

Marsha Warkentin and Raoul Ehr

Carl Reinhold

Linda Kopp

Cover: A fine example of a turn-of-the-century duplex on Milwaukee's South Side.

order from
The University of Wisconsin Press
114 North Murray Street
Madison, Wisconsin 53715

ISBN 0-299-97015-9
LIBRARY OF CONGRESS
CATALOG CARD NO.: 81-70932

Preparation of **Built in Milwaukee** was funded through the U.S. Department of Housing and Urban Development under the provisions of Title I of the Housing and Community Development Act of 1974 as amended. A matching grant was received from the State Historical Society of Wisconsin, funded by the U.S. Department of the Interior, Heritage Conservation and Recreation Service, under provisions of the National Historic Preservation Act of 1966, as amended. Historic preservation grants-in-aid are administered in Wisconsin in conjunction with the National Register of Historic Places Program by the Historic Preservation Division of the State Historical Society of Wisconsin. However, the contents and opinions contained in this publication do not necessarily reflect the views or policies of the Department of the Interior or the State Historical Society of Wisconsin.

Table of Contents

Introduction

I Historical Landscape 2

II Residential Architecture and Building Types 26

III Architecture of Commerce and Industry 72

IV Civic Structures 98

V Open Space, Public Parks, and Urban Design 110

VI Religious Buildings 130

VII Milwaukee Architects 138

VIII Area Survey Notes 144

North Side 146

Northwest Side 154

West Side 162

South Side 170

East Side 180

Menomonee Valley 190

IX Glossary 198

X Footnotes 200

XI Bibliography 208

XII The National Register of Historic Places in Milwaukee 211

Introduction

In 1979, the City of Milwaukee, with funding assistance from the State Historical Society's Historic Preservation Division, initiated a comprehensive architectural survey of the city. The project's goal was to identify and document structures and sites of architectural and/or historical significance built prior to 1930. The survey, completed in 1980, was carried out by three architectural historians and was conducted on a street-by-street and building-by-building basis.

A survey form, with an accompanying photograph, was completed for each of the approximately 6600 sites. Nearly one-third of the sites were included in proposed historic districts or local conservation districts. A variety of sources was used to document the buildings and structures. For buildings constructed after 1889, when building permits were issued systematically, the Building Permit Records located in Milwaukee City Hall provided an excellent source for construction dates, architects and builders. For sites older than 1889, and for those lacking building permit records, a combination of maps, atlases, city directories, archives, local histories, and newspapers was used. Property deeds were researched in only a few instances due to time constraints and the size of the survey.

In addition to survey forms, photographs, and mapped sites, the survey team compiled a research bibliography and index of Milwaukee's architectural history and geographical development. Thus, the eighteen month project not only documented individual sites, but also contributed to an overall understanding of the city's development and the architectural character of its neighborhoods.

The survey is used as an aid in determining the eligibility of sites and structures to the National Register of Historic Places; to help evaluate the impact of federally-funded projects; and to help establish boundaries for historic districts. Additionally, the survey provides an important tool for planning housing rehabilitation, commercial revitalization, and neighborhood conservation.

This book is intended to share the information developed during the survey. For years, Milwaukee's building history has been the subject of local interest. Many of its landmark buildings are well-documented. Often, however, the city lost individual structures of exceptional quality, as well as areas whose history and physical fabric, which, in retrospect, might have warranted conservation. In the past two decades, national public concern over unguided, or misguided, environmental change has prompted legislation to protect historically and architecturally significant structures, and to encourage their restoration. The National Historic Preservation Act of 1966, the National Environmental Protection Act of 1972, and the Tax Reform Act of 1976 all testify to a changing attitude among Americans regarding their rich architectural legacy. A growing interest in architectural conservation, rehabilitation, and adaptive re-use among homeowners and businessmen is the grass-roots counterpart to national legislation. Public concern for Milwaukee's historical environment has been one of the primary reasons for undertaking the survey and this book. It is intended that this book will help the people of Milwaukee understand their city's architectural past, create interest in conserving Milwaukee's diverse neighborhoods, and stimulate thought about appropriate future change in the urban environment. It is hoped that readers will gain an appreciation of how their homes, workplaces, and recreation areas fit into the city's past, and why they deserve a place in its future.

This book is based on data from the architectural survey, maps and iconography, and a review of the many published sources on Milwaukee. Materials from the Menomonee Valley Industrial survey (State Historical Society of Wisconsin/University of Wisconsin-Milwaukee, 1980) were also used.

Structures and sites of all kinds are described within the context of the growth and change of the city from its settlement to 1930. The text highlights not only the monumental, but also the ordinary and the typical in Milwaukee's building history. Our premise is that a tanning factory, a corner store, or a neighborhood of frame cottages is material for architectural interest as much as a mansion or a city hall. This book does not, however, provide a complete catalog of Milwaukee's built environment. It is selective by necessity and design. Because of the survey emphasis on pre-1930 buildings, the recently annexed outlying areas of the city are excluded.

This publication does not pretend to offer new scholarship in local history, geography, or architectural history. Rather, it has benefited from an excellent body of scholarly sources on Milwaukee. The work of Milwaukee's many nineteenth and early twentieth century historians is acknowledged, as is Bayrd Still's comprehensive urban biography published in 1948 (see bibliography). The architectural research and publications of individuals such as Richard Perrin, Mary Ellen Young, and H. Russell Zimmermann were forerunners in recording and championing the city's landmarks. Excellent recent books and theses which examine the city's geographical and ethnic development include Kathleen Conzen's *Immigrant Milwaukee, 1836-1860;* Craig Reisser's "Immigrants and House Form in Northeast Milwaukee"; and Roger Simon's "The Expansion of an Industrial City: Milwaukee 1880-1910". In addition, the Index to the *Milwaukee Sentinel,* which covers the years 1837 through 1890, was indispensable in recovering primary material on all facets of the city's past. Credit must also be given to the mapmakers, lithographers, and photographers of Milwaukee whose craft and artistry have left the city with a rich iconographic collection. Unfortunately, because of the scope of this publication, only a fraction of this fine visual record could be presented here.

State Historical Society of Wisconsin

"Milwaukie," the harbor, August 11, 1852. This drawing by a traveler, Adloph Hoeffler, gives some sense of the topography and architectural scale of the city at mid-century.

BUILT IN MILWAUKEE
AN ARCHITECTURAL VIEW OF THE CITY

I Historical Landscape

Foundations

State Historical Society of Wisconsin

"Milwaukee Fifty Years Ago - A View Up the River." Drawn about 1877, this romanticized view of the 1820s landscape looks north up the Milwaukee River.

I am convinced that there are many layers of history and that the final reading will be delayed until the gift of seeing past and future as one is restored to us.

— Henry Miller.

When looking at a specific place, one first sees its physical shape: its topography, scale, boundaries, and buildings. But closer views can also reveal how a culture's hopes, needs, values, and ideology shape and materialize in the environment. Thus, in outlining Milwaukee's broad geographical history from its settlement to 1930, both physical and cultural characteristics are included. This opening chapter is a "bird's eye view" of the city's growth, while succeeding chapters detail Milwaukee's building history and neighborhood character.

Water has been a central force in shaping Milwaukee's physical and economic landscape. The city owes its existence to the confluence of the Milwaukee and Menomonee Rivers into Lake Michigan. At the mouth of the rivers, an estuary provided a safe harbor along the western coast of Lake Michigan, and the rivers afforded access to inland regions. Long before the first white settlers speculated upon the promise of the site for a city, the Indians had recognized its advantages for human habitation. Archeological evidence indicates that the Indians occupied the area in prehistoric times. In his studies of Indian remains during the 1830s and 1840s, Increase Lapham found over one hundred earthworks and burial mounds (in the shapes of birds, mammals, lizards, and man) within the present city limits. Accounts of French explorers of the seventeenth and eighteenth centuries reported mixed bands of Indians living in the Milwaukee area, composed mostly of Potawatomi and Ottawa, with some Chippewa and Menomonees. In the middle of the 1700s, the site began to develop as a French-Canadian trading post, and by the 1830s it prospered under the direction of Solomon Juneau. By the early nineteenth century, the Wisconsin Indian population was in social and political flux due to the advancing frontier of white settlers. Communities of Potawatomi, Menomonee, and Chippewa Indians lived in and around Milwaukee, and traded with early white settlers.[1]

The name Milwaukee, reputedly meaning "the Beautiful Land," appears in travel accounts of the seventeenth and eighteenth centuries as Melleoiki, Millwakey, and Milwarck among other spellings. Pioneer Daniel Fowler was among many who postulated about the origins of the place-name Milwaukee. In his paper read to the Old Settlers' Club in 1876, he suggested that the name derived from the Indian word "Mahn-a-wawkie," meaning good land, and signifying "a good place for game, fish, and to harvest the marromin (wild rice)."[2]

Early accounts also reveal much about the appearance of the natural landscape at the time of exploration and first settlement. A "Map of Milwaukee in 1836" as recalled by early settlers reveals some of these land features while superimposing section lines and street names for contemporary reference.[3]

Low wetlands lined the banks of the Milwaukee and Menomonee Rivers. This estuary was alive with fish, waterfowl, and many species of birds. On the south side, a narrow promontory of land (Walker's Point) was surrounded by tamarack swamp and marsh which extended to the river's mouth. A wild rice swamp, covered with at least two feet of water, lay along the west bank of the Milwaukee River in an area roughly bound by Wisconsin Avenue on the north, Fourth Street on the west, and the Menomonee River on the south. Above Wisconsin Avenue, the ground was dryer and tamarack, black ash, tag alder and cedar grew along the riveredge lowlands. Cherry Street was the northern terminus of the wetlands. Soft and boggy land skirted the east side of the Milwaukee River. The area south of Clybourn Street was entirely marsh except for two islands and a strip of land along the beach. According to pioneer James Buck, this lake beach "was at least ten feet in height and from one hundred to two hundred feet wide." It was thickly covered with white cedar, balm of Gilead, crab apple, and oak.[5]

At the edge of the wetlands, steep bluffs rose to dry high lands. These bluffs, cut by springs and ravines, had rounded fronts and were heavily vegetated. On some bluffs, poplar and hazel trees were interspersed with a few black and bur oaks. Wild plum trees were found in one part of Walker's Point. On the east side above Wisconsin Avenue, a few oaks and a series of small sand dunes punctuated a thick growth of small bushes. Black, bur, and white oaks dominated the west side bluffs. Beyond the bluffs lay a gently rolling terrain of deciduous forest and prairie.[6]

Milwaukee's topography influenced the physical and political character of the early settlement. The watercourses divided the area into three sections: east, west, and south. Indian land cessions following the Black Hawk War opened southeastern Wisconsin to Yankee settlement in 1833. By 1835 lands had been surveyed and were ready for public sale. By then, however, a handful of promoters had claimed the lands which comprised the original nucleus of Milwaukee. Morgan L. Martin, in partnership with Solomon Juneau, staked out the eastern wedge between the lake and the river as a townsite. Byron Kilbourn, an Ohio engineer and surveyor, chose the west side of the Milwaukee River. The third developer, George H. Walker, established his claim south of the river junctions on a peninsula which became known as Walker's Point. Thus, Milwaukee's development began as three separate speculative ventures. Sectional rivalry among the original town-makers, "induced by the speculative origins of the towns and fostered by the existence of the river barrier," characterized Milwaukee from the beginning.[7]

The 1830s were the heyday of land speculation and townsite promotion in the territory between the Alleghenies and the Mississippi River. In

For the last million years the area which Milwaukee occupies was covered and shaped by glaciers and earlier versions of Lake Michigan. Prehistoric shorelines exist above the present lake level as terraces, wave-cut cliffs, and abandoned gravel and sand beaches. The soil is primarily glacial drift: unassorted till, stratified gravel, sand and clay, which cover a bedrock of ancient sea bottom sediments.[4]

Milwaukee in 1836.

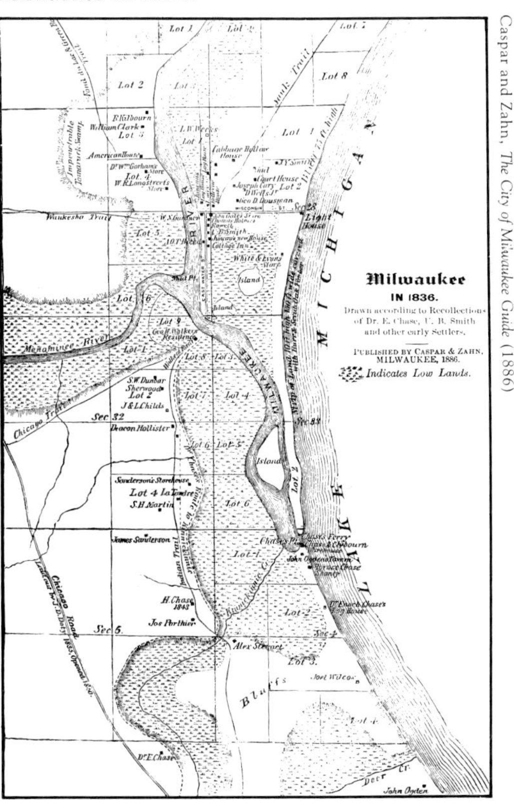

Caspar and Zahn, *The City of Milwaukee Guide* (1886)

Milwaukee, this not only produced competing settlements but also influenced the original layout of the village. In 1835 Kilbourn and Juneau filed their respective plats for the west and east sides. Both plats followed the gridiron plan of repetitive rectangular blocks which was a common layout

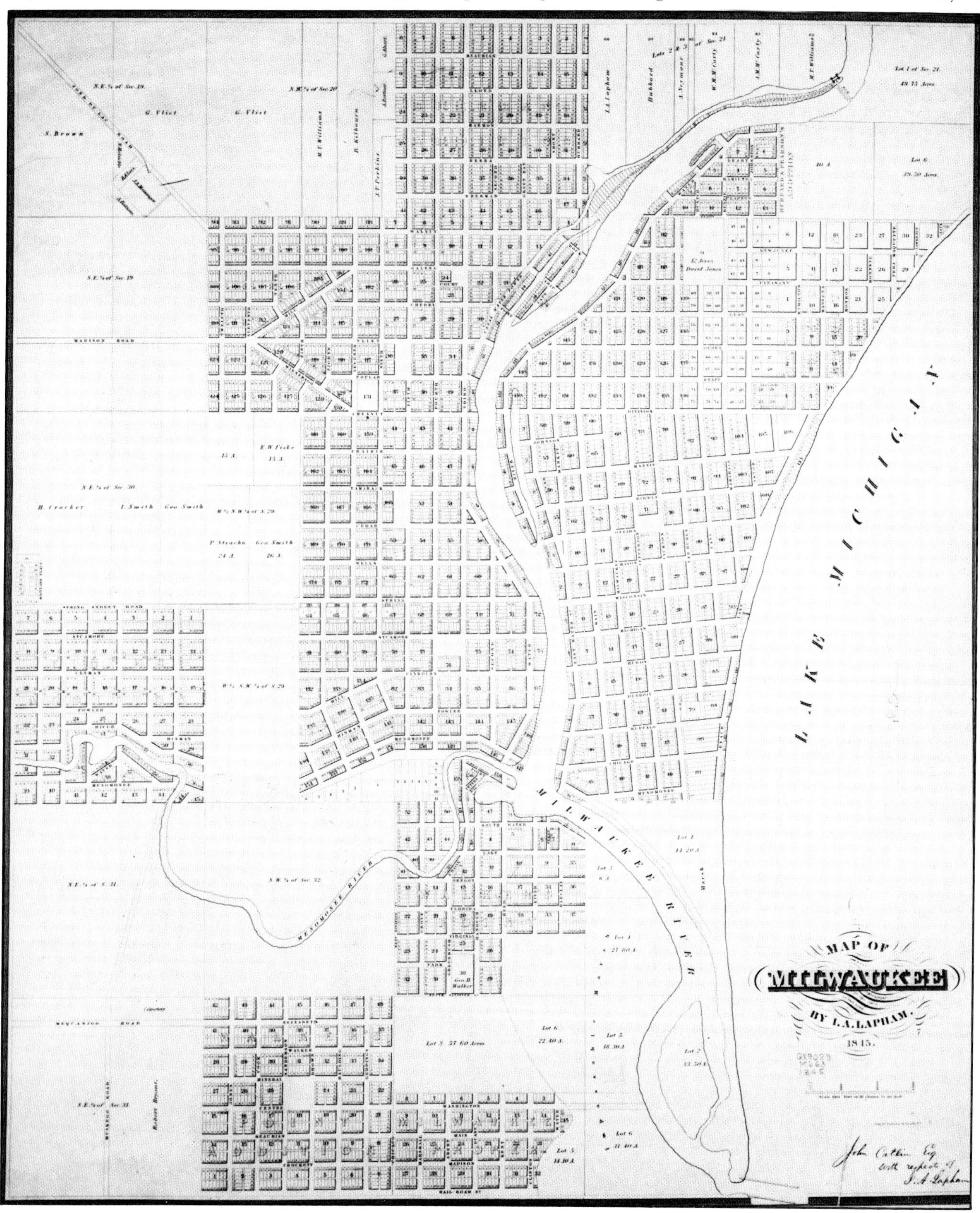

City Plan of Milwaukee in 1845, by Increase Lapham.

State Historical Society of Wisconsin

of western towns during the nineteenth century. This plan facilitated land survey, lot subdivision, and sales. Its uniformity appealed to promoters and prospective buyers alike. Both the Kilbourn and Juneau plats, however, shared the typical failing of the gridiron plan: they disregarded topography. The plats preserved the straight line and the right angle at the expense of the natural lay of the land and the individual features of the site. The only deviation in Milwaukee's checkerboard street pattern was East Water Street (now North Water) and West Water Street (now a part of Plankinton Avenue), which followed both sides of the Milwaukee River above the Menomonee. Winnebago Street formed a diagonal on the northwest side, but this was actually an incorporation of a pre-existing trail. Several randomly-placed public squares were also included in both plats, but because of competition between Juneau and Kilbourn, the east-west streets did not align evenly and had different names. The limits of the town were extended in 1845 by the addition of Walker's Point on the south side. Due to delays in clearing land titles, Milwaukee's third gridiron plat was not recorded until 1854.[8]

Several trails radiated from the village nucleus into the surrounding wilderness. They generally followed earlier Indian routes and connected Milwaukee with Green Bay, Chicago, and southwestern Wisconsin, as well as smaller nearby settlements in the interior. Although stagecoaches advertised to the contrary, most of these roads were little more than unimproved wagon paths in the 1830s. James Buck, in recalling some of the existing roads in 1836, cited the Green Bay Road, Muskego Road, Mukwonago Road, Western Road, and Chicago Road. Parts of these early routes remain today as Green Bay Avenue, Muskego Avenue, West National Avenue, and West State Street respectively. The Old Chicago Road, as described by Buck, no longer exists. Kinnickinnic Avenue roughly follows an Indian trail, and is said to have been a major southbound route along the lakeshore.[9]

Despite its formal gridiron plan, Milwaukee at this time was a small frontier village of scattered buildings. Writing in the early 1840s, Increase Lapham described some of the site's features:

> The city commences about a mile above the mouth of the river, at a place called Walker's Point, and extends about a mile and a half along the river. Below Walker's Point, the river is bordered by impassable marshes. The ground occupied by the town is uneven, rising from the river from fifty to one hundred feet, thus affording very beautiful stations for residences, commanding a full view of the town and bay, with its shipping. But few of these sites have yet been occupied and improved, as their peculiar importance and interesting views would lead us to suspect.[10]

Throughout the small riverfront community, radical alterations of the terrain had begun by the 1840s. Hills and bluffs were removed or graded (eliminating, no doubt, some of the commanding views) and the remaining soil was used to fill in the marshes and lowlands along the river banks. These and other costly "improvements" were financed by the local promoters (chiefly Byron Kilbourn and Solomon Juneau) to entice settlers to their respective townsites. By 1837, Kilbourn had spent about thirteen thousand dollars for the construction of roads and streets.[11]

In Juneautown, on the east side of the river, buildings clustered along Water Street near the intersection of Wisconsin Avenue. Kilbourntown, on the west side, was centered at the corner of Third Street and Juneau Avenue. Among the earliest structures were log cabins and "claim shanties," built by driving stakes in the ground and surrounding them with basswood lumber. Most buildings, however, were frame with clapboard exteriors. These were modest structures, one to three stories high. They included an intermingling of dwellings, stores, taverns, sawmills, and

Increase Lapham House, 325 W. McKinley Ave., 1848. Increase Allen Lapham (1811-1877) arrived in Milwaukee in 1836. His studies and publications in regional geology, Indian archeology, meterology, and the natural landscape established him as Wisconsin's first scholar. In his work for the government land office, he also prepared several early maps of Milwaukee. He lived in this Greek Revival Style double house (now demolished) for several decades after its construction in 1848. The Lapham House was still standing c. 1900 when this photograph was taken.

State Historical Society of Wisconsin

John Bechtel's Mansion House, N. Third St. at Juneau Ave. Nineteenth century photograph of an early hotel run by John Bechtel, who came to Milwaukee in 1847. This pioneer structure, in the Greek Revival Style, was typical of wood-clad buildings in early Milwaukee, and was probably constructed in the late 1840s.

Milwaukee Co. Historical Society

shops belonging to blacksmiths, coopers, and other tradesmen.

Most of the dwellings were "mere shells inclosed (sic) with siding, their flimsiness not infrequently disguised by a false front." As early as 1836, however, the first two brick houses were built of locally-made cream brick, a building material for which Milwaukee would later become renowned. The first brick store block, erected in 1840 at the northwest corner of Third and Juneau Streets, was three stories high, and housed the first theater in Milwaukee.[12] None of these buildings remain today.

Approaching Milwaukee in 1840, one would have seen a skyline dominated by the first courthouse and the newly erected St. Peter's Catholic Church. The courthouse, built in 1836, faced south on Cathedral Square (then called Juneau Square). The two-story building, fifty-one feet long and forty-two feet wide, featured a pedimented portico supported by four Tuscan columns. The church stood on Juneau Avenue west of Jackson. A new wooden bridge spanning the Milwaukee River at Juneau Avenue was also erected at this time. Built in 1840, the bridge was the first to connect the two rival settlements on either side of the river; before then, settlers relied on ferries.[13]

Between 1835 and 1840, the population of Milwaukee expanded from 125 to 1,692. Although the majority were Yankees from New York State and New England, Milwaukee's population was ethnically diverse from the beginning. The numbers of Indians and French-Canadians declined yearly, and in their place, the first groups of British, German, Irish, and Norwegian immigrants started arriving before 1840. The first black settler, Joe Oliver who worked for Solomon Juneau as a cook, arrived in 1835. The population was transient, with some settlers staying only a short time before leaving for other parts of Wisconsin and the Midwest. But some of Milwaukee's most prominent nineteenth century citizens, such as scholar-naturalist Increase Lapham and banker-businessman Alexander Mitchell, settled permanently in Milwaukee during its founding years.[14]

Milwaukee, 1854. Detail from a lithograph by George J. Robertson. This view, looking east on Wisconsin Ave. from about Fifth St., is the first illustration of Milwaukee to show a large number of buildings in detail.

State Historical Society of Wisconsin

Village to City: 1846-1880

Milwaukee Co. Historical Society

Economy

Although it was incorporated as a city in 1846, Milwaukee at that time was actually three villages "slightly connected together," because of the river barrier and the speculative rivalries of the thirties.[15] In the middle period of its growth, however, Milwaukee emerged as a city whose land use and commercial specialization connoted an increasingly urban society.

Milwaukee's desirable location and the westward migration of population were instrumental to its growth in the mid-nineteenth century. The steamboat added new importance to waterside locations. More significantly, Milwaukee's site at the edge of rich Wisconsin farmlands made its development as a commercial trade center possible and profitable. In the 1840s and 1850s Milwaukee became a principal wheat market and shipping point. By 1865, the city was the largest primary exporter of wheat in the world, and it held a major position in the wheat trade until 1880.

As Wisconsin agriculture began to diversify, so did Milwaukee's manufacturing activities. The city's economy grew around the processing of regional agricultural products. Major processing industries between 1850 and 1880 included flour milling, meat packing, tanning, brewing, and boot and shoe making. Most of these were small-scale establishments until the 1870s. While manufacturing activities were found in the heart of the city, they were concentrated primarily along both banks of the Milwaukee River below Michigan Street and above Juneau Avenue.[16]

Heavy industry began in the late 1860s when the Milwaukee Iron Company constructed the Bay View Rolling Mill at the lakeshore on the city's southern border. (The site of the mill, now gone, lies at the southern terminus of the Harbor Bridge ramp.) The city's location near regional iron ore supplies and marketing routes spurred its beginnings in heavy industry. Milwaukee's subsequent growth in the iron and steel industry derived from the source of supply provided by the Bay View mill.[17] Thus, Milwaukee's economic growth in the middle period can be attributed to its proximity to plentiful natural resources: agricultural land, iron ore, rivers, forests, and a lakeshore harbor.

Phoenix Mills. One of Milwaukee's largest flour mills was located at the corner of Cherry and Commerce Streets on the Milwaukee River. The mills were originally built in 1848 by Comstock and Chase, and rebuilt in 1876. This photograph shows one of the mill structures as it appeared in the late nineteenth century. It was constructed of local cream brick with Italianate details. The name of E. Sanderson, owner of the mill, appears in the center gable.

Grain elevator, c. 1870. The shipment and storing of grain was Milwaukee's first large-scale commercial activity, and grain elevators were the largest structures in the mid-century city.

State Historical Society of Wisconsin

Transportation

Developing transportation, the corollary to Milwaukee's economic rise, shaped the city's growth and physical appearance. Plank roads were the first mode of improved transportation. The first of these was the Watertown Plank Road, constructed in 1846 at private expense between Milwaukee and Watertown. Its success led to the construction of plank roads in other directions. The approximate routes of the Watertown, Wauwatosa, Lisbon, Mequanego (Mukwonago), New Fond du Lac, and Janesville Plank Roads survive today as State Street, Vliet Street, Lisbon Avenue, National Avenue, Teutonia Avenue and Forest Home Avenue respectively.[18] The fringes of the city developed first along these and other early routes. Country roads dotted with farmsteads became major urban arteries by the end of the century.

Harbor improvements begain in the 1840s. Filling in the marsh, dredging, and pier construction transformed the meandering river mouth to a deepened watercourse lined with buildings and wharves. The first railroad operated in 1851, connecting Milwaukee with Waukesha. By 1855 service to Chicago was available. At the close of the sixties, twelve hundred miles of railroads radiated from the city, including rail connections to New York. In 1873, ten railroad lines with fourteen branches ran tributary to the lakeshore city.[19] Major rail corridors stretched south along the industrializing river mouth, east-west along the Menomonee Valley, and north along the Milwaukee River. Depots, rail yards, and roundhouses became pronounced visual elements in a city whose economy relied upon a complex of transportation routes.

Union Depot, c. 1885. View north on S. Second St. from the corner of Seeboth. Now gone, this depot was built in 1866 by the Chicago, Milwaukee and St. Paul Railroad.

State Historical Society of Wisconsin

Population

The U.S. Census recorded a total population of 20,061 in 1850 and 115,587 in 1880. Milwaukee's expanding and diversifying economic base prompted a dramatic population growth from the 1840s to 1880. Much of this increase stemmed from the influx of European immigrants to the city which had become a major embarkation point in the 1840s and 1850s for immigrants traveling west through the Great Lakes. Germans, British, and Irish — in that order — made up the major immigrant groups in Milwaukee before 1880. (See table, "Size of Milwaukee's Population, 1848-1930.") The entire Midwest received large numbers of Germans in the mid-nineteenth century, but Germans comprised a disproportionate share of Milwaukee's population, totalling a third of the city's inhabitants. The combination of urban frontier opportunity and available farmlands attracted the first Germans, who were magnets for later settlers. The Germans were distinctive not only because of their numbers, but also because they were present in all occupational levels of the city's economy. While over half of Milwaukee's Germans were skilled workers or craftsmen, they also included a significant number of the city's professionals, and a majority of its laborers. Unlike the Irish and later arrivals, such as the Poles, Milwaukee's Germans were not easily classified according to one economic class. Likewise, the Germans could not be typed according to religion, since Catholics, Protestants, and Jews were among their ranks. Therefore, rather than forming an ethnic subculture, the Germans created a coordinate German society to the American one.[20]

Milwaukee Turner Society, 1034 N. Fourth St., 1882-83. The *Sozialer Turnverein Milwaukee*, founded in 1853, was one of several early Turner societies organized by Germans in the United States. The Turners devoted their energy to education, physical training, and liberal reform. They are now primarily a social organization. This is the largest of Milwaukee's Turner Halls, a cream brick Victorian Italianate structure designed by Milwaukee architect Henry C. Koch.

Size of Milwaukee's Population, 1848-1930

Year	Total	Percent of Native-Born	Percent of Foreign-Born
1840	1,712	—	—
1848	16,521	42	58
1850	20,051	36	64
1860	45,246	50	50
1870	71,440	53	47
1880	115,587	60	40
1890	204,468	61	39
1900	285,315	69	31
1910	373,857	70	30
1920	457,147	76	24
1930	578,249	81	19

Source: U.S. Census: reprinted in Still, p. 570-571, 574-75; Conzen, p. 14.

Other immigrant groups which added to Milwaukee's population before 1880 included Scandinavians, Poles, Dutch, and small representations from nearly every country in Europe. The first German-Jewish immigrants arrived in 1844 and by the mid-fifties the Jewish community numbered about 200 families. Poles had settled in Milwaukee as early as the 1840s. The first permanent Polish settler is reported to have been Anthony Kochanek who arrived in 1848. By the 1860s, there were about thirty Polish families in the city. Between 1870 and 1880, Milwaukee's Polish population jumped from 325 to 1,790. In addition, a free black community established itself in Milwaukee before the Civil War. Some were fugitive slaves, and others were free blacks who left or were expelled from the Southern states. The 1860 U.S. Census enumerated 122 black people living in the city, many of whom were prosperous businessmen. The census listed blacks in occupations ranging "from domestic and personal services to merchants and store keepers, two journeymen masons, and a dentist."[21]

German-English Academy, 1020 N. Broadway, 1890-91. In 1851, a group of Milwaukee Germans, dissatisifed with available public education, founded the German-English Academy. The school became an innovator in Milwaukee education, offering instruction in German and the first kindergarten in the city. This building was erected in 1890-91 to accommodate the need for more space and better facilities. The Milwaukee firm of Charles D. Crane and Carl C. Barkhausen designed the cream brick academy. Plans for the restoration and re-use of the now-vacant building are underway.

Expansion and Land Use

As Milwaukee's population grew and its economy diversified, the city's territory expanded to the north, south, and west. By 1860, Milwaukee's boundaries reached Burleigh Street on the north, Lincoln Avenue on the south, and Twenty-seventh Street on the west.

Most of this area was platted by 1880. The original gridiron plan of 1835 was continuously extended, with the exception that plat additions preserved old routes (discussed above) which radiated diagonally from the city. With only slight variations in block and lot sizes, this street pattern was repeated until twentieth century subdivisions initiated the curve in Milwaukee street layouts. Revision of the Milwaukee charter in 1856 put this precedent into law by stipulating that subdividing property into city lots "shall, in platting the same, cause the streets and alleys in such plat to correspond in width and general direction with the streets and alleys in said city adjacent to" the new additions. The 1874 City Charter also included this provision. Bluffs were leveled and marshes were filled so that the city's topography would conform to its checkerboard layout.[22]

Land use specialization paralleled the city's physical growth between 1846 and 1880. In the 1850s, the initial intermixture of dwellings, workshops, stores, and warehouses began to evolve into an urban landscape differentiated according to function. There was a growing separation between workplace and residence. By the 1860s, retail shops, offices, banking and insurance firms concentrated in a central business district roughly bound by Clybourn, State, Broadway on the east side of the river, and Second Street on the west side. Commission merchants, warehouses, and docks increasingly located downriver in the Third Ward. Additional commercial areas developed on the near South side across the river and climbed north along Third Street. Grocers and other neighborhood businesses began to leave the central district for residential areas. Mills and factories clustered along the Milwaukee River north and south of the business district, except for the brewers who mainly located in the vicinity of Juneau Avenue west of the river. Most of the numerous small workshops in the city were located along or near the riverfront, the main axis of mid-century Milwaukee.[23]

Milwaukee Female College, southeast corner of Milwaukee St. and Juneau Ave., 1852. Institutions established by and for women were rare in nineteenth century Milwaukee. The Milwaukee Female Seminary was founded in 1848 by Mrs. L. A. Parsons. Catherine E. Beecher, a nationally-known educational reformer, provided the impetus for expansion of the school. In 1852, her Gothic Revival plans for this building were accepted and the cornerstone was laid. The name was changed to Milwaukee Female College the next year. In 1899 the school moved to a new campus on the East Side, was re-named Milwaukee-Downer College, now incorporated into Lawrence University.

State Historical Society of Wisconsin

"Map of the City of Milwaukee, 1855" by Increase Lapham.

State Historical Society of Wisconsin

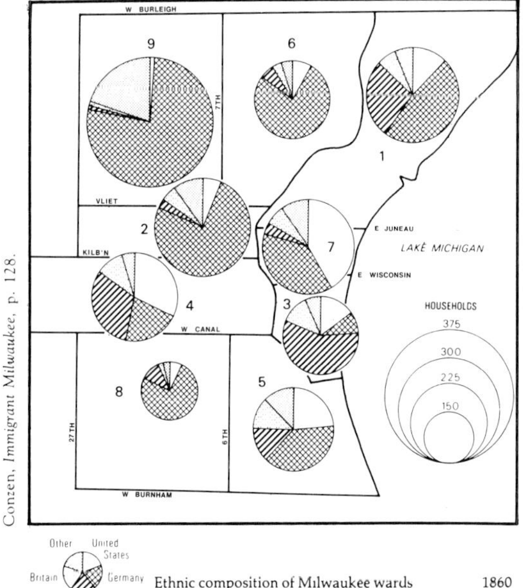

Conzen, *Immigrant Milwaukee*, p. 128.

Ethnic composition of Milwaukee wards 1860

Neighborhoods

Milwaukee's early neighborhoods surrounded the core of the city. Those closest to the city center combined residential and commercial land uses. At the periphery, the neighborhoods were almost entirely residential, with the exception of major commercial routes and small retail shops and services clustered at corners.

Early in the city's history, Milwaukee's neighborhoods developed patterns of segregation by ethnicity and income. In 1853, one recent German immigrant observed that "an especially noteworthy feature is the separation of the various nationalities into different quarters of the city."[24] To some extent, these residential patterns reflected the desire to live near others who shared the same cultural background. Residential patterns also reflected rent-paying ability, proximity to employment, concerns about social status, and stage in the family cycle.

Though political wards (precursors of present-day aldermanic districts) are arbitrary boundaries for measurement of residential patterns (neighborhoods are smaller units and may overlap ward boundaries), the ward map illustrated here gives us a good picture of the ethnic geography of Milwaukee in 1860. Census data, correlated with city directory information, reveals where Milwaukee's major ethnic groups lived in the mid-nineteenth century. Native-born Americans concentrated in central wards Four and Seven, areas valued for their closeness to the city center. Airy homesites on the east side bluffs attracted Yankees who owned or worked in downtown shops and businesses. Here, the lots generally were larger, the houses more substantial, and the population density lower than in the other urban neighborhoods. Prosperity enabled the Anglo-Americans to preempt choice lands for their own private residences.[25]

The Irish congregated in the southern sections of the Third and Fourth Wards. Because they suffered the disadvantages of poverty and limited job skills upon their arrival, they were relegated to the least desirable residential locations in the city near manufacturing areas bordering the Menomonee Valley and on low-lying lands in the lower Third Ward. The "Bloody Third," as it was perjoratively termed, contained the largest concentration of Milwaukee's Irish and remained the locus of their settlement until the 1890s when the upwardly-mobile Irish moved to other neighborhoods in the city. Despite poor housing conditions and unhealthy sanita-

State Historical Society of Wisconsin

Jefferson St. and St. Paul Ave. A 1930s photograph shows the densely-built rows of immigrant housing which formerly comprised much of the lower Third Ward. Most of these houses were constructed in the 1860s and 1870s. They were primarily wood-clad, with Italianate details, and on raised foundations because of the low-lying site. In the early twentieth century, the Italians succeeded the Irish as the predominant ethnic group in the lower Third Ward. All residential buildings were torn down in the 1950s and 1960s, leaving the area strictly for manufacturing and trade.

tion, the lower Third Ward was nonetheless near the available employment for the Irish — street construction, work along the harbor, day labor in the central business district, and domestic service.[26]

While the Irish remained a visible group in proportion to their relatively low numbers, the German neighborhoods made up Milwaukee's more "foreign environment" from 1846-1880. This was due to the almost exclusive use of German language and to distinguishing ethnic features of the buildings. Here Frederika Bremer, a Swedish novelist, noted "German houses, German inscriptions over the doors or signs, German physiogomies" on her visit in the 1850s.[27] By this time, in fact, Milwaukee was known among German-Americans as *Deutsch-Athen.*[28]

The German areas of the city developed not so much as neighborhoods but as communities of their own, with business districts, wealthy sections, and fringe areas of small frame workers' houses and shanties. German settlement originally stretched along the east and west sides of the Milwaukee River just north of the central business district (roughly between Wells Street and Juneau Avenue). From this "German Town," Milwaukee's coordinate culture spread to the north and west, in Wards One, Two, Six, and Nine. German settlement in the mid-nineteenth century was able to grow unimpeded in the northwestern quadrant of the city because of the availability of land. By the late 1850s, development on the northwestern side had proceeded about as far west as Sixteenth Street and north to North Avenue. In 1880, it had reached the city limits, west to Twenty-seventh Street and north to Burleigh Street. The lots in the newly-developing northwestern sections tended to be smaller than the city average. Newcomers generally moved to the edges of German areas where land values were comparatively low.[29]

Neighborhoods on Milwaukee's South Side (south of the Menomonee River Valley) were characterized in this era by a greater ethnic heterogeneity. The area also developed more slowly than the East and West sides because of extensive marshes and a contested land title. In the 1840s and 1850s, settlement concentrated in Walker's Point (see illustration of Increase Lapham's "Map of the City of Milwaukee," 1855). By the 1850s, the south side population was a mixture of Germans, Yankees, and Irish, with larger German growth on the western fringes by 1860. A small Scandinavian settlement also developed on the South Side. By 1860, brickyards, a tannery, and an engine works signaled the industrial future of the South Side. Between 1860 and 1880, industrial expansion attracted new immigrants to the South Side in greater numbers, especially the Poles, who began arriving in force during the 1870s. In addition to the Polish immigration, the founding of the Bay View Rolling Mill in 1868 at the southern edge of the city also precipitated growth on the South Side. A small village of millworkers, many of whom were skilled British and Welsh workers imported by the Milwaukee Iron Company, sprung up around the lakeshore mill. During this period, Bay View was a separate village, incorporated in 1879, and did not join the city until 1887.[30]

Throughout the 1846-1880 period, population density and land values on the South Side remained relatively low. Despite the variety of ethnic groups inhabiting the South Side, "in the popular mind as well as statistically, the area was characterized more by its (industrial) employment than by its ethnic status."[31]

Although Milwaukee's black population numbered only about 122 in 1860, there was no distinct black neighborhood at this time. Census data show that black residences were distributed throughout the city's east and west sides, with small clusters on Wells Street between North Third and North Sixth Streets, and in the lower Third Ward. A few were also located in Walker's Point. This population distribution continued through most of the nineteenth century, and it was not until the turn of the century that there was a discernable black residential area.[32]

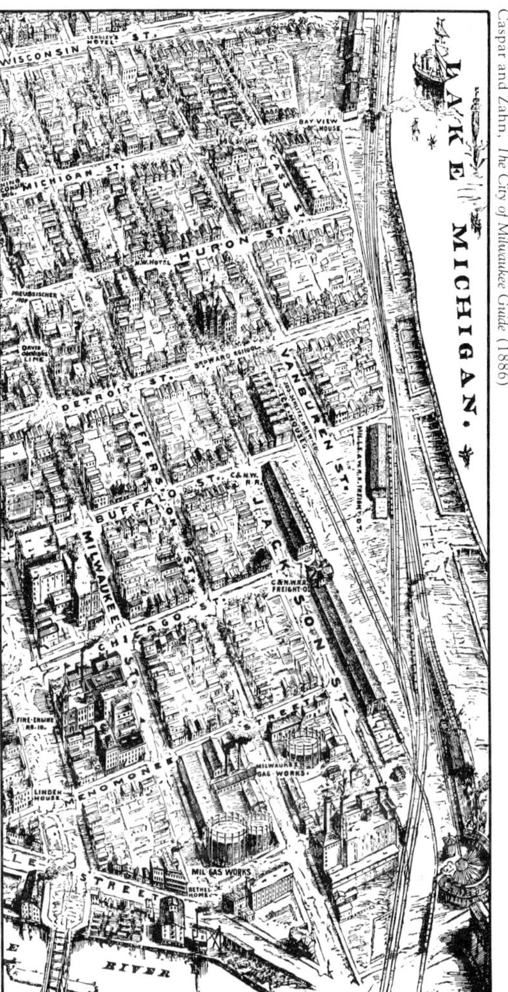

Caspar and Zahn, *The City of Milwaukee Guide* (1886)

A portion of the lower Third Ward, 1886.

State Historical Society of Wisconsin

Milwaukee, 1872. A detailed lithographic view which reveals the expanding business district on the east and near south sides. In the Menomonee Valley, several ship channels have been dredged and the marshland was partially drained and filled. Railroad structures have become a noticeable part of the urban landscape. Drawn by H. H. Bailey and printed by the Milwaukee Lithographing and Engraving Co.

Urban Services

Essential urban services (water, streets, sewers, fire and police protection) in Milwaukee were transferred from private to public responsibility during the middle period. Early "internal improvements" (which also included marsh-filling, bridge construction, and harbor dredging) were provided by a combination of the speculator-promoters (Juneau, Kilbourn, and major business interests) and the voluntary efforts of the citizenry. By law, all able-bodied men were expected to labor two or three days annually on the streets. After the Civil War, private subsidy of urban services proved woefully inadequate due to the rapid growth and physical complexity of the city. Many houses were unserved by sewers, and the private wells upon which people relied for water became increasingly polluted. This created serious health hazards, including cholera and smallpox. Milwaukee newspapers during the sixties were full of reports on the environmental issues. In 1865, the *Sentinel,* for instance, called attention to the "little stream trickling down (the city's streets), the stench from which precluded effectually any idea you may be inclined to form that it is pure spring water."[33]

Public concern over health, sanitation, and safety was the chief motivation for extending the domain of municipal government. The City Charter of 1874 gave the Board of Public Works responsibility for water, streets, sewers, bridges, sidewalks, wharves, and public structures throughout the city. The 1870s stand out as a decade in which major advancements in urban services were begun. The city built and operated its first municipal water works, constructed a sewer system, and expanded the number of paved streets. By 1880, the city had ninety miles of water pipe and ninety-eight miles of sewer main. Twenty-five miles of streets had been paved with wooden blocks, the most popular form of paving at the time. There were, in addition, a few blocks of brick and stone pavement downtown. In 1871, a full-time paid fire department was authorized, replacing previous volunteer methods. However, adequate fire protection did not occur until the turn of the century. The largest fire in the city's history, which struck the lower Third Ward in 1892, did much to agitate public action for fire codes and building regulations, as well as increased fire department personnel and equipment.[34]

Urban transit in Milwaukee also began in this era. The earliest horse car company, the River and Lakeshore Company (later the Milwaukee City Street Railway Company) commenced operation in 1860 with a franchise granted by the city. It ran a short downtown route between the two railroad terminals. After the Civil War, new routes were built to North Point (on the East Side) and to Forest Home Cemetery (on the Southwest Side). Substantial real estate in these suburban areas was owned by the street railway's investors, who had an interest in promoting the sale and development of their lands through improved transportation. But because of low population densities, the lines proved unprofitable and caused financial problems for the Milwaukee City Street Railway in the late 1860s and 1870s. Two other street railway companies were formed before 1880: the Cream City Railway Company (incorporated in 1876), which served the East Side; and the West Side Street Railway Company (incorporated in 1874), which operated most of its routes in previously settled sections of the West Side. By 1880, Milwaukee had a horse-drawn streetcar network which reached most parts of the city. Lines often ended near cemeteries and parks, giving urban dwellers access to popular recreation spots and

Milwaukee Co. Historical Society

Deutscher Markt (German Market), 1899.

rural retreats. Traffic funneled, however, towards the central business district, while workplaces outside the downtown area received little service. Crosstown connections (between east and west, north and south) were poor.[35]

Despite the introduction of the streetcar into the urban environment, Milwaukee remained an essentially pedestrian city during this period. Ridership on the streetcars remained low. In the late 1860s and 1870s about ninety percent of the population lived within two miles of the central business district, and fifty-eight percent within one mile. Even newly-developing areas at the edge of the city were only three to four miles from downtown. Reliance on foot travel placed a premium on central residential location in the pre-suburban era. The city's wealthy citizens tended to live near the city center, while outer areas were developed by newer immigrants.[36] In addition, Milwaukee's topography influenced the decentralization of trades and industry. Manufacturing stretched along the north-south course of the Milwaukee River, the east-west valley of the Menomonee, and along major rail corridors. This allowed most of the city's workforce to walk to their jobs. Milwaukee's streetcar system did not become a major means of commuting to work until the turn of the century.

Wisconsin Ave., looking west from the Milwaukee River, c. 1890.

Milwaukee Co. Historical Society

Industrial Metropolis: 1880-1930

State Historical Society of Wisconsin

Downtown street scene, 1890s.

> If it was the Europeanism of Milwaukee that lent the city distinction in the nineteenth century, industrialism was its prevailing feature in the twentieth.[37]

Economy

The period after 1880 was marked by Milwaukee's transition from a commercial trade center to an industrial city. The processing industries which had established Milwaukee as a thriving frontier city in its earlier years continued to remain among the leading producers in the city. Flour milling was the one exception. Milwaukee declined steadily as a milling center after 1890 because, as geographer Roger Simon noted, "the westward movement of wheat production coincided with discriminatory freight rates to make Milwaukee a less profitable location for milling."[38] By the 1920s flour milling lost its rank among the city's ten major industries.

All other processing industries, however, prospered and developed into large industries of national importance: tanning, brewing, and slaughtering and meatpacking. By 1909, tanning had become Milwaukee's top industry by value of product, and the city was the nation's leading leather producer. While ownership remained in the hands of local capitalists, tanning was not a localized industry. Following a national trend toward consolidation, a few large firms in Milwaukee engaged in international marketing with worldwide agencies. The three largest Milwaukee tanneries in the early twentieth century were Pfister and Vogel, A. O. Trostel and Sons, and A. F. Gallun and Sons. While tanning in Milwaukee declined in the 1920s due to decreased demand for leather goods, the city's

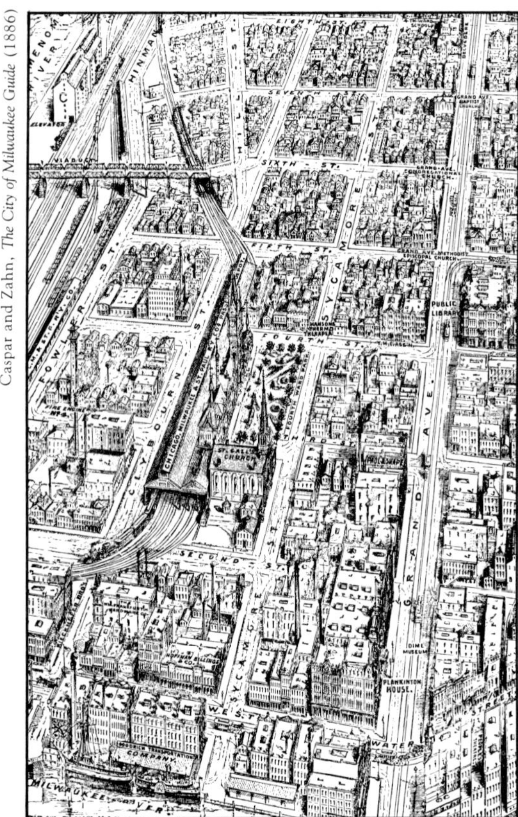

Caspar and Zahn, *The City of Milwaukee Guide* (1886)

The central business district west of the Milwaukee River, 1886. Milwaukee's grand new railroad terminal, erected in 1886 by the Chicago, Milwaukee, and St. Paul Railroad, is visible in this engraving printed by Caspar and Zahn for a guide to the city. The terminal was demolished in the 1960s.

tanneries remained among the wealthiest, as well as the oldest, industries.[39]

The brewing of malt liquors was Milwaukee's leading industry by value of product in the 1880s, and ranked second nationally at the time of the 1910 United States Census of Manufacturers. Although Milwaukee gained the popular approbation of "Beer Town," it was not the nation's largest brewing center in the 1880-1930 period. The city could, though, claim the largest single brewery (Pabst Brewing Company) in the 1890s. In addition, Milwaukee brewers pioneered in new processes of manufacture, installation of the first refrigeration equipment and bottling plants, and national advertising. Part of the success of the city's brewing industry can be explained by the fact that Milwaukee brewers were not just innovative businessmen but were professional brewers, many of them German-born and educated in the traditions of the trade.[40]

The brewing industry in Milwaukee, as elsewhere in the United States, suffered from World War I until the 1930s because of the national prohibition movement as well as (untrue) allegations that the breweries were subsidizing German war propaganda. After the "reform-fostered and war-invoked" prohibition amendment was passed in 1920, Milwaukee's breweries turned to the production of cheese, malt, candy, and near-beer until the end of prohibition in 1933.[41]

Milwaukee's industrial character, however, rested on the growth of the heavy metals industries in the city after 1880. The expansion of the Bay View Rolling Mills, which originated in the late 1860s, provided the iron and steel necessary for the development of a major machinery, tools, and implements industry in Milwaukee by the late nineteenth century. By 1909, the foundries and machine shops, iron mills, and tool and implement firms accounted for three of Milwaukee's top six industries. World War I stimulated the metals trades in the United States, and after 1913 the iron and steel industry was consistently the leader among the city's industries. Correspondingly, the 1920s saw the rise of automotive and related industries (such as gas and oil) in Milwaukee.[42] Located chiefly in the Menomonee Valley, the city's east-west waistline, the sprawling plants and smoking chimneys of the iron and steel industries competed with the sights, smells, and sounds of Milwaukee's older processing firms.

Of Milwaukee's industrial activity after 1900, the *Milwaukee Sentinel* reported that "in most cases the investments are made by Milwaukee capitalists. . . . In some cases, however, the industrial growth is the result of the incoming of capital from sources outside the city."[43] Ownership and management of many of Milwaukee's major industries prior to 1930 remained in the hands of descendants of the original founders. Yet, Milwaukee's industry participated in the American trend during this period towards corporate consolidation. While each firm expanded in size and production, the actual numbers of manufacturers in the city decreased.[44]

In the late nineteenth century, Milwaukee, like American society in

Bay View Rolling Mills (Illinois Steel Co.), 1883.

general, changed from a home-centered economy to one which focused on the factory and the machine. The traditional family-operated "cottage industries" such as blacksmithing, dressmaking, and foodstuffs were replaced by factories and retail establishments which supplied similar goods and services. This meant that the myriad of small workshops in Milwaukee, which often combined with places of residence and which formerly comprised much of the city's "work space", gradually declined. The large factory, commercial building, and industrial plant—though fewer in actual numbers than the small workshops of an earlier time—became the dominant physical elements in Milwaukee's urban landscape.

Location of Industries

The nature and growth of Milwaukee's industries not only led to bigger physical plants, but also extended the land area assigned for manufacturing. Industrial activity continued to concentrate along the Milwaukee River from the dam (below North Avenue) to Lake Michigan. By the 1880s, the long frontage of the Menomonee Valley developed as the city's major manufacturing area because of available land in the valley and its access to rail and water transportation. A variety of firms also located on the Milwaukee Road corridor in the northwest (roughly paralleling North Thirty-first Street), along the lakeshore south of the harbor, and on the banks of the Kinnickinnic Creek.[45]

This increased decentralization of Milwaukee's manufacturing in the late nineteenth century, in large part a function of its river-divided topography, enabled workers to move from the central areas of the city and still remain fairly close to the industrial jobs. Unlike many other major American cities at the turn of the century, the geographic distribution of Milwaukee's industry created new residential areas for workers outside the central city. Therefore, Milwaukee's "suburbs" of this period were not the exclusive domain of the prosperous. The historical research of Roger Simon, based on detailed census analysis, showed that those who moved to Milwaukee's new neighborhoods at the turn of the century "included less affluent workers than were probably suburbanizing in some other cities."[46] This pattern was fairly typical of midwestern cities of similar size at that time. Likewise, the central city was not comprised primarily of those who had to remain near sources of unskilled employment. In fact, downtown areas such as Yankee Hill, Grand Avenue, and Prospect Avenue were among the most prestigious residential neighborhoods in the city.

Herman Wudtke Collection

View up the Milwaukee River from below Michigan St., c. 1900. Milwaukee's tallest and most prominent downtown buildings at the time, the Pabst Building (1892) in the foreground and City Hall (1893-95), stand out against earlier commercial structures. Steamers, still a regular sight on the river, are tied up at Goodrich Docks.

View southeast from W. State St. and N. Eighth St., c. 1890. Steeples and smokestacks dominated the pre-skyscraper horizon of Milwaukee's downtown. The former Exposition Hall, site of the present Milwaukee Auditorium, can be seen on the left. Designed by Milwaukee architect Edward Townsend Mix in the 1880s, Exposition Hall was the first public building in the city with electric lights. In the foreground are cream brick residences in the Victorian Italianate and French Second Empire styles, dating from the 1870s and 1880s.

State Historical Society of Wisconsin

Milwaukee Co. Historical Society

Southwest corner of E. Wisconsin and Broadway, c. 1895. The *Milwaukee Sentinel* reported the comments of a visitor from Madison: "Ease and comfort, before business, say the quiet burghers. But what matters it? At sun down close the stores — at nine o'clock shut off the lights and stop the street cars, and everything is quiet. . . ."

Population

The salient characteristic of Milwaukee's population between 1880 and 1930 was its occupational distribution. A sharp rise in the proportion of industrial workers among Milwaukee's population accompanied the city's economic growth and change. In 1880, the number of factory workers in the city totalled 13,782, increasing to 45,297 by the end of the century. Between 1899 and 1909 the number of persons engaged in industrial work increased by fifty percent. In 1910, Milwaukee was only the twelfth largest American city in population, yet it ranked third (after Buffalo and Detroit) in the proportion of its workforce employed in "manufacturing and mechanical pursuits."[47]

Milwaukee's ethnic composition during this period included some seemingly contradictory statistics. While the percent of foreign-born persons (relative to native-born population) in Milwaukee declined steadily, the numbers of new immigrants rose through 1910. Yet in that year more persons of foreign birth lived in Milwaukee than at any other time in the city's history. Along with New York City, Milwaukee also held first place in its percentage of foreign stock.[48]

Milwaukee remained heavily Germanic in population and appearance after 1880. The most significant population change was the decline of foreign-born Germans and the increase of immigrants from eastern and southern Europe.[49] Most of Milwaukee's newcomers came from non-industrialized countries with oppressive class structures which denied occupational mobility. Forced to accommodate to an urban industrial environment, the new arrivals supplied workers for Milwaukee's expanding industries.

Immigrants from Poland added a new dimension to the city's ethnic structure, becoming not only numerically significant but socially and politically influential as well. By 1910, over 70,000 Poles lived in Milwaukee, comprising nineteen percent of the population. The Poles, who settled primarily on the South Side, were occupationally and religiously more homogeneous than the Germans. The Polish Catholic parish, the Polish

Milwaukee Co. Historical Society

Frank Wojciechowski Grocery, N. Water and Pulaski Sts., c. 1905. Immigrant Polish family in front of their store in the East Side Polish neighborhood.

language press, and the numerous fraternal organizations "guarded the identity of the nationality group and channeled its influence in the municipal life."[50]

Czechs, Slovaks, Hungarians, and Russians constituted another portion of Milwaukee's eastern European population. Polish, Russian, and Hungarian Jews increased Milwaukee's Jewish population to 10,000 by 1910. Colonies of Italians and Greeks were also established within the city during these years.[51]

Milwaukee's black population remained under 1,000 until the northward migration after World War I. Between 1910 and 1930, the black community expanded from 980 to 7,501. Although it was growing in numbers, Milwaukee's black population was increasingly segregated within the square mile downtown bound by North Third, North Twelfth, West Wright, and West Kilbourn.[52]

Despite the apparent ethnic patchwork in Milwaukee between 1880 and 1930, the numbers of these various new nationality groups were comparatively small. Germans and Poles dominated the ethnic complexion of the city. Consequently, Milwaukee was among the most ethnically homogeneous cities of its size in the country. Still, the city's population was more diverse in the twentieth century than that of the combined German and Yankee town of the nineteenth.

Growth Patterns and Land Practice

After a slow start in the mid-nineteenth century, Milwaukee's streetcar network expanded into a full-fledged transit system by the end of the 1890s. In 1896, all the smaller streetcar companies consolidated under the ownership and operation of one corporation — the Milwaukee Electric Railway and Light Company. Electrification of the street railways was completed in that decade. Considerable expansion of lines and connections between 1890 and 1910 improved transportation for urban dwellers, though the city's streetcars never adequately served crosstown travel or

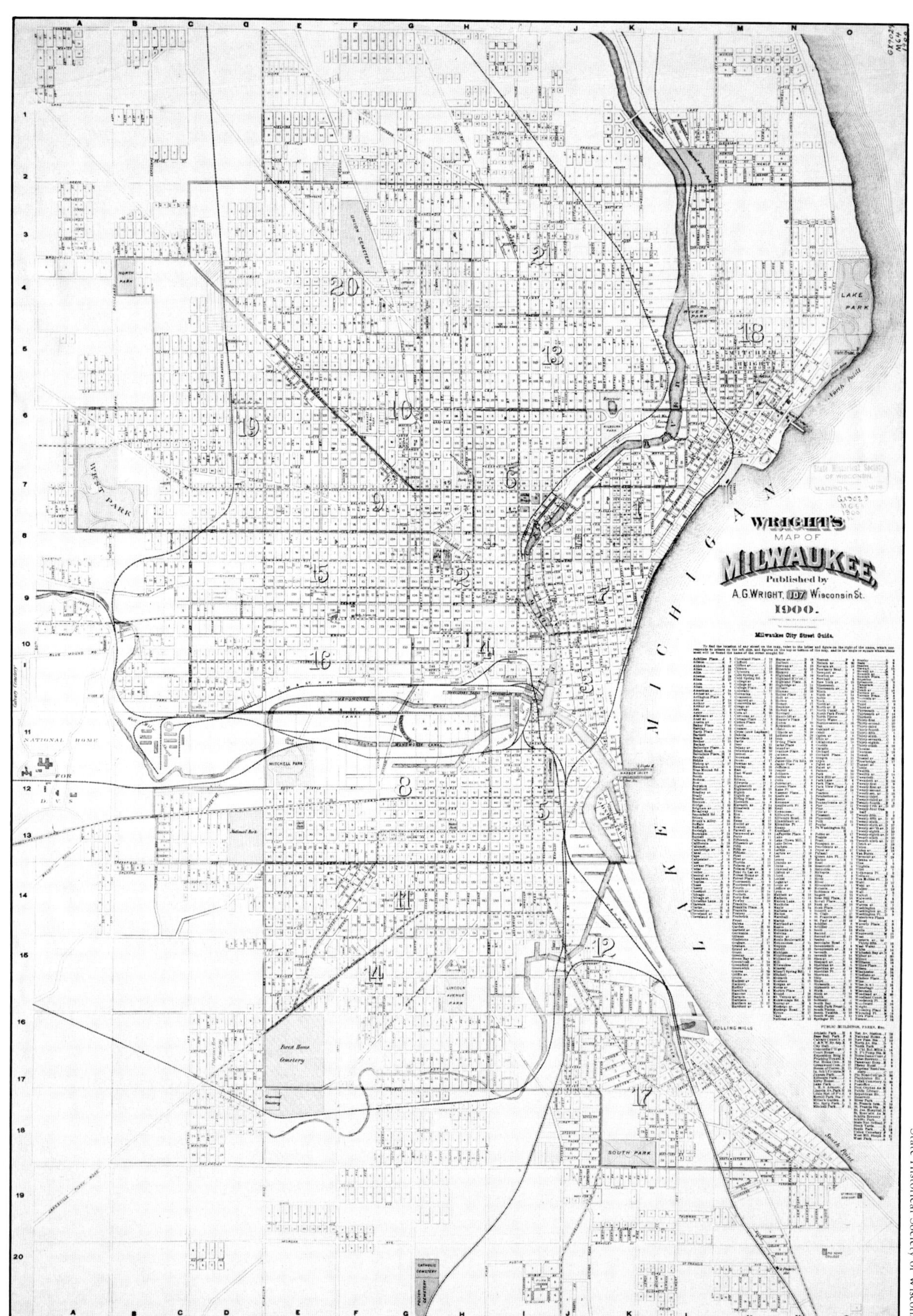

State Historical Society of Wisconsin

major manufacturing areas. In 1902, for example, five of Milwaukee's thirteen largest industries still lacked trolley service.[53]

Despite the street railways' shortcomings, they provided access to inexpensive suburban land. Partially because of the decentralizaton of industry, however, streetcars did not change Milwaukee's residential growth patterns at the turn of the century: They merely enabled continuation of the older development patterns described earlier.[54]

Combined with Milwaukee's rapid economic growth, the streetcars sparked physical expansion of the city in all possible directions. Wright's "Map of Milwaukee, 1900" (illustrated here) shows the extent of Milwaukee's growth by the turn of the century. By 1930, the city's developed areas included the territory roughly bound by Capitol Drive on the north, North Sixtieth Street on the west, and Oklahoma Avenue on the south.[55] As the city grew in area, it absorbed pre-existing villages such as Humboldt on the North Side and Bay View on the South Side. The city also spun off several separate industrial towns and residential suburbs by the end of the nineteenth century. Cudahy, South Milwaukee, and West Allis were all towns founded by large companies in the 1890s for their expanded industrial plants. North Milwaukee was a promotional venture of the railroads and Republican leaders for industrial relocation.[56]

The process of urban expansion in Milwaukee's newly developing sections after 1880 varied little from one section of the city to another. Subdivision plats, filed with the city, varied in size but seldom deviated from the established rectangular grid street layout. Property along major existing roads was subdivided earliest, the rest of a given area generally following in order of its distance from the central city. The development of blocks within a subdivision repeated the same pattern. Essential urban services usually followed a set order: streetcar lines, then water and sewer mains, and finally graded streets.

The lot sizes and quality of urban services in the city's developing areas to the north, south, and west depended on the socio-economic status of the prospective inhabitants in a particular area. In the highest income neighborhoods, such as North Point on the East Side, developers subdivided the land into large lots with a comparatively small number of lots on each block. Generally, urban services preceded housing construction. In middle income areas, such as the northwestern section of the city, an increasing number of duplexes were built on long narrow lots. Residents usually had streetcar service, water and sewer connections, and graded (not paved) streets by the time houses filled one-third of most blocks.

Lot sizes were not generally smaller on the South Side than in the northwestern section, but densities were greater. The Polish tradition, in Milwaukee, of raising flats to provide a basement dwelling, as well as constructing a cottage at the rear of the small lot, substantially increased the population densities of South Side neighborhoods. In addition, many South Side residents delayed installation of urban services for some years after the blocks were filled with houses. Abutting property owners subsidized most of the street, water, and sewer improvements. The Poles, who inhabited much of the South Side and who were primarily employed in industrial work, chose to purchase homes and pay off their mortgages before assuming the costs of urban services desirable for health and convenience.[57]

Even though the process of urban expansion in Milwaukee was fairly uniform, the city's neighborhoods, old and new, varied greatly in occupational and ethnic composition and in housing conditions. "Different groups staked out distinct sections of the metropolis for themselves . . . markedly different urban environments arose in scattered corners of the expanded city."[58] Later chapters on neighborhoods describe the ethnic population and housing characteristics of various areas within the city between 1880 and 1930, the period from which most surveyed sites date.

Baist's Property Atlas, 1898. Section showing the developing West Side. Pre-existing plank roads, farmsteads, and open land remain among the new subdivisions. Note the rectangular grid street layout and narrow lots of the recently-platted areas.

Duplex, 2021 N. Twenty-eighth St., c. 1907. Duplexes such as these, with rectangular plans and prominent gables, were built in great numbers at the turn of the century on long narrow lots in the developing West Side.

Milwaukee Co. Historical Society

Juneau Park, looking south along Lake Michigan, c. 1915. The Chicago and Northwestern Railway Depot, built in 1889, was located at the south end of the park. Since then, the terminal has been demolished, the lakeshore extended, and Memorial Drive has replaced the railroad tracks. The Milwaukee Art Center is now the most pronounced architectural element on the downtown lakefront.

Planning and Zoning

Overall guidance and planning of the city's physical growth dates from the turn of the century. The Board of Park Commissioners, established in 1889, was the first municipal body to consider the land use of the urban landscape as a whole. (See chapter on "Open Spaces, Public Parks, and Urban Design.") A city ordinance of 1902 regulated the height of buildings with respect to the width of streets. The Metropolitan Park Commission, appointed in 1907, attempted "to provide residence areas apart from the commercial and factory zones."[59] Overall planning was facilitated by the passage of the city's first comprehensive zoning ordinance in 1920. New York had pioneered in comprehensive zoning in 1916, and Milwaukee was the twelfth city in the nation to follow its example. The ordinance divided the city into use, height, and area districts (residential, local business, commercial and light manufacturing, and industrial) "according to the predominant types of building then existing or anticipated in the logical development of the community."[60] In 1923, the Wisconsin Supreme Court strengthened the concept of zoning in Milwaukee, and elsewhere, by recognizing planning as a means of promoting the public welfare and expanding the concept that aesthetic factors might be considered in regulation.

Summary

Observers of Milwaukee in the early twentieth century called it an industrial workshop, a city of homes and workers. The Works Projects Administration (WPA) *Guide to Wisconsin* aptly described Milwaukee's physical and cultural landscape by the time of the 1930s:

> Milwaukee, the largest city in Wisconsin, covers an irregularly glove-shaped area of 44.1 square miles along the crescent curve of a bay in Lake Michigan's western shore. Toward the east Milwaukee looks upon a marine landscape animated by freighters, car ferries, excursion steamers, and the white flecks of yachts and sailboat. Westward, highways lead past wooded farmlands to dozens of inland lakes where affluent Milwaukeeans maintain year-round residences and the mildly prosperous have summer cottages . . . North along the high bluffs overlooking the lake are the town houses of the wealthy, some new and impressive, some old and baronial, many built years ago as the homes of pioneer brewers, tanners, and lumbermen. Wisconsin Avenue, the main thoroughfare, runs westward from the lake, through the heart of the city. Business in outlying areas concentrates in frequent neighborly clusters of shops and offices. Newcomers sense . . . the suburban, rather than metropolitan face that the city presents: the low buildings of the downtown area where only a few rise higher than 300 feet, the acres of field and forest in one of the country's outstanding park systems, the free sweep of Lincoln Memorial Drive along the lake, the neat cottages in the German and Polish neighborhoods, the pastoral look of lawns and gardens in even the less prosperous districts . . . Assimilation of the German elements has accompanied the decline of German immigration to the city. Milwaukee no longer seems a city transplanted from the Rhine to the banks of the Milwaukee River; the German theater has disappeared with the beer gardens; "Milwaukee German" is heard less and less frequently. . . ."[61]

Looking south on N. Third St. from Wells St. at night, c. 1920. Automobiles, Charlie Chaplin, and an abundance of electric signs were new facets of Milwaukee streetscapes in the early twentieth century.

Milwaukee Co. Historical Society

Aerial photograph of downtown Milwaukee, 1930s. View northeast. Interstate Highway 794 now bisects the business district one block north of the railyards.

State Historical Society of Wisconsin

Residential Architecture in Milwaukee

Milwaukee Co. Historical Society

East Side house under construction, c. 1915.

As noted in the introduction, the comprehensive architectural survey identified more than six thousand buildings and structures. Over half of these sites were residences. The survey included houses of high style and fine workmanship, as well as hundreds representative of various periods of Milwaukee's development from ca. 1840-1940. Consequently, there is a good source of information — the survey forms — from which a chronology of historical styles, building materials, and building types can be established. Only extant buildings were surveyed, however, and it is therefore necessary to refer to historical photographs and drawings to elaborate on those aspects of Milwaukee's architectural history not revealed in the initial survey.

In this chapter on Milwaukee's residential architecture, we are seeking an understanding of what is typical and what is unique. What does one see in Milwaukee? How did the first Yankee settlers and subsequent European immigrant groups influence the residential building traditions of the city? How did the city's phenomenal economic growth determine the configuration and location of neighborhoods? How do residential building types (i.e. cottage, duplex, bungalow) and historical styles mesh? What were the city's indigenous nineteenth and early twentieth century materials and design resources?

Milwaukee and Its Early Dwellings

Alfred T. Andreas' 1881 *History of Milwaukee* reports that there were seven dwellings constructed by Indian traders before "Anglo-Saxons" began building in 1834. In 1834, five structures were completed, and in 1835, sixteen were built and three more started. By the end of 1835, according to Andreas, Milwaukee had twenty-eight finished and three partially-finished buildings, most of them dwellings.[1] In 1836, a "building mania" resulted in the construction of more dwellings and a courthouse. By 1837, about five hundred inhabitants lived in sixty dwellings, and fifty more were under contract for construction. Early buildings, of Indian traders and settlers like Solomon Juneau and George H. Walker, were constructed of rough hand-hewn logs similar to the first buildings of other pioneer settlements along the edges of the Great Lakes and throughout the Wisconsin Territory. Very quickly, however, an already-advanced building technology and vocabulary of architectural style became available, and the young settlement of Milwaukee kept pace with the development of more urbanized centers elsewhere in the Midwest. In the 1840s and 1850s, a severe shortage of housing beset the city as demand outpaced supply. *Milwaukee Sentinel* editorials encouraged the speculative construction of houses:

> There is a great demand for dwelling houses and those of our capitalists who own lots and have money would find a safe and permanent investment in erecting a few buildings to rent . . .[2]

State Historical Society of Wisconsin

State Historical Society of Wisconsin

William A. Prentiss House. Built in 1836, burned 1845. This engraved view is probably representative of the early Milwaukee residences constructed of sawn lumber.

Building Materials and Labor Supply at Mid-Century

The point we wish to bring out particularly here, is that Milwaukee herself affords the material with which to build a city . . .[3]

Milwaukee Illustrated, 1877.

Lumber

Although vast, Wisconsin's timber resources were strained by the mid-nineteenth century's demand for sawn lumber. Supplies were brought to Milwaukee via Michigan to supplement the local shortages. Lime for mortar, clay for brick, and building stone, however, were plentiful in the Milwaukee area. Local sawmills insured that board lumber was available to the first generation of Milwaukee builders. In 1834, Daniel Bigelow built a water-powered mill along the Milwaukee River, near Humboldt Avenue, producing oak and basswood lumber. In 1835, Otis Hubbard and James K. Bottsford built the second mill along the river. The first planing mill was built by Robert Luscombe and J. T. Perkins. This four-story, water-powered planing mill measured forty feet by eighty feet. The planer which produced doors, sash, millwork, and siding was reportedly Luscombe's invention.[4]

By 1847, a small, but indigenous building trade was established in Milwaukee. The city's first directory listed three lumber merchants, one planing mill (the Luscombe and Perkins), one painter and glazier (A. McFayden), and the LaPoint and Pfenning sash factory. The second directory of 1848 included an advertisement of architect John F. Rague, formerly of New York, in addition to several new lumber yards and building supply dealers.

PLANING MILL

SASH FACTORY,

AND

LUMBER YARD,

JOHN T. PERKINS

KEEPS CONSTANTLY ON HAND

SEASONED LUMBER,

OF ALL KINDS; ALSO

Flooring, Planed, Matched and Dressed Siding,

DOORS & SASH,

OF ALL SIZES,

AT HIS LUMBER YARD,

No. 278 Third Street, (Second Ward)

DOORS and SASH made to order on the shortest notice, at his Sash Factory on Canal Street.

J. T. Perkins Planing Mill. Advertisement from 1847-1848 Milwaukee City Directory.

ARCHIBALD McFADYEN,

HOUSE, SIGN,

AND

ORNAMENTAL PAINTER,

Imitator of WOOD and Marble,

GILDER & GLAZIER,

Number 225, WATER STREET, MILWAUKEE,

Has always on hand, ready mixed Paints, Oils, Turpe ne, Varnishes, Japan, Window Glass, & Sash.

WALL PAINTING

Executed in the most approved manner.

Archibald McFayden, House, Sign, and Ornamental Painter, 1847-1848. Milwaukee City Directory. This conventionalized drawing of a Federal Style building was often used in Milwaukee newspapers and directories in the 1840s and 1850s to illustrate real estate, hotel, and builders' and painters' advertisements.

Brick

Locally burned brick has been used by Milwaukee builders for residential construction since the late 1830s. Milwaukee's "cream brick" is burned from the Lacustrine clays which run in deep veins along Lake Michigan. Their unique color comes from the chemical reaction of minerals in the clay, which burn a buff color instead of the more typical red. Disagreement exists about Milwaukee's first brickmaker, but consensus dates the first brick house at 1836, and the first brick commercial block at 1840. The brickmaking industry began to boom in the 1850s with a large demand for Milwaukee bricks from other American cities such as Chicago and St. Louis and from abroad.[5]

Numerous newspaper articles in other cities called attention to the special quality of Milwaukee's brick products.

The city is built largely of a fine cream-colored brick, which is of a superior quality and enduring in color, and gives the place a peculiar appearance — having earned for it the cognomen of "Cream City".

E. C. Hussey, *Home Building . . . at about 400 Places from New York to San Francisco,* 1876

Milwaukee has long been celebrated for the beauty and superiority of its bricks, which are of light cream or buff color, admirably adapted to ornate modern city architecture, being more pleasing to the eye as well as more durable than the red bricks of eastern kilns.

Andreas, *History of Milwaukee,* 1881.

Burnham Brickyard Advertisement, 1890. George and John Burnham started their brickyards in 1843; in 1865 they split, forming two separate brickmaking businesses. By 1880, George Burnham and Sons was the leader of the brickmaking industry in the city, producing 15 million bricks and employing 300 men.

Geo. Burnham & Sons,

— MANUFACTURERS OF THE —

CELEBRATED MILWAUKEE CREAM-COLORED

ANGULAR BRICK OF ALL KINDS MADE TO ORDER.

— DEALERS IN —

HEMLOCK AND HARDWOOD LUMBER AND PINE AND HARDWOOD LANDS IN WISCONSIN AND MICHIGAN.

OFFICE AND YARDS: 671 PARK STREET

MILWAUKEE, - WISCONSIN.

State Historical Society of Wisconsin

Milwaukee Cement Works. The Milwaukee Cement Stone quarry was located along the Milwaukee River and covered nearly 200 acres. Kilns for burning limestone, stone crushers, and warehouses were among buildings illustrated in this 1877 lithograph. This cement works began production in 1876.

Joseph Shaver Marble Company, Seventh Street near Cherry, photograph c. 1895. There was no local source of high grade marble in Milwaukee, but the cutting, polishing, and manufacturing of imported marble was conducted at several locations in the city.

Milwaukee Co. Historical Society

Milwaukee Lime and Limestone

Our beautiful, hard, firm and durable brick have been noticed by scribblers innumerable, during the past season, so they are now pretty well known . . . but none have taken the trouble to inform the public of the other building materials with which we are abundantly supplied. Good brick would possess but little value without good lime and good sand — clean, sharp, gritty sand — is also indispensible to good masonry. Our lake shores and hillsides afford the latter material in great perfection, easily and abundantly obtained. The lime brought to Milwaukee is of the purest and whitest kind. There are four principal quarries where it is obtained, one of them (and one of the best) within the corporated limits of our own city. The stone from which (lime) is made is of a very rough, porous kind, allowing the heat to penetrate to the center of each fragment and thus securing a perfect calcination of the entire mass. The stratum of limestone that lies under this rough kind is of more regular structure and affords an excellent building material as may be seen in many of the basement stories of the buildings in Milwaukee . . . with such materials, it is our own fault if we do not have within a few years a BEAUTIFUL CITY as well as a great one.

Milwaukee Sentinel,
October 12, 1847

Early lime and cement producers established their businesses in the 1840s. Werner Trimborn (1802-1879), a native of Prussia, arrived in Milwaukee in 1847, and in 1851 established the Trimborn and Sons lime business which served many of Milwaukee's early masons. Trimborn, one of the first German settlers, worked up to six kilns for burning lime, located on his 530 acre farm in Greenfield, just outside the present-day city limits.[6]

The Balloon Frame and Builder's Guides

City Directories, the 1850 industrial census, and the *History of Milwaukee* by A. T. Andreas (1881) provide information on the ethnic background of Milwaukee's first house builders. Although skilled German craftsmen and carpenters were among the stable German population of 1850, successful builders at mid-century and beyond were often Yankees. Kathleen Conzen notes in *Immigrant Milwaukee* (1976) that non-native Americans had to spend time "familiarizing themselves with American ways before striking out on their own."[7] Later in the century, however, the traditional skills of European craftsmen were required as Milwaukee's finest homes were erected of hand-cut stone, carefully-laid brick, and finely-turned wood. Builders whose biographies appear in A. T. Andreas' 1881 *History of Milwaukee* were from Wales, Prussia, Germany, Holland, Newfoundland, Canada, Poland, Ireland, and England.

The builders of Milwaukee's first houses of the 1840s and 1850s did not have to possess great carpentry skill, since several new technological developments were available. Lightweight frame construction and some prefabrication of parts were possible using the "balloon frame". The balloon frame was constructed of lightweight, dimensional lumber and connected with mass-produced wire nails. Joints were nailed, rather than being fastened by the traditional mortise and tenon joinery of earlier American houses.[8] This framing method used a minimal amount of lumber, and enabled rapid house construction by relatively unskilled persons. By the time of the Civil War, the balloon frame largely replaced the hewn frame for urban domestic construction, although builders in rural areas continued to use hand-hewn timber frames until the early 1870s.[9]

Manuals such as *Homes for the People in Suburbs and Country* by Gervase Wheeler (1855) provided builders with construction details for the framing system. These builders' manuals not only explained the advantages and technique of the new balloon framing method, but also provided information on architectural details and styles.

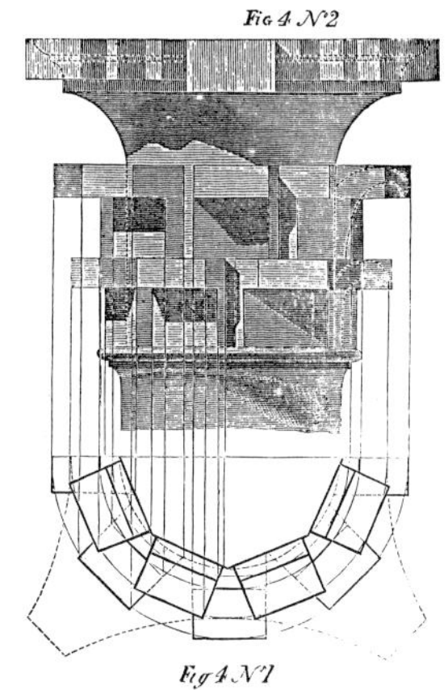

The Modern Architect; or, Every Carpenter His Own Master, Embracing plans, elevations, specifications, framing, etc., for private houses, classic dwellings, churches, etc. to which is added the new system of stair building. By Edward Shaw, Boston, 1854.

By the time Milwaukee was settled, ideas of American architectural style had long been exchanged through carpenters' or builders' guides. The first manuals used in America originated in England and the eastern United States, and were carried in the pockets of carpenters to the settlements of the West. Typically, these practical books illustrated details such as moldings, windows, staircases, and columns, and provided plans and facade elevations. They were written for the carpenter rather than the few amateur or professional architects of the day.

The earliest American books, such as the seven manuals written by Asher Benjamin (1771-1845) between 1797 and 1814, showed architectural details representative of the Federal Style. Later books, such as *The Modern Builder's Guide* (1833) by New York architect Minard Lafever (1798-1854), illustrated plates of Greek Revival facades and details.[10] Later editions of Lafever's book recognized advances in building technology, and provided carpenters with plans which utilized board lumber, rather than the laboriously hewn timbers of previous decades.

Nicolson's New Carpenter's Guide; being A Complete Book of Lines for Carpenters, Joiners, Cabinet-Makers, and Workmen in General. By John Hay, London, 1860. Nicolson's was among a number of English books also used by American carpenters. Although it is difficult to document exactly which books or manuals were used in Milwaukee, the book from which this illustration is taken was owned by D. C. Chatterton of Milwaukee.

Milwaukee Co. Historical Society

Joseph Keyes House (later August and Frederick Luening), formerly at Broadway at Wells, 1836. Photograph c. 1920. The Keyes home is evidence that some of Milwaukee's first houses were built on raised brick foundations. The raised foundation is testament to the poor drainage and swamp-like character of the early settlement. It also may indicate a change in street grade, as some areas were "cut down" as roads were constructed.

Houses of the First Three Decades: 1840-1870

Residential architectural styles in Milwaukee during the first three decades of settlement reflected the Yankee backgrounds of many of its citizens. Although most early buildings have been razed, photographs help to reconstruct a chronology of "pioneer" styles. It is evident that the first land speculators, lumbermen, and businessmen quickly constructed "proper and stylish" homes for themselves. The early architectural styles of Milwaukee display the adaptation of architectural motifs of the eastern United States to a new place and a new people. Milwaukee's natural resources and building materials lent a special character to its early architecture. The Greek Revival house, for example, was often built of the unique Milwaukee cream brick, and the early Italianate house displayed a limestone foundation, sill, and window trim from nearby quarries.

An early Milwaukee resident, the Swiss-born Reverend Bishop Dr. Johann Martin Henni, astutely observed the local use of prefabricated parts and Milwaukee's emerging expression of architectural taste.

Writing of dwellings, he states:

> One would suppose that in this building of houses, many men would find employment, but such is not the case. From base to ridgepole, everything comes finished from the factory. One gets boards for the floors already planed, windows with frames and glass, doors with locks—in short, everything is prepared by machinery and only a few laborers are needed to erect a complete building out of the several parts.[11]

"Taste for art", Henni noted, was "still in its infancy."[12] He critically noted that the early Milwaukeeans had no idea of "architecture proper, although every house is built to a certain style. A frieze or a few Doric half-columns nailed on a frame house is considered an ornament in Grecian, Italian, or East Indian Style."[13]

The "certain styles" to which Henni referred in 1851 are the Greek Revival, the Italianate, and likely, the Gothic Revival. Examples of Federal Style architecture were also found in Milwaukee in 1851.

A Note on Architectural Styles

A knowledge of architectural styles helps us to understand Milwaukee's past. Styles are representative of the ideas and concerns of various periods of history, as well as local resources such as building materials and a skilled labor supply. Although style is a useful way of classifying buildings, there are sometimes great differences among buildings of the same style. Relatively few buildings in Milwaukee are examples of "pure" style, because builders often combined elements of several styles in one building. This eclectic nature is particularly obvious in the merging of styles at the end of the nineteenth century, and in the period revival styles of the early twentieth century. The term "Victorian" is often used in connection with the styles popular during Queen Victoria's reign between 1837 and 1901. In America, the Victorian era is associated with colorful and picturesque architectural styles, as well as the creation of new building technology which fueled the development of modern architecture.

Federal Houses in Milwaukee

Photographs of early Milwaukee depict a considerable number of brick buildings, including dwellings and stores, which show Federal Style characteristics. These early buildings have disappeared almost completely from the first neighborhoods of the city where they were once abundant, particularly in the present-day downtown area.

American architecture of the late eighteenth and early nineteenth centuries was influenced by archaeological discoveries of ancient Greece and Rome. Architects studied illustrations of antique buildings, and produced crisp, linear designs for residences, stores, and public buildings. In New England, the term "Federal" or "Federalist" is associated with the Neo-classical buildings of the period 1785-1820. Although the less delicately proportioned Greek Revival Style assumed national importance as an American architectural style after about 1820, the slender proportions of the Federal Style nevertheless reached the early settlements of the Middle West. In Milwaukee in the mid-nineteenth century, "brick was an ideal medium for the crisp details of the (Federal) style."[14] Characteristics of local Federal Style buildings included a cubic or rectangular form, often three stories, with symmetrically-arranged windows. Some brick buildings evidenced tall parapet end walls, with twin gable-end chimneys.

State Historical Society of Wisconsin

Layton House, 2504 Forest Home Avenue, 1849. Photograph c. 1890. Designed by John Rague for John and Frederic Layton. Situated along what was originally a plank road, the Layton House was a popular hotel and stopping point for early travellers. Straight stone lintels at the windows and a simple brick course at the cornice are among the only decorative details of this severe, symmetrical design.

Layton House, photograph 1981.

1209 S. 7th St., 1860. This small frame house is representative of a handful of early Milwaukee houses which date from the 1840s and 1850s. Most defy classification along stylistic lines, but exhibit both "Federal" and later Greek Revival details. Significant early details include the "half moon" window in the gable end, four over four double hung sash, and a glazed transom over the entrance.

Milwaukee Public Library

Federal Style House, c. 1845. Originally located on Water Street, this 2-story brick house has the crisp, simple details and tall end wall parapets which were characteristic of Milwaukee's early Federal houses.

Benjamin Church House, now in Estabrook Park, 1843. Originally located at 1553 N. Fourth Street, this Greek Revival house was built by an early settler. It is an outstanding example of the style, with a full Doric-columned portico. Benjamin Church, a builder by trade, was born in New York.

William Howard House, 910 S. Third Street, 1854. Situated in Walker's Point, the Howard House is one of the best remaining examples of the Greek Revival Style in the city. Of note is the recessed entry framed by pilasters and a classical entablature; full sidelights and a glazed transom surround the door. William Howard, a canal and cargo ship worker, was born in Fort Ann, New York and came to Milwaukee in 1836.

4261 S. Whitnall, c. 1850. Early Milwaukee settler J. Ballard Cross arrived in the area in 1843 and became a farmer and wagon maker. Greek Revival characteristics of his house include returns at the gable ends and a classical entablature over the entrance. Originally, the house was clapboard-covered.

In 1849, the *Philadelphia American and Gazette* praised Milwaukee as a city "which has sprung up in western wilderness as if by magic . . . (it) is already growing tired of its brick and mortar hedged streets, and its 16,000 inhabitants are beginning to think of decorating its rural suburbs with a more ornamental style of building. Professional architects are paying their court to the capitalists of the place. . . ."[16]

Greek Revival

The Greek Revival was certainly the most prevalent of the house styles of the period 1840-1860. Assisted by the builder's book, the early carpenters constructed gable or hip roofed, square or L-plan dwellings with classical ornament based on the Greek and Roman orders. Columns, capitals, friezes, and moldings followed classical precedent, and the buildings' facades often emulated the temple form. Returns at the eaves or a full pedimented gable identifies the Greek Revival house of early Milwaukee. Six over six, double hung sash, and an entrance framed with pilasters and sidelights are also common style features.

Architectural historians note that the Greek Revival Style achieved national prominence during a time of great nationalistic spirit and European travel and discovery. American popular opinion identified with the struggles of the Greeks against the Turks in the great war of 1821-28. The Greek Revival Style was chosen for the design of countless public and private buildings in Eastern states, as well as territorial capitals, schools, banks and farmhouses in the West. The Milwaukee County Courthouse of 1836, executed in a classical manner with four Tuscan columns, no doubt reflected the local admiration for things Greek and Roman.

By 1849, in some circles at least, there was a consciousness of the building art which Henni's comments do not acknowledge. An editorial in the *Milwaukee Sentinel* noted:

> . . . we are glad to see a growing desire for something more than mere piles of brick and mortar, or scantling and boards. It costs little or nothing more to build a home comely and shapely, beautiful and with every convenience within than to build one just the reverse. . . .[15]

Early Gothic Revival

American architectural fashion diversified greatly in the 1840s, with new standards of domestic taste changing continually. The nation's housing at mid-century evidenced a gradual evolution of architectural plan and details at all income levels, from the simple worker's cottage to the wealthy businessman's "palace". A taste for the exotic and eclectic was evident in the development of the Gothic Revival Style, and can also be seen in some versions of the Italianate Style.

In the Gothic Revival, pointed arches and an overall symmetry replaced the rectangular openings and classical symmetry of the Greek Revival. Andrew Jackson Downing's publications, which illustrated picturesque houses in rustic settings, helped spark an interest in both Gothic Revival and Italianate styles of architecture in Milwaukee. Downing's books showed numerous residential designs, many of them drawn by architect Alexander Jackson Davis, for varieties of "Gothic" cottages and "Italian" villas. Versions of "Norman" cottages and "Swiss" chalets were also illustrated.

Downing's Gothic cottages were not the first Gothic buildings in America, as fascination with things "Gothick" had begun as early as 1756 with the popularity of British author Horace Walpole's novel the *Castle of Otranto*. Gothic church designs were popular in America in the 1830s and 1840s. Downing-inspired Gothic houses, showing the influence of Early English and Norman architecture, were built in Milwaukee and southern Wisconsin between about 1845 and 1860. Characteristics of the style include steeply-pitched gable roofs, pointed lancet windows, and decorative carving or cusping at bargeboards. Smooth-finished stone, or vertical board and batten siding were preferred materials for the exterior of the Gothic house. Only one "pure" example of the style stands in Milwaukee today, but Gothic Revival details can still be seen on various dwellings throughout the city.

A later version of the Gothic Revival, known as the High Victorian Gothic or Victorian Gothic, was popular in the 1870s and 1880s.

Herman Wudtke Collection

St. John's Episcopal Church Parsonage, 1848-50. Formerly at the east corner of S. 4th and Pierce Streets, now the site of the Boy's Technical School, this house evidences the vertical board and batten siding associated with the early Gothic Revival. Cusped bargeboards are also visible at the gable ends.

DESIGN FOR A COUNTRY HOUSE.

A COTTAGE IN THE SWISS STYLE.

House Plans. From Andrew Jackson Downing's *The Horticulturist* 1848-49.

3317 S. Kinnickinnic Avenue, 1855-56. Built by early settler Russell Bennett as a farmhouse (and illustrated in the 1876 *Illustrated Historical Atlas of Milwaukee*), the Bennett House survives as Milwaukee's best example of the early Gothic Revival. Although later additions and alterations have been made to the cream brick house, pointed arch windows with prominent hoods, and steeply pitched gable roofs are features of the original design.

Early Italianate and Italian Villa

Sixteenth century palazzo designs of the Italian Renaissance and the country homes of rural Tuscany provided the architectural vocabulary for a popular residential style of the mid-nineteenth century. The "Italian" Style, varieties of which are sometimes referred to as the "Bracketed Style", "Italian Villa", and "Italianate", was a popular mode of residential construction in Milwaukee between about 1850 and 1870.

The influence of the earlier Federal and Greek Revival Styles can be seen in the flat surfaces, cubic form, and formal symmetry of some early examples; whereas towers, cupolas, irregular plans, and surface richness characterize the later examples. Early examples have straight lintels and long rectangular windows; the three-story façade of some early examples resembles now-razed Federal period houses built in the city.

Many of the Italianate houses in Milwaukee have hip or gable roofs, round or segmental arched windows, and a variety of ornamental details including scrolls or brackets at cornices and entrance hoods, carved or pressed window enframements, wide pilasters or cornerboards, and chamfered posts at porches and entrances. On gable-roofed houses, returns at eaves (originally a Greek Revival feature), may still be present, but are of shorter proportions.

Samuel Luscombe House, N. 77th St. and W. Lisbon, 1851. The low pitch roof, overhanging eaves, and round arch windows are early Italianate features of this cream brick house.

Carl Kunckell Residence, 2221 S. 16th Street, 1857. An excellent example of the Italian Villa style, this house was built by a fur dealer and manufacturer of soda water. The L-shape plan, 14 foot square tower, and round-arched windows are key features of the design. Originally, the house and its six-acre estate commanded an excellent view of the surrounding area; over the past century the land surrounding the area has been re-graded leaving the Kunckell house above high retaining walls.

A Villa in the Italian Style, Bracketed. Figure 48 of Andrew Jackson Downing's *Cottage Residences* of 1850. Downing was one of the early advocates of the Italian mode. The square tower was a prominent feature, as were round-arched windows and broad overhanging eaves. Although Downing's design is shown in wood, brick and stucco were preferred materials.

1825 N. Second Street, c. 1858. The flat roof and cubic appearance of this 1850s house are reminiscent of the proportions of earlier Federal period houses. A modillioned cornice and moulded lintel and door surrounds are the main decorative features of this painted brick structure.

Italianate houses of cream brick had a special character due to their masonry construction. Lintels were often of carved stone. Great attention was paid to the craftsmanship of details such as the oculus (or round window) in the gable end, and water tables of rusticated limestone were often added at the foundation and first story level. Brick quoins were fashioned at the corners to emulate blocks of stone.

Although some of Milwaukee's Italianate houses show the builder's or architect's careful use of pattern books or Renaissance architectural detail, others indicate only the carpenter's selection of the wide array of stock ornamentation available at the local lumber yard and through mail-order. Although many fine details were hand carved, the machine-made, scroll-sawn and pressed wood ornaments made it possible to create a house of great richness very quickly.

Emil Schneider House, 813 South Third Street, 1870. One of three excellent late Italianate houses on South Third Street in Walker's Point, the Schneider House was built by a wine and liquor merchant who emigrated from Prussia in 1852. A low hip roof, bracketed cornice, and round-arch, brick-trimmed windows are original features of the house.

Edward Townsend Mix House, Waverly Place and Juneau Street, 1869. Photograph c. 1875. Architect Mix designed his own house in the Italian Villa Style, with an asymmetrical plan and square corner tower. No longer standing.

Milwaukee Public Library

1948 N. Third Street, c. 1860. This two-story frame house has prominent segmental-arched hood molds at the windows and entrance, and is representative of simple Italianate houses built before the Civil War.

Creative Eclecticism in Milwaukee: Houses built after the Civil War

2443 N. Gordon Pl., c. 1851.

Octagon

The short-lived "Octagon House" phenomenon was inspired by the writings of Orson Squire Fowler of New York. Fowler was fascinated with the eight-sided octagon shape, and his 1848 book *A Home for All, or the Gravel Wall and Octagon Mode of Building* proclaimed the advantages of the Octagon for residential construction. Although Fowler endorsed the gravel and cement wall, many Octagons were of wooden construction, but built with an interlocking pattern of horizontal beams rather than the standard stud wall. Wisconsin has a rich concentration of Octagon houses, but only one of the three known to have been built in Milwaukee remains.

Between the end of the Civil War and the turn of the century, American architects experimented with a variety of historical sources and symbols. Italian Renaissance, English Medieval, and French Baroque buildings were among many sources which helped shape the private and public architecture of the era. Advances in building technology, such as new saws and lathes, and new materials also offered new opportunities for architectural expression.[17] Architectural books and periodicals facilitated an exchange of ideas between architects of the East Coast and the Midwest, as many (but not all) styles "moved" to Milwaukee after a debut in New York, Boston, or Philadelphia. Another factor which fueled the eclectic nature of late nineteenth century architecture was a change in living habits and social customs. In Milwaukee, as in large cities elsewhere in the United States, prospective home owners turned their attention from the central city to the "suburb", and architects and builders responded with house designs well-suited for the new informal, relaxed atmosphere of the suburban setting. The suburb of the Milwaukee of 1875, however, was as near as Fifteenth Street and Wisconsin Avenue. By 1895, however, the suburban location was well beyond the limits of the old "walking city" and catered to a less affluent resident than the previous generation.

By 1880, architectural style and residential building fashion was widely discussed in Milwaukee newspapers. In an article titled "Taste in Building", the *Milwaukee Sentinel* editor attempted to define beauty in architecture, and admonished readers that "the individual who builds a tasty house is a public benefactor. He not only satisfies the public taste, but he helps to educate it."[18]

Many of Milwaukee's fine houses of the second half of the century defy classification along strictly stylistic lines. Rather, they are an interesting amalgam of styles, representative of the builder or architect's borrowing from several sources. Characteristically, the large house designed by an architect for a wealthy client on Prospect Avenue or Wisconsin Avenue has several companion houses of smaller scale in middle income neighborhoods built by carpenters with the aid of published plans. Such filtering of styles is a standard feature of the architectural character of Milwaukee. Each building has its own special character to which the builder or architect and various owners contributed. Buildings were often "modernized", resulting in Greek Revival houses with Queen Anne porches and various combinations of materials and details. Whether speculatively-built duplexes or individually-designed "gingerbread" cottages, the style of a house can help to reveal something of the personality of an earlier owner and earlier Milwaukee neighborhood.

State Historical Society of Wisconsin

Emil Wallber House. Stereograph view of the Wallber residence at Sixth and Galena being moved in 1875. Reportedly this was the first brick house in Milwaukee to be moved. Emil Wallber was later Mayor of Milwaukee (1884-1888).

House Moving

House moving was an early feature of Milwaukee's changing landscape:

> . . . houses are often seen travelling through the streets. This means that if to an American the place where his house stands seems no longer desirable, he has it placed on rollers and pulled to a better location; he has "moved" as ordinary parlance has it. However, during this jaunty trip (which sometimes lasts 8 days) the owner lives in the building, quite comfortable.[19]

In 1847, a *Milwaukee Sentinel* editorial noted that house moving was carried on "extensively" and reported that during the week of September 25, 1847, a thirty foot by forty foot house was moved "some distance without the slightest damage. The job was done by four Germans; Hensel, Lusk, Rolle and Gust, who certainly understand their business."[20]

By the end of the century, it was common to move homes and heavy brick commercial buildings. Henry Buestrin and Company proudly advertised in 1881 that they had moved the two hundred and fifty ton, ninety-five foot brick chimney at the Phoenix mills, with a base of eight feet, reportedly the first job of its kind ever attempted in America.[21]

2700-2704 S. Shore Drive, 1892. Cream brick houses (and one of brown brick) in Bay View are trimmed with limestone sills, lintels, and string-courses. Pressed brick panels further decorate the wall surfaces.

Milwaukee's Cream Brick Houses

The cream brick house of Milwaukee's neighborhoods may be of Greek Revival, Italianate, or Queen Anne Style, but its unique material is often its most distinguished feature. A gable or hipped roof, and carefully-crafted masonry details are the constituent features of this Milwaukee building tradition. Cream brick was popular until the late nineteenth century, when architectural taste shifted in favor of dark masonry materials such as Lake Superior brownstone and shades of brown and red brick.

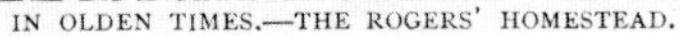

IN OLDEN TIMES.—THE ROGERS' HOMESTEAD.

THE MODERN STYLE—RESIDENCE OF FRED. PABST.

Victorian Italianate Style

In 1877, the Victorian Italianate residence of Frederick Pabst Jr. at Eighth and Juneau Street, designed by Henry C. Koch, was featured in the popular promotional book *Milwaukee Illustrated: Its Trade, Commerce, Manufacturing Interests and Advantages as a Residence City.* It was described as an example of the "Modern Style", while the Italianate James Rogers House on Sixth Street was illustrated as a contrasting example of a "relic of the olden time."[22]

In the 1870s, some of the homes built for Milwaukee businessmen and professionals evidenced this ornate "modern" style. Throughout the city, many elegant houses were designed in the Victorian Italianate, a highly decorated version of the Italianate Style. Carved trusswork at gables and porches, a variety of scroll-sawn wooden ornamentation at porches and entrances, and often, an abundance of iron cresting at the ridgepoles of the gable roof added a picturesque quality to standard Italianate features such as round-arched windows. Flat-topped, stilted segmental, and rectangular arch windows were introduced in the Victorian Italianate house, enriching the facade. Moldings and ornamentation were intended to lend dramatic shadow effects.

1535 N. Marshall St., c. 1875. Of particular note on this cream brick house is the fine iron cresting at the roofline and porch. Incised stone keystones and an ornate punched vergeboard further decorate this hip roofed house.

It is not uncommon to see Victorian Italianate houses built in 1890 of similar appearance to those of the 1870s. This was due to builders' use of stock millwork trim such as standard window enframements, and the popular pattern books. Shortly before and after the Civil War, a new set of books appeared for both architects and builders. Calvert Vaux published *Villas and Cottages* in 1857; Henry Hudson Holly published *Holly's Country Seats* in 1863 and *Modern Dwellings in Town and Country* in 1878. George E. Woodward, A. J. Bicknell, and architects Palliser and Palliser were among compilers of books illustrating the plan, elevation, and details suitable for city and "suburb" in the 1870s and 1880s. On the interior, innovations and improvements in heating technology, such as the forced air furnace made it possible to create open floorplans with more freedom than ever before.

Dr. Henry H. Button House, 1024 E. State, 1875. Designed for a civic leader by Edward Townsend Mix, the Button House is representative of the scale and quality of the many expensive Victorian Italianate houses built in Milwaukee in the 1870s.

Palliser's Model Homes for the People, 1876. The first of over twenty publications by George and Charles Palliser, architects who pioneered "mail-order" architectural services. Palliser's inexpensive paperback plan books offered many new styles, including Gothic, Italianate, and Second Empire. Milwaukee's architects took note of these plans, as did numerous "do-it-yourselfers."

PALLISER'S

FOR THE PEOPLE.

A COMPLETE GUIDE TO THE PROPER AND ECONOMICAL ERECTION OF BUILDINGS.

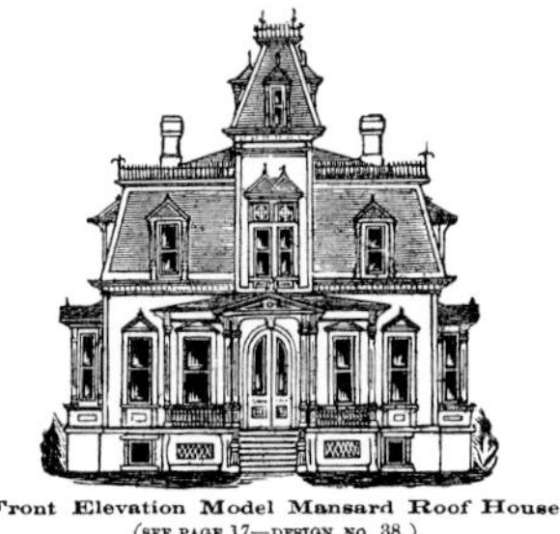

Front Elevation Model Mansard Roof House.
(SEE PAGE 17—DESIGN NO. 38.)

GEO. PALLISER, ARCHITECT,

5 and 6 Exchange Place, corner Wall and Main Streets,

BRIDGEPORT, CONN.

1876.

GOULD & STILES, STEAM JOB PRINTERS, BRIDGEPORT, CONN.

Gold's Perfect Heater. Advertised in George Palliser's Model Homes for the People (1876), the Gold heater was among many new patents for furnaces and heaters which appeared after the Civil War.

E. A. WHITFIELD, *Pres't.* A. H. SEAVER, *Sup't.* M. H. STAFFORD, *Treas.*

GOLD'S "PERFECT" HEATING APPARATUS,

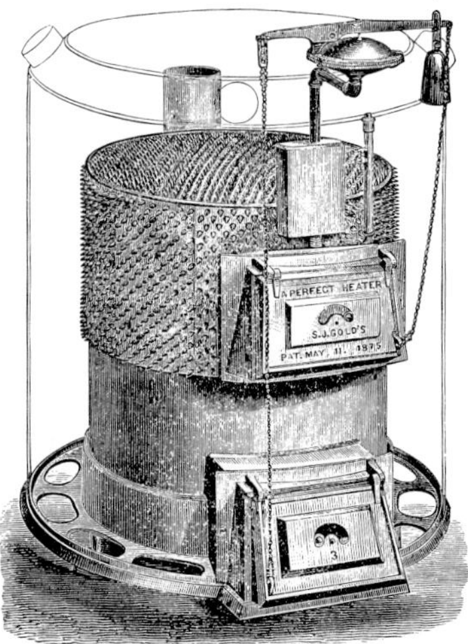

(Wrought Iron), Patented May 11, 1875.

The best Heater in the world, affording an abundance of heat fully equal to steam or hot water; constructed on the same principle as "Gold's Steam Heater," and the best apparatus for warming Private Dwellings, Churches, Schools, Hospitals, Stores, &c., affording a pure and healthful atmosphere. It will not burn out, nor rust out; positively gas tight at all times; no dust; no burnt, dry air; no artificial moisture required. Will consume all kinds of coal or wood with best results. SIMPLE, DURABLE AND ECONOMICAL.

Full Descriptive Circular, with Price List on application. Manufactured by

S. J. GOLD HEATER COMPANY,
No. 93 LIBERTY STREET, NEW YORK.

1624 N. Van Buren, 1890.

Victorian Gothic

Inspired by the writings of John Ruskin, English architects of the Victorian period designed colorful, but structurally "truthful" buildings in the 1850s and 1860s. In America, architects designed dramatically pinnacled and polychromatic buildings in cities such as Boston, Philadelphia, and New York. As the Victorian Gothic reached the Midwest, it was well-represented in the fine houses of Milwaukee built in the 1870s. The Victorian Gothic was more complex than the earlier Gothic Revival; hallmarks of the style are steeply pitched roofs, pointed arches, and intricate turned or carved gables. When of masonry construction, Milwaukee's pale brick added a distinctive luminosity to the Victorian Gothic, which was often executed elsewhere in dark brown or dark red brick, with multicolored stone or brick trim. Local writers called the Victorian Gothic the "New American Pointed Style" and applauded Milwaukee architect James Douglas as the local master of the style.[23]

2710 W. State St., c. 1868.

1712 W. Kilbourn, c. 1875.

928 W. Walker, c. 1880.

French Second Empire

The residence of Mr. Alexander Young on Grand Avenue and Tenth Street will be remodelled, by the addition of a French roof, after the renaissance style. The cost will be $5000.00.

Milwaukee Sentinel,
September 18, 1888

The "French roof" cited in this brief newspaper account was a mansard, which has a double slope, the lower usually longer and steeper than the upper. The name mansard is derived from Francois Mansart (1598-1666), a premier French architect who developed the roof type.

Houses built in the French Second Empire Style always have a mansard roof. Architectural historians attribute the popularity of this roof form to the building of an extension to the Palace of the Louvre between 1852 and 1857. In American residential construction, the distinctive mansard roof was often grafted onto a house form that resembled the rich facade of the Victorian Italianate. Brackets, elaborate window enframements, round-arched windows, and square or polygonal towers are common elements. A projecting pavilion carrying a mansard-roofed dormer is a standard feature of high-styled examples. Although the French Second Empire or "Mansard" Style was highly acclaimed and often used in the construction of some of Milwaukee's fine commercial blocks and elegant mansions of the 1860s and 1870s, it did not generally filter into post-Civil War housing stock. Therefore, there are few "domestic" examples to study in the city.

Milwaukee Co. Historical Society

MacArthur House, Marshall Street. Now razed, this elaborate example of the Second Empire style was probably built in the 1860s or 1870s. In addition to the mansard roof which is lit by round windows, there is an array of sculptural details. Oversized consoles, and highly decorated moldings and columns contribute to the overall effect.

Alexander Mitchell House, 1859 with additions and alterations 1860-1876, and later. Built for Alexander Mitchell, one of Milwaukee's leading businessmen and politicians, this Second Empire style mansion is the result of several series of additions. Between 1870 and 1876, the house received its mansard roof and square tower. The original house is attributed to builder John Bentley; the additions to Edward Townsend Mix.

1039 S. 3rd St., c. 1890.

Victorian Workers Houses in a Workingmen's City

> It has been so often said that no other city of its size in the world contains so many workingmen who own their own homes, that the saying has become an undisputed belief. Go into the wards where the laboring classes reside — especially those on the West and South Sides — and it is surprising to see the numbers of little houses, comfortable and cleanly, which bear the marks of ownership.[24]

The many rapidly constructed structures built to house the growing population of the 1870s and 1880s were less ornate than the grand Victorian Italianate houses of Prospect Avenue and Wisconsin Avenue, but nevertheless were important in Milwaukee's nineteenth century neighborhood architecture. One version of the worker's house was one or two stories in height, had small proportions, and a cottage-like appearance. (See "Housing Types in Milwaukee".) Another, larger version was usually two and one-half stories. Both types had gable roofs, with frame construction and clapboard covering. Characteristically, window enframements and door surrounds had peaked lintels with a punched design or a molded panel. Some Victorian Gothic features such as pointed or lancet windows were also present. Porch or entrance posts, when present, were chamfered or turned, and had scroll work or brackets. Gables were sometimes trimmed with decorated bargeboards or ornate trusses. Much of this ornamentation came from local planing mills and lumberyards.

1229 W. McKinley Avenue, c. 1883.

1030 S. 33rd Street, c. 1889.

1646 S. 28th Street, c. 1880.

714 W. Washington Street, c. 1895.

Stick Style

Stick Style buildings are expressive of the wooden framing system which underlies the wall. The Stick Style may be considered "one of the two most purely American styles of the nineteenth century."[25] The sources of this vertical, structurally expressive style are found in the residential designs published by Andrew Jackson Downing in the 1850s. Downing emphasized "truthfulness" in wooden construction. Vertical or horizontal boarding on the outside walls was expressive of the underlying stud wall underneath. Although there are few "pure" examples remaining in Milwaukee today, Stick Style details such as panelling and simple gable end trusses are observable on houses in various locations throughout the city.

Milwaukee Public Library

Wells Street Houses, photograph c. 1890. This view illustrates a row of eclectic late nineteenth century houses, like many which once stood in the city. Vertical board panelling, simple trusses in gable ends, and steep roofs were Stick Style features.

1725 W. State Street, c. 1890.

Eastlake

Eastlake ornament is a distinctive form of architectural decoration found on Victorian Gothic and Queen Anne Style houses. The mechanical lathe, gouge, and chisel created the knob-like decorations; bulbous, furniture-like posts; and distinctive, three-dimensional brackets which are the hallmarks of Eastlake design. Appreciation for this architectural fashion reached Milwaukee via London, with the publication of Charles Locke Eastlake's *Hints on Household Taste.* The Eastlake mode reached America in the early 1870s and was a popular form of architectural ornament in Milwaukee for over two decades.

Milwaukee Co. Historical Society

Unidentified North Side house, Photograph c. 1900. The builder of this late nineteenth century house used an array of Eastlake Style wood trim. Scalloped shingles, incised panelling, machine-cut trusswork, and turned and punched porch railings are of note.

1741-43 N. Farwell, c. 1885. This eclectic residential design of the mid-1880s has the lathe-turned and gouged millwork characteristic of the Eastlake Style.

2576 N. Fourth Street, c. 1880. Stick and Eastlake Style decorative devices are employed on this brick and wood trimmed house. The square tower has diagonal "stick-work"; the latticework and bulbous posts of the entrance porch are Eastlake features.

Richardsonian Romanesque

The permissive Queen Anne Style was a threshold for numerous architects and builders, who went on to design rusticated "castles" of brick and stone. Henry Hobson Richardson (1838-1886) was the prime shaper of this late nineteenth century style. Between 1885 and 1900, major avenues such as Highland, Wisconsin, Wahl, and Prospect, were the sites of rusticated stone mansions, whose Romanesque details demanded the expertise of skilled Milwaukee masons and stonecutters.

Architects working in the Richardsonian Romanesque, as this heavy masonry style is often called, drew on round Romanesque arches and low-sprung Syrian arches for openings in the thick walls, and combined round or polygonal turrets and projecting bays with conical roofs. Local architectural practitioners, such as Henry Koch, combined the Richardsonian Romanesque with the previously mentioned German Baroque features such as curved gables.

1672 N. Prospect Ave., 1887. Designed by H. C. Koch for wholesaler George H. Heinemann, this three-story house is faced with stone, brick, and shingles. The short stone columns with intricate capitals are a Romanesque feature; the prominent gables are treated with Queen Anne vergeboards and pressed wood panelling.

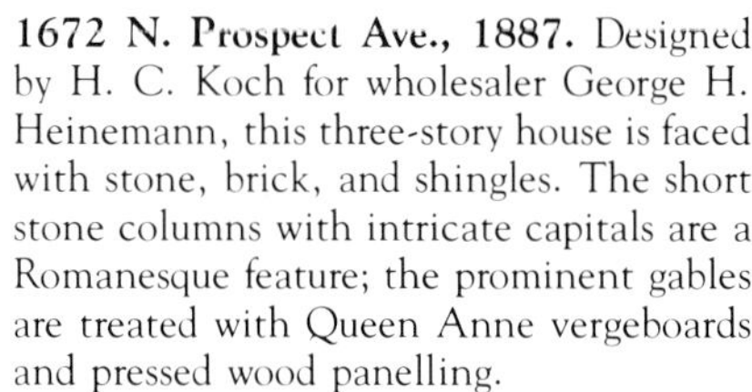

Francis Bloodgood Jr. House, 1135-39 E. Knapp and 1249 N. Franklin Pl., 1896. Designed by Howland Russel, with a steeply pitched French roof and parapets at the prominent dormers.

1060 East Juneau Ave., 1887. Built by T. A. Chapman for his daughter and son-in-law, this elaborate residence shows the influence of several styles, including the Romanesque of H. H. Richardson. Carved stone, terra cotta, brick and ornamental ironwork enhance the original design.

Châteauesque

High, pinnacled roofs, pinnacled round turrets, and wall dormers with prominent gables are characteristics of the Châteauesque Style briefly used by Milwaukee architects primarily in commissions for wealthy clients between c. 1890 and 1900. Although the so-called Châteauesque Style was based on the French Renaissance architecture of the reign of French King Francis I (1515-1547), it absorbed elements from earlier Gothic styles as well. In America, Beaux-Arts trained New York architect Richard Morris Hunt (1827-1895) was considered the foremost architect of the Châteauesque. Although several Milwaukee mansions were built in this style by architects such as Edward Townsend Mix and Henry C. Koch, unlike other earlier styles, it did not filter well into the ordinary housing stock of the city. Steep conical-roofed turrets, however, were used in a number of eclectic late nineteenth century houses.

Queen Anne

Beginning in the 1880s and lasting until about 1905, the Queen Anne was an important style of residential architecture in Milwaukee. On the surface, the Queen Anne Style was an amalgam of materials, shapes, and surfaces. Patterned shingles, elaborate turned and pressed millwork, glass and metalwork decorated the asymmetrical, irregularly massed house form. Brick, stucco, stone, shingles, and clapboard were often combined on a single exterior wall. Towers, turrets, balconies, and projecting bays further complicated the silhouette of the Queen Anne house.

The 1876 Philadelphia Centennial Exposition helped to create a taste in America for rural medieval English houses, on which the early Queen Anne Style was based. The well-published work of English architect Richard Norman Shaw in the late 1860s, and the work of Boston architect H. H. Richardson in the 1870s furthered the influence of the early phase of the style. In succeeding years, the Queen Anne acquired a less medieval appearance, entering a phase known as "free classic". This phase emphasized classical details and had a smoother appearance, enhanced by fewer exterior materials. The 1893 World's Columbian Exposition in Chicago, which celebrated classical architecture, contributed to this direction.

Milwaukee Public Library

Prospect Avenue Houses. Photograph 1890. The Sanford Kane House at 1841 N. Prospect is shown at right. Built in 1884, the Kane House is one of the city's best remaining examples of the Queen Anne Style. The Alonzo Kane House, at left was designed by James Douglas. The 1876 design has the distinctive stepped tower for which Douglas was known.

2732 N. Shepard, 1896. A three-story corner tower, classical-column porch, and patterned shingle trim are features of this Queen Anne house. Designed by architects Frank and Mueller.

2824 W. State, c. 1890.

The Queen Anne Style was frequently chosen for the houses of middle and upper income Milwaukeeans, and it absorbed two distinctive cultural currents of the late nineteenth century city. One was a preference by speculative builders to construct two-family, or duplex houses; the Queen Anne-derived duplex is a standard of many neighborhoods throughout the city.

Another factor influenced the Queen Anne and later styles in Milwaukee. German architects, often working for German clients on a grand scale, used a number of German motifs, including the curved or stepped gable and rich German Baroque ornamentation. Popular among many residents, some of the Northern European motifs present on the architect-designed houses filtered into the general housing stock of the late nineteenth century city.

1119 E. Knapp Street, c. 1895.

157 W. Saveland, 1903. This Queen Anne house is testament to the endurance of picturesque pattern-book houses into the first years of the twentieth century.

938 Layton Boulevard, 1892. This Queen Anne house, designed by Gustav H. Leipold, owes its architectural significance to a three story corner tower with a conical roof, shingled gable end broken by a broad arch and a wrap-around porch. The once-spacious yard of owner Louis Kretschman was divided in later years for the construction of another house.

922 S. 23rd St., 1901. Designed by Uehling and Linde for F. Kempsmith, this frame house exhibits characteristics of turn-of-the-century Queen Anne houses seen throughout the city. Panelled vergeboards, a polygonal corner tower, massed chimneys and mullioned windows were standard features.

Porch and gable trim, 1891. From the Sanger, Rockwell, and Company Catalogue.

118 *SANGER, ROCKWELL & CO.,*

DESIGNS FOR PORCH, SHOWING DIFFERENT STYLES OF COLUMNS.

Fig. 533

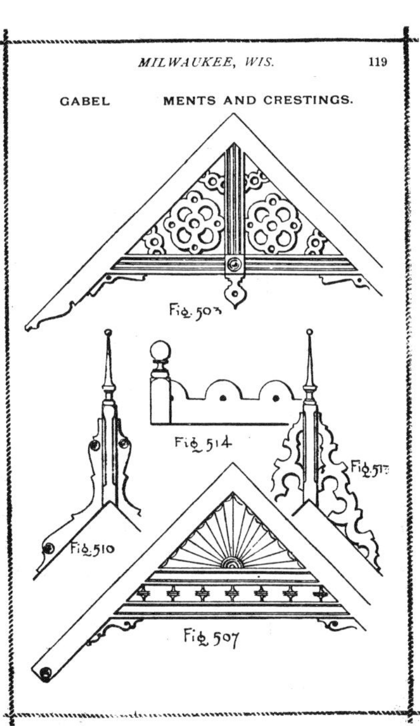

MILWAUKEE, WIS. 119

GABEL MENTS AND CRESTINGS.

Fig. 514

Fig. 510

Fig. 507

The Suburban Ideal in the City: Milwaukee and its Residences 1900-1930

Milwaukee Journal, April 23, 1922.

If you want to double your money in 2 or 3 years, then buy lots in our new subdivision on Walnut Hill, which is located north of the fairgrounds and extends from Vliet Street on the south to Walnut Street on the north and from Von Molke Park on the east to Western Avenue on the west. This is surely the finest tract in or adjoining the city ever offered to the public and will become one of the choice residence localities of the city. The land lays high and dry and commands a beautiful view of the city and surrounding country. . . .

Milwaukee Sentinel
June 22, 1889

The improved street railway facilities is another reason why there are so many "for rent" signs in the windows of houses in the Seventh, First, Fourth and the lower part of the Sixteenth Wards. It is no longer an inconvenience to reside at a distance of a mile and a half or two miles from the business portion of the city. There is a noticeable exodus of the people to the suburbs or outskirts of the city where most of the new houses have been erected. . . .

Milwaukee Sentinel
April 21, 1890

Here you will find the home site of your dreams. Out where the sun shines. Away from the crowded streets. Here you and your loved ones can enjoy the pure fresh air and stay healthy and strong. Here they can really LIVE instead of EXIST. This is the opportunity for the man who earns his daily living. It will interest him because buying real estate in the suburbs is not a rich man's game. It doesn't take a fat bankroll. Nor does it require a large investment. Still the fact remains that Milwaukee's real estate values in the outlying districts are considerably lower than in any other city of its size in the country. The man with a moderate income who has an honest desire to own his home is the type of man who is far-sighted enough to see that here is a chance for investment on easy terms. Some of the best subdivision property available which under ordinary conditions should increase in value at least two percent within the next three years is open to you.

Milwaukee Journal
May 13, 1923

With the establishment of savings and loan associations and companion home-building associations across the city in the 1880s, the opportunity for home ownership was strengthened. In the last years of the nineteenth century and well into the twentieth century, there was a general preoccupation with affordable single family housing, although the duplex enjoyed great popularity. Newspaper advertisements extolled the single lots and houses for sale. Although the city's boundaries continued to expand in the first years of the twentieth century, Milwaukee was more compact than other large cities, and relied less on the streetcar as a suburbanizing factor.[26] Milwaukee's "suburban" population was also generally less affluent than that which suburbanized other cities.[27] Tracts such as Walnut Hill (described in the previous quote) were geared at workingmen's homes, and Milwaukee and the surrounding area were the sites of several innovative workers' communities, such as Garden Homes (1921) and the Parklawn Public Housing Project (1937) on the city's northwest side, and Greendale (c. 1937) at the southern edge of the city.

While lumber dealers and plan books were the purveyors of moderately-priced houses such as the bungalow, Milwaukee's architects nevertheless were commissioned to design houses in the city's middle and upper income areas, particularly on the East Side. Although the era which saw the architectural excesses of industrialists' mansions such as the Plankinton House (designed by Edward Townsend Mix in 1886) had ended, substantial, stylish homes were still being designed for Milwaukee's prosperous businessmen and professionals.

The early twentieth century house in Milwaukee was well-equipped with the latest heating, plumbing, and electrical systems, but the exterior seldom revealed such modern characteristics. As discussed in the following section, the period revival house (based on such diverse sources as German half-timbered houses, Swiss chalets, English cottages, New England farmhouses and Mediterranean villas) dominated early twentieth century residential construction. Popular periodicals such as *Suburban Life* and *Country Life* encouraged the taste for the rustic, or suburban setting, and illustrated hundreds of possibilities for revival designs. Evidence of the reaction to historical styles appears in Milwaukee's residential architecture in the form of the Bungalow, the Prairie House and the International Style, and provides great contrast to the bulk of residential building of the period 1900-1930.

Milwaukee Journal, May 1, 1921.

Period Revival Styles

The c. 1910 portfolio of Milwaukee architectural firm Cornelius Leenhouts and Hugh W. Guthrie displayed the firm's residential and commercial work in the city. Included among the residential illustrations were styles "revived" from historical sources such as English Tudor, Spanish Colonial, and American Georgian. Firms such as Leenhouts and Guthrie provided clients with a choice of styles, from the highly ornamented to the severely undecorated. This broad stylistic range was summarized in the introduction to their portfolio, entitled "THE HOME";

> . . . given a good plan you can get a good design whether it is carried out in Colonial Queen Anne, Gothic, English Domestic, or any other style, as each has its own peculiar advantage or fitness, one being dignified and purposeful, the other aspiring and pretentious. . . .[28]

Neo-classical Revival and Beaux Arts Classicism and Their Impact on Residential Design

The 1893 World's Columbian Exposition, held in Chicago, provided America with an elaborate display of architecture based on classical models, particularly those of ancient Greece. The buildings of the 1904 St. Louis Exposition and the 1910 New York State Building at the Pan American Exposition in Buffalo similarly gave the country a new interpretation of classical architecture. In Milwaukee, as elsewhere, the Neo-classical Revival was best applied to the design of monumentally-scaled public buildings, and it was a popular choice for insurance companies, banks, and civic buildings.

In contrast to the strong, simple forms of the Neo-classical Revival, Beaux Arts Classicism wedded antique Roman motifs to seventeenth century French architecture, producing an ornate, highly picturesque style. Like the Neo-classical Revival, this style is best represented in buildings of large scale. "Beaux Arts" Classicism takes its name from the many late nineteenth and early twentieth century architects who received their architectural training and ideals at the Ecole des Beaux Arts in Paris. The chapters on the Architecture of Commerce and Industry and Civic Structures discuss the role of these styles in the creation of Milwaukee's major public and commercial structures. In Milwaukee, this new interest in the antique also had a significant impact on the next generation of residential architecture. The smooth, white surfaces, classical columns, and details such as Palladian windows of many houses built after c. 1900 are evidence of a revived interest in classical architecture, an interest that was abandoned after the popularity of the Greek Revival waned in the 1850s.

> The cream-colored brick in which the city at one time took especial pride has fallen into disfavor, and justly enough, for in color it is thin and cold, with no value except perhaps in contrast with new-fallen snow. It is particularly ugly in its cheap, rough grades, as used in blank party walls and on inferior buildings, where it turns, when stained with soot and weather, to a dreary, sickly, streaked gray — as utterly a forlorn building material as can be imagined. For all the better class of work nowadays the brown, red or pink brick of other localities is imported.
>
> *Architectural Record,* March, 1905

above

3112 W. McKinley, 1903. Designed by Herman W. Buemming.

The period revival house in Milwaukee, like the earlier Queen Anne and Romanesque house, absorbed the German and Northern European interests of the major architects who were often working for German-American clients. The English Tudor house in Milwaukee, for example, often has special Germanic details. Half-timbering and curved gables are among the subtle indicators of this cultural preference. The period revival designs of architects and their clients in Milwaukee filtered into the city's housing stock, as is evidenced by the many speculatively-built small houses of period revival character built in the twenties and thirties, which can still be seen in almost all sections of the city.

2951 N. Marietta Avenue, 1912. Created by Leenhouts and Guthrie for Tom Bentley, this truncated hip-roof design revives characteristics of both Georgian and Federal styles.

2442 N. 37th St., 1901. This small North Side residence has a gambrel roof, with a prominent broken scroll pediment in the shingled gable. A round window lights the attic.

2950 N. Shepard Ave., 1908. William Schuchardt designed this "half-timbered" house for L. Heilbrouner. Like many Period Revival houses inspired by English sources, prominent vergeboards and applied half-timbering dominate the facade.

529 E. Oklahoma Ave., 1925. Designed by John Menge, Jr., for F. Kleczka, this tile-roofed house has a Spanish flavor.

2130-32 Hi-Mount Boulevard, 1923. Designed by Russell Barr Williamson for the American Builders Service. Williamson's Prairie designs were promoted by the American Builder's Service as "Williamsonian."

I loved the prairie by instinct as a great simplicity — the trees, flowers, sky itself thrilling by contrast.

Frank Lloyd Wright,
An Autobiography

I began to see the building primarily not as a cave but as broad shelter in the open, related to vista; vista without and vista within.

Frank Lloyd Wright,
The Natural House

2430 Newberry Boulevard, 1922. Russell Barr Williamson designed this Prairie House for Dr. T. Robinson Bours. Of note are the horizontal band of windows tucked under the broad overhanging eaves, and the clay tile roof.

The Prairie House in Milwaukee

While Milwaukee architects such as Alfred Clas and George Ferry were creating English Tudor cottages and Spanish Colonial houses for clients on Lake Drive, a unique philosophy of domestic design was developing elsewhere in the Midwest.

Architect Frank Lloyd Wright (1867-1959), a native of Wisconsin, admired the beauty of the Midwestern landscape, particularly its long stretches of prairie. Wright's designs for houses of the early twentieth century emulated the clear horizon of the prairie with their low, ground-hugging masses. Low, hipped roofs with broad eaves sheltered the stucco or brick building. Brick was often of the "roman" variety, an oversized, flat unit. A strong, horizontal character, emphasizing the building's connection to the ground, was achieved with banded windows and bands of concrete, terra cotta, or wooden trim. The Prairie House represented a significant break from traditional European sources and created considerable controversy among architects.

The Prairie House, by Wright or other "Prairie School" architects such as George Maher of Chicago or Percy Dwight Bentley of LaCrosse shows the influence of the midwestern landscape, as well as the designs of architect Louis Sullivan and the architecture of Japan. Wright's small, but devoted following of architects and designers carried the Prairie house idea not just to Milwaukee and other American cities and towns, but to Europe and Australia. Prairie houses appeared in architectural journals, and were published in several popular magazines such as the *Ladies Home Journal.*

In some instances, carpenters and builders copied the horizontal massing and certain details of exterior trim, and the Prairie Style thus filtered into the housing stock of the period. In Milwaukee, there are at least five houses designed by Wright, including a group of duplexes. Fine examples of the Prairie Style work of several other architects were built across the city between ca. 1905 and 1920, with a significant number on or near Newberry

Boulevard on the East Side. Russell Barr Williamson appears to have created some of the "purest" Prairie work in the city. H. W. Buemming and Mark Pfaller are among other local architects who worked in the Prairie vein. It is interesting to note that Buemming and Pfaller otherwise worked with a full repertoire of historical styles, producing designs for Colonial Revival and Tudor Revival buildings as well as the more astylistic Prairie house.

The Milwaukee architect usually had to work within the relatively small, narrow configuration of the city lot; consequently the long, cantilevered roofs and horizontal emphasis of Wright's suburban and rural work were compressed into a tighter, more cubic design. However, the special features such as terra cotta or concrete decoration based on floral or geometric motifs, roman brick, and geometrically patterned stained glass are frequent features of the Milwaukee Prairie house.

1510 Layton Boulevard, 1919. With its cubic form and broad eaves, architect Mark F. Pfaller's own residence shows the influence of Wright's F. C. Bogk House of 1905.

2924 N. Shepard Avenue, 1913. Splayed buttresses, roman brick and horizontal banding with geometric ornament are Prairie Style features of this house. Architect was H. W. Weiner; Christian Schoknecht, mason.

1516 Layton Boulevard, 1922. The influence of the well-published works of Chicago architect George Maher is evident in the splayed entrance portico of this South Side residence. Designed by the Milwaukee firm of Backes and Pfaller for John S. Jung.

Detail

F. C. Bogk House, 1905. The only single family house in Milwaukee attributable to Frank Lloyd Wright, the Bogk House was executed in brick and trimmed with precast concrete.

735 S. 22nd Street, 1908. Wide, overhanging eaves and a low-pitched hip roof show the influence of the Prairie Style on vernacular building. Designed by architect Charles Tharinger for Alfred Jones, such simple plans were available through builders' plan books as well as architects.

The International Style

Influenced by the Modern architecture of Europe in the 1920s, and new building materials and construction techniques, the International Style in America represented a revolutionary, although relatively limited, change in residential building. The International Style is characterized by a striking lack of historicism, minimal detail, and precise geometric form. Smooth wall surfaces, flat roofs, cantilevered and projecting floors, and horizontal bands of windows (which often carry around the building) are standard features.

In Milwaukee there are few "pure" examples of this industrial-appearing style; it did not extend into the city's housing stock as previous architect-introduced styles had. However, the International Style philosophy of modern materials used with a lack of historical association did have some effect on the residential work of local architects. Many of the buildings in this style were constructed, however, after World War II.

In America the International Style was mixed with the streamlined decorative ideas called Art Deco, or Moderne, which had gained currency with the 1925 Paris Exposition Internationale des Arts Decoratifs et Industrielles Modernes and had prospered in this country with the angular, cubic setback skyscraper of the late 1920s. The style engendered a flat-surfaced dwelling, usually in brick, stucco, or concrete block, and sometimes employing translucent glass blocks, tubular steel railings, and metal casement windows.

1933 Home Show Winner, 3840 N. 55th Street. One of the first attempts in Milwaukee to build a single family house in the International Style. Architect Henry Phillip Plunkett's design was selected by a committee headed by architect Alexander C. Eschweiler as the winning design. Clad in metal, the basic cube of the main house is broken by a stair tower which leads to a roof top terrace.

149 W. Warnimont, 1937. No architect is documented in the design of this stucco house which has the round corners and "porthole" window associated with the "Streamlined Moderne" phase of the International Style.

3765 S. Third Street, 1936. Designed by Alfred H. Zarse for Herbert Kleinschmidt, the windows and metal railings of this two story, hip roofed house show the influence of the International Style. The stone veneer, however, diminishes the effect of smooth uniform wall surfaces inherent to the International Style.

Change

As older residential streets were absorbed by commercial uses, houses were converted to shops and stores. Often, an unusual blending of architecture resulted, with nineteenth century houses peering above twentieth century storefronts. Today, however, the residential appearance is often conserved and improved as the house becomes a business or professional office, while retaining its original appearance.

Herman Wuldke Collection

Val Blatz House, N. Van Buren St., corner Juneau Street, photograph c. 1958. A terra cotta and tile decorated laundromat was grafted on the eclectic brick and stone mansion of a Milwaukee brewer. No longer standing.

845 N. 11th St., c. 1875. This cream brick Italianate house has successfully been converted into professional offices, with all original details and surfaces intact.

1531 W. Lincoln, c. 1892 with 1930s glass tile facade. Known as Red's Lunch since the 1940s, this frame residence has a lower story facade with an octagonal Moderne window.

Housing Types in Milwaukee

This section reviews the distinctive types of housing in the city. Although styles have been discussed in this chapter on residential architecture, it is important to differentiate the one story cottage from the duplex, the single family house from the apartment house, and to observe the special house types and siting patterns of immigrant housing in the city. One of Milwaukee's most popular single-family house types, the bungalow, can also be considered a distinctive style of architecture.

The Cottage

One of Milwaukee's earliest speculatively-built house types was the one or one and one-half story gable roofed cottage. In some neighborhoods, there were uniform rows of these houses; in others, a few were situated along alleys or at the rear of other houses. The basic cottage was often "raised" by several generations of Polish residents (as is discussed in the following section). Many were built to house the workers of the city's growing industries; as a housing solution, they provided quickly constructed, inexpensive quarters for many generations of laborers. Although small, many were attractively trimmed with mass-produced millwork. Windows often have punched or machine-tooled enframements; porches have turned posts and jig-sawed "gingerbread". The bungalow is this century's parallel to the cottage of the mid to late nineteenth century.

2315, 2317A. W. Pierce St. The construction date of these frame cottages situated at the rear of a lot (behind a large house) is unknown. The three-bay, gable-roofed facade is a 19th century cottage standard throughout the city.

Millwork Trim, 1891. Figure 68 of Sanger, Rockwell and Company's catalogue illustrated this popular cottage window enframement.

MILWAUKEE, WIS. 89

DESIGN FOR COTTAGE WINDOW FRAME.

Fig 65.

The scarcity of city tenements this season that are adapted to small families has become the subject of common remark among the house-hunters. Almost all these persons who are seeking for houses this spring are in search of cottages "with the rooms all on the ground floor". Basement houses seem to be out-of-date. In view of this demand, which will of necessity increase rather than diminish every year, we would suggest to our real estate owners the policy of building, this season, more of this class of houses. A cottage house, or a row of them, will always command good tenants and good rents in Milwaukee.

Milwaukee Sentinel,
April 8, 1861

2550 S. Shore Drive, 1920. Built for F. H. Gerdis by H. Erdmann, this Bay View cottage has diminutive proportions and millwork details similar to examples built as much as 40 years before.

931 W. Walker St., c. 1900. Segmental-arch hood molds and a round gable window are of note.

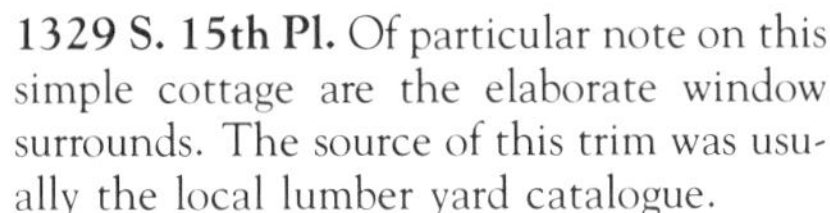

1329 S. 15th Pl. Of particular note on this simple cottage are the elaborate window surrounds. The source of this trim was usually the local lumber yard catalogue.

1111, 1107, 1105, 1103 W. Scott St., c. 1875. This row of gable roofed cottages is representative of speculatively built one-story houses constructed after the Civil War.

Rowhouses and Apartment Buildings: 1845-1930

Between circa 1845 and 1920, boarding houses were found in great numbers throughout the city, serving the housing needs of newly-arrived immigrants, single persons, and those families who could not afford to buy or rent a house. Many boarding house situations consisted of a room or two let out in a private home. Between ca. 1845 and 1885, when a family moved from a boarding house, they often moved to a rented or purchased detached house. Multi-family houses such as tenements or rowhouses were found only in relatively small numbers. The ability of both workers and industrialists to purchase their own homes was a strong feature of Milwaukee's nineteenth century housing pattern.[30] Land values in most areas of the central city permitted the construction of small single family houses on single lots, and inexpensive houses such as cottages were usually available for sale or rent. A number of multiple family housing types existed, however, from the city's earliest years of settlement. Two or three story double homes, with a party wall and separate entrances were built in the 1840s and 1850s, and some were of excellent construction and fine detailing. Larger "tenements", or buildings of more than three units, were built in the 1860s and 1870s, but few have survived. In 1874, a "west side capitalist" built a forty-five unit tenement at Seventh Street and Vliet Street. Such high density units, however, did not become popular until the turn of the century.

Herman Wadtke Collection

"Bellanger Row", c. 1850. Photograph c. 1900. Tall parapet walls incorporating twin end chimneys demarcate each unit of this Federal style two story row, formerly at the southwest corner of Broadway and Wells Streets.

1502-04 E. Irving St., c. 1855-60. This Greek Revival double house is representative of small party-wall units built before the Civil War. Of note are the six over six, double hung sash.

1008-18 W. Pierce, c. 1885. Each double entrance of this ten-unit row is decorated with a sunburst-motif porch; decorative brick panels in parapets above each porch add texture to second story wall surfaces.

706-08 E. Juneau Ave., c. 1880. This cream brick apartment house has careful masonry details including corner quoins and prominent keystones.

The Norman, corner of Grand Avenue and Seventh Street. This new apartment building will be ready for occupancy about April 16. Contains all modern improvements, including steam heat, passenger and freight elevators, etc. Flats are divided into four, five, six, and seven rooms. A first class restaurant will be run in connection with the buildings. Apply to E. J. Tapping, 136 West Water.

Milwaukee Sentinel,
June 22, 1889

In the late 1880s and 1890s, a number of fine multi-unit rowhouses and apartment houses were constructed on Yankee Hill and at the edges of downtown. The Queen Anne Style of their exteriors, with asymmetrical details, towers, and turrets disguised the multi-unit plan of the building. Smaller multi-family units were often based on the duplex plan, with prominent gables and standard duplex features such as columned porches.

Graham Row, 1501-07 N. Marshall, 1880. Three separate residences are contained in one of Milwaukee's few "true" rowhouses. Constructed of cream brick with sandstone and terra cotta trim, the Graham Row is representative of the eclectic nature of late nineteenth century architectural styles in the city. Bult by masonry contractor John Graham, Queen Anne and Romanesque styles are merged in the design.

Between 1900 and 1935, many masonry apartment buildings were built throughout the city. Some examples were planned around courtyards, and have well designed ventilation and lighting systems, evidencing the continual development of apartment planning in American cities in the early twentieth century. Stylistically, the apartment houses were representative of the period revival styles popular in the first decades of the twentieth century. Spanish or Mediterranean, English Tudor, Georgian Revival, and Gothic exteriors were found on apartment buildings which lined the city's boulevards and residential streets.

The city's finest large scale apartment buildings were built along Prospect Avenue during the same period. Some replaced the nineteenth century mansions built by earlier generations of Milwaukee businessmen and industrialists. This shift in near-downtown density and land use — from the multi-roomed private house to the multi-unit apartment building — reflected the area's changing pattern of life in the early twentieth century.

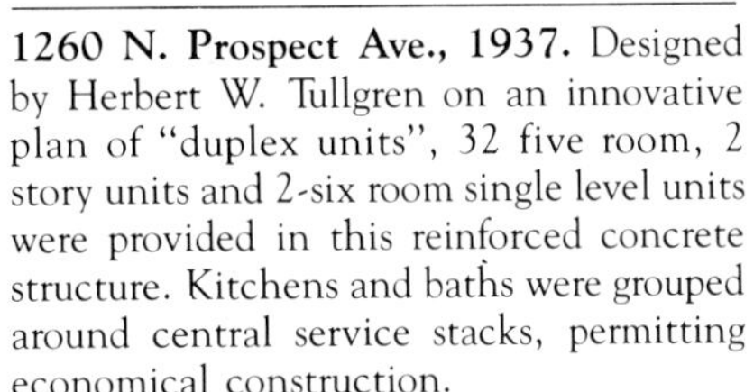

1260 N. Prospect Ave., 1937. Designed by Herbert W. Tullgren on an innovative plan of "duplex units", 32 five room, 2 story units and 2-six room single level units were provided in this reinforced concrete structure. Kitchens and baths were grouped around central service stacks, permitting economical construction.

The Everglades, 3118 W. Pierce St., 1928. Architects George Zagel and Bro. used terra cotta panels to decorate this Mediterranean-inspired apartment house. Spanish and Mediterranean motifs were favored by builders and architects of apartment buildings in the 1920s and 1930s.

Milwaukee Co. Historical Society

2617 Prairie (later Highland Ave.), c. 1900. Otto Uehling, architect and engineer, designed this cross-gable duplex with prominent Palladian windows.

The Milwaukee Duplex

The duplex was built throughout Milwaukee in large numbers between 1890 and 1921. Although native Milwaukeeans today refer to these houses as "duplexes", during their initial period of construction there was no widely used local term used to describe them. Henry Saylor's *Dictionary of Architecture* defines a duplex apartment as "one having rooms on two floors, with a private stairway between." This definition accurately describes the Milwaukee duplex, which was called by several names at the turn of the century. Annual building reports published in the *Milwaukee Sentinel* between 1894 and 1908 referred to the duplex as a "flat" or "two family flat". Building inspectors' reports listed the duplex as a "two family flat", but in 1914 the term "duplex flat" appeared. From c. 1914 through the 1920s, builders and architects as well as realtors used the term "duplex". Real estate advertisements which appeared in the *Milwaukee Journal* during the 1920s often used the term "duplex flat".

Duplex construction occurred initially in Milwaukee in the 1880s. Few building permits remain from the 1880s, however, and only a handful of sites therefore can be verified as "true" duplexes. But evidence of the duplex's popularity exists elsewhere. City Directories indicate that double occupancy was popular in the late 1880s and early 1890s. Fire insurance maps, which contain useful information about construction materials, do not differentiate housing types. Yet, between 1894 and 1919, building reports appearing in the *Milwaukee Sentinel* and those published by the city Building Inspector show that duplex building occurred in every city ward except downtown and the Menomonee Valley. Between 1904 and 1916, duplex construction peaked, with most constructions occurring between the years 1908 and 1914.

Some areas of the city, particularly on the Northwest Side, were built almost exclusively of duplexes. From 1904 until World War I, the wards (now aldermanic districts) north of Vliet Street and west of North Seventh Street were consistently leaders in duplex construction. Wards north of Brown Street and west of Teutonia Street contained at least fifty percent of all duplexes built in the city. On the East Side, duplex construction occurred in significant numbers north of North Avenue. The South Side experienced the least duplex construction, with a relatively small number constructed in each ward.

2451-53 Cramer, c. 1890.

As a house type, the duplex developed from the simplest of house forms — the gable-roofed house of rectangular plan. Because of Milwaukee's long, narrow lot configuration, most of the city's housing was sited with the gable end perpendicular to the street, and the duplex was no exception to this pattern. The earliest examples, of the 1880s, were simple gable-roofed blocks with a small porch and balcony at the second story. Between 1890 and 1925, the front gable remained a standard feature, but three new types appeared. One type had a hip roof with intersecting gables projecting from the main block of the house. Porches were often used only at the entry. The second type was based on the gable-roofed block, but varied the plan to include "T" and "L" configurations. Entries, flush or recessed, were paired at opposite corners of the front facade. A full front porch was a consistent feature of this type. A third type of duplex was introduced after World War I: a simple hipped roof block with an attic dormer and a full front porch were standard features.

The Milwaukee duplex, although an ubiquitous form, nevertheless revealed great diversity in its architectural treatment. Queen Anne, Bungalow, English Tudor and Colonial Revival were among popular duplex styles.

One constant, however, was the Milwaukee duplex builder's interest in the gable end which was almost always turned toward the street. Between 1890 and 1910, the gable end was variously shingled, stuccoed, panelled or clapboarded. A central window, or pair of windows, was centered in the gable and framed by shingled reveals, pilasters or freestanding columns, or simple millwork trim. Often, the gable end window was a three-part window, usually Palladian. Broad, panelled vergeboards were nearly always present, and brackets sometimes carried the eaves. The treatment of porches varied greatly, from simple full porches with sturdy columns to small entrance porches embellished with delicate trusswork. Towers and turrets were added to early examples. Duplexes built in the teens and after World War I were often relatively devoid of ornament, with jerkin-head gable or hipped roofs a common feature.

Almost every major residential architect and builder of the period 1890-1925 designed or built duplexes. Frank Hunholz, Fred Graf, George Schley, and George Zagel were prominent duplex builders on the Northwest Side; architectural firms included Buemming and Dick, Henry Messmer, Leenhouts and Guthrie, and Crane and Barkhausen.

1244-46 S. 19th Street, 1890.

1242-44 N. 24th Place, 1904.

1220-22 N. 21st Street, 1902. Designed by Jacobi and Wiskocil for Louis Schridrer.

2720-22 W. Burnham St., 1915. Designed by Frank Lloyd Wright for the City Real Estate Company. One of four duplexes in a row.

The Milwaukee Bungalow: Type and Style

2922 N. 46th, 1925. Splayed piers carry the entrance porch of this brick Sherman Park bungalow. Designed by architects George Zagel and Bro.

3029 N. Bartlett Street, 1913. Built for developer Louis Auer and Son after plans by H. V. Miller, this East Side house has the exposed rafters and jerkin-head roof which are common features of the Milwaukee bungalow.

As a housing type, the bungalow, or small house, is a testament to the endurance of the Milwaukee ideal of home ownership, which began in the nineteenth century. The popular notion of working-men and women owning their own homes, was evident in advertisements for the sale of laborer's cottages as early as 1860. The one or one and one-half story houses built in Milwaukee between c. 1902 and 1925 were also representative of the Bungalow Style, a link to the American Arts and Crafts tradition, which flourished briefly in the early years of the twentieth century. Although mass-produced, many Milwaukee bungalows exhibited principles of good workmanship and the use of natural materials that were revered by the spokesmen of the craftsman movement.

The Craftsman, a monthly magazine published between 1901 and 1916, promoted the ideals of editor Gustav Stickley, a Wisconsin-born designer, and the craftsman movement in America. Articles stressed the ideal of a democratic and functional architecture based on the integration of natural materials and forms, hand-made decorative arts, and naturalistic garden design. At the center of the craftsman philosophy was a concern for "home" and domestic life. *The Craftsman* encouraged the improvement of all aspects of domestic design, offering articles or advertisements for such items as "bungalow furniture" and wickerware, earthenware, table-runners, and hammered-copper book-ends made by the Roycrofters of East Aurora, New York. Stickley and his followers were indebted to William Morris and the late nineteenth century English Arts and Crafts tradition for the philosophy of a high standard of craftsmanship, and of design derived from natural forms intended to counter the new machine-oriented industrial order.

The simple rustic house most often illustrated in *The Craftsman* and Stickley's books such as *Craftsman Homes* of 1909, was the bungalow. It took many forms, from Japanese pagoda to Swiss chalet, but usually maintained its low gabled roof, low, open front porch and large chimney mass.

Milwaukee has an excellent collection of Bungalow Style houses inspired by *The Craftsman* and numerous "Bungalow Books". Bungalow plans were available from architects, but also through mail order catalogues and many published sources. Even Sears, Roebuck and Company provided bungalow plans in their *Modern Homes,* a mail order plan book.

4503 W. Wright Street, 1915. A prominent chimney mass and rectilinear truss work in the porch gable are notable bungalow features.

> "One need not necessarily be rich to give grace and charm to his habitation. Remember that an attractive bungalow costs no more than an uninteresting old-fashioned house. . . ."
>
> *Bungalow Magazine,* 1914

3267 North Cramer, 1920. Built by contractors Feiler and Mylers, exposed rafters, and pyramidal roof with eyebrow window are distinctive bungaloid details.

1929 N. 51st Street, 1915. Owner/builder T. P. Kennedy's Washington Park bungalow has splayed porch piers and prominent exposed rafters.

The Milwaukee bungalow was, in most cases, a modest home, but one that was carefully detailed and well constructed. Brick, stucco and stone were favored materials, and "honesty" of construction was emphasized over any other design principle. On many frame examples, a jerkin-head gable roof was a common feature.

Although bungalows were built as "infill" throughout the city, excellent concentrations existed on the East, Northwest, and West Sides. The larger house, built according to Craftsman principles, was found primarily on the East Side. The design of the larger Craftsman house varied greatly, from somber, stuccoed, hipped-roof examples, to rustic, shingled gambrel-roofed examples. Natural materials, a general lack of historical references, and a spacious front porch were standard features, however.

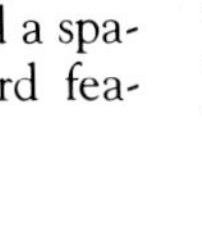

2813-15 N. 40th St., 1917. Bungalow and Queen Anne motifs are combined on this large Craftsman duplex. Such houses were advertised as the "Bungalow Duplex."

5816 W. Washington, 1919. Four unadorned columns carry the roof of this Craftsman design.

Milwaukee Co. Historical Society

Jacob Gipfel House. Photograph c. 1875. Although this house stood outside the Milwaukee city limits (at the intersection of Green Bay and Green Tree Roads), it serves to illustrate the half-timbered construction favored by some Wisconsin settlers. The heavy timber frame of this structure was filled with brick and mortar nogging.

Robert Machek House, 1305 N. 19th St., 1893-4. An eclectic house built by a Viennese wood carver. Machek used simulated half-timbering and Gothic, Renaissance, Baroque, and Oriental motifs in his elaborate design.

Immigrant House Types in Milwaukee

In assessing the immigrant's mark on the architectural fabric and cultural landscape of the city, Craig Reisser, in "Immigrants and House Form in Northeast Milwaukee," notes that despite the large number of German and Polish builders, true European house types were anomalies in the cultural landscape of nineteenth century Milwaukee. Although the majority of newcomers were European immigrants, their ready acceptance of cheap sawtimber, machine-made nails, and balloon frame construction and their low sources of income effectively submerged the vernacular Old World styles.[31]

Indeed, few examples of traditional half-timbered German homes (known as Fachwerkbau), are known to have been built in Milwaukee. The timbers of the half-timbered house were mortised, tenoned, and pegged together. The spaces between the timbers were filled with nogging, or burned brick, or with rubble masonry. One example, built in Milwaukee in 1839, was razed in the 1860s.

As Reisser notes, "Immigrant-constructed neighborhoods in Milwaukee exhibit differences in physical appearance from Yankee neighborhoods that are not attributable to differences in social status."[32] Among expressions of immigrant culture which are still observable are the raised or Polish flat, and the rear house.

Although the raised house gained popularity in late nineteenth century immigrant neighborhoods, houses of brick and frame construction in the mid-nineteenth century also were often set on high brick foundations, because of the low and marshy conditions which prevailed in the early settlement of the Kilbourntown and Juneautown plats. Thus some Yankee settlers endured the same basement quarters as later Poles and Germans. Photographs are the source of this information, as most of these early houses have been razed.

1916 N. 21st Street, c. 1892.

The Raised Flat

The raised or "Polish" flat is a unique survival of immigrant culture in Milwaukee. The walk-in basement apartment was an addition created almost exclusively by the Poles. In the study of immigrant housing in northeast Milwaukee, Reisser identified 169 flats in which Polish familes often shared living quarters with newly-arrived relatives.[33] These Polish families purchased inexpensive wooden houses with wood foundations, and then raised them several years later to create a basement apartment. Houses were often moved from another location and set atop a brick semi-basement to create the "Polish flat". This arrangement provided the owner with inexpensive housing, a rental unit, and space for relatives, when needed. Reisser notes that "nearly all dwelling units with walk-in basements were built in this additive manner." Many of these basement apartments were also connected to stores.

The Rear House

In addition to the raised or Polish flat, the rear or alley house is another survival of immigrant culture in Milwaukee. Many of the small houses situated at the rear of lots were built by Germans and Poles between c. 1880 and 1910. The practice of building or moving two houses to a lot allowed an immigrant family to first build the small house at the rear, and another large house as they required it. Both houses, however, were sometimes built or moved to the lot at the same time. The rear houses provided rental income for the immigrant family, and space for newly-arriving relatives. The rear house and companion house at the lot front were often similar in style, despite disparities in time of construction. The congestion caused by the rear house was a consequence of the intense desire among immigrants for home ownership, particularly Polish immigrants.[34] Reisser notes that in the first years of the twentieth century, Yankee reformers considered these rear houses to be among the primary housing evils of the era, regarding them as deteriorating, overcrowded, unsanitary firetraps".[35] Milwaukee's first zoning ordinance in 1920 restricted the construction of rear houses. Large gardens, squeezed in behind the raised flats and rear houses were a standard feature of the immigrant neighborhoods.

Immigrant Garden, c. 1925.

Milwaukee Co. Historical Society

Home Grounds and the Neighborhood Landscape

At least one nineteenth century Milwaukee writer noticed the care with which some Milwaukee residents kept their yards, or "home grounds", as they were often called. He called attention to the west end of Grand Avenue, now Wisconsin Avenue:

> . . . while the residences lining Grand Avenue compare favorably with those of any other portion of the city, the grounds of the west end of the thoroughfare are observed to me more extensive, giving opportunity for the display of skill in landscape gardening not afforded in the more compactly settled portions of the city . . .
>
> *Milwaukee Illustrated, 1877*[36]

Although old houses sometimes appear today almost as they did when built, few home grounds are still found in the fashion in which they were originally landscaped. Some details indicative of past taste in residential landscape design can still be observed in the city's neighborhoods, however. These details include paths and walks, rock walls or rockeries, fences, and curbs. Fences often reflected the style of the house they surround, as some of the old photographs in this chapter indicate.

Colonel William Jacobs House, c. 1850. Photograph c. 1890. Located at what is now S. 27th and W. National Avenue, Colonel Jacobs decorated the grounds of his porticoed Greek Revival house with a fountain, ornamental shrubs, and an unusual grotto and rock collection. The fountain was supplied by an artesian well discovered when drillers bored into a "gusher" near the south rim of the Menomonee Valley.

Milwaukee Co. Historical Society

Alexander Mitchell Garden, 900 W. Wisconsin. When Alexander Mitchell enlarged the house and grounds of his estate in the 1870s, elaborate gardens and an octagonal garden structure were also created. Today, the grounds provide an idea of the extent of one of Milwaukee's finest nineteenth century gardens.

Wealthy businessmen such as Alexander Mitchell hired the Scottish and Austrian gardeners who arrived in Milwaukee after the Civil War to design and maintain the extensive grounds around their elegant homes. Interest in landscape design was shared by many people, however, and there were numerous books and periodicals to advise the layman on the layout of gardens and yards, and the proper choice of plants. Among popular periodicals was *The Horticulturist*, published between 1846 and 1859 and books such as Frank Scott's *The Art of Beautifying Suburban Home Grounds* (1881) and Elias Long's *Ornamental Gardening for Americans* (1884).

State Historical Society of Wisconsin

Thomas Armstrong was born in Northern Ireland, where he learned his trade as a landscape gardener. He established his nursery and landscape business in 1854. Armstrong supplied plant material for some of the city's finest gardens, and also laid out home grounds and parks.

Sanger, Rockwell and Company, 1891 Catalogue. Lumberyard catalogues offered a selection of ornamental fence work, in addition to millwork trim for buildings. The Leidersdorf house has a fence similar to the one illustrated in the catalogue.

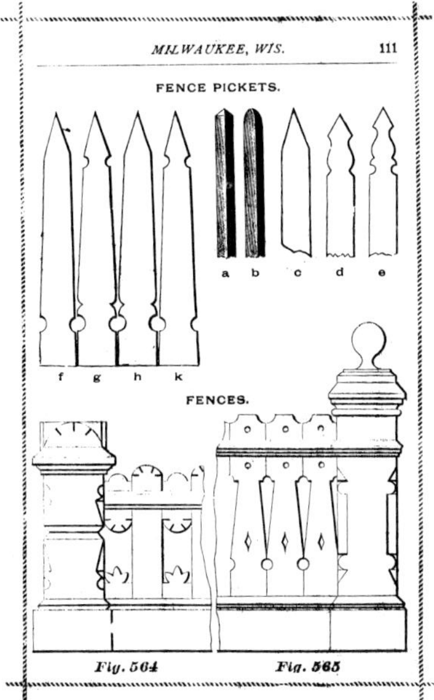
MILWAUKEE, WIS. 111

FENCE PICKETS.

a b c d e

f g h k

FENCES.

Fig. 564 Fig. 565

Leidersdorf House, National Avenue, photograph c. 1890. The Leidersdorf family is shown among their collection of conifers. The sugar maple along the boulevard was likely planted by Leidersdorf. Of note is the plank curb and street leading to the gravel driveway.

Milwaukee Co. Historical Society

Architecture of Commerce and Industry

Milwaukee Public Library

Milwaukee has called itself "the city that works." Commentators have proclaimed it "the workingmen's city."[1] In this chapter we look at the work*places* of Milwaukeeans. Commercial and industrial building in Milwaukee falls into four periods, based on the city's economic growth, developments in building technology, and phases of architectural expression. However, there is much continuity and overlap of older building forms from period to period. While some commercial architects and their clients experimented with the latest construction techniques and styles, others chose to replicate or modify earlier building traditions. The avant-garde in any era may draw much attention, but the simpler, more traditional designs have always constituted a greater portion of commercial buildings in the city. Also, the current appearance of structures often reflects layers of alterations and additions spanning several decades.

Throughout Milwaukee's history the buildings of commerce and industry encompassed a variety of uses, including retail, wholesale, manufacturing, service, transportation, and entertainment. Many buildings shown here represent straightforward, practical solutions to the technical demands of a particular trade or industry. Others combine structural innovation with sophisticated architectural expression. While some of Milwaukee's commercial buildings lack all pretense, others present a clear attempt by a business or corporation to project a certain image. Although they reflect a mercantilistic preoccupation with commodity, utility, and image projection, Milwaukee's commercial and industrial buildings are both architecturally and historically interesting.

Milwaukee Co. Historical Society

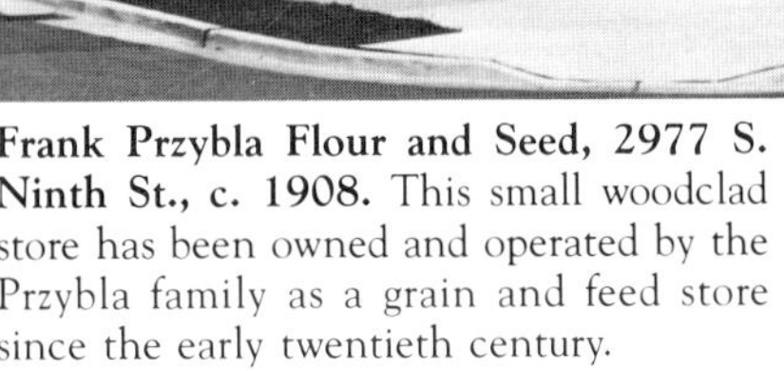

Frank Przybla Flour and Seed, 2977 S. Ninth St., c. 1908. This small woodclad store has been owned and operated by the Przybla family as a grain and feed store since the early twentieth century.

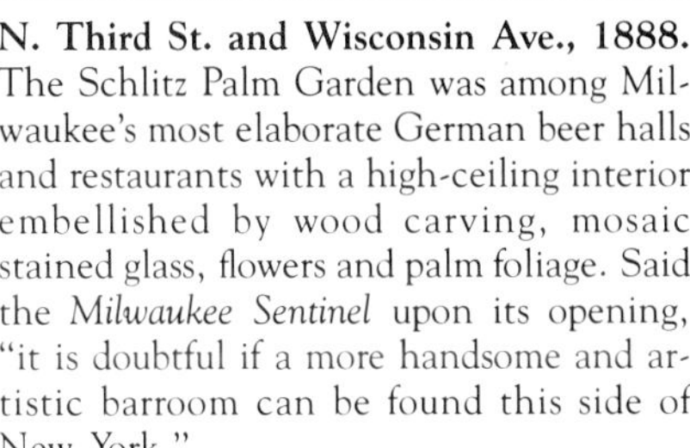

N. Third St. and Wisconsin Ave., 1888. The Schlitz Palm Garden was among Milwaukee's most elaborate German beer halls and restaurants with a high-ceiling interior embellished by wood carving, mosaic stained glass, flowers and palm foliage. Said the *Milwaukee Sentinel* upon its opening, "it is doubtful if a more handsome and artistic barroom can be found this side of New York."

Commission Row, 317-339 North Broadway, 1894-95. Since Milwaukee's earliest years, the lower Third Ward has been a center of wholesale and mercantile activity. Following a disastrous fire in 1892, grocery dealers constructed these commission houses. Designed by the Milwaukee firm of Henry C. Koch and Co., the row is still used for grocery wholesaling and warehousing.

Milwaukee Co. Historical Society

423 W. Juneau Ave., 1853. The Gipfel Union Brewery was founded by German-born Charles Gipfel and operated until about 1890. The brewery produced lager beer until 1872, after which it made only *Weissbier* (white beer).

Pioneer Trade and Commerce: 1835-1860

Frontier life demanded simple and economical solutions to building needs. In response to the services and goods required by townspeople and travelers, mills, offices, and shops were opened — saw mills and flour mills, liveries, and blacksmith shops, land offices and lawyers' offices, hotels and taverns, and stores which sold everything from salt to books.

With the exception of flour and saw mills, and a few warehouses, commercial buildings in Milwaukee prior to 1860 seldom deviated from the domestic scale of one to three stories. They were simple, rectangular or square shapes, most often with gable or flat roofs. Wood buildings commonly employed the balloon frame, but the traditional heavy timber mortise-and-tenon framing system could also be found in commercial buildings within the city. Exterior walls were flat surfaces of clapboard or brick, sometimes stone. Ornamentation was minimal, due in part to the scarcity of skilled labor and the limited economic resources of settlers, as well as a continuation of older building traditions.

Structure and plan were revealed through the undisguised handling of natural materials: wood, clay, and stone. Commercial life in Milwaukee was not yet complicated by great wealth and the desire to exhibit status and sophistication. The resultant simplicity and functionalism of Milwaukee's early commercial buildings is very appealing to the modern eye.

The earliest places of business in Milwaukee were log cabins and wood frame shanties. Within a few years after the city's founding in 1835, however, more substantial wood and brick commercial structures were erected. Among these, the conservative form of the Federal Style predominated. While the height of Federal architecture in the United States lasted from about 1785 to 1820, construction in this style continued well beyond this period in outlying regions and the newly-opened West.

In Milwaukee, the stepped parapet end walls characteristic of the style perhaps appealed to German settlers, who were familiar with similar gable treatments in their native land. The former Gipfel Brewery, which stands at 423 West Juneau Avenue, is the one remaining example of a Federal commercial building constructed of brick in the city.[2] Although the building was not among the city's finest Federal structures, its severe lines, flat unadorned walls punctuated by symmetrically placed windows, and the parapet end walls are representative of the Federal Style as it appeared in old Milwaukee.

Intermixed with the Federal Style buildings were shops, warehouses, and offices constructed in the Greek Revival Style. Milwaukee's pioneer settlers shared the American enthusiasm for Grecian design in the antebellum period. On the developing frontier, only a few prestigious buildings — usu-

Herman Wudtke Collection

Dousman Warehouse, 1839. Water Street, below Wisconsin Avenue along the Milwaukee River, was lined with warehouses, wholesale firms, and small shops and factories by the 1840s. This building, which was located just south of the Cream City Mills, served as a fish warehouse for many years (note the sign of the fish over the door). The pronounced gable returns, entablature, and lunette of the well-proportioned facade are features of the Greek Revival Style.

ally courthouses, banks, or churches — were built of stone in a manner imitative of Greek temples and monuments. Milwaukee's Greek Revival commercial buildings followed a more vernacular rendition of the style. Generally they were plain rectangular blocks with low-pitched gable roofs. Finished with clapboard or local cream brick, these buildings were sparsely ornamented with mill-board Grecian details such as pilasters, entablatures, and pediments. Unlike Greek Revival churches or dwellings in Milwaukee, colonnaded fronts and carved ornament seldom, if ever, appeared on the city's Greek Revival commercial buildings, which were stripped, abstracted expressions of the style.

Milwaukee's commercial architecture prior to 1860 was influenced not only by Greek precedents, but also by Gothic and Italian ones. By the middle of the 1840s, revival of Gothic forms became popular in the United States. In frontier cities like Milwaukee, the early Gothic Revival Style was revealed more often in the ornament (such as gable trim) and the

Kleinsteuber's Machine Shop, 322 W. State St., 1840s or 1850s. This photograph, which may date from the 1860s, shows the machine shop where Christopher Sholes, inventor of the typewriter, did much of his work on various inventions. The clapboard building, reminiscent of small New England shops in the Greek Revival Style, is no longer standing.

State Historical Society of Wisconsin

Layton and Co. Beef and Pork Packers, 1856. Englishman John Layton and his son Fred established their firm in 1845. Cutting and packing was done in this brick "ham house", which stood on the 400 block of N. Plankinton Avenue. A larger slaughtering and packing works was built in the Menomonee Valley in 1863 to accommodate the expanding business. Thereafter this building served as an office and warehouse for the company. The cornice and gable returns of the original Greek Revival design had been removed by the time of this photograph in the late nineteenth century.

Herman Wudtke Collection

State Historical Society of Wisconsin

Cream City Mills. An 1860s lithograph by Seifert and Lawton of Milwaukee shows a Greek Revival mill which was located on Water Street below Chicago Street. It was originally built for grain storage by George Dousman in 1835, and rebuilt in 1863. Matthew L. Keenan converted it into a flour mill in 1867.

Clinton House, c. 1840-1850. This Greek Revival hotel and boarding house stood on S. First St. between Seeboth and Pittsburgh. It served South Side residents and travelers of modest means as late as 1900, when this photograph was taken.

State Historical Society of Wisconsin

Halfway House Tavern and Inn, 5905 S. Howell Ave., c. 1850. Travelers between Milwaukee and Racine County stopped at this "halfway house". It was also a gathering place for the rural community of New Coeln, settled by a group of Germans in the 1840s. The cornice and gable returns of the Italianate structure have been removed, and the cream brick has been painted, but otherwise the exterior of the structure remains intact.

components (such as windows) of a commercial building than in its total plan and silhouette. Additionally, the Gothic Revival generally was not promoted as a commercial style, but as an ecclesiastical and residential one. Railroad depots, however, were an exception. Milwaukee's first passenger station, built in 1851 by the Milwaukee and Mississippi Railroad, was a small rectangular building with vertical board and batten siding, a steeply-pitched gable roof, and bargeboard trim characteristic of small wooden buildings in the Gothic Revival Style.[3]

Variations on the themes of Italian Renaissance architecture were very popular in commercial building in nineteenth and early twentieth century America. By the early 1850s simplified Italian Renaissance motifs began to appear on Milwaukee's commercial buildings. The Halfway House Inn and Tavern (later known as the New Coeln House, among other names) was located beyond Milwaukee's boundaries when it was built in the 1850s. But it demonstrates a type of Italianate commercial building which was constructed in Milwaukee for small shops and taverns until the 1870s. Typically these buildings were three-bay, cream brick cubes, and featured a hip roof with a cross gable, and round-headed or segmental arch windows with hoodmolds. Later examples, like those dating from the 1860s and early 1870s, often had gable roofs and pronounced ornamented cornices.

Cross Keys Hotel, 400-402 N. Water St., 1853. Social activity in early Milwaukee centered around the hostelries and taverns. Until its demolition in 1980, the Cross Keys Hotel was the last of the historic inns which once lined Water St. This photograph belies the handsome early appearance of the building, which had four stories, an ornamented Italianate cornice, a wrought-iron balcony, and large windows on the first floor facade.

Many early commercial buildings in Milwaukee were built as freestanding units. As Milwaukee grew from a frontier village to a city, however, an increasing number of commercial buildings in the business districts showed the builders' understanding of the urban street. Italianate commercial blocks of the 1850s, such as the one located at 165-169 South First Street, comprised some of the city's first truly urban commercial forms. The flat-roofed brick building followed the street corner in continuous bays of round arch windows and first story storefronts.

Enterprise and Eclecticism: 1860-1890

Nationally this was a time of accelerated growth and rampant individualism in the American economy. In the span of a few decades, Milwaukee transformed from a small frontier city into an urban manufacturing center. Commercial and industrial architecture echoed the transitions of the city's culture as a whole. Office buildings, stores, factories, and railroad stations in Milwaukee eclipsed all other structures in size and prominence. The height of commercial buildings downtown increased as the demand for office and retail space grew. New possibilities in structure, materials, and style were explored. Exteriors became increasingly intricate, employing a variety of shapes and outlines. Rooflines became equally complex. Mirroring the new commercial wealth, buildings were enriched by elaborate ornamentation such as carved stone, inlaid brickwork, and details of wrought iron and copper. At the same time, however, buildings were designed with more consideration of their functional requirements.

Leland Roth has observed that "the unbridled energy of the age, its confident enthusiasm, and brash parvenu taste resulted in an architecture that consciously attempted to be modern, vigorous, and more energetic than previous expressions."[4] In a city known for its stolid, restrained architecture, it is interesting to note that some of Milwaukee's most exuberant, and even zany, commercial structures were erected during this period. If the urban fabric of Milwaukee lost some of its harmony and coherence during this era, it also gained some excitement and pluralism. In the wake of changing tastes and values, a number of these buildings have disappeared.

The major change in commercial building after 1860 in Milwaukee, as elsewhere, followed the introduction of iron as a structural material. By the end of the century, this would culminate in the steel-frame, curtain-wall skyscraper. Experiments with iron construction occurred in the East during the 1840s and 1850s, when iron columns were substituted for the masonry of outer walls to support the floors of a building. Inventors James Bogardus and Daniel Badger of New York were primarily responsible for turning the casting of iron beams and columns into a major industry by the time of the Civil War. Whole buildings could be fabricated from factory-produced iron parts, including interior frame and exterior shell.[5]

In 1860, Milwaukee businessman James Baynard Martin commissioned English-born builder-architect George H. Johnson to build an office block with a complete cast iron front. Still standing at the southeast corner of East Wisconsin Avenue and Water Street, the Iron Block is Milwaukee's last remaining building with a cast iron facade. Although the Iron Block was not the only structure of this type erected in Milwaukee, it was the city's most ambitious attempt at cast iron commercial building.

The framing of the Iron Block is conventional brick and timber, but the north and west facades are cast iron manufactured at Daniel Badger's Architectural Iron Works in New York City. The Iron Block's design, like many of its contemporaries, was influenced by Italian Renaissance sources. The skeletonized Venetian style, with its repetitive arcades and sharp detail, was well-suited to mass-produced iron construction.

Significantly, the Iron Block contains what is possibly the oldest remaining elevator in the city, dating from 1879. The first passenger elevators, adding to the development of the skyscraper, were installed in cast-iron buildings.

Until the 1890s, iron framing was used most often in conjunction with brick bearing walls in Milwaukee's large commercial buildings. The great interest in iron was also expressed in the richly ornamented ironwork on interior light courts. These courts, or atriums, were a popular feature in late nineteenth century office blocks as the larger building size dictated a need for natural light.

Architects and builders in this period adopted a wide variety of architectural styles for places of business. Among these, the Italianate Style was most common in Milwaukee. Italia-

205 E. Wisconsin Avenue, Iron Block, 1860.

Union Architectural Iron Works and **Galvanized Iron Works.** Milwaukee firms specializing in architectural iron work advertised in city directories and trade journals throughout the nineteenth century.

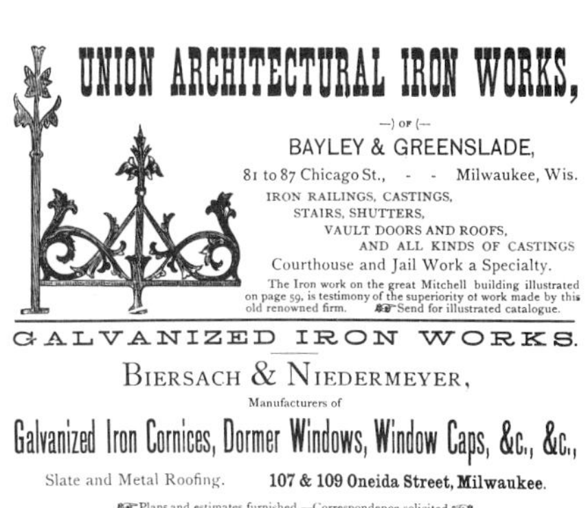

nate was the practical building style of the day. Italian design sources — from the Renaissance as well as late Romanesque, from northern and southern Italy — were used eclectically in the creation of commercial facades. This style has also been called Commercial Italianate, or in its more elaborate form, Victorian Italianate.

These buildings can be distinguished from earlier Italianate examples by their more ornate treatment of windows and elevations. The characteristic round and segmental arches are decorated with highly articulated moldings. Pilasters, belt courses, and corbel tables add to the compartmentalized effect of the facades. Buildings are crowned with overscaled bracketed cornices, sometimes with a pediment for added vertical emphasis.

From the 1860s to the 1880s, hundreds of Italianate stores, offices, and shops were constructed along the downtown streets and in neighborhood business districts throughout the city. The 700 block of North Milwaukee Street, the 600 block of North Broadway, and the 1000-1100 block of North Third Street still contain impressive concentrations of these buildings. The largest Victorian Italianate structures in the city, such as the Republican House pictured here, are no longer standing.

The east side of the 700 block of N. Milwaukee Street. This street facade contains some of the city's most extraordinary small to medium-sized Italianate commercial buildings of the mid- to late-nineteenth century. As an ensemble, it constitutes an important document of the way the central city looked at that period.

State Historical Society of Wisconsin

Republican House, c. 1885. This Victorian Italianate hotel was located at the northwest corner of Third and Kilbourn, and was among Milwaukee's grandest hostelries. This building replaced an 1836 hotel, which was originally called Washington House. The name was later changed to commemorate the birth of the Republican Party.

807-809 S. Second St., c. 1863. Frederick Vullmahn constructed this building for his boot and shoe shop, with living quarters for his family upstairs. Like John Schmitt's store, the punched-out millwork designs on the window enframements were a standard feature on wood Victorian Italianate buildings.

1647 N. Twelfth St., 1870s. John Schmitt, dealer in wines and liquors, posed with friends in front of his store in about 1885. Clapboard Victorian Italianate stores such as these, with bracketed falsefront gables and peaked cornices over windows, were the newest additions to the neighborhood streetscape in the 1860s and the 1870s.

320 E. Clybourn Ave., 1874. Milwaukee architect Edward Townsend Mix designed this Victorian Italianate building for the Wisconsin Leather Company, established in 1846. The cream brick structure has been painted, but its facade has changed little in one hundred years.

John Pritzlaff Hardware Co., 143 St. Paul Ave., 1874 with later additions. In 1843, two years after settling in Milwaukee, German-born John Pritzlaff became a porter for a city iron merchant. He established a hardware business in 1850, which eventually became the largest in Milwaukee. One of his first stores, dating from 1861, still stands at 1033 N. Third St. In 1874, Pritzlaff constructed the first section of this cream brick and stone building, which still retains its original cast iron storefront. The Italianate round arch windows and bracketed cornice were repeated in subsequent additions made between 1879 and the end of the century.

During the two decades following the Civil War, the French Second Empire Style and the mansard roof became fashionable. In America, French Second Empire was for a time the "official" style for grand urban buildings, municipal as well as commercial. Often they were the largest and most prestigious, or at least the fanciest, buildings in American cities and towns. In Milwaukee, financier and business tycoon Alexander Mitchell, whose penchant for French Second Empire can be seen in his mansion at 900 West Wisconsin Avenue, constructed the city's outstanding example of the style. In the Mitchell Block (1876-78), designed by Edward Townsend Mix, all the important elements of the style are present. The five-story granite and limestone building has a mansard roof with dormers, pavilioned elevations, and lavish overlays of Baroque detail. Its horizontal layering and sculptured appearance are also characteristic of the style. In a desire to emulate the French Second Empire fashion, mansard roofs were sometimes added to older commercial buildings to "modernize" their images.

Merchants Mills, 343 N. Broadway, 1875. Although more common in its day, the Victorian Gothic treatment of commercial and industrial buildings is a rare sight in Milwaukee today. Few examples were found in the survey. The most important building in the style was the old Northwestern Mutual Life Insurance Company (no longer standing) designed by Edward Townsend Mix. The Merchants Mills block was built for Jewett and Sherman, purveyors of coffee and spices.

Just as the Second Empire Style borrowed from French Baroque sources, the Queen Anne Style combined English designs primarily from the seventeenth and early eighteenth centuries in a free-form manner. Queen Anne commercial buildings were relatively few in number in Milwaukee. Most were small-scale stores and shops. They can be identified by their irregular silhouettes, with multiple high-pitched roofs often accented with round or polygonal turrets. Surface materials vary in texture and color, and may be brick (usually red-brown), clapboard, shingles, stone, or combinations thereof. A variety of window types are prevalent, particularly three-part bay windows. Some Queen Anne buildings, such as the James Conroy Building, exhibit early English Renaissance motifs while others employ later, classical details. Most of Milwaukee's commercial Queen Anne buildings date from the 1880s and 1890s, but corner stores were constructed in this style as late as 1910.

Interest in and revival of Romanesque architecture, a round-arch medieval style, began in the 1840s in

Kneisler's Tavern, 2900 S. Kinnickinnic Ave., 1890. The irregular pentagonal plan, turrets, shingled gable, and sunburst motifs over the storefront windows are Queen Anne features of this well-conserved Bay View landmark.

above right

James Conroy Building, 727 N. Milwaukee St., 1881. With the advent of the Queen Anne Style in Milwaukee, red and brown brick began to supplant the use of traditional cream brick in building construction. Of note is the treatment of the top story, which has two high gables, patterned brick, and a central chimney (the tall chimney cap has been removed). James Conroy erected this building for his ice cream and catering business, founded in 1868. The first floor was a salesroom and ice cream parlor.

Milwaukee Club, 706 N. Jefferson St., 1884. Although not a commercial structure, the Milwaukee Club is associated with the commercial and industrial life of the city as an exclusive businessmen's club, begun in 1882. Edward Townsend Mix designed the Queen Anne red brick structure with a prominent polygonal turret.

America. By the 1880s, the forceful Romanesque-inspired designs of Henry Hobson Richardson had created a distinctively American style of architecture, which became known as Richardsonian Romanesque. Richardson's Cheney Block (Hartford, Connecticut, 1875-76) and Marshall Field Wholesale Store (Chicago, 1885-87) influenced the designs of Milwaukee's best remaining examples of commercial buildings in this style.

Northwestern Mutual Life Insurance Company, 611 N. Broadway, 1885. The interior has a central court which extends from the second floor to a rooftop skylight of ornamental iron construction. Portions of the original interior, including marble trim, terrazzo flooring, and paneled wood wainscotting, still remain.

The Northwestern Mutual Life Insurance Company's headquarters, completed in 1885 from the plans of the prominent Chicago architect Solon Spencer Beman (1853-1914), illustrates the imposing sense of massiveness, rock-faced masonry, and rhythmic arcades which are trademarks of Richardsonian Romanesque. Granite and limestone, from which this building was constructed, were popular materials, as were brownstone and red brick. The Hotel Pfister, executed in local Wauwatosa limestone and Milwaukee cream brick, on a steel frame is a simpler rendition of the style.[6] The *Hotel Pfister Souvenir*, published upon its opening in 1893, described Henry C. Koch and Company's design as "modernized Romanesque." The eight-story hotel, it said, "is not a showy building on the outside, but has the appearance of substantiality, which is its chief charac-

Steinmeyer Building, 205 W. Highland Ave., 1893. Photograph of the Richardsonian Romanesque block shortly after its construction. By this time the firm of Bauer and Steinmeyer, established in 1865, was operated by the family of William Steinmeyer, and was the largest grocery business in Milwaukee. Grocery firms such as these were forerunners of modern-day supermarkets. "The stock carried by this firm," an 1892 promotional booklet claimed, "comprises a full line of staple and fancy groceries, including canned goods, condiments and table delicacies of every description."

teristic throughout."[7] The Steinmeyer Building, a wholesale block designed by Milwaukee architects George B. Ferry and Alfred C. Clas in 1893, is finished in red brick. The flat wall surface, minimal detail, and repeating arches give the structure a taut, integrated form, a new trend in post-Civil War commercial buildings.

Although these buildings were large for their day, they were often structurally conservative, using bearing walls instead of an iron or steel frame for support. The Chicago and Northwestern Depot, which was among Milwaukee's largest structures when it was erected in 1889, was supported by heavy walls of granite, brownstone, and red pressed brick. (By comparison, the train shed, measuring eighty-five feet wide by six hundred feet long, employed the technological advances which had been made in iron trusswork.)[8]

Visually, the Richardsonian Romanesque style advanced the idea that commercial buildings did not have to have complicated shapes or rooflines to be impressive or authoritative. Nor did they have to be laden with an eclectic array of historical ornament. Richardsonian Romanesque pointed in the direction that American commercial architecture would take by the end of the nineteenth century.

Chicago and Northwestern Railway Depot, 1889. Railroad terminals were symbols of great prestige in the nineteenth century. Cities demanded monumental stations to stand at their railroad gateways. Charles Sumner Frost of Chicago (1856-1931), architect of several prominent railroad buildings in the Midwest, planned Milwaukee's passenger depot for the Chicago and Northwestern Railway. It was located at the eastern end of Wisconsin Ave. on the lakeshore and was demolished in the 1960s.

State Historical Society of Wisconsin

Button Block, 500 N. Water St., 1892. This handsome Richardsonian Romanesque office building, with an arcaded exterior of brownstone and red-brown brick, was constructed for Charles Pearson Button, owner of the Phoenix Knitting Works.

831-33 N. Jefferson St., 1890. For a time in the twentieth century, the urban elegance of the Richardsonian Romanesque Style was not appreciated. Recently, however, this brownstone building has been carefully restored. (Another downtown commercial structure, the Matthews Building at 301 W. Wisconsin Ave., is also undergoing restoration of its Romanesque facade.) Arnold and Quistorf's Tavern originally occupied this building, now the home of Elsa's on the Park.

Looking east on State Street from about 9th Street, photograph about 1915.

Urbanism and Industrial Growth: 1890-1915

During this period American commerce and industry increasingly consolidated into large corporations. Small enterprises, which rose in the mid-nineteenth century from the efforts of individuals and partnerships, expanded into corporately-run businesses overseen by boards of directors and influenced by diverse investors. Centralized industry and commerce contributed in part to a growing population shift from rural areas and small towns to cities such as Milwaukee, especially after 1900. Milwaukee's mills and factories grew to even greater size in physical plant, production, and marketing. With great size came complexity. Industrial processes and trade relationships began a period of standardization in response to an increasingly complex socio-economic structure.

Not surprisingly, the commercial architecture of these years reflected the trend toward control and the search for clarity in the larger culture. Two forces shaped commercial building after 1890. One was stylistic, and the other was technological. Architects returned to the classical styles which emphasized order, symmetry, and restraint. Historicism continued to play a role in commercial design. However, there was also an attempt to express the structure and function of buildings more clearly. Some Chicago architects of the late nineteenth century, and the individual styles of Louis Sullivan and Frank Lloyd Wright, achieved this ideal most artistically. The development of the steel frame skyscraper and inventions such as electric lighting radically altered the appearance and functioning of commercial structures.

To the contemporary observer, these buildings seem altogether more "serious" than those of the previous era. Perhaps their designs represented a kind of antidote to the labor unrest, social turbulence, and radical cultural changes in America at the turn of the century. Certainly Milwaukee did not lose its local architectural character, but its new commercial buildings reverberated the pulse of the nation more than in the past.

Milwaukee Interurban Terminal, 231 W. Michigan St., 1903-05. Another variation of Neo-classicism can be seen in the former central terminal for the Milwaukee Electric Railway and Light Company. The building was designed by Milwaukee architect Herman J. Esser and contained the interurban's general offices, terminal station, car house, and training facilities.

Although few of Milwaukee's architects at the turn of the century were trained at the Ecole des Beaux Arts in Paris, no doubt many visited the World's Columbian Exposition held in neighboring Chicago in 1893, which catalyzed national interest in Greek and Roman architectural models. Perhaps the most successful buildings of this classical resurgence in Milwaukee were produced by the local firm of George B. Ferry and Alfred C. Clas. Noted for their design of the Milwaukee Central Library (see Civic Structures), as well as numerous other structures in the city, Ferry and Clas were also responsible for the design of the office building which stands at 526 East Wisconsin Avenue. The Northwestern National Insurance Company, completed in 1906, is housed in a compact Bedford limestone structure with recessed openings between coupled columns. Its mansard roof with ornate dormers and its tripartite windows with circular panes are indicators of French Renaissance influence. The Second Ward Savings Bank, now the Milwaukee County Historical Society at 910 North Third Street, is also an attractive design in the same French Renaissance vein. The Milwaukee firm of Charles Kirchoff and Thomas L. Rose were the architects of the building, completed in 1913.

The Neo-classical Revival was the sterner relative of Beaux Arts Classicism. Banks constructed branch offices in the Neo-classical Revival style all over the city between 1890 and 1915. Temple forms and free-standing columns of classical antiquity were devices for creating buildings Greco-Roman in spirit and detail. Classical prototypes had been similarly popular for bank design during the years of the Greek Revival in the early nineteenth century.

On a grander scale, corporations often chose the Neo-classical Revival for the power and monumentalism of the style. The Northwestern Mutual Life Insurance Company commissioned Chicago architects Marshall and Fox to design their third home office in Milwaukee (the second, at 611 North Broadway, was discussed previously). Completed in 1914, the massive block of white granite was

Northwestern National Insurance Company, 526 E. Wisconsin Ave., 1906.

Second Ward Savings Bank, 910 N. Third St., 1911-13. A triangular plan was often used for commercial buildings on odd-shaped corner sites. N. Plankinton Ave. originally ran north to State St., along the east facade of this former bank building.

Northwestern Mutual Life Insurance Company, 720 E. Wisconsin Ave., 1914.

Pabst Theater, 144 E. Wells St., 1895. The Pabst Theater, financed by Captain Frederick Pabst, was built to replace the burned Stadt Theater. German plays, operas, and concerts were produced here until the 1920s. The remaining section of the Stadt Theater building originally adjoined the end east of the Pabst, and was the site of the Pabst Theater Cafe. It was a showplace in the city, and its walls were adorned by works of Milwaukee's German panorama painters.

Germania Building, 152 W. Wells St., 1896. George Brumder's publishing house, the Germania Publishing Company, was located here. The firm was founded in 1873 to accommodate the needs of Milwaukee's large German population for books, magazines, and newspapers in their own language. The German-language press declined in the 1920s, and by the 1940s, the Brumder estate had sold the building.

reviewed by architect Peter B. Wight as a "chaste revival of classical and especially Roman details." Wight, who was not an advocate of the revival of classical architecture in the early twentieth century, noted "if the designs and arts of the Romans can be consistently revived in concert with modern engineering devices, this building demonstrates it."[9]

Milwaukee provided its own interpretation of classical revivals, at the turn of the century. While eastern cities such as Boston and New York extolled the Italian Renaissance in their prominent new buildings, Milwaukee built theaters, office blocks, and factories with German Renaissance elements. Civic structures such as City Hall, and residences such as the Captain Frederick Pabst mansion, are local landmarks in this style which signify the city's Germanic heritage. Often these buildings featured Flemish motifs, such as elaborate curved gables, and German Baroque ornamentation. It was no coincidence that they were usually designed by Milwaukee architects of German extraction (Henry C. Koch, H. Paul Schnetzky and Eugene R. Liebert, and Otto Strack, for example) for clients such as Frederick Pabst, the German Stadt Theater, and the Germania Publishing Company.

The Pabst Theater, built in 1895 from the plans of Otto Strack, has strong Baroque overtones. The German-born architect was familiar with European theater design, reportedly supplementing his knowledge with a study of the planning of Adler and Sullivan's Auditorium Building in Chicago (1886-1890).[10] The Pabst Theater's conservative exterior design belies the fact that its planning (including acoustics and facilities) and fireproof construction were advanced for its time.

The Germania Building (1896), known as the Brumder Building after World War I, is a pentagonal office block which dominates the triangle formed by Plankinton Avenue, Wells and Second Streets. The architects were H. Paul Schnetzky and Eugene R. Liebert, a local firm whose commercial and residential designs often had a distinct German character. Despite the building's profusion of Renaissance detail, the design as a whole is greater than the sum of its ornamented parts, which differentiates it from commercial architecture of the mid-nineteenth century. The copper-clad domes have been called "Kaiser's helmets."

In addition, several of Milwaukee's brewery buildings from the late nineteenth century, which are illustrated later in this chapter, evidence German Renaissance features.

Between 1890 and 1915, development in building technology paralleled a return to classical, and simpler, commercial styles. Although the technology of the skyscraper evolved over the span of several decades (chiefly in Philadelphia, New York, and Chicago), William LeBaron Jenney has been credited with the construction of the first true skyscraper, the Home Insurance Building in Chicago (1883-1885).[11] The primary requirement of the skyscraper was to support the entire structure on a metal frame, freeing the exterior and interior walls from any bearing function and reducing them to protective screens. The term "skyscraper" was first used in an 1889 article entitled "Chicago's Skyscrapers" in the *Chicago Tribune*.[12] The steel-frame skyscraper matured in Chicago during the 1880s, and by the 1890s Milwaukee erected its first commercial high-rises. Tall buildings with load-bearing walls continued to be constructed in Milwaukee during the 1890s, but the steel frame became standard for large commercial buildings by 1900.

The Pabst Building, which was located on the Milwaukee River at the corner of East Wisconsin Avenue and Water Street, was among Milwaukee's first skyscrapers and its tallest building for several years after its construction in 1892. It was rivaled only by City Hall in its visual prominence. While the base and the middle section of the building were modifications of the round-arch Richardsonian Romanesque style, the roofline and tower were suggestive of Flemish Renaissance buildings. This rich final flourish was another architectural reflection of the city's and client Frederick Pabst's German background. In later years the

Wholesalers and Manufacturers Directory (1905)

roofline was altered and the tower removed, seriously diminishing the original design. Before the Pabst Building's demolition in 1980, it was one of a handful of buildings in Milwaukee by the well-known Chicago architect Solon Spencer Beman. Beman was best known for his work on the model industrial town of Pullman, Illinois.[13]

Architects and builders experimented with architectural expressions for the new skyscraper building type. Romanesque, Renaissance, and Neoclassical styles were among those explored for tall buildings. Henry C. Koch, whose German Renaissance designs brought him architectural recognition in Milwaukee, provided the city with one of its most notable early skyscrapers. The Wells Building, constructed in 1901 at 324 E. Wisconsin Ave., has a classical three-part composition: a two-story base with broad windows and an arched entry; a multistory middle section of uniformly-spaced windows; and a terminal section with a bold projecting cornice rich in terra cotta ornamentation. It is evident that Koch had seen the work of Chicago architect Louis Sullivan, interpreting his designs rather than imitating them in the Wells Building. Although there is some resemblance to Sullivan in the general massing and ornamental scheme, Koch's ornament is Renaissance rather than the Sullivanesque blend of naturalistic and abstract forms.

Milwaukee Co. Historical Society

Wells Building, 324 E. Wisconsin Ave., 1901. This photograph shows Milwaukee's newest skyscraper shortly after it was constructed.

The Commercial Style arose in Chicago in the 1890s as a direct outgrowth of experimentation with tall buildings. The character of Commercial Style facades derives chiefly from the fenestration rather than the wall surface, and ornament is subordinate. The result is that the buildings have a skeletal appearance. Windows are usually rectangular, large, and regularly spaced. The "Chicago window," a three-part window with a wide fixed central light flanked by two narrower double-hung sashes, is another common feature.

Railway Exchange Building, 233 E. Wisconsin Ave., 1899.

The Railway Exchange Building (233 E. Wisconsin Ave.), Gimbels Brothers Store (101 W. Wisconsin Ave.), the Caswell Building (152 W. Wisconsin Ave.), and the Plankinton Building (161 W. Wisconsin Ave.) are all good examples of the Commercial Style along Milwaukee's downtown thoroughfare. The Railway Exchange Building, constructed in 1899, has the brownstone and dark brown brick veneer often seen in Commercial Style buildings of the 1880s and 1890s. Significantly, William LeBaron Jenney of Chicago was the architect. Jenney's innovative work attracted talented young designers to his office. One of Jenney's well-known students, Daniel H. Burnham, planned the first phase of the Gimbels Brothers Store in 1901-02. The white glazed terra cotta tile facade and the riverfront colonnade lend it a Neo-classical appearance. The colonnade, however, was part of later additions to the building by Milwaukee architect Herman J. Esser.

The Caswell Building, designed by the Milwaukee firm of Van Ryn and DeGelleke in 1907, is a handsome corner block with a white glazed brick exterior, characteristic Chicago windows, and a recessed arched portal over the main entry. The horizontal line, rather than the vertical, is dominant in the composition. Compared to the earlier Railway Exchange Building, there is less expression of wall surfaces and more that of a transparent glass skin over the structural skeleton. Across the street is the John Plankinton Building, designed by Chicago architects Holabird and Roche in 1916. Unlike many Commercial Style structures, the white terra cotta tile facade of this store and office block is richly ornamented with sculptural relief on the spandrels and cornices.

Gimbel Brothers Store, 101 W. Wisconsin Ave., 1901-02 with later additions. Adam Gimbel founded his "Palace of Trade" in Vincennes, Indiana in 1842. The firm moved to Milwaukee in 1887 and opened its first store in a rented building on Wisconsin Ave. By 1901, the expanding business began construction of the present building.

Caswell Building, 152 W. Wisconsin Ave., 1907.

3113 W. Burleigh St., 1946. The marked horizontality, long cylindrical windows, and small "portholes" of the streamlined facade of this factory building identify it as Moderne Style. Designed by architects George Zagel and Bro.

Watts Building, 759-61 N. Jefferson St., 1925. Ornate Moorish designs are incorporated into the terra cotta facing of this store building by the Milwaukee architectural firm of Martin Tullgren and Sons.

Corporate Image and the Avant-Garde: 1915-1930

The period between the First World War and the Depression was one of general prosperity for Americans. Architecturally, there was great movement upward and outward. Architects and engineers of tall buildings perfected the riveted steel frame created in Chicago during the last two decades of the nineteenth century. Commercial buildings rose to new heights in the urban landscape, as use of downtown land grew more intensive. The desire for ever greater height was also fed by corporate image-making. The skyscraper graduated from being a novelty to an established status symbol in American commerce.

At the same time, there was widespread horizontal expansion in American cities. During the 1920s, the suburbs became the focus of intense building activity in Milwaukee. In part this growth was stimulated by the electric railway system, but by the mid-1920s the private automobile began to reshape the city. Commercial buildings in the new suburbs often reflected the styles and the lower, more horizontal scale of suburban housing. Correspondingly, this was the last phase of the traditional "corner store" in urban neighborhoods, before the automobile altered shopping patterns of Milwaukeeans.

Stylistically, commercial architecture between 1915 and 1930 was marked by two strong contrasts. It was a period in which modernism and nostalgia developed simultaneously. There was an attempt to establish a new "industrial aesthetic" in architecture: a severe, geometric, utilitarian expression free of historicism, felt by some to be more appropriate in an industrialized culture. The impetus for this "Modern Movement" came from contemporary work in France, Germany, and Holland, and resulted in building styles called International Style, Art Deco, and Moderne. Much of what we, fifty years later, associate with "modernity" in design, stems from this era.

On the other hand, commercial designers looked backward as well as forward. Period revival commercial buildings, most often Spanish Colonial, Moorish, or Tudor in Milwaukee, became the fashion for small shops and stores. This nostalgia, sometimes with an exotic flare, is represented best in the gas stations and the movie palaces of the time. Interestingly, both were built in response to two new technologies, the automobile and the motion picture, which had great influence on American culture.

The major innovation in twentieth century building was reinforced concrete construction, emanating from experimental work in concrete during the nineteenth century in France, England, and the United States. By the second decade of this century, concrete construction had become popular in this country. Enthusiasm for it matched the earlier passion for cast iron. In Milwaukee before 1930, however, concrete was used more often in components of commercial buildings (foundations, floor slabs, ornamentation) than for complete skeleton framing.

Terra cotta, an ancient building material made of clay, also figured prominently during these years. In the Midwest, it was regionally important in the architecture of Louis Sullivan, Frank Lloyd Wright, and the Prairie School. Several companies in Milwaukee specialized in terra cotta brick and moldings. Glazed terra cotta tile and surface ornamentation were used in commercial buildings all over the city in the early twentieth century, replacing the hand-carved stone used in the nineteenth. (Note, for example, the terra cotta facing on Gimbels and the Plankinton Building discussed above.) During the 1920s, the use of terra cotta reached a peak in "elaborate treatment, texture, and polychroming" on Milwaukee's commercial buildings.[14] Many of these stores and office buildings were period revival, and Spanish-influenced designs were particularly popular. The example here is among the finest of this genre in Milwaukee.

Early modern commercial architecture in Milwaukee is represented by a sizable, but not outstanding, collection of Art Deco, Moderne, and International Style buildings. Only a few are highlighted here. The Wisconsin Gas Company, at 626 E. Wisconsin Avenue, is one of the major Art Deco skyscrapers in the city. The local firm of Eschweiler and Eschweiler moved beyond their earlier historicism to create a modern expression in granite, brick, and limestone. The twenty-story building is massed in a series of cubical setbacks, characteristically Art Deco, which rise to a large beacon light in the shape of a gas flame. The exterior materials punctuate the building's verticality, graduating in color from a dark granite to shades of red and pink brick, to cream brick at the top. Surface treatment reflects the Art Deco style of ornament, which is rectilinear in low relief on flat planes. Aztec-like zigzags crown the cornices, and sunburst copper panels decorate the spandrels.

The Milwaukee Journal Building, located at 333 W. State Street, is a classicized variation of the Moderne style. Architect Frank D. Chase of Chicago desired "to present a marked contrast to the ornateness which distinguishes much of the existing architecture in Milwaukee."[15] The building's flat surfaces and rectilinearity are characteristically Moderne, but the pink Kasota limestone exterior and the atypical round arch windows and entry modify the usual Moderne severity. The smooth wall planes are enriched with low-relief carving, the work of sculptor Arthur Weary. A carved stone frieze, three hundred fifty feet long with characters six feet high, portrays a historical narrative of communications. The depictions begin with Cro-Magnon stone carving and culminate with the modern press. In addition, carved stone lunettes above the third story windows feature twenty "marks" (insignia) of famous printing craftsmen. Large cast iron panels with bas-relief ornament the main entrance and the spandrels of the large lower story windows.

Although many Moderne buildings were constructed of concrete or cut stone to accentuate the hard-edged, bare "industrial aesthetic" of the style, the Northwestern Hanna Fuel Company Building is faced with a warm light orange brick. The office building was built in 1934 from plans by the firm of Martin Tullgren and Sons. Its geometric form, semi-cylindrical buttresses, and semi-circular aluminum canopies over the doors are identifying

Wisconsin Gas Company, 626 E. Wisconsin Ave., 1930.

Milwaukee Journal Building, 333 W. State St., 1924.

Northwestern Hanna Fuel Company, 2150 N. Prospect Ave., 1934. This small office building is a good example of later work by the Milwaukee architectural firm of Martin Tullgren and Sons. Herbert Tullgren, son of Martin, actually designed the structure which shows an interesting adaptation of terra cotta to modern design.

A. O. Smith Corporation Research Building, 3533 N. Twenty-seventh St., 1930. In 1902, A. O. Smith's parent company, C. J. Smith and Sons, designed and built the first pressed steel automobile frame in America for the Peerless Motor Car Company. A. O. Smith also pioneered in automated frame assembly, and produces automobile frames to this day. This building is part of the firm's industrial complex on the site, and was erected for research in machine design.

Moderne features. The buttresses, which dominate the facade, are faced with orange terra cotta. On the panels between the first and second story windows, terra cotta relief sculpture depicts workers engaged in various coal mining operations. The planning incorporates open work areas and a recreation room for employees, and was advanced for office buildings of its time in Milwaukee.[16] The appearance of workers in the ornamentation of this building, as well as on the *Journal* Building and other Moderne structures, reflects the ascendant political concerns for the working man in the 1920s and 1930s.

The International Style was not always translated successfully in American commercial buildings. Milwaukee's A. O. Smith Research Building is an exception. The design is not a dogmatic interpretation of the International Style, but derives inspiration from the European modernists as well as the Chicago tradition in commercial architecture. Holabird and Root of Chicago were the architects, with engineering design by E. W. Burgess of the A. O. Smith Corporation. The seven-story structure was built in 1930, shortly after the debut of the International Style in the United States. True to modernist principles, the building's architectural expression lies in its smooth uniform wall treatment and its complete absence of ornamentation. The glass frontage of the steel-frame building is arranged into vertical panels of convex triangular bays. Aluminum is used for the vertical spaces between the windows and for the shallow spandrels. A base course of black stone and corners of buff stone provide striking surface contrasts.[17] Upon its completion, the A. O. Smith Building was called "the most daring example of modern architecture in the city."[18]

The automobile spawned a whole new range of commercial building types. Gasoline stations, "the feedbag[s] of twentieth century transportation," were the first structures built in response to the automobile.[19] They first appeared between 1900 and 1910, as simple sheds of brick or metal. By 1915, oil companies were building stations to catch the motorist's eye.

Exotic themes were used to identify a particular retailer's products in the customer's mind, thereby making buildings into signs or symbols. Windmills, teepees, lighthouses, and Egyptian pyramids were among the models employed for gas stations and other roadside structures between 1915 and the 1930s.

Oriental architecture was the inspiration for a chain of filling stations owned by the Wadham's Oil and Grease Company of Wisconsin. In 1916 the company retained Milwaukee architect Alexander C. Eschweiler, noted for his Period Revival residential designs, to develop a prototype which would be portable, inexpensive, and — most of all — distinctive in appearance. The first "pagoda" Wadham's station (now demolished) was built in 1917 at the corner of N. Fifth Street and Wisconsin Avenue, and was painted in the bright company colors of red, black, and yellow. Wadhams constructed a large, but undetermined, number of pagoda stations in Milwaukee until the 1930s, when mergers led to the disappearance of the company name and their familiar station design.[20] Only a handful remain.

Milwaukee Co. Historical Society

Wadham's Oil Co. Filling Station, Wisconsin Ave. at N. Twenty-seventh St., 1925. The most elaborate examples of pagoda stations in Milwaukee have been lost. This 1930s photograph shows a station with a three-tiered pagoda roof and gasoline pumps with individual swooping canopies.

Wadham's Oil Co. Filling Station, 104 W. Walker St., 1930. The gable ends of this still-operating gasoline station are decorated with stained glass "W's" (for Wadham's).

The Corner Store and Tavern: A Chronology

The corner grocery, shop, and tavern have been fixtures in Milwaukee neighborhoods since their beginnings. Most had living quarters above the store, where the proprietor often resided. Early examples no longer remain. Below is a small selection of corner stores and taverns, which represent various styles and periods from the Civil War to the 1920s.

642 W. Garfield Ave., Henry Erbach Bakery, c. 1875. Early Italianate store with a square plan and hip roof, typically constructed in Milwaukee from the 1850s through the 1870s.

above right
1701-03 W. Lincoln Ave., Frank Kaminski Grocery and Saloon, c. 1890. A type of wood-clad corner store, with a high falsefront bracketed gable, commonly built in Milwaukee neighborhoods from the 1860s to the 1880s.

2501 N. Thirty-fifth St., 1905. Major Milwaukee breweries built and leased taverns to local proprietors. Flat roofs, segmental arch windows, and corbeled tables are characteristic of brewery-owned taverns at the turn of the century.

1405-07 W. Lincoln Ave., Joseph Czaskos Store Building, 1906. Good example of the Queen Anne Style with multiple gables and a round turret. The South Side has a good collection of Queen Anne Style corner stores.

2567 S. Twelfth St., 1907. Georgian Colonial Revival Style shop with a gambrel roof, and clapboard and shingle siding.

824-26 S. Sixteenth St., 1913. Neo-classical symmetry and detail are evident in this neighborhood market.

1629-31 W. Lincoln Ave., Joseph Mentkowski Butcher Shop, 1908. Between 1880 and 1910, high stepped gables, often ornamented with shingles, finials, and novelty windows, were a popular feature of storefront design.

5001-03 W. Center St., 1923. The Prairie-influenced design of this brick store reflects the suburban styles of duplexes and single-family houses erected in surrounding West Side neighborhoods at the time. George Zagel and Bro., architects.

Milwaukee's Breweries: A Sampling

Milwaukee has long been associated with the brewing of malt liquor. "The manufacture of beer," said an 1886 *Industrial History of Milwaukee*, "has contributed more to make this city famous than all other interests combined." The city's first brewery, the Lake Brewery, was founded in 1840 by three Welshmen. However, the German breweries of the 1840s and 1850s developed into major industries and established Milwaukee as a national brewing center. Below are only a few of Milwaukee's brewery buildings; discussion of others can be found elsewhere in the book.

Milwaukee Co. Historical Society

Simon Meister Brewery, 406 W. Juneau Ave., 1853. One of Milwaukee's small early breweries, now demolished. The building had cream brick walls, with stepped gable-end parapets and a series of six octagonal windows in the attic story.

Jacob Obermann Brewing Co., 502 W. Cherry St., c. 1866. Obermann, a native of Germany, founded a brewery on this site in 1854. This cream brick building, with a corbelled and pedimented cornice, was built about 1866, and is the only remaining structure of the brewery. Obermann became part of the Jung Brewing Co., now also defunct, in the late nineteenth century.

Valentine Blatz Brewing Co., SW corner Broadway and Juneau Ave.. First established by John Braun in 1846, the brewery was purchased in 1851 by Valentine Blatz, who expanded it into one of Milwaukee's largest breweries at the turn of the century. The remaining structures of the once-vast complex are Milwaukee cream brick with Wauwatosa limestone trim, constructed mainly between the late 1870s and the 1890s. The Bedford stone, Romanesque Style office building at 1120 N. Broadway was built in 1890 from the plans of Milwaukee architect H. Paul Schnetzky. The buildings are now used for storage by the Pabst Brewing Co.

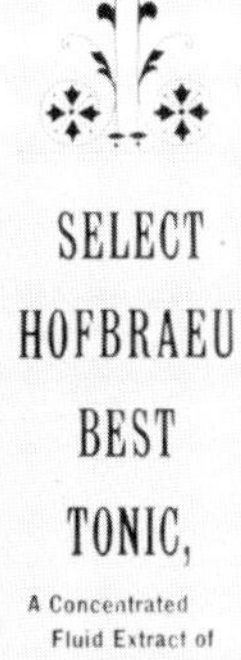

State Historical Society of Wisconsin

Pabst Brewing Co., 1890s lithograph. Jacob Best and his four sons founded Milwaukee's oldest operating brewery, begun in 1842 at the corner of N. Ninth St. and Juneau Ave. It was known as the Best Brewing Co. until the name was changed to Pabst in 1889.

Pabst Brewing Co., N. Ninth St. and Juneau Ave. The present brewery complex dates from 1872 and later. Constructed of cream brick and limestone, the ensemble features arcaded facades, crenellated turrets, and stepped gable ends popular in Milwaukee's industrial architecture at the turn of the century. The Hospitality Center, at 915 W. Juneau Ave., was designed in 1934 by Milwaukee architect Thomas Van Alyea and resembles the architectural character of the older buildings.

IV Civic Structures

State Historical Society of Wisconsin

Milwaukee County Court House, photograph c. 1860 (?). This Greek Revival Style building was erected on Court House Square in 1836, the year Wisconsin became a United States Territory. Thirty-five years later the building was razed to make room for a new structure. Note the young elm trees and the sapling-dotted park with its gravel walks.

State Historical Society of Wisconsin

Milwaukee County Court House, photograph c. 1890-1900. This view shows the Kilbourn Avenue and Jackson Street elevations of the second court house. This Roman Revival structure was designed by Leonard A. Schmidtner and constructed in 1872. The park space lay on the Wells Street side of Court House Square.

Not surprisingly, in a growing city, most of Milwaukee's public structures constructed prior to 1875 have disappeared. The scale of these buildings was quite small, even by the standards of the last decade of the nineteenth century. Architecturally, the basic styles of Milwaukee's three principal governmental buildings of this early period — the first and second court-houses, and the old city hall — bore some relationship to the forms of classical antiquity. They were either Greek Revival or some variation on the Italianate. Before the writings of John Ruskin and the onset of the Victorian Gothic, few governmental buildings anywhere in America strayed from the classical. On the other hand, many non-governmental public buildings, such as schools and fire stations, took on the great diversity of residential and commercial styles of the mid and late nineteenth century.

Milwaukee's surging growth in the decades around the turn of the century was well-matched by the zeal of its politicians and residents for municipal improvement. Bayrd Still comments that:

> The [political] platform pledges . . . in the forty years between 1870 and 1910 reveal the changing concept of municipal responsibility that accompanied the growth of the Wisconsin metropolis . . . By 1910 the expenditures of the fire, police, and health departments had increased manyfold; the existence of public waterworks, parks, and natatoria reflected a deepened concern for the welfare of the citizens; . . .[1]

Civic pride was also reflected in the drive for new public buildings. The small-scale buildings of mid-century were soon replaced with larger, more technologically-advanced structures. Three architectural firms in the city, Edward Townsend Mix, H. C. Koch & Co., and Ferry & Clas, dominated this period and gave Milwaukee some of its most significant public structures. Mix adapted the prevailing styles of the period to the needs of the city in elegant and imposing designs. Koch, the most original of the designers, developed new structural syntheses which were symbolic of the Germanic character of the city. Ferry and Clas responded to the monumental ideas of the Neo-classical Revival following the World's Columbian Exposition by creating unique designs in the new civic style.

The influence of the 1893 World's Columbian Exposition in Chicago on the design of American civic buildings was enormous. Although the whole country was affected, Milwaukee was partially insulated from the influence of the antique by Koch's personal virtuosity and prolific output. Nevertheless, the classical staged a strong resurgence. The influence of architects, generally from the East, who had been trained at Ecole des Beaux Arts, permeated the civic design movement. In the Neo-classical Revival and, particularly in Beaux Arts Classicism, the grand scale and some of the more regal detailing of the Baroque period were adapted to unique designs which were otherwise synthesized from the Renaissance and antiquity. There were, however, references to more modern buildings as well, such as the well-known adaptation of the central dome of the Fine Arts Building in Chicago for Milwaukee's Central Library by Ferry and Clas.

Indeed, following the Exposition, many Milwaukee architects felt compelled to make classical references in their work regardless of the building's function. Even natatoria were classically-derived. Fortunately for the architectural diversity of the city, other styles were also used, especially in designing schools, where the popular Collegiate Gothic, or Jacobethan, associations were sought. There was a transition in the 1920s, again in school design, away from the traditional forms to the cosmopolitan streamlined style associated with Art Deco skyscrapers in America and, to a lesser degree, the rise of Modern architecture in Europe.

Milwaukee Public Library

Heading East on the State Street Bridge, photograph c. 1932.

City Hall is the most symbolic building in the downtown landscape. More than any other structure, it proclaims "Milwaukee" and reflects the leading role of the Germanic populations that built the city in the late nineteenth century.

Construction on the design by Henry C. Koch and Company began in 1893, and the building was dedicated two years later. City Hall is distinguished by two neo-Baroque Rathaus-like towers which rise eight stories above the pavement. Built on filled-land in the Milwaukee River valley, the structure rests on a "forest of wooden piles driven into reclaimed marshland."[2] Three imposing granite arches engulf citizens who enter the building from the south. A sandstone and brick facade rise above to meet the copper roof and its surmounting towers.[3] Although the interior finishes have been partially modernized, the original monumental diamond-plan central atrium space pierces the full height of the building.

The Milwaukee County Court House, of Roman Neo-classic character, is another dominant feature of the downtown scene. Built in 1930, it was a structure which, at the time of its completion, loomed over the central city. Designed by the New York architect Albert Randolph Ross, the building made a strong symbolic statement about the power of government. The imposing presence of the Court House was amplified by the oversized Corinthian colonnade and imperial siting on Ninth Street high above Kilbourn Avenue. The plaza below was designed in the 1960s by the New York landscape architectural firm of Clark and Rapuano in collaboration with Donald Grieb Associates on a concept by Howard, Needles, Tammen & Bergendorff. The white clock tower, reminiscent of the arches

Milwaukee County Court House, photograph 1979.

at the Seattle World's Fair of 1962, was designed by the Grieb firm. It commemorates the civic contributions of Otto Schoenleber, founder of the Ambrosia Chocolate Company.

The grey granite castle that is the Federal Building, 515 E. Wisconsin Avenue, was the product of the popularity of the Richardsonian Romanesque Style in the 1880s and 1890s. This building, and countless other courthouses across the country of the same period, were derived from H. H. Richardson's scheme for the Allegheny County Court House in Pittsburgh. The Milwaukee structure was designed by Willoughby J. Edbrooke, supervising architect of the United States Treasury Department. "Among its noteworthy features are the carved ornament on the exterior, the spacious light court, surrounded by broad corridors and surmounted by an iron and glass skylight, and the splendid oak-panelled courtroom numbered 390, which has been called "the most distinctive courtroom in the United States."[4] The Federal building's south wing was added in the period 1929-1932, with subsequent alterations made in the 1940s. Although the building was originally known to most Milwaukeeans as the main post office, today it serves as an office building and courthouse.

The Central Public Library at 814 W. Wisconsin Avenue constitutes Milwaukee's strongest presentation of the lessons of the World's Columbian Exposition. Designed by Ferry and Clas in 1895, the main facade owes a debt, as architect William R. Ware noted, to the University of Leipsig Library (1891-2) by Arwed Rossbach.[5] At the time, the Milwaukee building was thought to have borne a relationship to Charles Atwood's Fine Arts Building at the Chicago Exposition. Actually, although the domed central pavilion is a similar idea, the Milwaukee building belongs more to the High Renaissance in its generally Palladian plan and main elevation than to the Roman concept which inspired Atwood.

Symmetrical in plan, the library's central pavilion is flanked by wings which end in lesser pavilions. The building rests on a one-story exposed basement decorated with banded rustication. The Corinthian order is used throughout: a double height porch dominates the central pavilion, the wings have pilasters, and the end pavilions bear engaged columns. Serliana, or Palladian windows, in the end pavilions resemble fenestration schemes of English classical buildings after Inigo Jones (1573-1652). Mannerist plaques, Baroque cartouches, wreaths and other decorations, and imperial eagles embellish the surfaces of the structure.

Originally the building housed both the library and the Milwaukee Public Museum. In the 1960s, however, separate facilities were erected for the museum. City offices now use the vacated museum space in the library building. The main entrance lobby retains its original appearance — complete with its coffered inner dome.

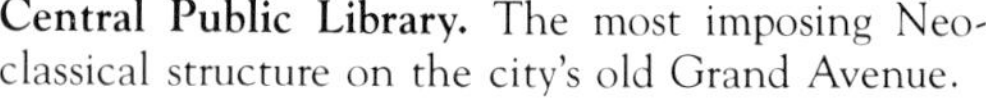

Central Public Library. The most imposing Neoclassical structure on the city's old Grand Avenue.

Schools[6]

In the 1830s and 1840s, public improvement and real estate speculating took precedence over public education and the construction of schools in the political arena. When the Milwaukee River had been bridged, and the east and west wards had finally been joined, the city then turned attention to the finer points of organization including the matter of schools. In 1846, the year of Milwaukee's incorporation, the Common Council appointed its first Board of School Commissioners — three commissioners from each of the five wards. Classes were held in existing buildings until 1849 when the brick schoolhouses were built in each of the wards. After a brief period of financial setbacks, the school system made a strong comeback erecting several well-appointed structures. By 1859, the system had grown large enough to require its first superintendent. Rufus King, editor of the *Milwaukee Sentinel,* was appointed. King was followed successively by Jonathan Ford, J. R. Sharpstein, and Edwin DeWolf. In 1864, during DeWolf's term, the board chastised the city for the opulent manner in which the school buildings were outfitted, noting:

> Our primary schools are overcrowded, our teachers overworked, and the result unsatisfactory. The city has, we fear, spent money injudiciously, one-half the sum spent on our costly school houses, expended in erecting plain primary school buildings, would have accomplished more for the cause of education. The evil is not past remedy . . . If the city will now expend one-fourth as much for the children of the primary schools, then Milwaukee may hope to proudly claim preeminence in its public schools as it does now in the matter of school architecture.[7]

High schools were operated only sporadically and without authority until 1867 when the legislature enacted the law establishing a high school for the city. It opened the next year in the Seventh Ward School House, but was moved successively to the First Ward School House, the Baptist Church (around 1873 after a fire), and then back to the First Ward building. In 1877, it moved to the Milwaukee Academy Building (built in 1865) on the corner of Cass and Knapp Streets.

By 1880, in addition to the high school, there were fourteen district schools and several primary facilities for younger children. During the superintendency of James MacAllister, which began in 1874, the old personal, historically-related names for the schools — Mitchell, Lapham, Humboldt, Lincoln, etc. — were dropped for reasons of order and efficiency in locating the buildings.

In 1858, the board had established a normal school to train teachers for the system. It had been housed in a number of buildings until 1875 when it moved to a structure on the corner of Seventh and Prairie (now Juneau). The municipal normal school became the nucleus of a larger teacher training role for Milwaukee. In 1880 the state legislature mandated that a state normal school be established in Milwaukee. Historian Bayrd Still reported: "The city was to supply a site and building worth $50,000. The city turned over property on Wells Street between Eighteenth and Nineteenth Streets and in 1885 provided a building valued at $53,000; the legislature authorized an annual appropriation of $10,000. The school opened in the fall of 1885 with a faculty of seven and forty-six students."[8]

The original core of the normal building was designed by Edward Townsend Mix. In this period of Victorian eclecticism in architecture, Mix sought to combine a Renaissance facade idea (modelled after the Gesu Church in Rome) in an elongated, vertical composition highlighted by Ruskinian polychromy and Gothic and Romanesque details. He capped each of the major wings of the building with a steeply pitched roof which rested on a secondary curved roof of the type one might find in a Baroque or Second Empire building. The curves were designed to reflect the curved

Herman Wudtke Collection

The Old First Ward School House. The old First Ward School was one of the five original "red brick school houses" erected in 1849 by the City. It was located at the northwest corner of Van Buren and Division Streets (East Juneau Avenue). Built at the period when the bracketed Italianate was overtaking the Greek Revival Style in popularity, this building illustrated an ambivalence appropriate to its time. It was razed about 1880 during the first era of school improvements.

Herman Wudtke Collection

The Old Fourth Ward Public School House, photograph c. 1870. One of the original five school houses, this structure was probably designed by John Rague and built by mason John Messenger. The design of the building expresses a very elegant understanding of the Italianate Style. The view shows a very Germanic, high style house of mid-century, some new tree plantings in the foreground, and the St. James Church spire in the background. Today the site is the corner of N. Eighth and West Michigan where the Eighth Street School is situated.

Normal School (Wells Street Junior High). The original polychromy of the building is evident in this early view.

State Historical Society of Wisconsin

elements in the main facade. Elegant chimneys modelled after the English Queen Anne Style punctuated this unusual roof. Additions were made to the building in 1894, 1918, and 1932. When Downer College expanded to take the responsibility for teacher training, the building was converted to use as the Milwaukee Girls' Trade and Technical High School. Until recently, it was the Wells Street Junior High School.

In the 1880s and 1890s, despite economic depression, the school board embarked on a major building program to keep pace with the rapidly increasing population. Today, several significant architectural statements remain from that period of intense activity. The Fifth Ward Primary School, now part of the Vieau School at the corner of Fourth and Walker (1894), by Ferry and Clas was one of the more Germanic and Gothic designs for public structures produced by that office. The building was expressed as four buttressed walls, pierced by overscaled, segmentally-arched windows which were crowned by corbie stepped gables. The elevations were embellished by the addition of ornamentation which emphasized the verticality of the design, including finials and arrow motifs over the window arches.

Milwaukee Co. Historical Society

The Sixth-District Branch School, photograph c. 1900. The polychromy and detailing of this Queen Anne Style school building, which formerly stood near the corner of Hubbard and Brown, are well rendered in this view. This structure probably served as the branch facility for the Garfield Avenue building at 2215 N. Fourth.

The freshest interpretations of the predominant Romanesque Style emerged from the office of H. C. Koch and Company. Koch received several commissions for schools, the earliest of which may have been for the Fourteenth District School on Eighteenth Street, between Kilbourn and Wells, built in the late 1870s.

The finer extant examples of his work include the Garfield Avenue School, 2215 N. Fourth Street, and the nearby Golda Meir School, 1542 N. Fourth Street, originally the Fourth Street Public School. The Garfield Avenue building was designed with a central hallway around which light-filled rooms were grouped in irregular clusters. The exterior of the structure was a late-nineteenth century caricature of Palladianism in that it was composed of three oddly asymmetrical masses. Furthermore, the masses were articulated by tripartite window systems, which were hugely overscaled. The impression given is that the building is lighter than it should be. It is not Roman in the sense of bearing-wall structures as envisioned by both Palladio and Richardson.

On the other hand, the Golda Meir School is truer to the Romanesque load-bearing format in its demonstration of a careful handling of materials and massing and attention to detailing. The basement of the building is rusticated stone. From the basement rise the piers on which the double-height window arches are sprung. Atop the arches smaller windows pierce the walls at the uppermost story. Koch took advantage of the hilly site by thrusting the basement upward, one story-height, in the middle of the structure, thereby allowing the central mass of the building to rise comfortably higher than the wings.

During the last decade of the nineteenth century, the chief competitor to Koch for school commissions was the firm of Van Ryn and DeGelleke. In the new century, this firm turned away from the fading popularity of the Romanesque and explored the design vocabulary of the English Renaissance, today called the Jacobethan, or "the Collegiate Gothic". In America, the chief examples of this style were the University of Chicago and Yale University, and the best known architects of the movement were Yale's principal designers, John Russell Pope and James Gamble Rogers.

The Jacobethan, like its historical antecedent, was characterized by brick walls broken by large, often banded multi-paned casement windows in a vertical composition emphasized by terra cotta quoins usually in a contrasting color. Bay View High School, 2571 S. Lenox Street (1915), with its grand setback from the street, recalls castles erected by the liege lords of Elizabeth I for her holiday retreats. The earlier Riverside High School, 1615 E. Locust (1912), hugs the street in the tight spatial fashion of the English colleges and their American emulators. The Jacobethan was eminently suited to the new steel construction technology of the period which allowed larger windows and, appropriately for classroom design, more natural light to the interior.

In the 1920s, the precision with which the academic details of the Jacobethan Style had been executed gradually diminished. Buildings began to take on a sparer appearance. Interest in flat surfaces moved to the forefront of design. One manifestation of this flat expression was a renewed interest in the classical ornament which encouraged the Adamesque (Georgian period) and French Renaissance detailing on the polite, less-than-robust commercial buildings of the period.

The other major manifestation was the modernity of the buildings which we now classify loosely as Art Deco or Moderne. The Moderne in this country encompassed a great variety of streamlined flat-surfaced architecture. The best known examples, perhaps, were the angular setback skyscrapers of the 1920s and 1930s. The Moderne was somewhat refined by the rather limited impact of European work — the International Style including the work of Le Corbusier, the Jugendstil of Holland and the Deutscher Werkbund, the wellsprings of Modern architecture. America's own presentations of the state of art of the Moderne were the World's Fairs in Chicago (1933) and New York (1939). Though these fantasy buildings resembled Hollywood sets, they did constitute one aspect of the experimental thrust of American architecture in this period.

Lincoln Junior High, 820 E. Knapp, designed by Guy E. Wiley (1928); Messmer High, 742 W. Capitol Drive, by Herbst and Kuenzli (1929); and Kosciuszko Junior High, 971 Windlake Avenue, represented the transition between the Collegiate Gothic and the Moderne. Solomon Juneau High, 6415 Mt. Vernon Avenue, by Van Ryn and DeGelleke (1931), illustrated a horizontal solution in the Moderne Style, but Rufus King High, 1801 W. Olive (1932), and Pulaski High, 2500 W. Oklahoma, designed by Guy E. Wiley (1938), were even stronger because of their projecting central towers, setback composition, and clean detailing.

State Historical Society of Wisconsin

Fourth Street School (Golda Meir School).

Rufus King High School, 1801 W. Olive St. The simplicity of the setback design combined with the axial placement of the central tower resulted in a powerful street end vista.

Fire Stations[9]

Milwaukee Co. Historical Society

Old Engine House No. 7, formerly on the corner of Kinnickinnic and Maple. In 1876, architect H. C. Koch was authorized by the Common Council to remodel the old Bentley School to a "hose tower and engine house".

Milwaukee's fire engine houses constitute a colorful part of the city's architectural history. The very early stations (prior to 1885), were designed by various local architects in the grand styles of the day — Italianate, High Victorian Italianate, and Gothic. Soaring campaniles, often four or five stories in height, were erected as bell, hose, and watch towers. The towers were often highly decorated, reflecting the styles of the buildings below. Among the remaining engine houses, the earliest is a building at 411 N. Third Street, now altered and in private ownership. Another early building which retains something of its original appearance is the Chief Lippert No. 1 (1876), named for Henry Lippert, the first chief officer of the department. A strong, late Italianate design in cream brick, the building has a finely detailed bracketed cornice with a gable inset. The old doors have been converted to windows, and the tower has undoubtedly been diminished in height and altered in detail. It is now (1979) in use as an Inner City Arts Council Facility.

In 1885, under the leadership of Chief James Foley, the department embarked upon a new program to control and standardize the design and construction of fire houses. He directed Sebastian E. Brand, foreman of Engine 9 and an ex-mason, to design all new structures. Brand's work expressed both the increased concern for functionalism and a stolid masonry interpretation of Victorian styles. He often mixed Gothic and Classical detailing in generally vertical elevations. At least ten of Brand's designs — spanning nearly three decades — survive today, either in continuous use as fire engine houses or with a new use. Many of the smaller buildings were remarkably similar employing a two-story, three-bay design.

In this scheme, a central engine door was flanked by two smaller bays with narrow windows. Otherwise straight cornices were varied on some structures by an inset gable over the central bay. A corner tower was sometimes added.

The largest and most elegant of brand's designs was Engine House No. 3 at 100 West Virginia Street. The Common Council authorized its construction in 1900, but Fifth Ward residents opposed the move because they assumed that the site was to be used as a market place acquired with revenue from a special tax assessed directly to them. Nonetheless, the city issued $50,000 in bonds presumably for the purchase of the site, and construction began. The building bears the date 1900, but it was completed a year later. The two-story symmetrical design incorporated two engine doors on either side of a central bearing mass and extraordinarily tall corner towers. The cream brick facade was capped by a cast metal cornice of Victorian Italianate design into which the vine-wreathed date was impressed. The towers, originally two and one-half stories taller and surmounted by late mansardic roofs with cresting, have been truncated.[10]

About 1913, the city's Bureau of Bridges and Public Buildings took charge of the design and construction of fire houses. As horses were replaced by trucks, Brand's work was supplanted by that of Charles E. Malig of the bureau who, like his predecessor, was a fixture in the engine house design role for several decades. Among Malig's more interesting contributions, were the so-called "bungalow" stations. These were one-story structures with a garage attached to an office quarters which looked like small Greek temples. The bungalow stations were created to match the scale of the houses in the neighborhoods in which they were built. Several remain including the facilities at 407 N. Hawley Road and 2901 N. Thirtieth Street.

Milwaukee Public Library

Engine House No. 18, 2602 N. Richards, photograph 1937. A typical modest design by Sebastian Brand executed in 1890.

Engine House No. 35, 407 N. Hawley Road. One of several bungalow-scale designs by Charles E. Malig, this structure was completed in 1927.

Engine House No. 3, 100 West Virginia Street. The largest facility of its type, the colossal twin towers of Engine House No. 3 soared over Walker's Point in 1901, the year of their completion. The equipment, rather dimly seen here, includes a pumper, a buggy (for the chief?), a hose truck, and a hook and ladder.

R. L. Nailen and James S. Haight, *Beertown Blazes*

Natatoria[11]

Milwaukee's natatoria, of which five examples remain, constituted the first effort to provide public baths by an American municipality. Compared with similar European institutions built in the 1840s, the city's natatoria came rather late. In part, this was due to the availability of waterways and beaches unique to this city. However, increased industrial pollution, particularly in the river systems, prompted mayoral candidate Emil Wallber to make the provision of public baths a key issue in his campaign in 1884.

Wallber was elected, but the first bath was not constructed until 1889. It is now gone, but the second structure at 1646 S. Fourth Street (1894) survives as a restaurant in which the galleries are occupied by diners and the pool by dolphins. The facility was originally equipped with dressing rooms and exotic "rain baths" (showers). The central section of the roof was sky-lighted. The exterior design by Milwaukee architects Schnetzky and Liebert owed its inspiration to the Renaissance and the church architecture of Leon Battista Alberti (1404-1472) and Giacomo Barozzi Vignola (1507-1573). More immediately, one might assume the influence of the Chicago Fair was a referral to the inspiration of the Classic.

Of the four surviving natatoria, the two older facilities were designed by private firms: the West North Avenue Natatorium (No. 1609) by Charles Lesser in 1902 and the East Center Street Natatorium (No. 243) by H. Messmer and Son in 1908. The last two — Greenfield Avenue (No. 1645 W.) and South Tenth Street (No. 2361 S.) — were designed by the Bureau of Bridges and Public Buildings (1911 and 1917 respectively, probably by Charles Malig). All four have similar two-story gallery plans clothed in a red brick Neo-classical shell.

South East Side Natatorium, 1646 S. Fourth Street. The current bichromatic paint scheme on the exterior of the building recalls the buildings of the late Gothic and early Renaissance in Florence and Venice.

The National Soldier's Home

The National Soldier's Home, erected in the late 1860s for disabled veterans of the Civil War was, and remains, the premier Victorian Gothic Style structure in the State of Wisconsin. The building was designed by Edward Townsend Mix. A huge five and one-half story tower rose well above the rambling four-story mansard-roofed mass of the main building. The principal details of the building — its fenestration, corbelling, and dormers — were executed in the late nineteenth century version of the pointed style. The predominant material was Milwaukee Cream brick, but Ruskinian accents were achieved through polychromatic treatment of the stringcourses and roof slates.

To heighten the picturesque effects of the site, the grounds were landscaped in a romantic fashion with curvilinear drives and a small lake which remains today. An excellent rustic gate, highly prized by both the residents who built it and visitors, formerly graced the entrance to the grounds. In the late nineteenth century, particularly before the city parks were constructed, the site was a place of public recreation. Though lavishly designed and well-touted for their inspirational effects, the grounds of the home must have been rather melancholy. Harger commented in 1877: ". . . and it is one of the pretty sights to witness the interest a squad of wooden-legged, battered veterans take in a simple game of croquet."[12] Today the old structure still serves the United States Veterans' Administration Center. Several other buildings, including an outstanding Ruskinian Victorian Gothic chapel, remain on the grounds, constituting an important assembly of nineteenth century institutional structures.

State Historical Society of Wisconsin

Milwaukee Public Library

The Old Huron Avenue Bridge (Clybourn), photograph c. 1870. This rare view depicts over 100 people and at least three fire engines on the iron swing bridge. Undoubtedly the photograph was carefully staged so as to demonstrate the strength of the structure which was built in 1869.

S. 11th St. Bridge over Burnham's Canal, 1886. This iron swing bridge replaced an earlier wooden swing bridge over Burnham's Canal. Built by Milwaukee Bridge and Iron Works, this is Milwaukee's oldest, and the last intact public swing bridge.

Movable Bridges[13]

Prior to the 1860s, many bridges in Milwaukee and elsewhere were built as fixed structures. As the network of canal and rail systems grew in the mid-nineteenth century, pressure was placed upon government to construct movable bridges to allow the free passage of shipping guaranteed by the United States Constitution, and still enable crossings at reasonable grades. Milwaukee's position as a Great Lakes port city justified bridge improvements as early as the 1850s. The first movable bridges in the city were made of wood. In the last half of the nineteenth century, the closing of the Lower Missisippi River during the Civil War, the rise of the railroad, and the innovative technologies in metals combined to hasten new bridges and new methods of construction. With three rivers and a lakefront harbor, Milwaukee strove to be near the forefront in bridge construction in order to compete with other ports.

> Milwaukee is said to have more bridges than any city its size in the country. Its streams are crossed by 18 swing bridges of iron, 2 swing bridges of wood, 2 stationary bridges of wood, and 4 stationary bridges of iron. There will be 37 bridges in all when the $50,000 Michigan-Sycamore Street bridge is constructed. It is expected, by the way, that east siders will call it the Michigan Street bridge; west siders will speak of it as the Sycamore Street bridge, and south siders will take their choice. There are also six railroad bridges. . . .[14]

There are three types of movable bridges: swing, bascule, and vertical lift. Only the first two types were built in great numbers by the City of Milwaukee before the recent era. Movable bridges depended upon the stability of iron and steel for their successful development. For longer spans, particularly, the ratio of strength to weight in steel was a critical element. Steel was also associated with the mechanical engineering technology which led to the construction of the motors and bearings that were strong enough to move the bridges.

A swing bridge rotates on a central pier in the middle of a waterway. Wooden swing bridges were first used in the 1830s, and the iron swing bridge was developed in the United States in about 1860. The city's earliest swing bridge probably was the Juneau Street Bridge, a wooden structure across the Milwaukee River which stood between 1851 and 1871. Pioneering iron swing bridges were built in the Midwest, particularly on the Mississippi River. Before 1895, the iron swing bridge was the most common type erected in Milwaukee. The first two designs were of the Howe Truss type on Cherry Street (1862) and on East Pleasant Street

Juneau Street (Chestnut) Swing Bridge, photograph c. 1932. The view depicts the bridge in the open position as pedestrians, cyclists, and drivers wait for a boat to pass on a wintry day.

(authorized 1869, but not built until 1886). There are several railroad bridges of the swing type extant in the city, however, all but one of the municipal bridges, the Eleventh Street Bridge, have been replaced. (The Oneida Street bascule bridge (1912) appears to have used the old leaf (roadbed) structure of the swing bridge which preceded it.(

Bascule bridges work on the principle of a hinge and counterweights. Developed in the Middle Ages as the drawbridge, the bascule design was perfected in the late nineteenth century. In 1836, the Territorial Legislature authorized Rufus Parks, Solomon Juneau, Pleasant Fields, and Augustus Bird to build the first bridge across the Milwaukee River. Placed at Oneida Street, it was of the bascule type and of wood construction. Swept away by floods, the bridge was replaced twice by swing bridges before the current structure was built.

American innovations in bascule bridge design originated in Chicago in 1893; the old Clybourn Street Bridge (1895) designed by the City Engineer's Office represented an early example of the rolling variety. It has since been replaced by a more modern structure. The Broadway and Wisconsin Avenue bascule bridges, now replaced, followed in 1901.

The construction of larger ships and the competition that arose among Great Lakes ports after the turn of the century necessitated the improvement of the Menomonee River Valley bridge and canal system. The Plankinton Avenue bridge (1904), a double leaf bascule type built on a design by Fred Moore of the Milwaukee Bridge Company, and still in use, represented the city's first effort. This site was also historically important as the place where in 1840 Byron Kilbourn first spanned the waters between Kilbourntown and Walker's Point.

Other extant early bridges are the East Water Street and Kinnickinnic Bridges, both of the period 1908-1909, built by the Milwaukee Bridge Company from designs prepared by city engineers.

Kinnickinnic Avenue Bridge. This view of the 1908 single leaf (one moving piece on each side) bridge looks toward the Port of Milwaukee and Jones Island. The overhead trusses for the trolley lines have been removed.

Milwaukee Public Library

E. Water Street Bridge. Also called the North Water Street Bridge, this bascule structure was built 1908-1910. It replaced an iron structure built in 1881. This crossing was the site of the old Walker's Point Bridge, built in 1845 and carried away in a flood in 1866. The current structure, shown here before the overhead trusses were removed, damaged the steamship "Kin — Dave" in 1920 when the tender apparently failed to time the movement of the bridge with that of the vessel.

Milwaukee Public Library

V Open Space, Public Parks and Urban Design

Lake Park.

Open space is a vital part of Milwaukee's urban form. Whether it is a square which offers a fuller view of a building, a park with a pond and shade trees, or a waterfront site which commands distant views and offers recreational opportunities, open space is an important part of how we perceive the city. In this survey, historic open spaces were inventoried as part of the comprehensive study of the city's growth. In those instances in which a landscape design was significant, attributions to designers and historical context were attempted. Structures in parks and open spaces were surveyed, and the landscape ideas of the spaces were analyzed. An understanding of the original purpose of the spaces, their time in history, stylistic expression, and original connections with significant individuals in Milwaukee and elsewhere was sought throughout the survey process. These observations are summarized here.

Water Features, Streets, and Squares: The Armature of Open Space

> "The life of the city verges toward the Lake Michigan shore with its three parks, beaches, yacht clubs, Coast Guard Station, municipal water filtration plant, and long government pier, the haunt of lay fishermen. Three rivers emptying into the lake — the Milwaukee from the north, the Menominee (sic) from the west, the Kinnickinnic from the south — roughly quadrisect the metropolitan district. . . ."
>
> *Wisconsin: A Guide to the Badger State, 1941.*[1]

Now forty years old, this description of the water features and adjoining improvements of the City of Milwaukee summarizes its geographical situation and accounts for many of its public open spaces. The lake and rivers are, and were historically, the preeminent physiographic features of the city and its principal open spaces. As open space, these bodies of water offered opportunities for commerce, transportation, and recreation. Their shores also provided inspiration for the landscape designs evidenced in the great nineteenth and early twentieth century parks. As the city expanded to its shores, some park schemes were realized, others were not. Today these water features, the river corridors and the great edge of Lake Michigan, are still critical elements in the open space network of the city. For many Milwaukeeans, they provide an important source of recreation and leisure, and are significant aspects of the total composition of this singularly habitable city.

The idea of the street system as open space was also an important one in the early development of the city. The street was a fundamental public guarantee of light and air. Milwaukee's mid-nineteenth century streets were only crudely improved; yet, a dusty or muddy space was often better than none at all. It is improbable that the uneasy street grids of Milwaukee's three original plats were done with the recognition of their Roman precedent. More likely, the grid reflected the simple utilitarian approach to surveying and a tacit recognition of the Land Ordinance of 1785. This was true for Byron Kilbourn's surveyor, who laid out his grid according to the established town and range lines. Unfortunately, Kilbourn never intended that the Milwaukee River at the eastern edge of his plat be bridged, and Solomon Juneau laid out his plat east of the river in an equally independent, albeit different fashion, ignoring the town and range lines. To the consternation of city fathers of later periods, these central city streets have remained askew to this day. Yet, the idea of the street as open space has persisted. The Milwaukee boulevard system is, in part, a product of thinking about the street as open space.

Another way that the open space was manifested in the early days of Milwaukee was in the creation of public squares. At that time, before 1850, surely few people thought about creating open space reservations. Open land was, after all, to be seen almost everywhere. Yet even in the 1830s and 1840s, some public-spirited citizens recognized the need for donations and purchases of land for public use which would extend the use of the street as open space. It was in this way that the square was added to Milwaukee's urban landscape.[2]

Though not the first public square, one of the most important was Market Square on East Water Street, a German commercial district in the mid-nineteenth century city. Kathleen Conzen writes:

> East Water Street, as it ran through the area was like the main street of a country town while the market place was a unique social center of German life in the community. Beer halls and saloons, boardinghouses, and meeting halls clustered around shops near the market and spilled across the river into the Chestnut Street area. . . .[3]

Market Square was a triangular piece of land on East Water Street near

State Historical Society of Wisconsin

E. Water Street, Toward Market Square, photograph c. 1870. Partly because of its central placement, City Hall is an important part of this view. Notice, however, the use of the street and the square as open space. The predominant theme of this downtown street was commercial — beer sales are signified by the barrels at the left and the tankard sign at the lower right, and the other signs are also eyecatching, especially the watchmaker's and the druggist's which have incorporated symbols of their trades. Even some of the street lights have panes etched with advertisements.

Milwaukee Co. Historical Society

Market Square. This westward view depicts the Wells Street facades of the old City Hall and the old Nunnemacher Grand Opera House. To the left is Nunnemacher's Grand Central Hotel.

State Historical Society of Wisconsin

Matthias Stein House on Market Square, c. 1870. Note the large cast iron fountainhead in the lower left foreground and the hitching post upon which the man is leaning in the right center forground. The curb stones appear to be plastered with advertisements although they are illegible in this picture. Other advertisements announce the presentation of Hamlet, over which is papered the phrase "Black Fiend". On the telegraph pole is a broadside which reads "Go Down Moses". Stein's house and gunshop are prominently featured, but notice also the German hotel to its right. One senses that Market Square was thought to be an important place in the city, both for its historical and contemporary significance.

State Historical Society of Wisconsin

Court House Square. The predominant mood of the Square was set by the elms and the building. There existed a strange discord between the Romanism of the building and of the fountain and the Gothic benches.

Mason Street.[4] Originally, the area was part of a steep hill on which Matthias Stein built his house in 1837. Although the hill was removed to fill the marshes to the north and west, Stein's house was preserved and was the first building on the square at the new grade.

Similar in function to medieval squares, Market Square was a center of civic and commercial life in the mid-nineteenth century. The most significant building on the square was the market hall, the second story of which was converted to a German theater by Joseph Kurz in 1853. Seven years later, the city purchased the building for use as a city hall. When the courthouse was completed in 1872, municipal functions were moved to that building and the Market Square building was abandoned. In the 1880s East Water Street remained an important economic center, but the square gave way to a new symbol of civic pride in the 1890s — the landmark City Hall.

Also of symbolic civic importance was the city's most elaborate ornamental square, Court House Square, now called Cathedral Square, bounded by Wells, Kilbourn, Jefferson and Jackson Streets. The land was donated by Morgan L. Martin and Solomon Juneau in 1837. Originally, the square was the site of the city's first courthouse building, a frame Greek Revival structure (1836). In 1872 this building was replaced with the new courthouse designed by Edward Townsend Mix and constructed of Lake Superior Sandstone. This building, too, was removed, but during its prime it was surrounded by landscape improvements in the high style of the late nineteenth century. The handsome stand of elm trees, gravel walks, and a cast-iron fountain created an elegant scene. Much appreciated by the citizenry, the park was used for concerts and promenading in seasonable weather. Although the landscape improvements of that period have disappeared, the square remains an important pedestrian crossroads which is given greater presence by St. John's Cathedral (1853) on the Jackson Street side.[5]

Milwaukee's first public square was the Fourth Ward Square on Clybourn between Third and Fourth Streets, donated in 1835 by Byron Kilbourn, Solomon Juneau, J. McCarty, A. Clybourn, and A. Fowler. Although its early appearance is undocumented, we know that by 1870 is had been landscaped with walks and trees. In 1886 the square became the forecourt of the new Union Station designed by Edward Townsend Mix. The space still exists today as Zeidler Park after Carl Zeidler, past mayor of the City.

The other early squares were Clarke Square (1837) at Eighteenth and Mineral donated by M. J. Brown, and N. and L. Clarke; Walker Square (1837) between Walker and Mineral Streets, donated by George Walker; Lincoln Park or Lincoln Triangle (1846) originally part of a forty-acre tract now at the intersection of Bradford, Maryland and Farwell Streets; and the First Ward Triangle (1847) at the intersection of Franklin Street and Prospect Avenue, donated by James Rogers.

In 1880, chronicler Alfred T. Andreas observed that "although Milwaukee has a number of public parks none of them, unless it be the Court House Square, rise above those of other cities."[6] This was clearly the hasty comment of the itinerant publicist. In fact at least one public park, Seventh Ward Park, at the lakefront (now Juneau), was created in grand style by the eminent Chicago landscape architect Horace William Shaler Cleveland. Perhaps a more appropriate criticism of Milwaukee's public parks would have been that there were not enough of them. In part, this lack of truly public space may be attributed to the existence, from the mid-nineteenth century until the 1920s, of a number of popular commercial pleasure parks and summer gardens on the German model. These places, which sometimes charged no admission, offered diversions of great variety often in a park-like setting. If the public park movement in Milwaukee started slowly in comparison with other American cities, it may be explained by the unique structure of leisure in Germanic Milwaukee.

Milwaukee's Commercial Pleasure Parks and Summer Gardens

Milwaukee Co. Historical Society

Pabst Park. This panoramic scene of Pabst Park at the turn of the century evokes the *gemuetlich* spirit of the fully-developed private pleasure park. The park was located at Burleigh near Third Street, today the site of Garfield Park.

The commercial pleasure park combined the interests of summer garden promenading and picnicking, music and drama, sport, and wildlife menageries, with the service of beer to entice an eager, fair-weather patronage. In spite of notable German antecedents for true public parks, the commercial park was also a well-established tradition in German-speaking countries. These European-styled parks offered more variety in amusements and facilities than the contemporary American public parks which were devoted almost entirely to ornamental landscape design.

By the 1850s many German-Americans had become artisans, and by the 1870s and 1880s they were important business managers and owners. As wealth and leisure time and, undoubtedly, business pressures increased for these upwardly-mobile people, the pleasure park provided a needed place of relaxation from the workaday world. Anti-German sentiment during World War I, Prohibition, and the economic and social patterns of the growing, changing early twentieth century city spelled the demise of the commercial pleasure park; thus ending a unique chapter in Milwaukee's social and landscape history. From W. W. Coleman's *Milwaukee: das Deutsch-Athen Americas* (1880) we have a detailed summary of these resorts in their heyday:

Strothman's Grove, Forest Home Avenue, photograph c. 1890(?). Philip Strothman was variously listed in the city directories as a tobacconist and laborer. It is possible that the grove was at the scale of a beer garden, but its remote location undoubtedly added to its rural charms.

Milwaukee Co. Historical Society

Milwaukee Co. Historical Society

National Park. The more rigorous adventurers and picnickers of the late nineteenth century frequented National Park where the accommodations were less refined than at other parks.

State Historical Society of Wisconsin

Schlitz Park, the Observation Tower. The park was sold to the city in 1909. Today none of these structures remain, although the view from the military crest of the hill is still grand.

The beautiful parks and commercial public gardens, in part in the city, in part in the region surrounding, so well known as summer destination points, recommend themselves as much for their natural beauty as for the musical and theatrical productions and the excellent beer. Among these parks "Quentin's Park" is the foremost: it is sited on the highest point on the northside with a splendid plan and views of the entire city — both of the bay and inland. Other popular places are the "Milwaukee Garden"; the Shooting Park; Eimermans Park on the northwest side; the hill garden at the Miller Brewery on the plank road, which has recently been attractively improved and has become one of the beauty spots of the region, set as it is over the rolling hills of the Menomonee Valley. Similarly popular are the Berninger Garden near the Falk Brewery; Knurr's Greenfield Park; Green's, Schubert's, and Conrad's establishments; Wootsch's South Park; Reich's very popular place on the Milwaukee River, our small city's Humboldt; the Lueddemann Garden on the lakeshore; and others. Near the last named garden with its romantic Indian lodge, lies, farther north, picturesque Lake Dells, a private park with travel accommodations in their forest, and lakeshore lodge which the owners are proud to open to the public. A splendid macadamized road, Lake Avenue, passes along the lakeshore, going through wooded areas with spectacular views of the lake, and past elegant estates and friendly farms to Whitefish Bay, a popular stopping place for hikers and strollers.[7]

Milwaukee Co. Historical Society

Schlitz Park

Originally known as Quentin's Park, this ample pleasure ground lay at the north end of Seventh Street. In July, 1879 the Schlitz Brewing Company purchased the seven acre property. The hillside site commanded an impressive view and was improved by the addition of a lookout tower. The main concert pavilion provided seating for 5,000 people, and was also used for dancing. The brewery operated a hotel in connection with the park, and it entertained customers and visitors with a menagerie of wild animals in addition to all of the usual sporting and cultural activities. Illuminated by three hundred fifty multi-colored gas lamps, Schlitz Park must have been a stunning attraction for Milwaukee's evening pleasure-seekers of the last century. Acquired by the city as Lapham Park in 1909 and 1910, the land is currently part of Carver Park, renamed in the late 1960s for the important Black scientist.

The Milwaukee Garden

The Milwaukee Garden was founded by H. Kemper in 1850. In 1854 Pius Dreher purchased this summer garden which had seats for 3,000 people, on a three-acre site located on Fourteenth Street between State and Prairie (now Juneau). It also included a dance and concert hall, a double bowling alley, a theater building, two fountains, and a menagerie. Gas lamps provided lighting for evening visitors.

American Landscape Architecture: The Rural Cemetery and the Public Park

The need to provide sanitation and more urban open space was a significant theme in Milwaukee in the last half of the nineteenth century. The park movement was an important expression of how the people of the city regarded themselves; namely, with a sense of pride and stewardship of the future. Nineteenth-century open space planning — the creation of park-like cemeteries and public parks — symbolized a mature approach to urban development. The landscape ideas and techniques which gave impetus to this city's late-nineteenth century open space system were grand and well-conceived. They were, however, neither wholly original nor unique to Milwaukee.

In 1831 Jacob Bigelow, a Boston physician, Asa Gray, a Harvard botanist, and a group of Boston-area influentials gathered together to propose a new idea for the location, design, and construction of burial grounds. The idea was to have an ornamental space — a place which would show the effects of improved nature — which would function both as a burying ground and as a scientific arboretum. They acquired a site near Boston at the edge of Cambridge, Massachusetts. They named the grounds Mt. Auburn (after Oliver Goldsmith's "Sweet Auburn" immortalized in a popular poem (1770) about a deserted and destroyed village of the great period of the English landscape estate). Bigelow and Gray hoped to observe the changes in the site over time as the area around the cemetery was urbanized — noting, at the same time, the general health of the community.

The rolling topography of the site was accommodated by a romantically-conceived plan, the character of which was dominated by the curvilinear carriageways designed by Alexander Wadsworth and H. A. S. Dearborn. The location of Mt Auburn Cemetery, combined with the ornamental character, caught the imagination of mid-nineteenth century Americans, anxious to express their grief according to the fashionable notions of the period. The romantic rural cemetery became a popular institution of that custom, and in later years a recreational destination point. Although the arboretum concept was lost in many of the designs which emulated Mt. Auburn, the character of the romantic landscape persisted. Based upon the pastoral English ideas of natural landscape, this still rather ill-defined sense of landscape improvement proved to be influential in designs not only for cemeteries, but also for parks and suburban subdivisions.

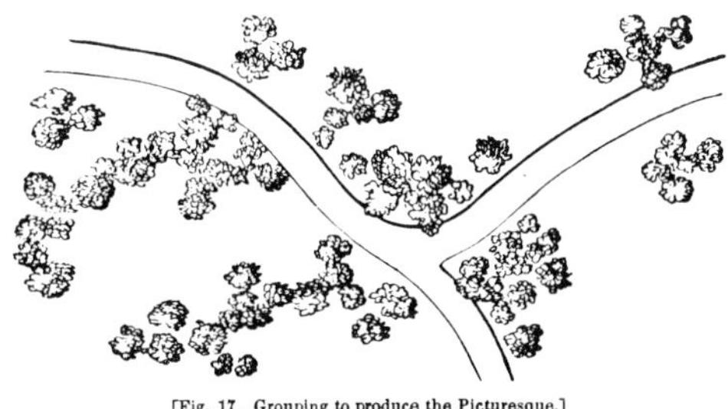

[Fig. 17. Grouping to produce the Picturesque.]

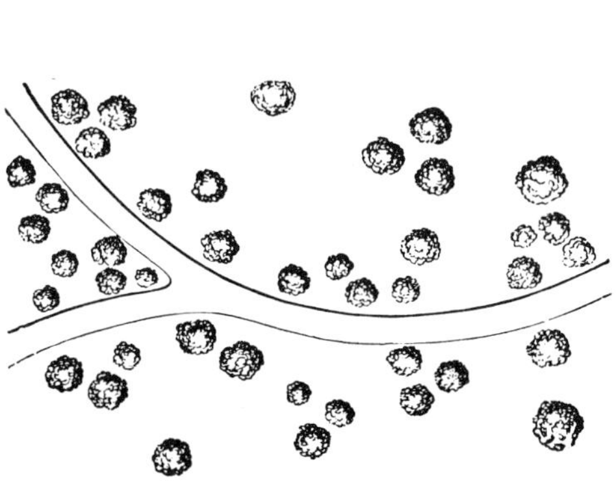

[Fig. 16. Grouping to produce the Beautiful.]

In the 1840s when Milwaukee was young, the cities of the East were growing rapidly and often without regard for the provision of public open space. Growth was deemed desirable, however random, and cities competed with each other for development. Recognizing the congestion that was resulting from this unplanned growth, Andrew Jackson Downing of Newburgh, New York became the spokesman for ornamental open space in and around the city in the form of public parks and suburbs. Downing was an outspoken arbiter of landscape taste and a tireless promoter of his ideas. He was the editor of *The Horticulturist,* a monthly journal devoted to matters of gardening, both practical and ornamental. He wrote several important and widely-read books on landscape and architectural design including the monumental *A Treatise on the Theory and Practice of Landscape Gardening* (1841), *Cottage Residences* (1842), *The Fruits and Fruit Trees of America* (1845), and *The Architecture of Country Houses* (1850). In architecture, he became a well-known advocate of the Gothic Revival Style and a popularizer of the informal suburban villa house type. In landscape architecture, he was responsible for the introduction of the English ideas of the natural landscape, the Picturesque and the Beautiful. Although not always understandable from Downing's text, Picturesque ideas were to be expressed in the landscape by the introduction of coarse, irregularly-shaped trees such as oaks, hemlocks, and pines in randomly spaced masses. The Beautiful was created by planting round-headed trees such as beeches and maples placed in more regularly-spaced groups.

Downing was one of the earliest significant publicists for the American public park movement. In the October, 1848 issue of *The Horticulturist* he wrote the now well-known dialogue between a traveler and his American friend on the subject of municipal parks.[9] In the course of the dialogue, he praised the parks of Munich and Frankfurt. These parks were not only great landscape creations, but also, unlike their predecessors, were developed and supported with money from public coffers. In 1850 Downing again referred to this idea of public support, and specifically to the London parks from which he had just returned, in his famous plea for a park for the City of New York. Although William Cullen Bryant had supported public parks earlier in his editorials in the *New York Post,* Downing's words carried the moment.

Downing's work both in design and park activism opened the way for a new American effort in landscape design and planning which focused on the work of Frederick Law Olmsted. The son of a shopkeeper in Hartford, Connecticut, Olmsted became a farmer and journalist, traveling widely in the South and abroad. In 1852 he published *Walks and Talks of an American Farmer in England* based upon a trip, during the course of which he saw Birkenhead (1843-45), Sir Joseph Paxton's design for a public park at the edge of Liverpool. This park, with its carefully designed grade-separated road and walkways was an important influence on the designs for Olmsted's many public parks. In 1857 Olmsted was appointed superintendent of the Central Park, the product of Downing's agitation in New York City. Later, with Calvert Vaux, he won a design competition for the park.

For the next half century, Olmsted dominated landscape design. Probably the first American to call himself a landscape architect, Olmsted with Vaux, and later his half-brother John Charles, became the chief landscape designers of parks, suburban towns and subdivisions, exposition grounds, estates and home grounds. Olmsted was also a strong voice in the conservation movement, being an early activist in the efforts to preserve Niagara Falls and to create a National Park System. In the Civil War he had been employed as the chief sanitary officer of the Union Army, and his concern for health issues carried into his later landscape practice. His personal accomplishments and the accomplishments of his firm were numerous and varied. He and his firm were largely responsible for the superior functional treatment of the nineteenth century ornamental landscape, particularly of parks and park systems of the type designed for Milwaukee, and especially in connection with the solution of urban sanitation problems.

As much as Olmsted dominated American landscape architecture, the work of Horace William Shaler Cleveland was of more immediate, if not lasting, influence on the Midwest and the city of Milwaukee. Cleveland's early career has been only partly documented,[10] but we know that he was a contributor to *The Horticulturist* in the 1840s. Probably by the late 1860s he had moved west to Chicago. In 1871 he wrote *A Few Hints on Landscape Gardening in the West* followed the next year by the influential treatise, *Landscape Architecture as Applied to the Wants of the West.* In this short book he advocated the use of boulevards in urban design as firebreaks and as links in an open space system. His experience with fire safety had been a personal one in that the materials of his office had been all but completely destroyed in the famous Chicago fire of 1871. As a consultant, he worked on individual projects in Milwaukee and Madison, and he served as the superintendent and landscape architect for both the Chicago and Minneapolis park boards.

The coincidental rise of the landscape architect and the park movement in America in the late nineteenth century had a powerful effect on the way the growth of cities was managed. Reformers clamored for the procurement and development of these "lungs of the city." Landscape architects responded with designs for individual parks of great ornamental charm and with the notion of boulevard linked park systems, the most important organizing idea of city growth to emerge in the nineteenth century.[11]

Forest Home Cemetery[12]

In 1850, the rector, wardens and vestrymen of St. Paul's Episcopal Church chose a site for an, as yet, unnamed new cemetery four miles from downtown and one and one-half miles from the city's southern limits. The original 72.58 acre tract was purchased from Polly, Eleanor and John Hull on July 6th of the same year. Publicist Silas Chapman described the site as "situated at the junction of the Janesville Plank Road and the Kilbourn Road," (now Forest Home Avenue and Layton Boulevard, respectively) on land which was "well wooded, and gently undulating."[13] The name, Forest Home, was adopted in May, 1851.

The original acreage was designed by Increase Allen Lapham, the state's foremost scientist and scholar of natural history, geology, prehistory, and meteorology. The design followed closely the rural cemetery ideal of a romantically conceived and picturesquely planned distant location. Curvilinear carriageways formed irregular blocks of various sizes. Lapham had visited Cambridge, Massachusetts in 1847, and he probably saw Mt. Auburn, which was well-known even at that time. A map maker and draftsman of some skill, he also evidenced interest in landscape gardening and cottage architecture. Lapham's design for Forest Home marks the first creation of this type of cemetery in the Upper Midwest, the nearest earlier example being Spring Grove in Cincinnati built in 1845.

Although there is no record of plantings in the first decade, in 1860 the minutes of the cemetery committee recorded the purchase of evergreens, elms, and other plant materials. Today, a large stand of mature white oak testifies to the original oak opening character of the landscape, and a grove of purple beeches at the south end of the pond signify horticultural interest of a bygone time. The most significant landscape design feature, however, was (and is) the picturesque rockery fountain which marked the entrance. Ornamental rockwork was an element of landscape improvement recommended by Downing. Few examples of such excellence survive today.

Simple early marble tablets, obelisks and sculptural grave markers of the later Victorian era, and the large randomly sited turn-of-the-century Neoclassical vaults such as that of Valentine Blatz and his family, are also significant elements in the romantic appearance of the site today. The principal cemetery buildings include a chapel loosely based on the English Gothic designed by Ferry and Clas in 1890 and an office building by Alexander Eschweiler built in 1909.

Forest Home Cemetery. The rockwork fountain.

Milwaukee's Public Parks Before the Park Commission — 1868-1889

> Indeed Milwaukee is a pleasant surprise to all who visit it. Nature was lavish in her gifts, affording three hills admirably suited for the site of a picturesque, beautiful city. Owing to the diversity in surface the drainage facilities are excellent, thus keeping the city pure, cleanly, and healthy. . . .
>
> *Milwaukee Illustrated,* Charles Harger, 1877.[14]

In the mid- and late-nineteenth century it was not uncommon to read such booster-inspired language about any city in the country, particularly in the Old Northwest. The names of the places were changed, but the language which referred to natural physical advantages in Downingesque terms was remarkably consistent. These raw, natural sites remained only to be acquired by an interested public and improved by the hands of the designer.

In the 1850s and 1860s, the *Milwaukee Sentinel* advocated for the creation of public parks to little avail.[15] In 1869, as a part of the preface to the Proceedings of the Common Council for that year, Mayor Edwar O'Neill also struck the theme of public parks:

> If we would retain the enviable name so long enjoyed by our city as affording the most delightful place of residence of any in the country, we must begin to realize the fact, that we have reached a point in our history, when it becomes necessary to cast aside the ways and thoughts of the village, and to assume the duties and responsibilities of a metropolitan city. We not only want water works and sewerage, but we are beginning to feel seriously the want of public parks, which will afford our citizens a place of healthy and innocent recreation.[16]

Milwaukee's first four public parks were created either as ward parks or in combination with some other municipal function, as might have been implied by Mayor O'Neill's association of waterworks and sewerage with parks. They were: Seventh Ward Park (later Juneau Park, 1872), Kilbourn Park and Reservoir (1868, 1872, 1875), Waterworks Park (1872), and the Flushing Tunnel Park (1887, later McKinley).

Juneau Park was officially acquired in 1872, although plans were developed for the site in October, 1870. The designer, H. W. S. Cleveland, wrote a letter characterizing the park for readers of the *Milwaukee Sentinel:*

Juneau Park, photograph c. 1880. Although the chief design component of H. W. S. Cleveland's scheme for Juneau Park (or Seventh Ward Park) was the walkway system which led people to the lakeshore, the most elegant idea was the water cascade, bridge and rockwork pond which constituted the chief ornamental features of the park.

Milwaukee Co. Historical Society

> The position and character of the tract are such as to confine the whole scope of its possible decoration within comparatively narrow limits, and yet its features are so peculiar, and comprise so much that is picturesque in themselves and their surroundings, that it has seemed to me that no artificial ornamentation was required beyond the simple development of their natural character.[17]

Cleveland's design, which was compared to New York's Central Park in the *Sentinel,* was a well-conceived scheme for the difficult site. It included recommendations for walkways, a spring-fed stream, drainage, plantings, and a shoreline retaining structure. Because of the precipitous character of the site, the walks had to be built at fifteen percent grades, much steeper than current standards would allow in snowy climates. Cleveland's planting suggestions reflected a knowledge of the region which was uncommon at the time. Given the existing character of the natural landscape, the use of sugar and norway maples and of white ash trees instead of elms was symbolically fitting. Similarly, the concept of using the existing springs to make an ornamental stream and basin system was appropriate to the unique bluff sites. The concerns for drainage and shoreline control reflected the advanced ability which Cleveland was able to offer his clients at a time when most landscape gardeners knew little of these issues.

The creation of the other three early parks was tied to public improvements in sanitation.[18] The municipal water system, of which the reservoir was one visible public part, and the water tower and pumping station, the other, was finally designed in 1871 after much study and deliberation. Although Kilbourn Park was donated to the city in 1868 by Byron Kilbourn, it is possible that ornamental improvements were not made until a decade later. The park probably was acquired chiefly as a reservoir site, but in 1879 the *Milwaukee Sentinel* reported that walks and a carriageway had been laid out upon the site: "imagine the whole, green and rich with foliage or stately with fir trees of unbending dignity and you have the park as it is to be."[19] Additional purchases of land occurred in 1872 and 1875.

Today, the elevated section of the park which is the reservoir site must be fenced for security purposes. The lower open knoll, however, still commands an excellent view of the near East Side. On its slopes, hiding among a group of silver maples, there is a lovely weeping beech tree which testifies to the subtlety of horticultural attention of the last century. The

The first filling of the reservoir (?), photograph c. 1872 (?). An unknown photographer witnessed water pumped from Lake Michigan to the North Avenue location.

Milwaukee Co. Historical Society

hillside of the reservoir is dotted with small pine groves, and a large formal bedding arrangement commemorates the American Legion.

The pumping works were located on the lakeshore at North Street in direct line with the reservoir. The standpipe was built above and enclosed by the masonry water tower structure (in the Victorian Gothic Style) designed by Charles A. Gombert. The system allowed water to be pumped from the lake all the way to the reservoir, from which the pressure of gravity allowed water to flow through the pipes to homes, shops, and factories. The grounds around the water tower were conceived as a small ornamental park with a view of the lake.

The sewerage system of the city was small and ill-planned until 1880. At that time, a considerable effort was mounted to re-engineer the system so that the three rivers would not be polluted by the outfall from the antiquated system. A treatment plant was designed by Chicago engineer E. S. Chesborough for the Menomonee Valley, and pipe was laid into the lake off Jones Island. The Flushing Tunnel, which was used to back-flush the Milwaukee River, was built in the mid-1880s under what is now McKinley Marina Park on the north shore. The Flushing Tunnel Park was the last open space added to the city's holdings without benefit of an overseeing body specifically charged wtih the creation of a park system. As Milwaukee and its industries began to expand, the need for more parkland became increasingly obvious.

The Water Tower Park, photograph c. 1885. Hundreds of small saplings once dotted this small serpentine plan park.

State Historical Society of Wisconsin

The Milwaukee Park Commission: The Early Years, 1889-1915

The rise of the park commission may be traced to early local Republican reform politics in the 1880s. In that decade, Milwaukee electoral politics witnessed a sharp increase in the power of German-American voters who generally gave their support to Republican candidates. In 1884 German-born attorney Emil Wallber was the Republican candidate for mayor. His endorsement of civil service reform was the party's priority issue, but he was also a champion of public facility improvements, including parks. Wallber won both the 1884 and 1886 elections. Then in 1888, the Democrats forged an alliance with the Republicans in order to hold back the rising electoral forces of the young Labor Party. The coalition candidate, Thomas Brown, narrowly defeated Herman Kroeger, the labor contender. The pressure for reform, as illustrated by the electoral contest in which each candidate struggled to out-promise the other, was strong. In 1889, the reformers pushed a bill through the state legislature authorizing the establishment of the Board of Park Commissioners of Milwaukee.

Christian Wahl, a retired industrialist from Chicago and a world traveller, was the leader of the Milwaukee park movement and the commission's first president. In his approach to the city's decision makers, Wahl cited the familiar "lungs of the city" arguments and the European precedents of Hyde Park, London; the Bois de Boulogne, Paris; the Tiergarten, Berlin; and the Prater, in Vienna as models upon which Milwaukee might create its own "healthy breathing spots".[20] In June, 1889 the commissioners met for the first time. By October of the following year, they had selected six sites "so located as to afford accommodation to the greatest possible number and still adhere to the general scheme of having a chain of parks around the city connected by handsome boulevards."[21]

The sites were Lake Park; River Park (later called Riverside); Coleman Park (later Lincoln Avenue and finally Kosciuszko); Howell Avenue Park (later South, and finally Humboldt); Mitchell Park; and West Park (later Washington). Published in the commission's first annual report in 1892 was the one million dollar price tag for the land acquisition. Topographical surveys maps were also included showing the character of the existing terrain.

The second year's report announced that Frederick Law Olmsted and Company had been contracted to design Lake and West Parks. It was explained that the World's Columbian Exposition work in Chicago "enabled them to offer more liberal terms than would have been the case had they not had the work in the West."[22] The contract provided for consultation at $12.50 per acre and a three-year retainer. The firm's Milwaukee work has received little attention in published scholarship. The elder Olmsted's personal involvement in the Milwaukee project is questionable since at this time he was heavily involved in both the Chicago project and an elaborate estate design for George Vanderbilt in North Carolina. He was also subject to frequent bouts with illness. In any case, the firm's park planning style was well-established at this period, and many of the designs were actually executed by John Charles Olmsted. Warren H. Manning, then a young member of the firm specializing in horticulture and later an important landscape architect in his own right, executed some of the firm's planting design studies. His letters to his wife during this period indicate that he made frequent trips to Milwaukee to survey the sites and meet with the commissioners.

In the first group of study plans for Lake Park prepared by the Olmsted office in 1892, little topographical change was contemplated, and a relatively modest system of carriageways and pedestrian promenades was proposed.[23] By 1893, however, the large meadow at the southern end of the park, which today serves as the golf course, was designed. The creation of this meadow necessitated filling a large ravine. By the time of the final plans in 1895, the ambitious thinking which had given rise to the meadow had also spurred the creation of an elaborate grade-separated drive and promenade system designed to exploit the blufftop views. Two-level bridges accommodating both carriages and pedestrians were shown over large ravines. Belvederes, a refectory and other lookout points were established. The northern half of the park was designed as a maze of bridges, embankments, meadows, and groves intended to delight the viewer regardless of mode of transportation. Interestingly, the buildings shown were rather small — the main pavilion as built was twice the size of the structure contemplated by the Olmsted firm. A large pier and a modestly-scaled shore drive were shown at the edge of the water. Connections to River Park and West Park were anticipated by the improvement of Newberry Boulevard and by the design for a street railway station at the head of Locust Street, respectively. As one could expect, the park was built in a slightly more economical, though very elegant, fashion. The bridges were designed by local architect and engineer Oscar Sanne, and constructed in the period 1893-1898. The pavilion by Ferry and Clas was built in 1902. The lakefront drive, projected by the Olmsted firm, was finally completed in 1929 on a plan by Alfred C. Clas.

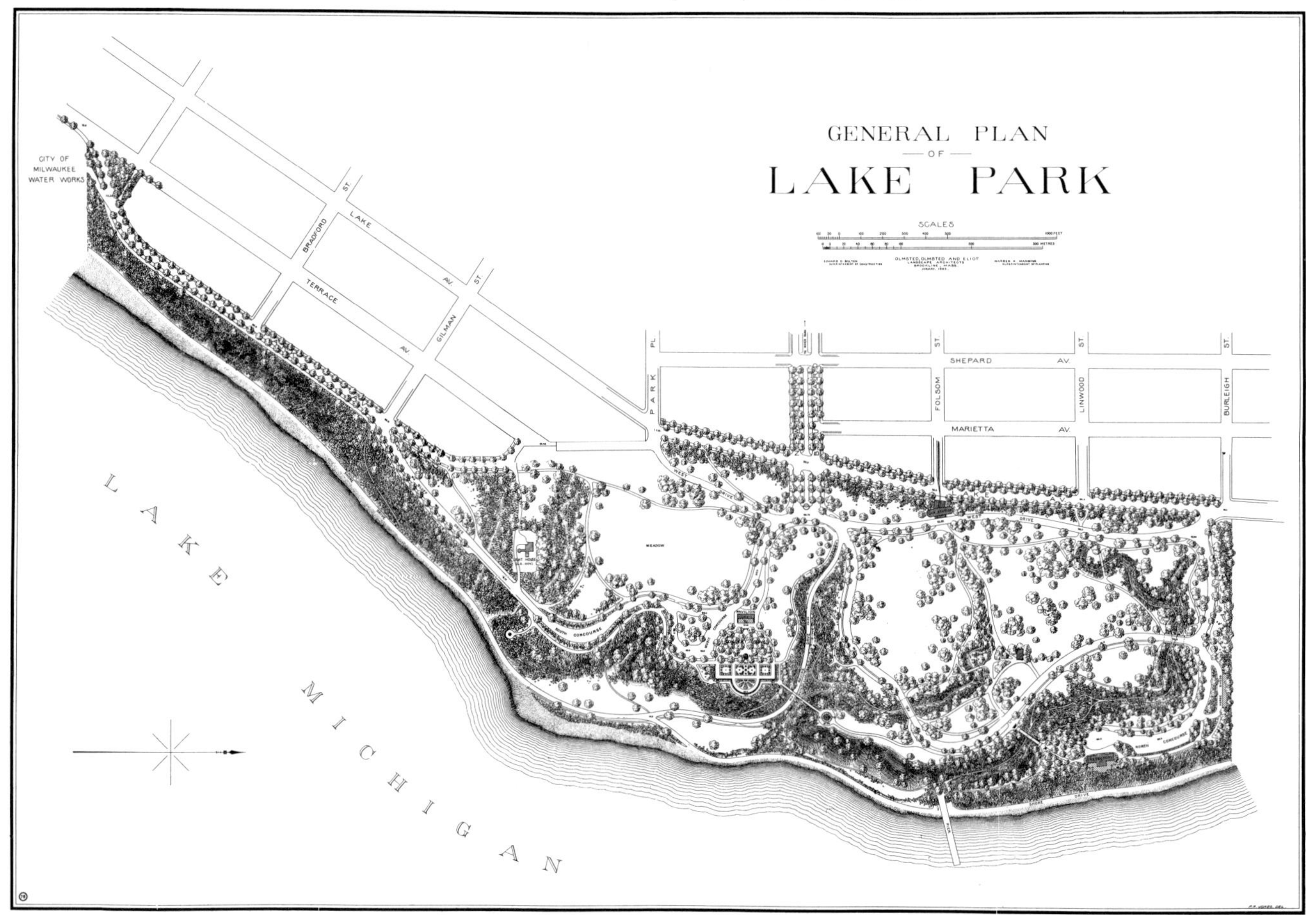

General Plan of Lake Park, 1895, The general spatial concepts of the park by the firm of Olmsted, Olmsted and Eliot were executed as shown. The principal changes occurred in the complex circulation plan which was far less grandly executed. Note the ravine drive. In the plan it is shown at a reasonable grade afforded by an elaborate bridge. As built, the drive is less contrived but steeper. Many of the park's functions as indicated in the plan have changed over time as more recreational demands have been placed upon the space.

State Historical Society of Wisconsin

Lake Park, photograph c. 1905. Many of the park's plantings were quite small or non-existent when this view was taken, and the sense of spatial "zones" which now occurs in the park because of the plantings was not originally perceivable; hence, this rather disorienting view southward from the lighthouse area. The Water Tower and the houses along Wahl Avenue are visible.

Milwaukee Co. Historical Society

Lincoln Memorial Drive, photograph c. 1930. This extraordinary view of the drive shortly after its completion illustrates Clas had also contemplated a semicircular colonnade at the lake bluff (where the War Memorial and Art Center Building by Eero Saarinen was constructed).

Frederick Law Olmsted National Historic Site

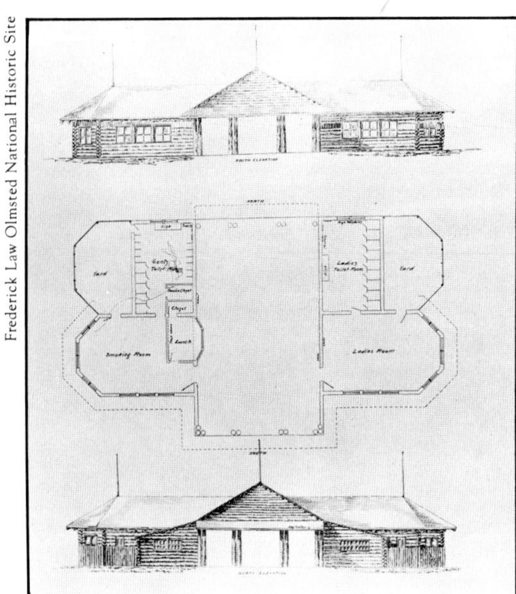

Design for Refectory Building, West Park c. 1892. While the design for this log refectory building, which was among the early sketches by the Olmsted firm, was an interesting concept, its rustic flavor was not wholly appropriate to the urban character of Milwaukee's residents.

West Park, on Vliet and Forty-first Streets, was a one hundred and twenty acre tract in the growing west end of the city. The original intention of the Olmsted firm was to create a simple, medium-sized pastoral park for passive recreation. Whereas a rather direct loop circulation system was shown in the preliminary plan, the final plan proposed a more complex grade-separated system with carriages and pedestrians on different levels. To the early schematic plans, which showed a meadow, a lake, a picnic grove and a small shelter, were added a playground and a vista concourse in the final plan. Later designs, including the final illustrative plan, reflected the Commission's desire to accommodate the gift of a small herd of deer by Gustav Pabst and Louis Auer by the creation of a deer paddock. In subsequent years, this gift proved to be the cornerstone of the Milwaukee Zoo which was originally located in the park in 1910.

Today, the most significant building in the park is the Emil Blatz Temple of Music. Constructed in 1938, the Temple is an integral part of neighborhood activities. The park's statuary clearly shows the influence of the surrounding German community. At the entrance, is the equestrian statue of Frederick Von Steuben, dedicated in 1921. Near the Blatz Music Temple are the imposing double monuments to the romantic poet, Johann Wolfgang Von Goethe and Friedrich Schiller. Dedicated in 1908, the pair was moved in 1960 to make way for freeway construction. Washington Park reached its current size of one hundred thirty nine acres in 1967. The freeway borders the west side of the park and separates it from Washington Blvd., a part of the original open space system.

The Olmsted firm also prepared a number of sketch plans for River Park. They are, however, fragmentary. The unique problem of this site was that it was bisected by the Chicago and Northwestern Railroad tracks. Once the Northwestern Railroad Company generously bridged the tracks, the park began to take form. Today, the easterly meadow area is devoted to recreational activities, while the western section across the railroad bridge retains two lovely oak groves high above the Milwaukee River, possibly envisioned in the Olmsted designs.

The planting palette for the Milwaukee parks designed by the Olmsted

West Side Park, Preliminary Plan (Washington Park) 1892. On this plan sheet appear the notations of a member of the Olmsted office, probably Warren Manning, relating to possible changes in the boundaries of the park. This plan, number four in the office files for this project, predates the idea of the deer enclosure. Notice the large picnic grove in the lower right section of the plan. This feature was not part of the standard Olmsted design for a park and was probably specifically tailored to the Milwaukee clients' needs. In this and all subsequent designs, the perimeter of the park was to be heavily screened from the adjacent neighborhood.

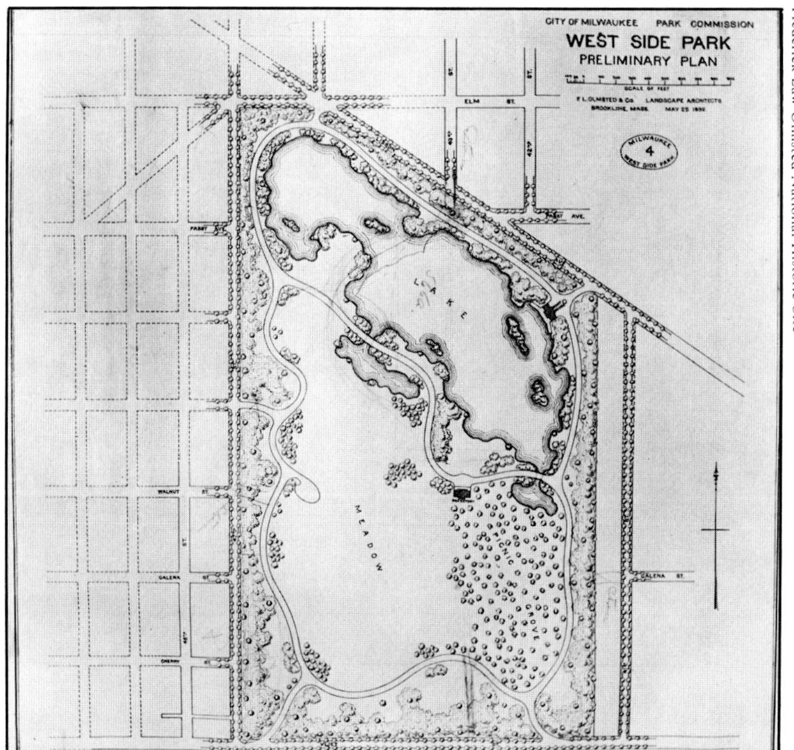

Frederick Law Olmsted National Historic Site

firm differed significantly from that used by the firm in eastern work of the same period. This distinction was due, perhaps, to Warren Manning's intense preoccupation with plant material. Certainly, some of the choices illustrated appropriate judgment and seem to work well even today. For example, the use of bur oak — almost never seen in the East — seems a good choice for this region, and the nut trees and conifers (the latter groups of which only rarely appear in Olmsted designs) were inspired selections. The use, however, of such ragged and short-lived trees as the boxelder and the silver maple as substitutes for the norway and sugar maple reflected an eastern bias about the appropriateness of the latter species in the West. Typical of the lavish scale of the period, enormous numbers of trees were specified and planted. In 1896, for example, eighteen hundred trees were planted in Washington Park alone.

By the end of 1894, five years after they had begun their work, the park commission members reported that they were financially overextended. This condition hampered their efforts throughout the next two decades. Nevertheless, important work pushed ahead. Excavation commenced on the lake in Washington Park, and the street railway station designed by local architect Howland Russel was constructed. In 1897 the commissioners turned their attention to the boulevard issue. They lamented that there was no law enabling the city to pay for the construction, planting, and maintenance of the center strips of the city's designated boulevards. The following year, the last year of Christian Wahl's presidency, brought significant physical improvements to the four major parks — Lake, West, River and Mitchell — and to Newberry Boulevard. The most impressive accomplishments were the beginning of construction on the Mitchell Park Conservatory designed by the local architectural firm of H. C. Koch and Company, and the construction of Newberry Boulevard. This latter occurrence suggests that the boulevard issue had been, at least partially, resolved.

The years around 1900 brought symbolic changes to the park system. In 1900, the park names were changed to recognize the importance of American history and of the ethnic character of the neighborhoods in which the parks were located, and in 1902 the passage into the new century was marked by a transformation of the park commission's philosophy on open space. The commissioners reported enthusiastically that: "Golf is altogether the best open-air game ever devised by man as all sorts and conditions of people can play it; for it suits the physical ability of everybody."[24]

The commissioners announced their intention to dedicate Washington Park, thought complete four years earlier, to athletics. Tennis grounds were to be installed. Previously only modestly scaled outdoor athletic gymnasia had been provided in the park for sports. The introduction of golf and tennis heralded new concepts in park design: from then on, recreation had equal importance with scenery in planning considerations.

In the 1905 Annual Report, the commissioners compared the acreage of their system with those of eleven other cities of comparable and smaller size including heavy industrial centers such as Toledo, Ohio, Lynn, Massachusetts, and Hartford, Connecticut. All, including Lynn, with only one-quarter the population of Milwaukee, had greater acreages. The statistical data may have been exaggerated to demonstrate the point that Milwaukee did not have a comparable area devoted to parks, and it illustrated nothing about the quality of the improvements of the parks. Several of the cities listed, however — particularly Minneapolis and Kansas City — had remarkable park systems. The commissioners, expressing dismay at Milwaukee's rank, argued for a more effective governmental structure and additional funds for acquisition, design and construction. A decade later, the city council still had not created the necessary machinery to renew and expand the system efficiently.

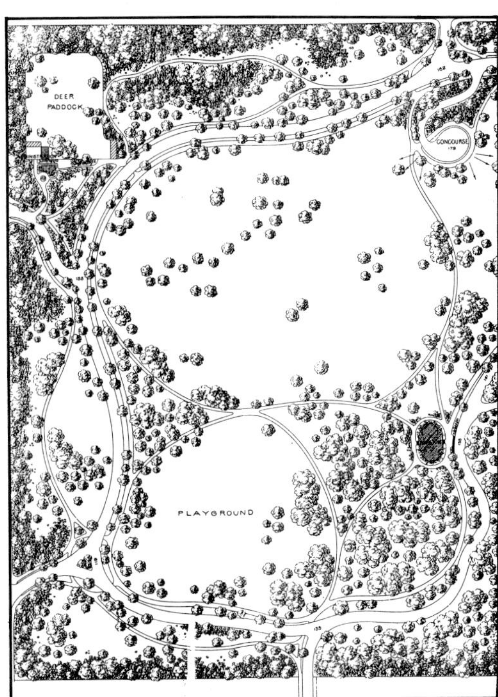

West Park, General Plan, 1895. (detail) This final plan shows the arrangement of picnic and play spaces adjacent to a meadow with a viewing concourse. Notice the complicated grade-separated circulation plan.

Mitchell Park Conservatory, photograph c. 1900. The Mitchell Park Conservatory was one of the most elegant park buildings of its age. The beautiful lancet arch form of its surfaces emulated the best work of the English designers of the mid-nineteennth century, especially John Claudius Loudon and Sir Joseph Paxton.

Milwaukee Co. Historical Society

Milwaukee Co. Historical Society

Humboldt Park, Boating on the Pond. The photographs were taken nearly a century apart.

Milwaukee Co. Historical Society

Humboldt Park. The idea of the *Lilienteich*, or lily pond, was probaby first introduced in Milwaukee in West Park, although it is not known whether the idea came from the Olmsted firm or from local interests. The Humboldt Park lily pond still makes a beautiful display in late June or early July. The old park has evolved into one of the best designed neighborhood parks in the city. The separation — both visual and real — of passive and active areas makes it usable to all without interference from one another.

Yet, the commission continued to move forward in the first three decades of the twentieth century. It continued to acquire land and make gradual improvements to the sites, especially in the quality of recreational facilities. In 1901, Mitchell Park, which had become known for its glass houses, was enlarged on the plans of Warren H. Manning. Today, the park is still the city's principal horticultural and botanical center under glass, but the old building has given way to new glass domes.

Humboldt and Kosciuszko Parks had been acquired in 1890, but site improvements had proceeded slowly. In Humboldt Park (Howell and Oklahoma) the ponds were completed in 1893. After World War I, a granite memorial was placed in the park. The existing service building was added in 1932, replacing an earlier boat house. Kosciuszko's (Lincoln between Sixth & Tenth) first major addition was the equestrian statue of the park's namesake installed in 1905. A small frame shelter building from the turn of the century serves as a senior center today, and an elegant Tudor styled service building also remains. The old boat house designed by Ferry and Clas has recently yielded to a new structure on the pond.

Between 1905 and 1915, Chicago's achievements in its West Park System, under the leadership of landscape architect Jens Jensen, were the models of park design and programming used in Milwaukee. The Chicago West Park system combined ornamental and recreational grounds, a huge building inventory, and a superior program of education and recreational training. A desire to emulate the Chicago successes and increased concern about providing play space became the motivating forces in park planning and politics in Milwaukee as the Socialists began to gain electoral power in the period of Emil Seidel's leadership and particularly after his election as mayor in 1910.

Milwaukee's model neighborhood park of the period was Sherman Park on North Forty-first Street. Acquired in 1891, the Perrigo Tract (as it was then called), lay just outside the city. After the area was annexed and development began to occur just after the turn of the century, a shelter was erected (since replaced by the current building constructed in the 1920s). In 1931, the Board of Public Land Commissioners staff report on neighborhood parks which proposed the creation of twenty-four more playgrounds, referred to Sherman Park as the outstanding example to be emulated in the planning task ahead.[25]

During the period 1907 to 1910, a significant beginning was made with the acquisition in 1909 of South Shore Park (a large neighborhood park in Bay View) and fourteen smaller tracts. In 1912, the city commissioned *A Recreation Survey* and a study entitled *How Much Playground Space Does a City Need?* by Rowland Haynes of the Playground and Recreation Association of America.[26] Pulaski Park, on the Kinnickinnic at Twentieth Street, was added to the system in 1915 and was enhanced by the additions of a statue of General Casimir Pulaski and an "Alpine" park pavilion by Ferry and Clas. As the first decade of the new century ended, the popular idea of neighborhood centers in the parks had already gained political strength. This idea was united with new concerns for a metropolitan park and parkway system, and civic center, eventually becoming the basis for city, and later, county, planning for Milwaukee.

Metropolitan Parks, City Beautiful and City Functional

The year 1893 brought two seminal contributions to the rise of city planning in the United States, one from the east coast and the other from the Midwest. In Boston, Charles Eliot's plan for the metropolitan park and parkway system was adopted. The Metropolitan Park Commission was formed to guide the open space planning for that growing region. In Chicago, the "greatest meeting of artists since the fifteenth century" created the World's Columbian Exposition on the shores of Lake Michigan. In spite of its imperialistic architectural imagery, the "White City", as Chicago's Fair came to be known, was proclaimed by social critics as the symbol of democracy.[27] The architectural and landscape architectural forms were adopted by a new group of urban progressives anxious to reform the city and to create a City Beautiful, the nucleus of which would be a Neo-classical civic center. This reform movement was the beginning of formal city planning in this country.

The first important city plan in the City Beautiful mode was executed for Washington, D.C. In 1901, the McMillan Commission, under the leadership of Daniel Hudson Burnham, chief architect of the Chicago Fair, and with the advice of Frederick Law Olmsted, Jr., created the axial plan for the mall, the Washington Monument, the memorials, and the White House which today dominates the city center. Eight years later, Burnham began his plan for Chicago. By that time, the Chicago plan was one of several designs for large American cities by major architects which advocated the creation of a classically-designed civic center and a grand boulevard and mall system. In the meantime, landscape architecture had been established as a discipline at Harvard University. Among the first recipients of a degree from that program was John Nolen, who devoted great energy to facilitating the transition from the civic improvement schemes of the City Beautiful phase to the analytical era of the City Functional, the beginning of comprehensive city planning.

Realizing that the City of Milwaukee was growing faster than its ability either to anticipate or accommodate change, the Common Council appointed eleven citizens as the Metropolitan Commission and authorized them to explore the problems of planning for the Cream City. Over a sixteen-month period, they issued a series of four "Tentative Reports" on the subjects of a civic center, neighborhood centers in the parks, riverfront

Scheme for City Hall Approach, 1910. Alfred C. Clas's urban design ideas were summarized in a pamphlet entitled "Civic Improvement in Milwaukee, Wisconsin", a synopsis of his address to the Greater Milwaukee Association in 1916. This drawing of a design for the City Hall approach was published six years earlier in *Architectural Review*. This easterly end of the Kilbourn Avenue axis envisioned by Clas was part of an extremely sensible, if grand, design which, had it been executed, would be an elegant promenade today. The style of the drawing ably emulates the beautiful watercolors for the Chicago plan by Jules Guerin published a year earlier.

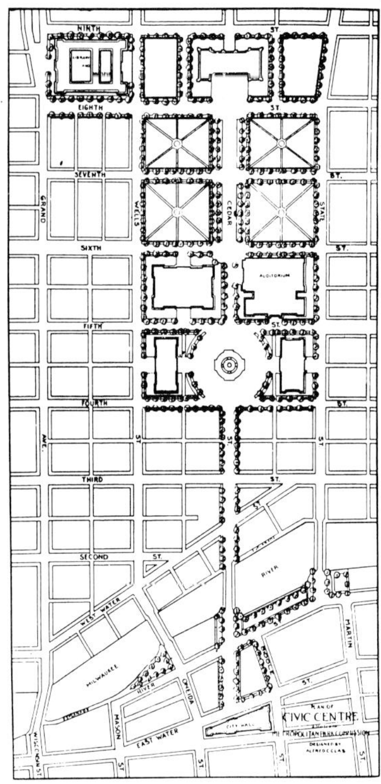

First Civic Center Scheme, 1909. Alfred C. Clas was the most energetic of the City Beautiful Era designers. To him should go a large measure of the credit for the initial expression of urban design ideas which have continued to be influential in downtown planning through the decades.

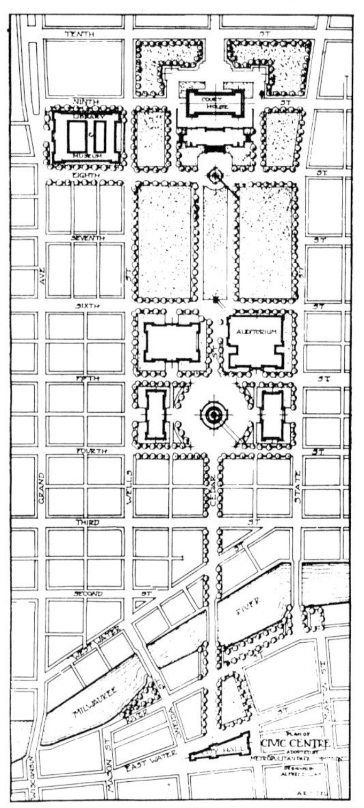

Revised Scheme for Civic Center, 1910.

parks and parkways, and boulevard construction. Of these, the riverfront report was the most fruitful in promoting active programming in the coming decades, largely through the later work of commission member Charles B. Whitnall.

In the meantime, Frederick Law Olmsted, Jr. and John Nolen prepared a joint consultants' report on the civic center scheme. This design had been produced by the talented local architect Alfred C. Clas. Clas proposed an axial relationship between city hall and the proposed new courthouse on the line of Kilbourn Avenue which would become a mall lined with public and quasi-public buildings. The consultants recommended enlarging the open space by adding two more blocks and strengthening the axial character with the insertion of obelisks. They indicated a slightly more indirect circulation plan in the French manner closing Seventh Street, and they also refined the superior height of the courthouse in relation to the rest of the buildings in the scheme. Combined in 1911, the four "Tentative Reports" and the Olmsted and Nolen report constituted the "Preliminary Reports of the City Planning Commission." The Metropolitan Commission, thus, passed out of existence. The City Planning Commission metamorphosed slightly in 1915 into the Board of Public Land Commissioners.

In 1916 the most cogent piece of planning literature of the period was issued — Werner Hegemann's report entitled "City Planning for Milwaukee: What It Means and Why It Must Be Secured." This document was submitted to a coalition of groups including the Wisconsin Chapter of the American Institute of Architects, and representatives of local real estate and civic interests. A maverick figure in planning, Hegemann burst upon the American scene with fresh ideas about the importance of housing renewal and design, and rapid transit.[28] He had been educated in Europe — at Charlottenburg, Munich, the Ecole des Beaux Arts and the University of London — and had worked all over the world. In 1912 he was prosecuted for exposing the miserable conditions of housing in the city of Berlin. Upon his arrival in the United States he entered into partnership with Joseph Hudnut and Elbert Peets. Together they planned a number of communities for Pennsylvania, where Hegemann had previous connections, and for Wisconsin, including the financially disastrous Lake Forest City near Madison.

The value of the Hegemann report lay not only in the extraordinary range and substance of his recommendations, but also in the rigor of his argument and the candor with which it was delivered. For example, in the park section he exposed to public discussion the argument between park and harbor planners over the use of the near southside lakefront and the Menomonee River Valley. He demonstrated a solution in Berkeley, California, which accommodated the interests of both parties in a similar confrontation. Noting, nevertheless, that park planning allied with civic center planning were the strongest existing elements in urban planning and design in Milwaukee, he reinforced arguments for riverfront parks and parkways (the Whitnall ideas), connecting boulevards, and neighborhood parks. The Hegemann report represents, for the first time in Milwaukee, a comprehensive statement about the coordination that must occur among planners of urban design features and city services — civic center, parks and parkways, housing and rapid transit. It also constitutes, therefore, the completion of the transition from park planning and civic improvement to comprehensive city planning.

The symbolic power of the civic center idea, however, dominated the efforts of the new Board of Public Land Commissioners.[29] One of their earliest (1919) major reports, entitled "The Grouping of Public Buildings", contained the recommendations of engineer Roland Stoelting who proposed three schemes for the clustering of civic buildings. All three concepts destroyed the great axial scheme proposed by Clas and modified by Olmsted and Nolen. Although the board strongly favored a court house and related civic buildings on roughly the same site proposed by the Old Metropolitan Park Commission, the report was unclear on this very point. In the meantime, a lakefront site was also proposed. The board rejected that site altogether, but as the question of a civic center went before the people in referendum in 1920, some citizens must have been confused. The civic center idea was a non-partisan issue at this time, and it passed by a three to one margin. Funding for its construction, however, was not authorized. In 1925 the scheme was dealt a setback by a repeal vote. Land acquisition had its own inertia, however, and in 1931 the new courthouse was completed on the site proposed in 1910. Clearance and redevelopment of the site have continued to this day, and the plan's potency is still a major force in downtown urban design.

The 1920s and 1930s were decades of change in the park movement. Charles B. Whitnall and his ideas dominated the period.[30] The County Park Commission had been created in 1907, but it was not until Whitnall came to it with his ideas about the role of parks and parkways in the decentralization of the city that the commission performed its great work. Whitnall was a self-taught student of urban planning. He relied heavily on the writings of the Scottish town planner Patrick Geddes, who, like Whitnall, devoted his early years to the study of plants. Geddes held the proposition that the city would be superseded by a more geographically widespread form which he called a "conurbation". Whitnall used the idea of the conurbation to think about how Milwaukee County might grow, but he added his own concept of the importance of river systems in the recreational life of the region. Whitnall's idea was to reserve the riverways for recreation and, thereby, insure their conservation not only as play space, but for sanitation and scenic quality as well.

In 1923 he presented his plan to the commission. In 1924 it was published in the first Annual Report of the County Planning Department, the commission's staff arm. The plan contemplated the acquisition and construction of an eighty-four mile parkway which would link existing elements of the city as open space system to the county. In the city, Whitnall envisioned a park corridor along the Kinnickinnic River to West Allis (State Fair Park), and along the Milwaukee River through Shorewood eventually linking with another loop on the Little Menomonee and Root Rivers.

The Kinnickinnic link was a particularly difficult one to forge. It lay largely within the city where land was already finely parcelled and developed, and quite valuable in comparison with comparable acreages outside of the city. Whitnall's persuasive pamphlet, "How the Kinnickinnic Should Look", was an enlightened effort in public sector planning. In a decade when most of the rest of the country had tired of progessivism and reform, and when only Jens Jensen of Illinois was contemplating similar ideas, Whitnall and the County Park Commission pressed ahead. This stewardship of urbanized riverways, originated by Whitnall and strengthened and codified in the modern environmental planning movement, was a significant theoretical contribution.

In 1927 the home rule law was passed in Wisconsin. With home rule came diminished ability for the city's Board of Park Commissioners to work independently of the other commissions and departments. Park land acquisition had swelled the acreage of the system, but maintenance was low. The Depression only made matters worse.

In 1936 the question of city-county park system consolidation was put to the voters, and was passed. On January 1, 1937 the old Milwaukee Board of Park Commissioners became history and the county administrative and planning structure took over. Today, after nearly a century of planning and development, the Milwaukee County Park System is one of the most beautiful in the country.

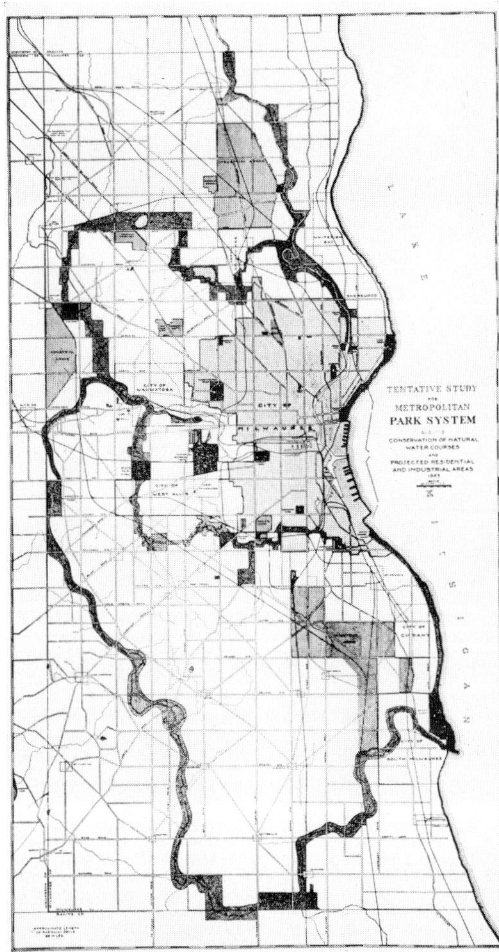

Whitnall's Study Map for a County Park System, 1923. Charles Whitnall's scheme for a linked river corridor parkway system projected substantial improvements in the County's watercourses.

"How the Kinnickinnic Should Look", 1931. Whitnall's pamphlet on the improvement of the Kinnickinnic River contrasted this view with photographs of the County Park Commission's completed work on Underwood Creek, the Olmsted-designed Riverway in Boston and Brookline, Massachusetts, and the improvements on the Yahara River in Madison. His photo essay was presented in the same idealistic spirit of reform literature of earlier decades, but the substance of the message was different. Few planners or designers of the time understood the importance of waterways as a resource for the creation of diverse and scenic open space systems.

VI Religious Buildings

Westminister United Presbyterian Church, 2306 E. Bellview Pl., 1895. Designed by W. D. Kimball, with alterations by Leenhouts and Guthrie.

Ministers and priests were among the pioneer settlers of Milwaukee, and church spires have pierced the city's skyline since the 1840s. Prior to the construction of the first church buildings, services for members of Baptist, Catholic, Congregational, Methodist and Presbyterian congregations were held in schools, homes, and stores. Many nationalities were represented in the first congregations; within the Catholic Church there were English, Polish, German and Bohemian congregations; the Presbyterian church held English, Dutch, and Welsh services. By 1889, there were 111 churches representing twenty-one denominations. Throughout the city, churches and their companion schools and rectories were an important cultural and religious element in the development of Milwaukee's ethnic neighborhoods.

Whether neighborhood church or downtown cathedral, the design of Milwaukee's churches often reflects the ethnic heritage of the congregation. The Gothic spires of Yankee and German congregations contrast with the onion-domed churches of Eastern European and Middle Eastern immigrants. Stylistically, Milwaukee churches in the historical survey are representative of the ecclesiastical architectural fashions between the Civil War and the late 1920s. English and German Gothic, French Romanesque, Renaissance and Neo-classical churches of both monumental cathedral and country church proportions influenced the design of many

Milwaukee churches, but Eastern European sources including the onion-domed churches of Byzantium are also evident. In many cases, congregations have modified designs with their own ethnic symbolism, often in the form of stained glass windows and interior murals and paintings. However, the influence of the Gothic Revival in Europe and America in the nineteenth century has had the most profound overall effects on the churches of the city. Gothic Revival features such as sharp gables, pointed arch openings, finials, prominent rose windows, and slender spires are the predominant architectural elements in Milwaukee's ecclesiastical buildings.

Although Milwaukee's architects fully exploited the local available cream brick and limestone, many churches have finishes imported from all over the world. Gold leaf, marble, mosaic and terra cotta are among the materials which enrich the surface of many masonry churches, while excellent effects were obtained on frame churches by the use of applied ornamental millwork trim.

The survey documented approximately 150 churches and related buildings (including rectories and schools). Those illustrated here represent the ethnic diversity of the city's congregations as well as the stylistic variation of the facades. In most instances, the original name of the church is given first in the caption, followed by the name of the current congregation or use.

State Historical Society of Wisconsin

First Baptist Church, corner Wisconsin Avenue and Milwaukee Streets, photograph c. 1890.

Temple Emanu-El, Broadway and E. State, 1872. No longer standing.

St. John's Cathedral, 812 N. Jackson St., 1847-1853. German born carpenter-architect Victor Schulte provided the plans for St. John's, Wisconsin's first Roman Catholic Cathedral. The Neo-Baroque tower by George B. Ferry was built in the 1890s (replacing the original one which had been exemplary of the German *Zopfstil* (or Baroque) design of Schulte's). A fire severely damaged the church, but the second tower survived.

St. Mary's Roman Catholic Church, 844 N. Broadway, 1846-47; additions and alterations 1866-67. Built for Milwaukee's first German speaking Roman Catholic parish, St. Mary's shows the influence of the *Zopfstil* favored by German designer Victor Schulte.

North Presbyterian Church, 1001 N. Milwaukee St., 1854-55. Now the Milwaukee School of Engineering Bookstore, this pre-Civil War Gothic Revival church has had a series of changes, including an 1891 renovation in which the building was raised 4½ feet.

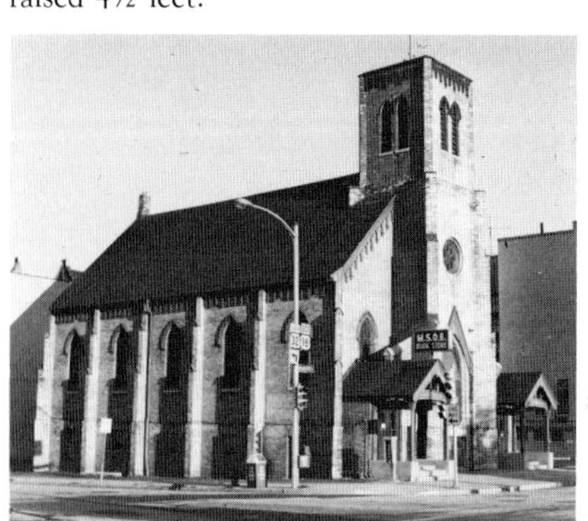

Salem Evangelical Lutheran Church, 6814 N. 107th St., 1863. This Civil War era church has Italianate brackets and semi-circular arched stained glass windows.

Welsh Congregational Church, 2739 S. Superior St. Milwaukee Iron Company workers from Wales organized Bay View's Welsh Congregational Church (also known as the First Independent Congregational Welsh Church) in 1868. The congregation built this simple gable-roofed church in 1873, and decorated it with segmental-arch stained glass windows. By the early years of the twentieth century, the number of Welsh residents had diminished, and the building became Ascension Chapel, an extension of the Evangelical Lutheran Church of the Ascension.

St. James Episcopal Church, 833 W. Wisconsin Ave., 1867-68; rebuilt after fire, 1872-74. Probably the oldest limestone church in Milwaukee, and the oldest surviving Episcopal Church in the city, this English Gothic Revival building was designed by Detroit architect Gordon William Lloyd. Of particular note are the Tiffany stained glass windows in the fourth bay of the east aisle. St. James parish was formed in 1850 as the Episcopal church for Kilbourntown, and served the Yankee community.

Salem Kircher Gemeinschaft, 1037 S. 11th St., 1874. This small South Side church is representative of many built throughout the city after the Civil War. The rectangular plan, central tower and spire, and lancet windows are typical features. The building now serves the St. Michael's Ukranian Catholic congregation.

Trinity Evangelical Lutheran Church, 1046 N. 9th St., 1878-1880.

Evangelical Lutheran Zions Kirche, 2030 W. North Ave., 1883. Corner towers or turrets flanking a central tower are a common feature of several cream brick churches of the 1880s. The octagonal spire rests on a square clock tower.

Mt. Zion Assembly of the Apostolic Faith, 2576 N. 5th St., 1897. Designed by Henry C. Rische, this Gothic Revival church was originally built for a German Evangelical congregation. The millwork trim is of Gothic inspiration.

St. Peter's Evangelical Lutheran Church, 1215 S. 8th St., 1885. St. Peter's was organized in 1860 by German Lutherans who left the Norwegian Evangelical Lutheran Church. Andrew Elleson designed this twin-towered edifice, executed in cream brick with limestone trim.

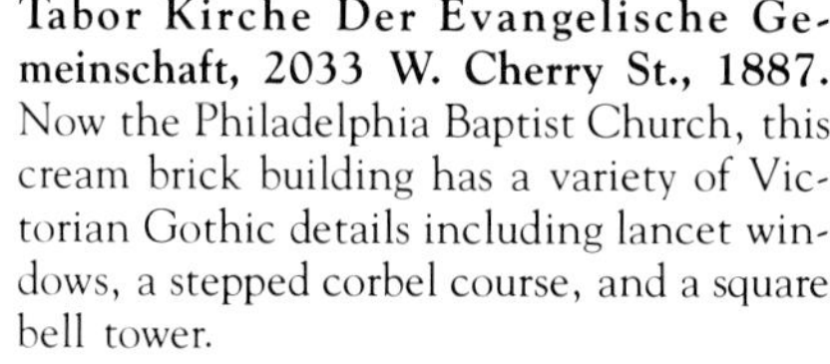

Tabor Kirche Der Evangelische Gemeinschaft, 2033 W. Cherry St., 1887. Now the Philadelphia Baptist Church, this cream brick building has a variety of Victorian Gothic details including lancet windows, a stepped corbel course, and a square bell tower.

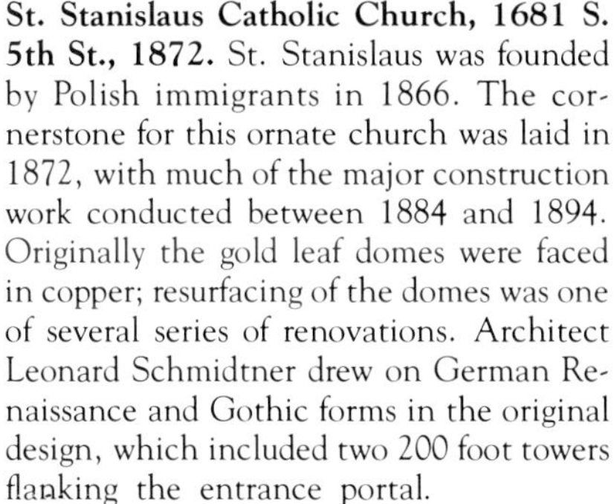

St. Stanislaus Catholic Church, 1681 S. 5th St., 1872. St. Stanislaus was founded by Polish immigrants in 1866. The cornerstone for this ornate church was laid in 1872, with much of the major construction work conducted between 1884 and 1894. Originally the gold leaf domes were faced in copper; resurfacing of the domes was one of several series of renovations. Architect Leonard Schmidtner drew on German Renaissance and Gothic forms in the original design, which included two 200 foot towers flanking the entrance portal.

Roman Catholic Church of the Gesu, 1145 W. Wisconsin Ave., 1892-94; additions 1902, 1927. Inspired by French Gothic churches, Henry C. Koch and Co. designed this twin-towered edifice with prominent rose windows. The walls are of gray limestone; the towers are enriched with carved stone finials and crockets. The stone entrance portico was added in 1902 after the design of Herman J. Esser.

Holy Rosary Roman Catholic Church and Rectory. 2003 N. Oakland Ave., 1885. This cream brick complex of church and rectory was designed in a wood-trimmed version of the Queen Anne style.

Tippecanoe Presbyterian Church, 125 West Saveland Ave. The Tippecanoe Amusement Hall and Tippecanoe Lake were the focal points of the community of Tippecanoe which became a well-known private park in the late nineteenth century. In the early 1890s, Captain John Saveland manufactured a two-acre lake from an artesian well on his property. Saveland apparently hoped that the lake would inspire the growth of an exclusive residential area. (It did not, although a few large homes were built.) Saveland turned the rest of his land into a private park, including an amusement hall, completed in 1893. The hall, which was converted from Issac Austin's barn with the help of community residents, was dedicated in July 1894. The park thrived for several years and the Tippecanoe Amusement Hall served a variety of community functions such as dances, school graduations, funerals, and recitals. In 1915 the Milwaukee Presbytery bought the Amusement Hall, which was at first used by Grace Presbyterian Church. In 1917, Tippecanoe Presbyterian Church was organized and services were held in the hall. The building was extensively remodelled in 1928 to its present appearance. Although the shingle and stucco treatment evocative of a rural English Gothic church are part of the remodelling, the high stone foundation is an original feature of the original barn and amusement hall.

St. George's Byzantine-Melkite Church, now Syrian Roman Catholic Church, 1617 West State Street. This is likely the only surviving Byzantine-Melkite church in the state of Wisconsin. Reverend Ronald Golini, in his history of the congregation, states that "for many years, the church served as the cultural and spiritual nucleus of the Syrian-Lebanese community." In 1895, the first immigrants from Syria arrived in Milwaukee, settling in an area bordered by Kilbourn and Highland Avenues, and Sixteenth to Twentieth Streets. Their experience with the Eastern Church, plus their unfamiliarity with English of Latin liturgy compelled them to seek their own parish and priest. The first services took place in an unused dance hall at 627 West State Street. In 1915 the congregation purchased a house at 1615 West State Street for a place of worship. On September 30, 1917, the cornerstone for the present building was laid. In true Byzantine Style, three bulbous domes cap the central and end towers. The circular stained glass window in the facade depicts the patron Saint George. Erhard Brielmaier and Sons were recorded as the architects.

Plymouth Congregational Church, 2717 E. Hampshire, 1913, and later additions. Now the Plymouth United Church of Christ, this building was designed by Alexander C. Eschweiler. It is a good example of the less decorated English Gothic mode popular in the early twentieth century.

Temple Emanu-El B'ne Jeshurun, 2419 E. Kenwood, 1922. This synagogue represents the merger of Milwaukee's two oldest Jewish reform congregations, Emanu-El and B'ne Jeshurun. Robert and Henry Messmer were the architects of the Neo-classical design, executed in Indiana limestone.

Milwaukee Architects

Trinity Evangelical Lutheran Church, 1046 North Ninth Street, 1878-1880. Designed by Frederick Velguth, a German-born master builder, this Victorian Gothic church has an exceptional facade of traceried arches.

When Milwaukee was settled in the 1830s, the architectural profession in America was still in the early years of development. During the first years of settlement, many builder-contractors also called themselves architects, despite their lack of formal academic training. By the end of the nineteenth century, however, Milwaukee's architects and engineers were prominent professionals in the community. They benefited from training in architectural schools and universities as well as the traditional apprentice system. Although architects from cities such as St. Louis, Chicago, Minneapolis, and New York received commissions in Milwaukee, most of the city's commercial and public buildings have been designed by local architects.

A few early architects seem to have only "passed through" Milwaukee, appearing in directories for a few years and then disappearing. Others, such as Henry Messmer and Henry C. Koch had practices which extended over several decades and their firms were carried on by their sons. The well-publicized residential commissions of architects such as James Douglas, Edward Townsend Mix, and George B. Ferry provided local carpenters and builders with inspiration for several generations of modest houses built in Milwaukee's expanding neighborhoods. (Of course, only a fraction of the city's residences were designed by architects, as carpenters and masons created the bulk of the city's housing with the aid of pattern books and prefabricated parts.)

Although many of the first generation of Milwaukee architects had Yankee backgrounds and received their training in the East, a number of architects such as Victor Schulte, Fred Velguth, Henry Messmer, and Otto Strack were German-born. The German heritage of the architectural profession can still be observed in directory listings of Milwaukee architectural firms today. As these brief biographies of a selection of only nine Milwaukee architects indicate, the city's early architects came from diverse backgrounds, and brought varied training and skills to their commissions.

John Francis Rague (1799-1877)
John Francis Rague was among the first architects who advertised in Milwaukee's City Directory. Rague studied with New York architect Minard Lafever and came to Milwaukee in the 1840s. Among Rague's work was the Federal Style Layton House Hotel, built in 1849 and still standing (in a much-altered state) at 2504 Forest Home Avenue. Rague moved to Dubuque, Iowa in the 1850s, and became well-known throughout Wisconsin, Illinois and Iowa. He is credited with the design of the Illinois State Capitol at Springfield, Bascom Hall, North Hall and South Hall at the University of Wisconsin-Madison, and the Territorial Capitol in Iowa City.

JOHN F. RAGUE,

ARCHITECT,

And Twenty years a practical builder in the city of New York, will draw

Plans Specifications, and Contracts for Buildings.

OFFICE.

Opposite the Bank Buildings, Over Noyes' Grocery Store.

James Douglas (1823-?)
James Douglas began his career as a builder, eventually turning to the design of buildings. Born in Scotland, he arrived in Milwaukee in 1843. Reportedly, Douglas helped to build the first bridge across the Milwaukee River at Water Street. Between 1847 and 1863, Douglas and his brother Alexander operated a firm as "J. A. Douglas, Architects and Builders". After a nine-year period working for the Mutual Life Insurance Company of the State of Wisconsin, Douglas returned to architecture and specialized in residential design. A. T. Andreas praised Douglas as "introducing a new American style of art" and referred to his designs as the "Douglas Style." Another historian, James Buck, called attention to Douglas' distinctive stepped tower designs, which Buck compared to ant-hills, or "Termes Mordax." The Douglas Style was usually a variation of the High Victorian Gothic, often with steeply pitched roofs, numerous dormers, and a variety of carved or turned millwork and stone trim.

1363 N. Prospect, 1876. One of few surviving residences by James Douglas. A five story stepped tower was removed, and alterations made to the facade, but the verticality and Victorian Gothic details of the original design are still evident at the roofline. Another Douglas design still stands at 1425 N. Prospect Avenue.

Edward Townsend Mix (1831-1890)

> Milwaukee, which he has done so much to adorn and beautify, is a lasting monument to his aesthetic taste and architectural skill. . . .
>
> A. T. Andreas,
> *History of Milwaukee,* 1881

Edward Townsend Mix was Milwaukee's leading architect after the Civil War. Born in New Haven, Connecticut, he studied with Richard Upjohn, and established his Milwaukee practice in 1857, after a partnership with Chicago architect William Boyinton. Celebrated for his designs for the Mitchell Building and the Chamber of Commerce Building, he was also sought by wealthy landowners on Yankee Hill, Prospect Avenue, and Wisconsin Avenue to design their large residences. Although Mix's own residence at Juneau and Waverly Place (1869) was of simple, understated Italian Villa Style, many of the houses he designed for clients were highly decorated with carved stone, wood, and ironwork. Although Mix maintained his Milwaukee practice into the early 1880s (he later moved to Minneapolis) his popularity declined somewhat as a younger generation of German-American industrialists often selected architects with German backgrounds.

Matthew Keenan House, 775-781 N. Jefferson, c. 1857. The Victorian Italianate double house is attributed to Edward Townsend Mix, and remains one of few houses still standing in the central downtown area.

Milwaukee Co. Historical Society

Henry Messmer (1839-1899)

Henry Messmer was born in Rheinbeck, Switzerland, and learned his trade in Switzerland and Germany. He came to Milwaukee in 1866 and was in partnership with L. A. Schmidtner before starting his own office. Architect of brewery buildings and warehouses (including buildings for Obermann, Asmuth and Kraus, and F. Miller), he was also recognized for church designs. Sons Robert A. (1870-?) and John (1884-1971) eventually entered their father's firm. John graduated from the University of Wisconsin at Madison with a Bachelor of Science degree, and was noted as a building supervisor and engineer.

1663 N. Astor St., 1885. Designed by Henry Messmer for Phillip Hartig, the Vice-President of the Schlitz Brewing Company.

Henry C. Koch (1841-?)
Henry C. Koch was born in Celle, Hanover, Germany, and emigrated to the United States with his parents in 1842. A graduate of the Milwaukee German-English Academy, he "commenced his studies as an architect in 1856, in the office of George W. Mygatt . . . at that time one of the leading architects of the West." In 1866 he entered partnership with Mygatt, becoming sole partner of the firm in 1870. Koch enjoyed a national reputation as the designer of churches and courthouses, but left an outstanding collection of public and private buildings in Milwaukee. Koch was a master of the eclectic versions of the Queen Anne and Romanesque Styles; northern European touches such as curved gables were his hallmark. In addition to the twenty courthouses Koch designed, he was architect of the Milwaukee City Hall of 1895. The Hotel Pfister (1893) and the Gesu Church (1893) are also among extant designs of the firm of H. C. Koch and Co.

Koch's son, Armand Koch (1879-1932) attended the Massachusetts Institute of Technology and the Ecole des Beaux Arts. He practiced with his father until 1910, and later established an independent office. Among Armand Koch's commissions was the Wells Building at 324 E. Wisconsin Avenue, finished in enamel terra cotta.

H. C. KOCH & CO.,

ROOM 160 NEW INSURANCE BUILDING,

CORNER BROADWAY AND MICHIGAN STREET,

MILWAUKEE.

TAKE THE ELEVATOR. *TELEPHONE NO. 254.*

Henry C. Koch House, c. 1895, photograph c. 1915. The house Koch designed for his family was located in the 1500 block of West Wisconsin Avenue. The Frederick Pabst House (designed by George B. Ferry) is at far left.

Milwaukee Co. Historical Society

Milwaukee Co. Historical Society

Frederick Pabst House, 2000 W. Wisconsin Ave., 1890-93. Photograph c. 1895. Pabst was president of the Pabst Brewing Company, and one of the leading German-born citizens of Milwaukee during the 1890s. Architect George Ferry's design is based on 17th century English and Flemish Renaissance architecture; the curved gables were favored by many Milwaukee architects of the period.

George Bowman Ferry (1851-1918)
Born in Springfield, Massachusetts, George Ferry attended the Massachusetts Institute of Technology and graduated in 1872. In 1881, he began practice with Alfred C. Clas, as Ferry and Clas. The firm designed several major downtown buildings, including the Public Library and Museum, the Plankinton Hotel, and the Northwestern National Insurance Building. Among Ferry's best known residential commissions was the Frederick Pabst House of 1892, still standing at 2000 West Wisconsin Avenue. The curved stepped gables, a German Baroque motif, show both Ferry's versatility as an architect (he often worked in the Neo-classical Style) and the preferences of the client.

Residence at Milwaukee, Wisconsin, 1888, George B. Ferry, architect. Illustrated in the *Inland Architect and News Record,* volume 12, 1888, as a competition entry.

Alexander Chadbourne Eschweiler (1865-1940)
Born in Boston, Eschweiler attended Marquette University and studied architecture at Cornell University. He organized Eschweiler and Eschweiler in 1892, including his sons Alexander C., Jr. and Theodore. Among the firm's commissions were Downer College and the Milwaukee Downer Seminary, the Wisconsin Telephone Buildings, the Gas Light Building, and many residences. English Tudor motifs were favored by the firm for residential work; brown, red, and amber stone and brick, planar, untrimmed wall surfaces and generally unadorned are hallmarks of the Eschweiler style. Georgian Revival and German-inspired designs were included in their residential repertoire, however.

Russell Barr Williamson (1893-1964)
Russell Barr Williamson was born in Indiana, and attended the Art Institute of Chicago. Between 1914 and 1917, he worked with Frank Lloyd Wright as an apprentice, and later a designer. Williamson's work as an independent architect began shortly thereafter in Milwaukee. He often worked in partnership with local builder's services such as the Milwaukee Realty and Construction Company and the American Builder's Service. In the post World War I era, with a demand for low cost standardized housing, Williamson adapted the Prairie Style to the requirements of mass production and new materials such as concrete. The influence of Wright's studio is evident in the overhanging eaves, horizontal bands of windows, and unadorned wall surfaces of his residential designs, many of them planned as duplex or fourplex units.

Russell Barr Williamson. This residential design was advertised by the American Builders Service in the *Milwaukee Journal*, April 22, 1923. The ad noted that "Williamsonian homes have graceful lines and artistic beauty."

opposite left
2826 E. Linwood Ave., 1903. Designed by Alexander C. Eschweiler for E. B. Cottrill, the architect shows his preference for the English Tudor Style. Eschweiler's multi-gabled design has a simple brick facade decorated with stone and half-timbering.

VIII

Area Survey Notes

From its foundation, Milwaukee has been a cluster of cities within a city. Each area of the city and the smaller neighborhoods, communities, and districts which comprise it offer unique and characteristic glimpses into the architectural and historical development of the city. The Area Survey Notes constitute a collection of observations about sections of the city described, arbitrarily, by the map shown here. Except for the industrial expanse of the Menomonee Valley, these areas were chosen to show, primarily, the residential and commercial character of the various parts of the city. This section provides information about significant buildings and their settings which help to define the cluster of smaller cities which make up Milwaukee.

North Side

Northwest Side

West Side

South Side

East Side

Menomonee Valley

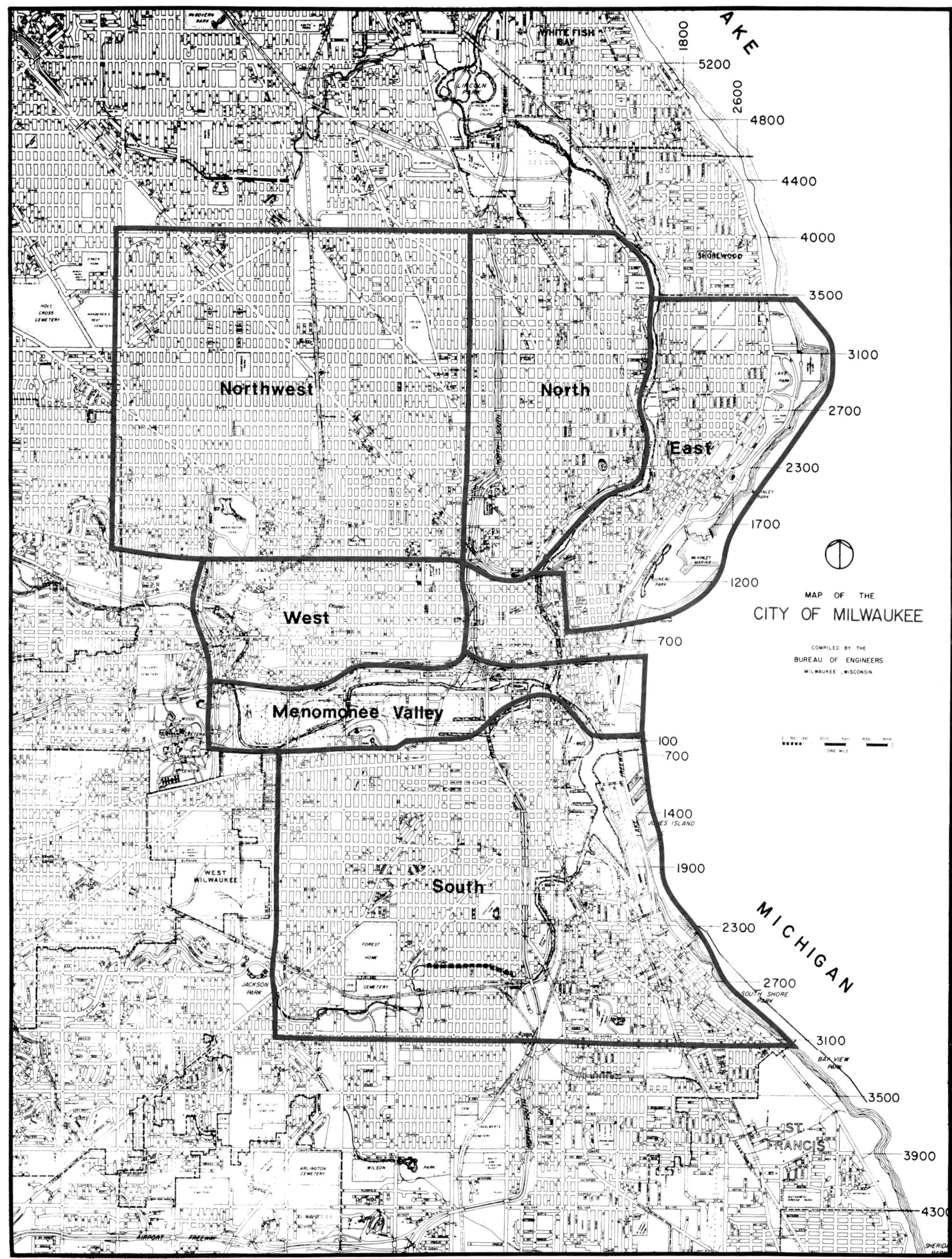
LAKE
MICHIGAN
MAP OF THE
CITY OF MILWAUKEE
COMPILED BY THE
BUREAU OF ENGINEERS
MILWAUKEE, WISCONSIN
Northwest
North
East
West
Menomonee Valley
South
WHITE FISH BAY
SHOREWOOD
WEST MILWAUKEE
ST. FRANCIS
JACKSON PARK
JONES ISLAND
SOUTH SHORE PARK
BAY VIEW PARK
FOREST HOME CEMETERY
AIRPORT FREEWAY
5200
4800
4400
4000
3500
3100
2700
2300
1700
1200
700
100
700
1400
1900
2300
2700
3100
3500
3900
4300
1800
2600

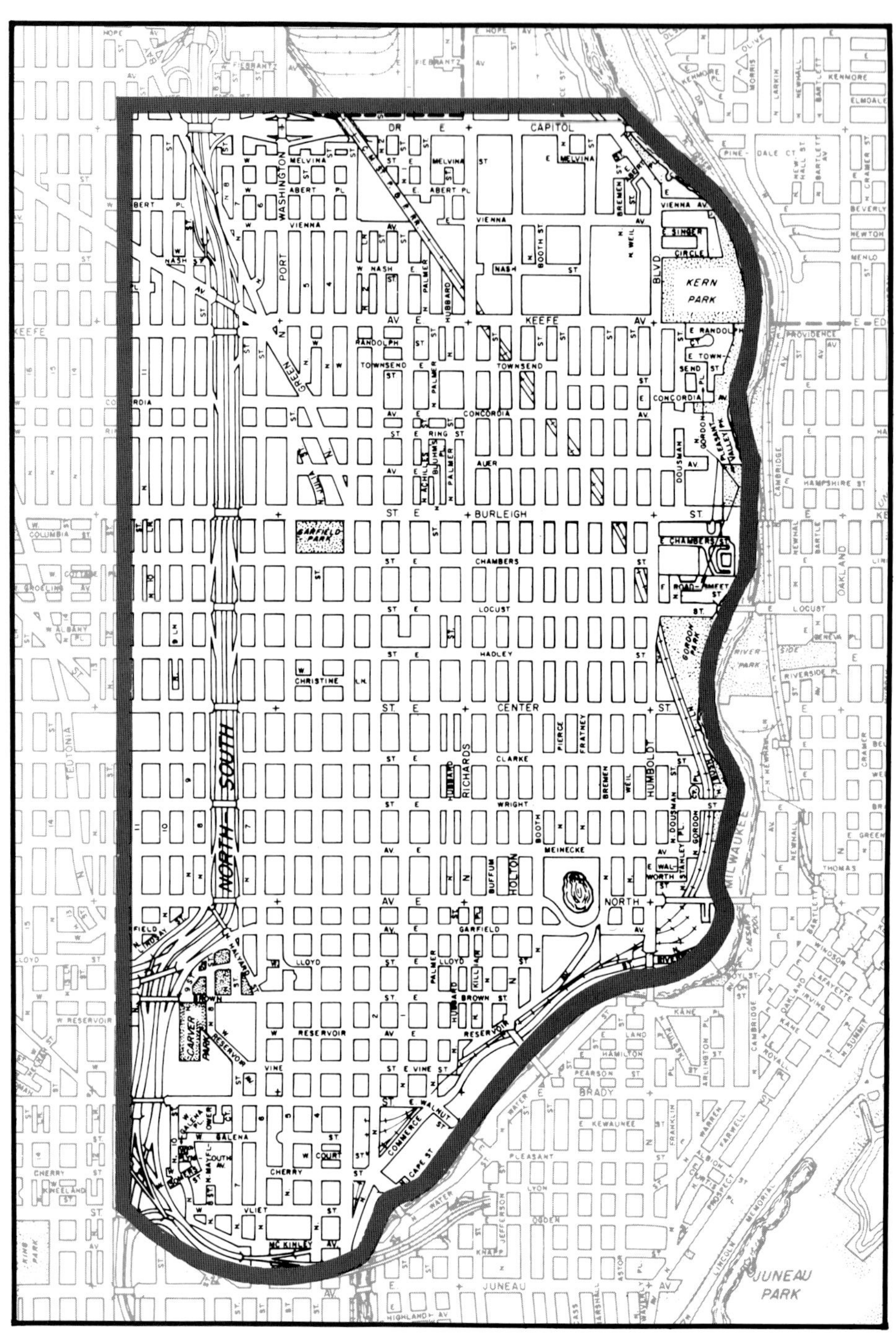
CAPITOL
KEEFE
KERN PARK
BLVD
BURLEIGH
GARFIELD PARK
CENTER
RICHARDS
HUMBOLDT
HOLTON
NORTH
NORTH – SOUTH
CARVER PARK
MILWAUKEE
OAKLAND
TEUTONIA
JUNEAU
JUNEAU PARK

North Side

The North Side

1858 Walling Map of Milwaukee.

American Geographical and Statistical Society

The North Side is one of Milwaukee's oldest settled areas. Its bluffs and proximity to the Milwaukee River were attractive to the city's earliest settlers and industrialists. When Byron Kilbourn laid out his village of square blocks and a courthouse square in 1835, the area north of present-day Wisconsin Avenue was a dry, level plain which ran north along the river as far as Brady Street, and west to the vicinity of North Sixth Street. From this plain rose forested bluffs which stretched to the west. Much of the land west of the river was a dense forest, broken only by Indian trails.[1] The southern edge of the North Side provided well-drained building sites, while Juneautown and Walker's Point to the south were both swampy. The owners of early industries found the Milwaukee River basin an excellent location site and along a direct transportation route to Lake Michigan. Home builders found the area near the bluffs highly appealing, with views extending to the marshes and the growing city below. Today, the North Side (defined here as the area between E. Capitol Drive at the north, Twelfth Street at the west, Ogden at the south, and the Milwaukee River at the east), retains some of the most interesting topography in the city.

Frank Whitnall House, 2914 N. Dousman, 1851. Frank Whitnall was a pioneer florist and nurseryman. This house was once part of a site known as "Whitnall's Knoll" which included ten greenhouses. This was later the residence of Frank's son Charles, Milwaukee's foremost promoter of public parks.

The earliest settlers on the North Side were farmers and traders. Among them was Garrett Vliet, who built a house near Walnut and Eighth Streets, a site which later became Schlitz Park and later Carver Park. In 1844 Benjamin Church built his small Greek Revival house on the hill which is now Fourth Street near West Court Street. (The well-known house of this early Milwaukee builder today stands in Estabrook Park.) Many settlers built their houses along or near the plank roads established

Joseph Schlitz Brewing Company, 235 West Galena St. The Schlitz Brewery grew from the small brewery established by August Krug in 1849. Joseph Schlitz, Krug's bookkeeper, took over after Krug's death in 1856. Joseph Schlitz became president, August Uihlein, secretary, and Henry Uihlein superintendent of the Joseph Schlitz Brewing Company. Henry Uihlein succeeded Schlitz as president in 1875. By 1885, the complex of brewery buildings covered approximately seven acres. Cooper shops, ice houses, bottling works, stables, grain sheds, and malt houses were among the many buildings comprising the brewery. Architecturally, the brewery is an interesting amalgam of German Renaissance architectural details, including towers, turrets, and heavily rusticated arches.

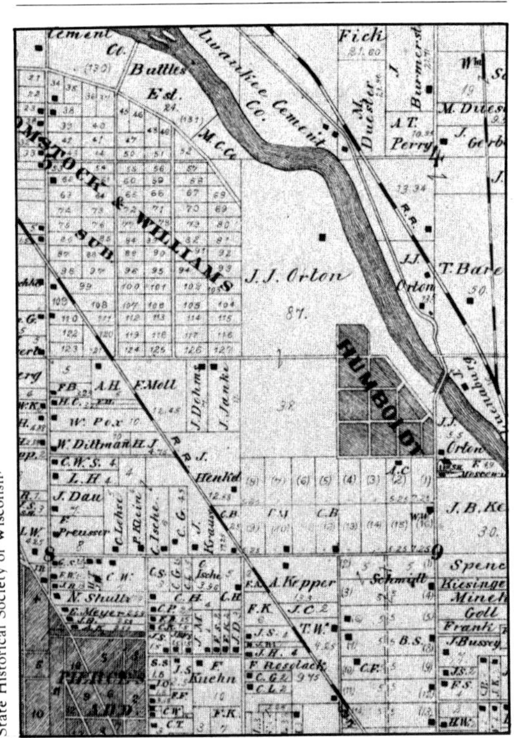

State Historical Society of Wisconsin

in the 1840s, which connected outlying towns to the grid streets of the Kilbourntown plan. Vliet Street joined the Wauwatosa Plank Road; Walnut Street fed into the North Fond du Lac and Lisbon Plank Roads, and North 12th Street joined the Cedarburg Plank Road, now Teutonia Avenue. The Green Bay Plank Road became North Third Street. Between the diagonals cut by plank roads, land speculators in the 1850s divided large tracts of land along the river bluffs near Third Street according to the square block pattern established by Kilbourn. After the Civil War, land developers platted the long narrow blocks which would become characteristic of much of Milwaukee's neighborhood development. Long narrow blocks were first evident on the North Side in the "School Section" which extended across the Milwaukee River and included an area from North Avenue to Burleigh Street.

Industrial development on the North Side began in the mid-1830s with the establishment of small gristmills and sawmills along the Milwaukee River. Among the first improvements to the river was the Milwaukee and Rock River Canal, intended to eventually connect Milwaukee with the Mississippi River. The first section of the canal and a lock and dam was built in 1838. The canal was used as a mill race when it opened in 1842, but remaining sections to the Mississippi River via the Rock River were never built. The LaCrosse and Milwaukee Railroad, built in 1852 along the Milwaukee River, further encouraged the growth of flour mills, breweries, and tanneries. Major breweries in or at the edge of the North Side included the Krug, later the Schlitz, Brewing Company, and the Jacob Obermann Brewing Company. The Obermann Brewery was located on Cherry between Fifth and Sixth Streets. While the North Side breweries were contributing to the city's fame as "America's Beer Capital", allied industries also developed. Within the brewery district (extending approximately from Vine at the north to Juneau at the south, between the Milwaukee River and North Twelfth Street) were found malt companies, barrel stave makers, coopers, ice companies, and small iron works.

Two unincorporated villages, once located outside the city limits, are part of the present-day North Side. One, known as Humboldt, had a role in the early industrial development of the area. The small village of Humboldt was platted in 1850 on a site formerly known as Mechanicsville. Situated above the dam of the Milwaukee River, near present day Humboldt Boulevard and Capitol Drive, the village was intended to attract the workers of the river's nearby flour and paper mills. Among the street names of the village were Leibnitz, Schiller, and Goethe, in keeping with the German birthplaces of many of the workers. In 1876 the *Milwaukee Sentinel* reported that the village was foundering as an industrial and residential site. This was due largely to the fact that Humboldt was not directly accessible by river because of the dam to the south (located near North Street), and transportation costs to nearby markets were high. Wagons brought goods to and from Humboldt "until the Humboltians found them too slow for the times." By 1884, the village was "in ruin" and was subsequently absorbed by residential development as Milwaukee's northern limits stretched along the river.[3] Directly to the south of Humboldt was "Pleasant Valley", which began as a private park in the 1870s and later became Blatz Park.

Another independent settlement known as Wilhelmsburg or Williamsburg survived intact until it was annexed to the city in 1891. At the intersection of the Green Bay Plank Road (now North Third Street) and Burleigh Street, this small community was established in the 1840s and was settled by "wealthy Pommern and Mecklenburger" from Northern Germany. The unincorporated village had a post office, stores, taverns,

Milwaukee Illustrated (1877)

Milwaukee River Above the Dam, c. 1877. This engraved view of the east side of the River shows the small group of summer homes built in the 1870s. The bridge at right is the North Avenue bridge.

W. Kroening Store, 540 North Avenue, c. 1880. The cream brick store of W. Kroening still boasts its gable end trusswork, incised limestone keystones, and original storefront.

325 W. Vine St., 1895. This building in the heart of the old North Side German neighborhood was constructed as a grocery warehouse, and for a time served as a horseradish factory.

Charles Fahsel General Store. North Third Street near Burleigh. Photograph c. 1885. Fahsel operated a general store in the settlement known as "Wilhelmsburg". Members of the family are pictured here in front of their combination store and residence.

greenhouses, market gardens, and a mill. Many Williamsburg residents were employed by the Lakeshore Railroad (now the Chicago and Northwestern) and by cement, flour, and paper mills.

The North Side, although settled initially by Yankees and French-Canadians, was overwhelmingly German and Polish throughout the nineteenth century. German families began to arrive in large numbers in the 1850s, and settled primarily to the west of North Pierce Street. By the 1890s, Polish and Jewish immigrants (of Polish-Russian origin) began to arrive on the North Side. A large settlement of Poles was centered in the area between the River and Richards Street, from North Avenue to Keefe Avenue. Jewish families settled in a small district bounded by N. Eleventh, N. Thirteenth, West Vine, and West Lloyd Streets, which reportedly contained more synagogues than any area of equal size in the United States.

Pre-Civil War residential neighborhoods on the North Side centered around local industry such as breweries, mills, and tanneries, and neighborhood stores and churches. Homes of wealthy local businessmen were built in close proximity to the cottages of their workers, a pattern which continued throughout the nineteenth century. The Uihleins, for example, resided on the heights of "Uihlein Hill", within sight of the Schlitz Brewery and other area industries, as well as the small houses of their employees. Brewery-owned taverns and stores lined North Third Street, a principal shopping street, and dotted the corners of North Side neighborhoods.

Much of the North Side was within the "walking city" and outlying areas, particularly beyond North Avenue, did not experience substantial residential development until after electric streetcars were built in the late 1890s, providing land speculators with a new market of commuters for whom to lay out large tracts of lots. Many of the new residential subdivisions then attracted the growing numbers of Polish and German immigrants, continuing the North Side ethnic pattern established in the 1850s. On the North Side, like the Near South Side, Polish home building associations were established to aid Polish immigrants in owning their own homes.

Comstock Hill/Uihlein Hill. A portion of the high ridge between W. Walnut, W. Cherry, N. 5th and N. 3rd was designated in 1835 as a courthouse square by Byron Kilbourn. When Solomon Juneau's proposed east side site was chosen instead, the small square off present-day Court Street remained undeveloped, eventually becoming the playground of the old Humboldt School built in 1876 and later replaced by the Fourth Street School. In 1851, Cicero Comstock built his mansion and rotary spade factory between 4th and 5th on West Galena. The factory was situated in front of his elegant Italianate residence. Comstock Hill became known as Uihlein Hill, when Alfred and Henry Uihlein of the Schlitz Brewery built their mansions on its eastern edge along N. 5th and W. Galena Street. Despite the portentous beginnings, little from an earlier time survives on this North Side ridge. Only the Gothic Revival Style rectory of the Czechoslovakian St. John de Nepomuc Society built in 1859 remains. Other buildings on the hill built by the Society have been razed.

418-420 E. Garfield, c. 1880. A pair of brick cottages and a small frame cottage on Milwaukee's North Side are representative of the scale of nineteenth century cottage-building throughout the city.

The North Side is a cross-section of the building types and styles that characterize the city as a whole. Immigrants' cottages, brewers' mansions, tannery buildings, the routes of plank roads, and a now-covered canal are all to be found here. North Avenue was the city boundary line for many years. When named, North Avenue reflected the supposition that it would be the city's north limit. Historically, the brewery district which grew up along and north of Juneau Avenue was considered the boundary between the downtown and the North Side. North Twelfth Street, a horsecar and electric streetcar route, was another dividing line between the north and northwest sections of Milwaukee.

A fine collection of brick houses representative of the early Italianate Style are among the oldest buildings still remaining on the North Side. Situated on the bluffs east of Third Street, most were built between 1850 and 1860 for German or Yankee businessmen who worked at the brewing, tanning and milling businesses along the river. Small, two story brick houses of the same period are also concentrated in this area. A variety of one story cottages, often situated at the rear of larger houses, were built extensively in the area south of North Avenue. As noted in the section on immigrant house types, the North Side has a large collection of raised flats and rear or "alley" houses built by German and Polish immigrants. Although the quarters were often cramped, the small rear houses and raised houses are testament to the immigrants' desire to own their own homes. A concentration of raised flats and rear houses built by Poles can be observed between Humboldt Boulevard, Richards Street, Auer Street and North Avenue.

2376 N. 5th St., 1878.

527 W. Vine, ca. 1860. This unusual raised flat has an atypical limestone foundation and details such as six-paned windows which indicate an early date of construction.

The Near North Side's neighborhoods built on the hills overlooking the city are evidence of the close connection between home and workplace. Excellent views of the river were shared by all income groups. Representative of the mix of managers' and workers' homes is the area east of N. Third Street and between North, Walnut and Hubbard. The flour mills of the nearby river and the tanneries and breweries of the area provided employment for many residents. Although much of the area was platted in the 1850s as part of the 47-square block area known as Sherman's Addition, residential construction did not begin in earnest until after the Civil War.

The North First Street residential area, extending from approximately Clarke to North Streets, was an enclave of upper income residents, including some of the city's leading German businessmen and professionals. Many of the fine houses of First Street were designed by well-known German architectural firms such as Uehling and Linde.

2463 N. First Street, c. 1893. Designed by John Roth Jr. for Charles Stolper, president of the Stolper Cooperage Company, this three story house has an elaborate corner tower with swag and garland frieze, and a third story open porch.

Hicks Heights. Hicks Heights, between Hadley and Locust on First Street, was advertised in 1923 as the "healthiest spot in Milwaukee." As planned, Hicks Heights incorporated a cul-de-sac design with a small park. The realtor, Louis Hicks, provided house plans to buyers of lots. Hicks Heights was situated on the farm property which formerly belonged to Daniel Richards (1808-1877).

Duplexes, 2700 block N. Weil

Humboldt Avenue, east of the Milwaukee River, gives way to Humboldt Boulevard at North Avenue, west of the river. Humboldt Boulevard once intersected the small village of Humboldt, and takes its name from that settlement. In the 1870s, the portion between North Avenue and Locust Street was the site of summer recreation for businessmen such as Adolph Meinecke and John Alcott who built handsome summer homes along the Milwaukee River, which parallels the Boulevard. Permanent residents of Humboldt Boulevard did not arrive until the end of the century, however. The first residences were built by prosperous Germans, who were succeeded by Poles. Although the Boulevard is the site of many duplexes and bungalows built in the first decades of the twentieth century, a few small cottages are evidence of the time when Humboldt abutted the western slope of the river; the unusual Octagon house on Gordon Place is likely a remnant from the early recreational period of the Humboldt area's history.

John F. Burka House, 2435-37 N. Humboldt Boulevard, 1906. The first Pole to build a house on Humboldt, Burka later moved his family's earlier frame cottage to the rear of the lot.

Cornice detail, North Third Street.

North Third Street. The end of the Old Green Bay Trail and the Green Bay Plank Road, North Third is one of the oldest commercial areas in the city. Throughout the nineteenth century, its stores and shops served the German community. Architecturally, North Third has one of the best concentrations of early commercial buildings, including fine brick Italianate examples.

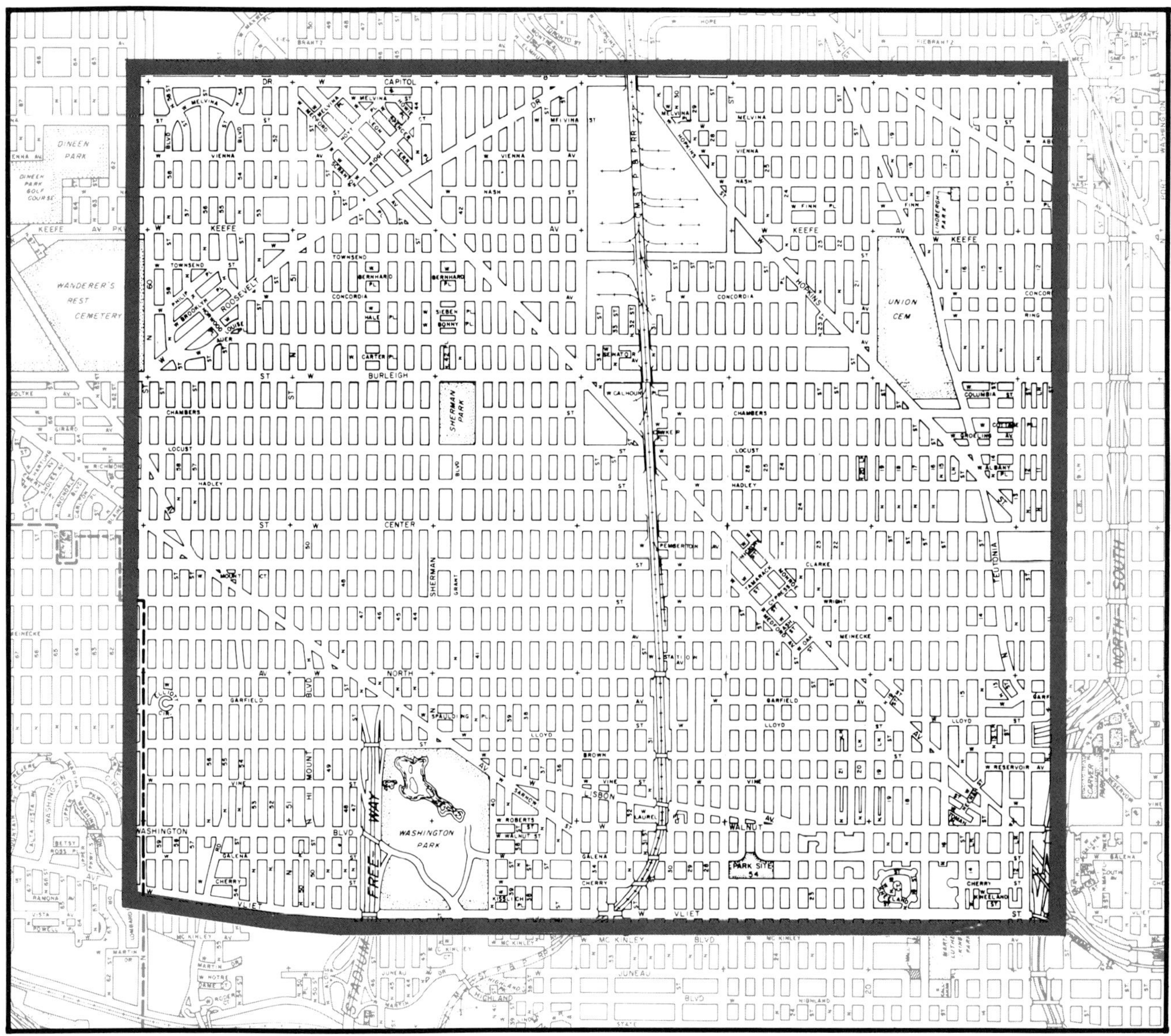

Northwest Side

Northwest Side

Responding to the waves of nineteenth century immigration, Milwaukee expanded its boundaries in all directions. Nowhere was this more evident than to the northwest. Traditionally, the wards which lay west of North Twelfth Street and north of Vliet Street were considered the northwest sector of the city.[1] In one of its last bursts of pre-World War II annexations, Milwaukee extended its lines to Capitol Drive on the north and North Sixtieth Street to the west.[2] It is within these boundaries — North Twelfth Street, Vliet Street, Capitol Drive, and North Sixtieth Street — that the northwestern part of the city was built prior to World War II. Beyond this area is the post-World War II city, which still contains significant pioneer settlements as well as contemporary developments. These peripheral sites are also included in this description of the Northwest Side.

Teutonia Ave. and N. Twelfth St.

The Northwest Side is defined only by a repetitive street system and has no boundaries created by natural features. In plan, it is a tidy, uniform grid broken only by the radiating avenues of the former pioneer plank and post roads. A tour of Meinecke Street from east to west illustrates the generational changes and growth of the area. Starting at North Twelfth Street, one immediately crosses Teutonia Avenue, originally the New Fond du Lac Plank Road. One of the early plank routes in Milwaukee County, Teutonia is dotted with reminders of post-Civil War commercial activity.[3] Here one finds the three-bay, cream brick and frame structures embellished with Italianate details which are exceptional buildings, not found in such concentration in other parts of the city. These served farmers and travelers with blacksmithing, provisions, and refreshment.[4]

Moving westward, the neighborhoods are comprised of compact duplexes and frame cottages which focus on the corner store, brewery, tavern, and ethnic church. For the predominantly German residents, the places of all daily activities had to be easily accessible by foot. Although the blocks are fairly uniform in character, a variety of Queen Anne and Georgian Revival Style architectural treatments diversify the area. These houses were sited as close to the front of the lot as the building would permit. This allowed a second or "alley" house to be built at the rear. This practice was not regulated until 1914 when the amended City Code established setbacks for multi-dwellings on a single site.[5]

Continuing west, the next noticeable change in the street grid is Fond du Lac Avenue, one of the three plank roads routed to the city of Fond du Lac. A small cluster of nearly square blocks run parallel to the avenue.[6] Fond du Lac Avenue marks the edge of the streetcar suburbs. From Fond du Lac Avenue to Grant Boulevard, the house forms remain the same: duplexes and larger frame single family houses. On these blocks, the corner commercial activity disappears and commercial strip development begins. In contrast to the eastern sections of the Northwest Side, residences sited here are set back from the street creating a more open street view.

1917 N. Nineteenth St. Small wood-frame cottages such as these were built in the earliest urbanized sections on the Northwest Side, near the old plank roads. Most date from the 1870s and 1880s.

The North Thirty-first Street industrial corridor marks an abrupt change in land use patterns. It divides the streetcar and auto era suburbs and reflects the economic base which shaped the area's residential and commercial character. The industries of the Thirty-first Street corridor provided area residents with a source of employment which was, importantly, within walking distance.

Approaching Grant Boulevard, the architectural character alters. The rows of gable and hipped-roofed houses give way to blocks of more stylish, individualized Georgian Revival designs. Palladian windows and shinglework motifs evidence careful craftsmanship. The familiar alley house has been replaced by the garage, often built three to five years after the construction of the house.

The suburban subdivision of the automobile era stretches from Grant Boulevard to North Sixtieth Street (present city limits). This area is characterized by spacious lots, fewer homes per block, and landscaped boulevards connecting parks and parkways. Period Revival houses and well-crafted bungalows line the streets of this completely residential subdivision.

Lisbon Avenue, another former plank road, is the last road to break the prevailing street grid. It is lined with commercial strip development, dating from the late 1890s.

Wauwatosa Township in 1876, showing a portion of the rural Northwest Side west of N. Thirty-fifth St. From the 1876 *Historical Atlas of Milwaukee County*.

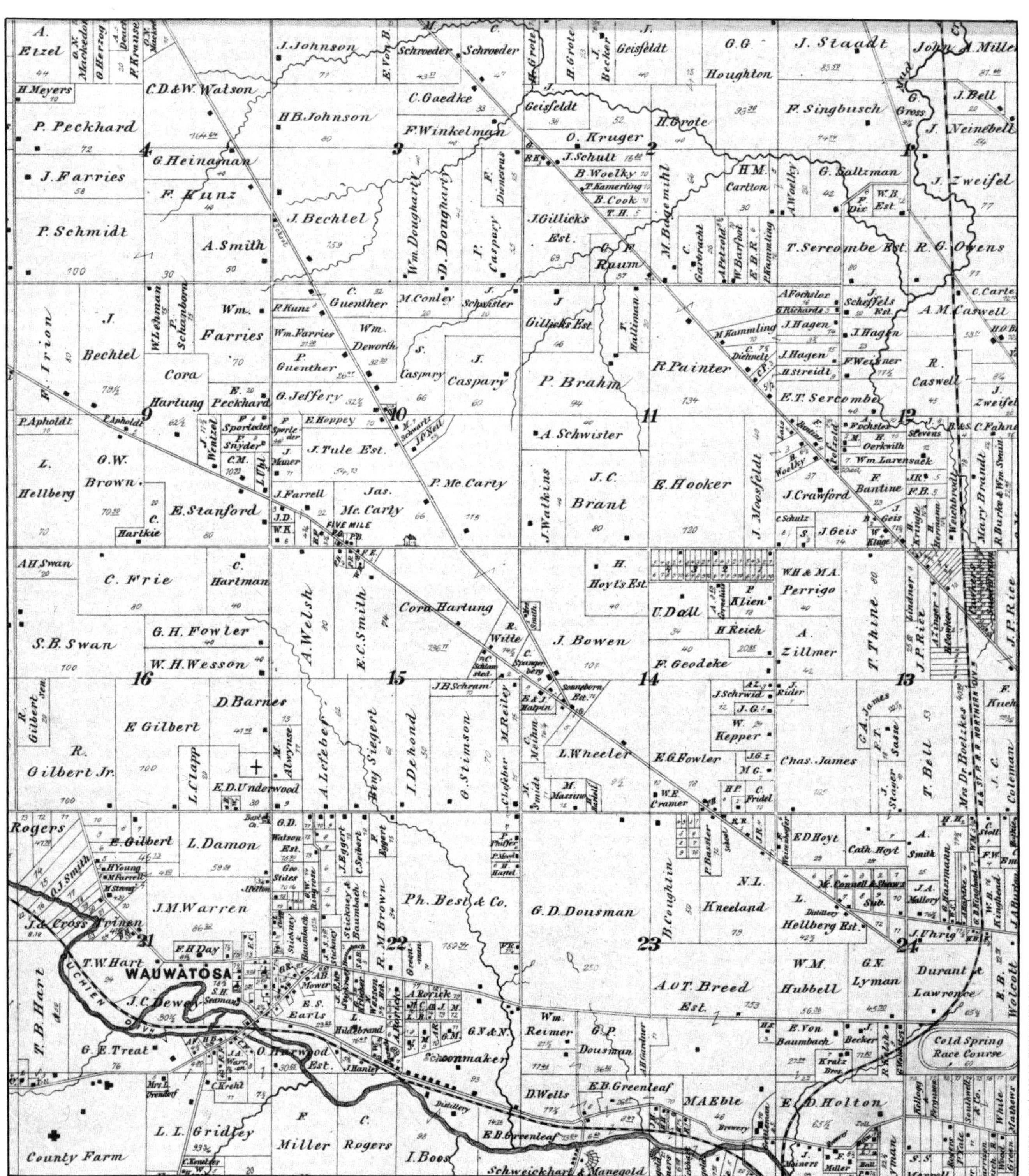

State Historical Society of Wisconsin

Early Development

Much of the Northwest Side is comprised of lands formerly belonging to the towns of Granville and Wauwatosa. Milwaukee County, established in 1834, carved large sections of land into civil, corporate towns.[8] Settlement was checked in parts of Granville and Wauwatosa because the Federal government granted vast tracts of land to the Milwaukee Railroad and Rock River Canal Company in 1838 for canal construction. The canal company filed bankruptcy in 1844-45 and the land grant holdings were then turned over to the Wisconsin Territorial government for public sale.[9]

Proposals were made during this time for the construction of a network of plank, post, military, and charcoal roads connecting Milwaukee County with the surrounding region. Authorization to levy taxes for road and bridge building was given in 1845 to a county board of supervisors. However, the privately-funded plank road proved to be the most popular "improvement" in the 1840s and 1850s. Financing was largely by stock company subscription.[10] By 1860, plank roads radiated to various points of the state. Many of their original routes are still evident today. Where a plank road crossed a north-south intersection, development of schools, churches, post stations, and toll stops occurred. Rural settlement was either on or within close proximity to the route. This land development pattern later stimulated the subdivisions of land companies and real estate agents. Today, none of these functionally named post stations and toll stops — "10 Mile House at Wattsville", "Post Office", "Schwartzburg Station", and "Williamsburg"[11] remain.

A few structures survive on the Northwest Side from the period of early agricultural settlement prior to the Civil War. This small collection of farmsteads and rural estates exhibit representative architectural styles popular from 1850 to 1890.

Franz Joseph Uhrig House, 1727 N. Thirty-fourth St. Uhrig, a St. Louis brewer, selected a twenty-acre site at the corner of Western Ave. (now N. Thirty-fifth St.) and the Lisbon Plank Road (now Lisbon Ave.) for his summer country home. In 1851, his "Villa Uhrig" was completed. Designed after his Italianate residence in St. Louis, it is constructed of local cream brick.

Samuel Luscombe House, 7709 W. Lisbon Ave., 1855. In addition to modest farmsteads, larger rural estates were also built along the plank roads. This twin-pavilioned Italian Villa is constructed of cream bricks probably burned at a nearby kiln. The original owner, Samuel D. Luscombe of Massachusetts, was a manufacturer of wooden tubs and pails, and was later a lumber dealer. Two subsequent owners, James Stewart and Edward Sandford, were captains of Great Lakes merchant vessels.

State Historical Society of Wisconsin

FARM RESIDENCE OF **EDWARD STANFORD ESQ.** WAUWATOSA TP. MILWAUKEE CO. WIS.

Residential Development

Initiated by land companies and site developers, residential development of the Northwest Side occurred in a leap-frog pattern. The topography of the area was a flat rolling plain with few marshes, swamps, or low spots. Developers had no trouble in securing buyers or obtaining the extension of municipal services to this well-drained, desirable building area.[12]

The original 1856 grid extended to North Twelfth Street, and beyond this line the land companies held small to medium-sized tracts averaging ten to twenty acres. Land company holdings were largely along the plank roads and were either platted by the company, or in most cases, sold to a site developer for subdivision. As the city extended its corporate boundaries, the land companies immediately grabbed peripheral tracts for speculation and resold them to the site developer. To ensure that block size, street width, and street orientation would be uniform, the Milwaukee City Council enacted a subdivision code in 1873 to prevent a repetition of the Juneautown/Kilbourntown incident of off-angle streets and irregular blocks.[13] The "Philadelphia System" of house numbering was also instituted so that each block would begin on the hundred.[14]

In the late nineteenth century, the city attracted a large number of foundries and metal fabricating operations. Because sufficient land was not available, these new industries generally chose to decentralize from the older job centers in the harbor area, Old Third Ward, and along the upper Milwaukee River at the base of Humboldt Avenue. The North Thirty-first Street railroad corridor provided excellent industrial sites northwest of the city. Foundries, food processing firms, and a large number of building materials manufacturers, including paint, planing mills, and sash and door companies located here between 1880 and 1910.[15]

Construction of electric streetcar lines paralleled industrial development on the Northwest Side. From 1880 to 1890, routes were extended to the eastern edge of the area and a more extensive network was built during the early twentieth century creating major arterials along Fond du Lac Avenue, Vliet Street, Walnut Street, North Avenue, Hopkins Avenue and North Thirty-fifth Street.[16]

German immigrants came to the Northwest Side in great numbers in the "second wave" after the Civil War. They were absorbed quickly by the city's new industries. Among them were a large number of builders, artisans, and craftsmen whose work is evident throughout the area and the city. The German immigrants adapted building plans to the narrow, long lots in constructing their residences, shops, and churches. The next generation was often employed in supervisory and professional occupations, and lived in close proximity to the original homesite.[17]

Bordering on the eastern edge of the Northwest Side, along North Thirteenth Street was one of the immigrant neighborhoods of Russian-Polish Jews. Having fled the ghettos of Eastern Europe and Russia during the 1890s, they were generally unskilled workers who worked as itinerant peddlers and rag dealers. Many found later success as merchants, skilled tradesmen, professionals and scholars in Milwaukee. Of the rich culture which once existed in this Jewish neighborhood, the only remaining physical example is the former synagogue, B'nai Jacob, located at 1930 North Thirteenth Street. As this immigrant group prospered, they moved to new home locations along and near Grant and Sherman Boulevards.[18]

1930 N. Thirteenth St., 1886. Originally built for a German Lutheran congregation, this small frame church subsequently housed Congregation B'nai Jacob in the early twentieth century and is now owned by Bethany Church of God and Christ. The steeple has been removed.

Duplex, 2065-67 N. Twenty-eighth St., 1899. A variation of the standard duplex form, this clapboard and shingle house has an intersecting gable plan instead of the traditional single-gable. Pressed wood swags and garlands decorate the broad frieze of the gable. A duplex of this size left little of the thirty foot wide lot for a yard. Milwaukee architect F. W. Andree designed the house for Charles Ehlert, a real estate agent.

Duplexes

The duplex or double flat was an attractive house type which adapted easily to the long, narrow lots on the Northwest Side. By placing one unit atop the other, the real estate developer or speculative builder achieved maximum use of each parcel. The homeowner then also had a ready second income to assist the financing of his investment. Furthermore, the depth of the lot afforded the opportunity to place the house towards the front and build a second, or "alley" house behind.

Because of the profuse construction of duplexes within the 1910 northwest wards, the duplex has been identified in Milwaukee as a traditional housing form. This proliferation of the duplex parallels a second wave of streetcar suburbs and early commercial strip development as seen in the Northwest Side.[19] Duplexes of the early twentieth century were generally larger and exhibited craftsman-like details in their architecture. The lots were widened to forty-five feet, resulting in fewer dwellings to the block. With the practice of siting the house at the center of the lot, the streetscape evolved into a more open suburban environment. The duplex on the Northwest Side was usually of frame or brick construction with clapboard cladding. A few, however, were constructed of cinder blocks, or cut stone.

Duplexes, Northwest Side.

Bungalows

The tract bungalow was built with the enthusiasm of the earlier duplex, and both house types offered economical home ownership. Emerging in the mid-1920s as the preferred housing type, the bungalow was built extensively in an area of the Northwest Side north of Keefe Avenue and west of Sherman Boulevard. Lacking unique stylistic elements, the Northwest Side bungalow was usually built as a regular gable or jerkinhead-gable cottage of one and one-half stories. Constructed by speculative builders, the bungalows stretched for blocks. Walter Truettner, a key figure in bungalow construction, billed himself as the "Bungalow Man" in local newspapers, and his work is seen throughout the Northwest Side.[20]

Bungalow, 2357 N. Forty-sixth St., 1919.

Automobile-Era Subdivisions

City officials were aware of the need for better than average homesites for the rising middle classes of the post-World War I economy. Landscaped boulevards and parkways had been set aside since 1896.[21] As part of the park system, these streets attracted the finest examples of residential architecture yet found in Milwaukee. Sherman and Washington Boulevards were declared in 1914, with the code amended in 1935, to include Hi Mount, Grant, Sarnow, Fifty-first, Forty-seventh, and Sixtieth Streets.[22] To draw home builders to this area, real estate agents created attractive developments with wide lots, ample setbacks, and full improvements. The widely advertised Washington Park subdivisions were a group of five developments (Residence Park, platted 1914; Jackson Park, platted 1910; Jefferson Heights, platted 1920; Keystone, platted 1917; and Boulevard Park, platted 1909-1914), which skillfully used the boulevard designations.[23]

The predominant architectural styles of the early auto-era suburbs in the Northwest Side are the fully-developed Bungalow and the period revival cottage. Unlike the tract bungalow, the larger Bungalow Style house was influenced by Prairie School and oriental elements, and displays an enrichment of form and detail. Characteristically, the bungalow is sited on a larger lot than the Northwest Side duplex.

The period revival cottage of these areas includes small houses with Georgian Revival, English Tudor, Spanish Colonial, and Italian Renaissance designs. The period revival houses were well-crafted inside and out, with attention to historical antecedents. A considerable number were built between 1915 and 1940 and were attractive to middle income families, many of whom had been raised in a neighboring duplex. Local materials are evident with extensive use of Lannon stone veneer from the Waukesha quarries. The finest examples of the Period Revival Cottages line the various boulevards in the area, including Washington, Grant, and Hi Mount.

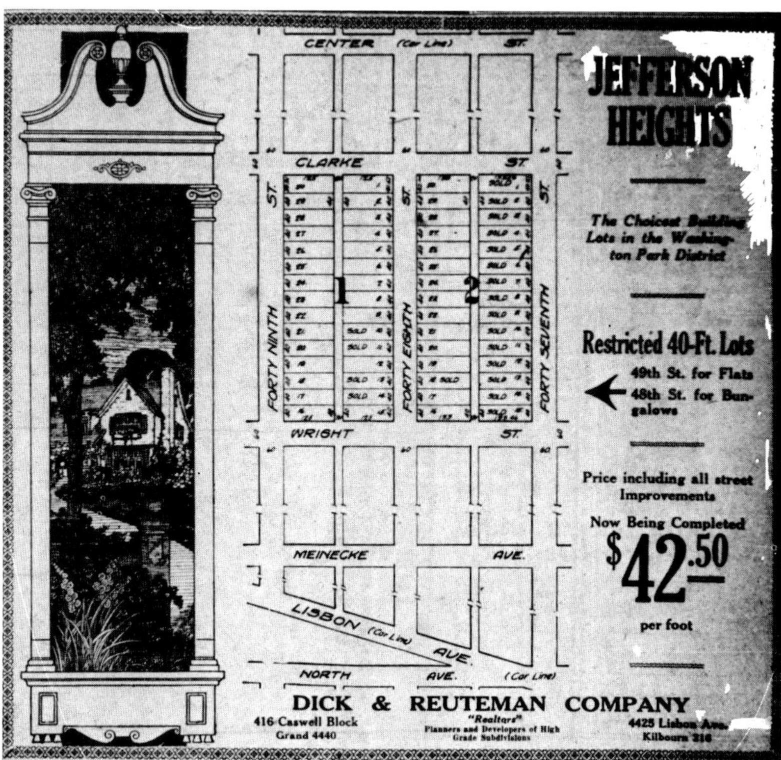

Newspaper advertisement for Jefferson Heights, in the *Milwaukee Journal,* May 14, 1922.

Innovative Projects on the Northwest Side

Near the periphery of the Northwest Side are two developments which show experimentation in the design of living environments and mass-produced housing prior to World War II: Garden Homes and The Parklawn Public Housing Project.

Garden Homes

Garden Homes was the first American cooperative housing built under an agreement between a municipality and its residents. It also represented the first attempt by a municipality to aid in housing a growing work force. Several conceptual precedents for the project existed in English Garden City projects, several model private sector efforts, and at least one American public sector program.

Garden Homes, photograph 1981.

Inspired in part by the thinking of Ebenezer Howard and his followers, who advocated the decentralization of the city by creating self-sufficient communities outside the city, the idea for the project was also nurtured by Milwaukee's consultants' reports between 1915 to 1920. City planner Werner Hegemann was familiar with the model housing erected by English industrialists and with the new designs that were emerging from the Continent. He described some of these projects in his report *City Planning for Milwaukee* (1916). Arthur Comey, the city's consultant on the drafting of a zoning ordinance, was also the staff planner for the Massachusetts Housing Commission which had made several experiments in industrial housing in Lowell. Comey had also been a planner of various privately funded garden city-inspired projects including Billerica Garden Suburb (in collaboration with Warren H. Manning).

In 1920, Mayor Daniel Hoan appointed the City's Housing Commission which endorsed the work in Massachusetts and initiated the design and construction of Garden Homes. The local architect of the project was William Schuchardt, a commission appointee. Schuchardt provided basic five and six room plans executed in stucco. The modest houses were sited on small, but adequate yards affording light and air to all sides of the dwelling. Located on a twenty-nine acre site at the intersection of Teutonia and Atkinson Avenues, the houses went into construction in September, 1921. By 1923, one hundred five single family homes, ten duplexes and one apartment building were completed. Most were successfully leased to families. By 1925, dissatisfaction with the lease arrangement began to surface. Due to a misunderstanding of the benefit assessment tax for street improvements, the residents thought that the original price per housing unit included street improvements. The residents subsequently petitioned for individual ownership. By 1927, all the units were sold and the Garden Homes Corporation was liquidated.[24]

Parklawn

A similar development to the Garden Homes was the Parklawn Public Housing Project of the WPA. One of several constructed nationally during the 1930s, it was endorsed by the administration of Mayor Daniel Hoan. A vacant site at Hope Avenue between Sherman Boulevard and North Forty-seventh Street was selected because it did not involve condemnation of private property.

The project was designed by the Allied Architects of Milwaukee, an association that represented the city's finest architects, Gerrit J. de Gelleke, principal; Peter Brust; A. C. Eschweiler; Herbert Tullgren; R. A. Messmer; and landscape architect, Phelps Wyman. A total of sixty-four fireproof buildings were built, which provided 518 units of three, four and five room rentals. It is still owned and leased by the Housing Authority of the City of Milwaukee.[25]

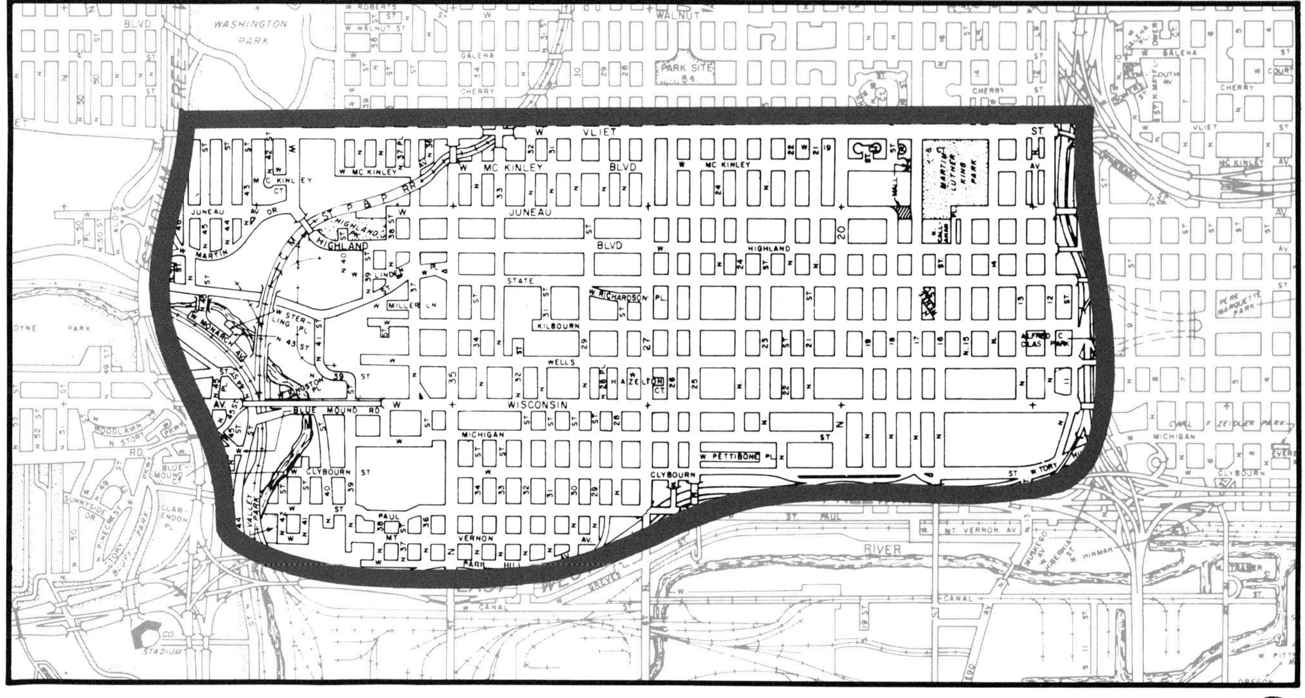

West Side

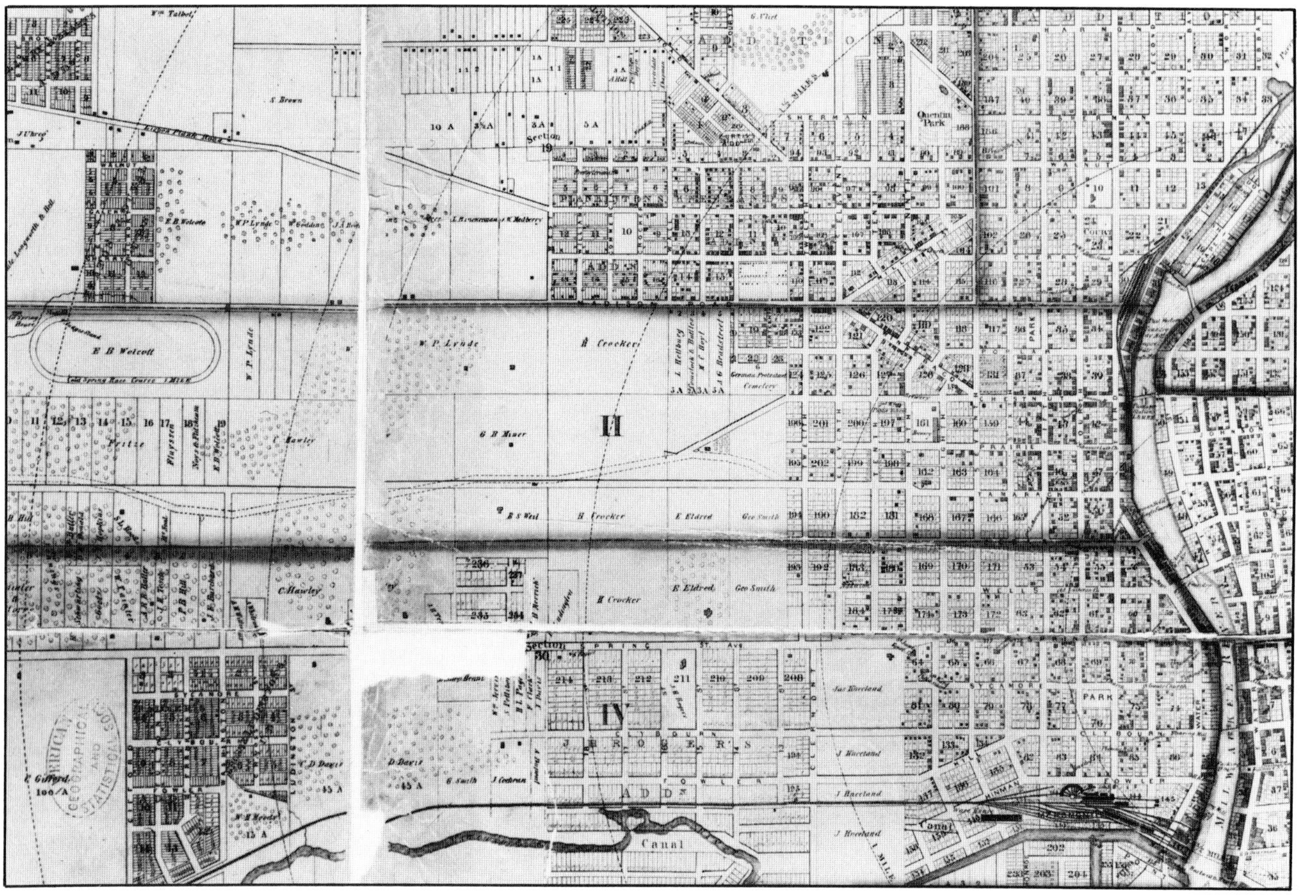

American Geographical and Statistical Society

West Side

Originally, the West Side of Milwaukee was defined as the land area west of the Milwaukee River and north of the Menomonee Valley. Guide books, atlases, and souvenir booklets of the nineteenth century confirm this definition. Late in the nineteenth century, the West Side's boundaries began at the western edge of the expanding central business district. Highways constructed in the 1960s now define this area of town. Expressways ring the West Side: I-43 on the east (adjacent to North Eleventh Street); I-94 on the south (following the northern rim of the Menomonee Valley); and the Stadium freeway on the west (along the Upper Menomonee Valley). Vliet Street is the northern boundary of the West Side, and the beginning of the Northwest suburbs.

The West Side was originally forested land broken only by Indian trails and grassy meadows. Bluffs along the edge of the Menomonee River Valley offered commanding views to the south and east. Natural springs provided water for early settlers.[1] Extensive grading prior to the construction of roads and houses has leveled the original irregular terrain.

Early Development

During the period of its pioneer settlement, the rural landscape of the West Side was interrupted by very few roads. The first, the Watertown Plank and the Wauwatosa Plank were constructed in the 1840s. Their winding east-west routes roughly followed the direction of present-day State Street and Vliet Street West of Thirty-fifth Street. The old Watertown Plank Road still pursues its original route along State Street. Spring Street (later Grand and now West Wisconsin Avenue), was a third major corridor. Smaller lanes and paths connected the first farmhouses scattered along these early roads. By the late 1850s, farming activity began to decline on the near-western fringes of the growing city. North of Wisconsin Avenue, the land was divided into rectangular tracts of various sizes, replacing irregular farm parcels.[2] Those who accumulated wealth during the pioneer period built their residences in this area on large tracts of land. Some of these landowners included businessmen such as Cyrus Hawley and William P. Lynde, and civic leader R. R. Butler, who served as mayor of Milwaukee. Their property lay between what is now North Twentieth and North Thirteenth Streets, and along Wisconsin Avenue, Wells Street, and Juneau Avenue.[3]

Early manufacturing activity on the West Side, which preceded the annexation and urbanization of the area, was located in the Upper Menomonee Valley. The breweries along the river banks played an important part in establishing Milwaukee as a major beer capitol in the world. The Plank Road Brewery, situated along the Watertown Plank Road, was the first brewery established in the Upper Menomonee Valley. Organized in 1848 by Charles Best (who also founded the Pabst Brewing Company), it was one of the pioneer breweries in Milwaukee. Another brewery, A. Gettleman Brewing Company, was located nearby and founded in 1854. The limestone bluffs along the valley conveniently provided caves for summer storage of the breweries' beer.[4]

Best went bankrupt in 1854 and Frederick Miller purchased the Plank Road Brewery in the following year. Miller enlarged the facilities, extending the caves to a depth of 600 feet. The Miller Beer Gardens were opened in 1878 and became a popular gathering place for Milwaukeeans. Situated on the bluffs above the brewery, the gardens offered an unsurpassed view of the Menomonee River Valley. In 1888, when the brewery's name was changed to the Menomonee Valley Brewery, it had reached an unprecedented production of 80,000 barrels a year. In that same year, a spur of the Chicago, Milwaukee, and St. Paul Railroad was completed to the brewery, enabling national distribution of the product.[5]

Sylvester Pettibone House, 2051 W. Wisconsin Ave. Of the considerable number of properties shown on the 1858 map, very few remain on the West Side. Sylvester Pettibone, farmer and contractor, built this Italianate house in the early 1850s along what was then Spring Street. In its original form, the house was a three-bay block constructed of cream brick, with a hip roof, belvedere, and full porch. The east wing, added in the 1870s, maintained the character of the original design. Although remodellings in the early twentieth century dramatically changed its appearance, the Pettibone residence remains similar in form, materials, and style to pre-Civil War houses built at the edge of the city.

opposite
Milwaukee's West and Northwest Sides, 1858. Plank roads, newly-platted streets, existing houses, and forested land are drawn in detail on H. F. Walling's "Illustrated Historical Atlas Map of Milwaukee and Environs."

Milwaukee Co. Historical Society

Frederick Miller's Plank Road Brewery, photograph c. 1880.

Miller died in 1888, leaving control of the business to his three sons and son-in-law. They reorganized the brewery in 1889 under the name of the Frederick Miller Brewing Company. The brewery continued to grow and was purchased in 1961 by A. Gettleman Brewing Company. Today, Miller Brewing is owned by the Phillip Morris Company and is one of the national leaders of the brewing industry. Still operating at its original site in the Upper Menomonee Valley, at 4000 West State Street, the brewery's facilities include an extensive array of brew houses, malt storage buildings, silos, and warehouses.[6]

Urbanization

The urbanization of the West Side resulted from the expansion of the city center and economic growth in the Menomonee Valley. The Kilbourntown plat of 1836 encompassed lands only as far west as North Thirteenth Street (North of Vliet Street) and North Ninth Street (south of Vliet). By 1846, the corporate limits had extended west to Twenty-seventh Street. Finch's Subdivision, on the present site of Marquette University, was the only outlying residential tract platted at that time. Before 1876, areas had uniformly progressed to the western city limits at Twenty-seventh Street. The block and lot pattern repeated the established rectangular grid street layout of the earliest plats. Simultaneous to this urban expansion, peripheral tracts were sold for rural estates. On Spring Street (West Wisconsin Avenue), where several of these estates were built, the lot sizes continued to vary, deviating from the standardized layout of the rest of the West Side.

Very little residential development occurred west of Twenty-seventh Street between 1850 and 1870. After the city annexed lands between North Twenty-seventh Street and North Thirty-fifth Street in the 1880s, property was subdivided and the street grid pattern was continued. Because of larger-than-average sized building lots between Juneau Avenue and Wells Street, the blocks are large, deviating from the surrounding street pattern. The land west of North Thirty-fifth Street, between Vliet Street and the Menomonee Valley, was part of the Town of Wauwatosa until the early twentieth century. Open tracts of various sizes mixed with platted areas in the 1880s and 1890s. The Chicago, Milwaukee, and St. Paul Railway owned large parcels of land adjacent to rail corridors in the Menomonee Valley. The area was annexed to the City of Milwaukee between 1900 and 1920.[7]

The development of the West Side provided the city with some of its most architecturally distinguished neighborhoods. West Side neighborhoods have a variety of building types and architectural styles, and reflect the diverse ethnic origins and socio-economic levels of their inhabitants.

Lower, middle and upper income groups all built homes on the heterogeneous West Side. Likewise, the area attracted a mixture of ethnic groups. In the mid-nineteenth century, the West Side was populated by an almost equal number of Americans, Irish, and Germans, with British immigrants forming a smaller percentage of the total. Later in the nineteenth century, the Germans settled extensively on the West Side. German workers, employed in processing industries such as tanning, brewing, and meat packing, built modest cottages near their jobs in the Menomonee River Valley and in the Old Third Ward (east of the Milwaukee River and south of Wisconsin Avenue). Prosperous German businessmen and industrialists also selected the West Side for their homesites. After the Civil War, newcomers found the large lots and rural environment of the western edge of the city inviting. They built expensive homes around Concordia College and along major boulevards and avenues. Following the disastrous fire of 1892 in the Old Third Ward, the Irish settled themselves in the Merrill Park area south of Wisconsin Avenue between North

Thomas D. Cook Double House, 853 N. Seventeenth St., 1875. Milwaukee architect Edward T. Mix designed this Victorian Italianate double house for Thomas Cook, a stone merchant.

Christopher H. Starke-Charles and Matilda Baerwald House, 1327 W. Kilbourn Ave., 1897. Most Kilbourn Ave. residences were built in the 1880s and 1890s. The largest of the period are concentrated in the 1300 and 1400 blocks. Originally the homes of business executives and merchants of primarily German origin, the architecture is eclectic. Queen Anne and Romanesque styles are interspersed with houses influenced by German and Flemish architecture.

Twenty-seventh and North Thirty-fifth Streets. The Irish, predominantly semi-skilled and unskilled workers, were employed in the railroad car shops located in the Menomonee Valley.[8]

Kilbourn Avenue

Kilbourn Avenue is an east-west avenue which bisects the West Side. Originally called Cedar Street, Kilbourn Avenue was the site of a number of high-styled, mid- to late-nineteenth century residences. Kilbourn Avenue was probably regarded as an attractive address since Wells Street to the south was a streetcar line and State Street to the north connected with the Watertown Plank Road. Today, surrounding arterials have minimized traffic on Kilbourn Avenue. The construction of apartment houses, hospital expansion, and Marquette University development has reduced the area's residences to a handful. These are situated in clusters, with ornate, larger homes on Kilbourn and simpler cottages on the side streets.

The earliest extant homes in the Kilbourn area date from the 1870s, and nearly all are of masonry construction. The first building code of 1888 established limits for fireproof construction. According to the code, all non-brick or non-masonry covered buildings on the West Side were supposed to have been removed from the area bounded by State Street to Wisconsin Avenue west to North Twenty-fourth Street. New construction was subject to the same limitations.[9] By 1914, the west limits had moved eastward to North Twelfth Street as city officials realized that heavy urbanization would not stretch so far west.[10]

Highland Boulevard

Highland Boulevard gained prominence in the late nineteenth century as a residential street comprised of native and second-generation wealthy German industrialists and businessmen, such as brewer, Fred Miller; hardware dealer, F. C. Pritzlaff; sausage maker, Fred Usinger; and metal fabricator, William Geuder. Created in 1896 by the Common Council as the first public parkway, Highland Boulevard extended from Washington Ave-

Joseph B. Kalvelage House, 2432 W. Kilbourn Ave., 1898. Farther west on Kilbourn Avenue is a large, formal German Baroque Revival house, a showcase of late Victorian decorative arts. Milwaukee architect Otto Strack, born and trained in Germany, designed the pressed tan brick structure, locally referred to as "Kalvelage Schloss." The major features of the facade are a German parapet-gabled central pavilion, and an entrance porch decorated with half-figure atlantes of terra cotta.

Prairie Ave., later Highland Blvd., prior to mansion-building, photograph c. 1885.

Highland Blvd. at the turn of the century. These Romanesque-influenced stone mansions, recently completed at the time of this photograph, have been replaced by apartment buildings.

Highland Blvd. today.

nue (North Twenty-seventh Street) to Western Avenue (North Thirty-fifth Street). An esplanade forty feet wide, it was minimally landscaped with grass and trees.[11] Locally referred to as "Sauerkraut Boulevard", the area was almost exclusively comprised of Germans.

Highland Boulevard and the surrounding area was annexed by the city in 1885. Some development preceded its designation as a boulevard.[12] The first significant building period occurred in the late 1890s and continued to the beginning of World War I. Historical photos record an elegant street of mansions interspersed with smaller ornate homes similar to those on Kilbourn Avenue. Imagination must be used to visualize Highland's original appearance because only isolated architectural examples from the period remain. Redevelopment of the boulevard has occurred in the form of apartment buildings, offices and Concordia College expansion. Although Highland Boulevard was a prestigious address during the late nineteenth century, it was not an architectural rival to Grand or Prospect Avenues. Highland Boulevard mansions were variations of the Romanesque Revival, Classical Revival and English Tudor Styles of the period.

The smaller residences of Highland Boulevard were the homes of middle income merchants and business executives. Similar in scale, materials and design to those on Kilbourn Avenue, they incorporated a variety of Queen Anne and German Renaissance elements into their picturesque massing. The largest extant concentration on the Boulevard is in the 2900 and 3000 blocks. Typical of late nineteenth century eclectic architecture, these homes are of masonry construction with gabled or hipped roofs, and a profusion of facade ornamentation such as dormers, gables and turrets.

Concordia

Directly south of Highland Boulevard is the Concordia neighborhood. Platted in 1848 as Dousman's Subdivision, it originally included the land between what is now North Twenty-seventh Street and North Thirty-fifth Street, and the land between Juneau Avenue and Spring Street (West Wisconsin Avenue).[13] Over the succeeding fifty-five years, this tract was resubdivided into smaller plats which prompted different rates and patterns of development. Located between two exclusive residential streets (Highland Boulevard and West Wisconsin Avenue), Concordia was an affluent neighborhood of middle and upper income groups.

The Concordia area was annexed by the city as far as Kilbourn Avenue in 1874 and to Highland Boulevard in 1885.[14] Prior to intensive development in the 1890s, there were a few farms and some residential construction. Two early residences remain from the period when the only road through this area was the old Watertown Plank Road, now the approximate route of State Street.

The Concordia neighborhood attracted residential development in the 1880s. One impetus was the relocation of Concordia College from Ninth Street and Highland Avenue to the present site donated by philanthropic Germans on Highland Boulevard.[15] The college was founded by the Wisconsin Lutheran Synod in 1880, broke ground in 1881 at the State Street campus, and opened for classes in 1882.[16]

Wells Street and Kilbourn Avenue were the principal residential streets which attracted business and professional men largely of German descent as well as a number of Yankees and settlers from the eastern United States. The architecture, influenced by German Renaissance forms, also reflects the eclectic styles of the period, such as Queen Anne, Victorian Gothic and Romanesque. Wells and Kilbourn closely resembled the fabric of the old Kilbourn Avenue neighborhood, but had a considerable amount of frame construction. The housing was of average scale and its massing and design were highly picturesque. The residential development here, however, never reached the grandeur of Highland Boulevard or Grand

3130 W. Wells St., 1897. Charles C. Rogers, a grain commission merchant, was the original owner of this late Victorian Gothic house, with cream brick walls (now painted), steep pointed gables, and multiple projecting bays. John Booth and Fred Fribers are recorded as the builders.

Albert Baubletz House, 3019 W. Kilbourn Ave., 1894. One of several Queen Anne Style residences in the Concordia area, this asymmetrical, multigabled clapboard and shingle house was designed by architects Koch and Leopold.

Avenue. On the side streets intersecting Wells and Kilbourn, the houses were typical of late nineteenth century frame cottages and duplexes built throughout the city to house supervisory and skilled industrial workers.

Although a considerable number of the wealthier residents had carriage houses, and probably did not use public transportation, the Wells Street horsecar (and later trolley) line was an integral element in the growth of this neighborhood. Originally built to transport patrons to the Miller Beer Gardens, it ultimately gave the West Side residents direct access to the rest of the city.

The area between North Twenty-ninth and North Thirty-fourth Streets on Kilbourn and Wells retains the strongest visual image of how this neighborhood may have appeared originally. There are a number of excellent examples of early houses, and no two are similar. Collectively, they are among the finest examples of the late nineteenth century residential architecture in the city. The masonry examples at 3119 (1899) and 3209 West Wells (1891) and at 3033 West Kilbourn Avenue (1895) are high-style interpretations of the popular Germanic forms used by the local architects. Equally impressive are the Queen Anne frame houses at 2825 (1888) and 3019 West Kilbourn (1894) and at 3413 West Wells (1895). Of the frame examples, a unique residence at 936 North Thirty-first Street (1890) is one of Milwaukee's few examples of the Shingle Style.

North of Kilbourn along State Street, residential development occurred primarily after 1900. On State Street between North Twenty-seventh and North Twenty-ninth Street, there are large frame Queen Anne Style residences similar in age, scale, and material to those of Kilbourn Avenue and Wells Street.

Wisconsin Avenue

First known as Spring Street Road and renamed Grand Avenue in 1876, Wisconsin Avenue was a street of prestigious homes, beginning with the Alexander Mitchell Estate (1859) at 900 West Wisconsin Avenue and ending with the Henry Harnischfeger Mansion (1905) at 3424 West Wisconsin Avenue.[17] In architectural exuberance and social standing, its only rival was Prospect Avenue on the East Side. Central city expansion, however, has reduced the avenue to a shadow of its former appearance. Isolated examples remain which allude to the opulent past.

Development of Wisconsin Avenue began during the pioneer period of the city. In the earliest recollections, this route was a consistently used reference point when describing West Side locales. The avenue was planked in 1854 from the central business district to North Twelfth Street and paved to North Twenty-seventh Street (city limits) in 1877.[18]

Mansion building began about 1870 when Sherburn S. Merrill, Chicago, Milwaukee and St. Paul Railroad (Milwaukee Road) manager, built his elaborate estate on the south side of what is now West Wisconsin Avenue and North Thirty-third Street.[19] Realizing Spring Street was an inappropriate name for an avenue of aspiring proportions, Merrill advocated that the street name be changed to Grand Avenue. During the 1880s and 1890s an astonishing array of eclectic Victorian residences were built. These were the palaces of meat packers, industrial barons and financiers. The avenue was also known for its religious architecture which rivalled the churches built on the East Side's Yankee Hill District. Calvary Presbyterian, 935 West Wisconsin Avenue (1870), St. James Episcopal (1867) at 833 West Wisconsin Avenue and the Grand Avenue Congregational (1887), 2133 West Wisconsin Avenue, indicate the religious traditions of the early area residents.

Henry Harnischfeger House, 3424 W. Wisconsin Ave., 1905. Milwaukee architect Eugene R. Liebert, whose residential work often reflected the Germanic background of his clients, designed a German-influenced period house for Henry Harnischfeger, founder and president of the Harnischfeger Corp., manufacturers of large cranes and machinery. The brown brick facade terminates in a stepped gable with tile coping. The second-story porch is adorned with knights-in-armor, symbolic of the original owner's name, which means "armor polisher."

Merrill Park

Historically, Merrill Park was a neighborhood of industrial workers and tradesmen. It is named after Sherburn S. Merrill, an official in the Chicago, Milwaukee and St. Paul Railroad, who owned the land prior to subdivision. He platted the first section in 1883 between North Thirty-third and North Thirty-fifth Streets, St. Paul Avenue and Park Hill Avenue. In subsequent years, other additions were platted as "Merrill Park", which extended the subdivision from North Thirtieth to North Thirty-fifth Street and from West Clybourn Street to Canal Street. As the neighborhood developed, the area from Twenty-sixth to Thirty-ninth Streets from West Michigan Avenue to West Park Hill Avenue was also considered Merrill Park.

Residential development of Merrill Park occurred primarily between 1880 and 1910. During this period, Milwaukee was emerging as a center of heavy industrial equipment. The West Milwaukee Car Shops, located directly south of the neighborhood in the Menomonee Valley, opened its plant in 1880. With its close proximity to the valley and to the breweries on the old Watertown Plank Road, Merrill Park attracted a mixture of Germans, Irish and Yankees employed by these firms. The Irish were the largest single ethnic group in the neighborhood and dominated the area's political, social and religious affairs. They were generally laborers employed as switchmen, firemen and brakemen. However, the combined population of Germans and Yankees clearly outnumbered the Irish, and the Germans were skilled workers in the car shops' foundries and machine shops. As an area of ethnic diversity, Merrill Park was as Irish Catholic as it was German Lutheran and Methodist.[20]

The houses in Merrill Park are generally modest single family and duplex frame dwellings. The Queen Anne and Georgian Revival Styles are well-represented.

Merrill Park station of the Chicago, Milwaukee, and St. Paul Railway, photograph c. 1920.

State Historical Society of Wisconsin

Pigsville

Pigsville, to the west of Merrill Park, is probably Milwaukee's smallest distinguishable neighborhood. Developed at the same time as Merrill Park, Pigsville was an isolated section of Milwaukee. Houses were built along the narrow river basin of the Upper Menomonee Valley between North Thirty-ninth and North Forty-fourth Streets. The sharp bluffs which surround the neighborhood have retained the identity of Pigsville, while the Menomonee River divides the area into "west bank" and "east bank" and two distinct communities. The area was considered so isolated by the City of Milwaukee, that the residents of Pigsville continually petitioned for annexation, which finally occurred in 1925.

The derivation of the name Pigsville is suggested by several theories. It was presumed that George Pigg operated a stagecoach tavern in the area, but census reports reveal Pigg was a laborer living in the Third Ward who had moved to a farm in Sauk County by 1860. The Census records no other Piggs living in Milwaukee during the rest of the nineteenth century. Another popular story is that of a farmer by the name of Fries who had a farm under what is now the Wisconsin Avenue Viaduct where he raised more pigs than any other animal. The *Milwaukee Sentinel* first referred to the area as "Pigstown" in 1894 and by the early 1900s the area was commonly known as "Pigsville".

The two largest ethnic groups in Pigsville were the Germans who settled first, followed by the Slavs. There were also significant numbers of Croatians, Serbs, Czechs, Poles and Russians. Both banks were ethnically mixed with the Germans primarily in the northeast corner, and the Slavs in the southwest corner. In general, the people in Pigsville were laborers and tradesmen employed in the valley breweries, car shops and foundries.[21]

View of Pigsville, photograph c. 1940. Pigsville residences resembled the South Side with numerous raised basement houses and small cottages. Pigsville's abundant green space contributed to its small town flavor.

State Historical Society of Wisconsin

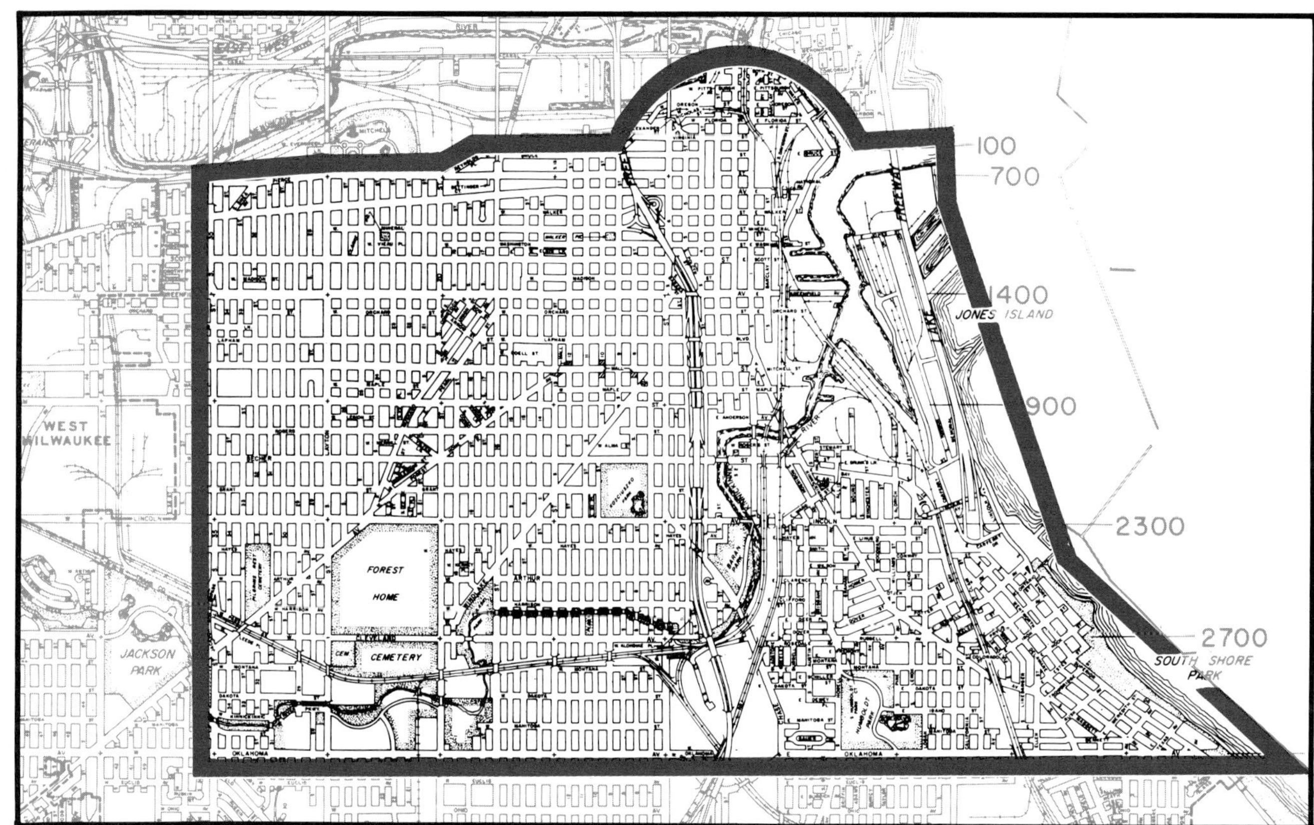
100
700
1400
JONES ISLAND
900
2300
2700
SOUTH SHORE PARK
WEST MILWAUKEE
JACKSON PARK
FOREST HOME
CEM.
CEMETERY
CLEVELAND
OKLAHOMA

South Side

Herman Wudtke Collection

Workers at Oberhauser's Blacksmith Shop, photograph c. 1900. Potter Ave. in Bay View.

Milwaukee's South Side is a diverse area of distinct neighborhoods and ethnic enclaves. Its historical landscape includes the farmsteads of pioneer settlers, one of the original three "villages" of Milwaukee, Walker's Point, and a former company town, Bay View.

The pre-settlement landscape of the South Side was composed of marsh and tamarack swamps along the riverbanks and streams; bluffs and ravines thickly vegetated with brush and trees; and forest and open prairie to the west. Remnants of Indian settlements were located at certain points along the Kinnickinnic River, which winds eastward through the middle of the South Side to the mouth of the Milwaukee River. "Indian Fields," in the vicinity of Forest Home Cemetery, covered almost a square mile of land, and was the site of extensive mound-building and agricultural activity. Corn was cultivated there by the Indians. Indian trails criss-crossed the South Side. Major routes were the Chicago Trail (incorporated into part of Kinnickinnic Avenue) and Mukwonago Trail (now West National Avenue), which led to Indian settlements in the Wisconsin interior along the Fox River.[1]

Historical Development

Earliest settlement on the South Side began in 1834 when George H. Walker, one of the original three proprietors of Milwaukee, staked his 160 acre claim and established a trading post on a finger of land south of the Milwaukee and Menomonee Rivers. This thin marsh-surrounded peninsula, which became known as Walker's Point, began at the Milwaukee River about midway between Pittsburgh and Oregon Streets and broadened in a southwest direction. The west side of what is now South Second street skirted bluffs ten to twenty-five feet high.[2] Walker's Point was the focus of South Side development prior to the Civil War, and has retained its name and identity to this day.

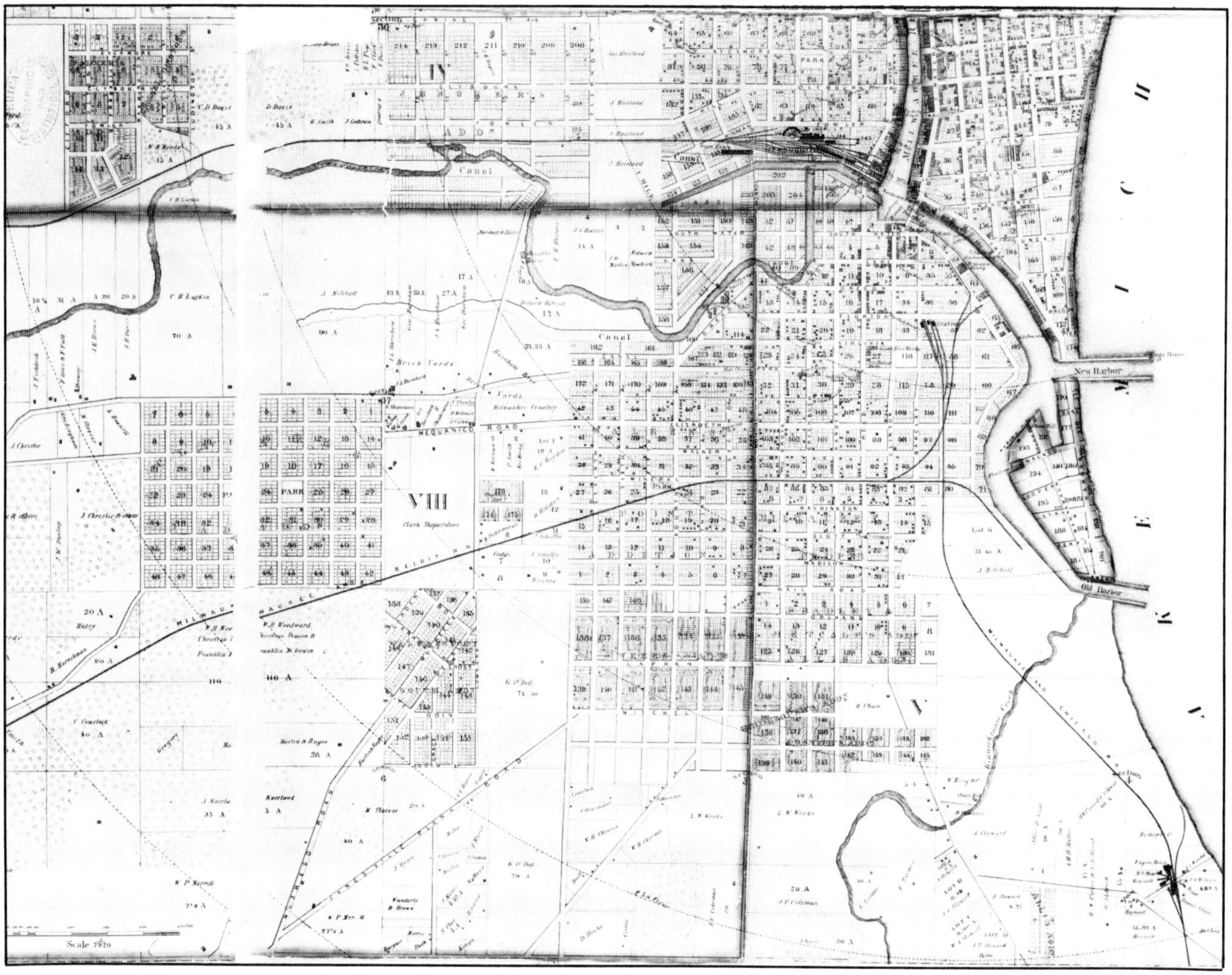

The South Side in 1858. From H. F. Walling's "Illustrated Historical Atlas Map of Milwaukee and Environs."

Morgan L. Burdick Farmhouse, 473 E. Waterford Ave. M. L. Burdick was one of Milwaukee County's first settlers, arriving in 1834 from Jefferson County, New York. In that year he staked a claim on a quarter-section of land, and in the late 1830s he returned to settle on the site. Burdick farmed the land, raising Praise-worthy apples and other produce, until his death in 1886. This small cream brick house, with segmental arch windows, is the only remaining structure of the early farmstead.

The first South Siders were Yankees, primarily from New York State and New England. Settlers who arrived in the 1830s included Horace Chase, John Ogden, Morgan L. Burdick, Joel Wilcox, Uriel B. Smith, George Wentworth, Russell Bennett, and Joseph Williams. Many streets on the South Side today bear their names, and a few of their houses remain. "Chase's Point," as Horace Chase's claim at the mouth of the Milwaukee River was called, was the informal headquarters for the Town of Lake, created in 1838, which originally encompassed all of the South Side except Walker's Point.[3]

By the 1840s small cabins and farmsteads dotted the South Side east of South Thirteenth Street and north of Lincoln Avenue. The settlers filled the marshes, graded the bluffs, and cleared the forests. Turnips, potatoes, oats, and rutabaga were among the first crops grown. At the same time, the South Side showed signs of early urbanization. George Walker filed the South Side plat, a gridiron street layout for Walker's Point, which was incorporated into Milwaukee in 1845. The next year a bridge was built over the Milwaukee River at Water Street, connecting the north and south sides of the city. The riverbanks near the bridge, known as Walker's Point Bridge, were gradually built up with warehouses, docks, and small retail businesses during the 1840s and 1850s. Dredging and maritime activities (such as shipbuilding, commercial fishing, and manufacturers and dealers in naval goods) altered the natural face of the South Side waterfront. Wolf and Davidson's Shipyard was established in 1858 at the mouth of the

Kinnickinnic River, becoming Milwaukee's largest shipbuilders by the 1870s.[4]

The growth of maritime-related occupations attracted Scandinavian immigrants to Walker's Point to work as seamen, ships' carpenters, and clerks for Great Lakes shipping firms. By the time of the Civil War, Norwegians, Danes, and Swedes settled on the South Side, organizing their community life around their Evangelical Lutheran congregations. Greater numbers of British, German, and Irish immigrants added to the heterogeneous South Side population in the mid-nineteenth century.[5]

Even though the South Side initially grew more slowly than other areas of the city, its industrial future was evident by the 1860s. Ironworks and foundries were built in Walker's Point. Among the earliest, erected in the 1850s, were the Bay State Foundry and the Globe Iron Works. On the southern edge of the Menomonee Valley, the Burnham Brothers Brickyard, Pfister and Vogel Tannery, and the Menomonee Valley Brewery attracted laborers. In the mid-1860s, Edward P. Allis' Reliance Iron Works relocated on the South Side. South of the city limits, at the mouth of Deer Creek on the Milwaukee Bay, the Milwaukee Iron Company constructed a rolling mill in 1868-69.[6]

The South Side began to assume its present physical form and appearance in the late 1870s and 1880s. Industrial development in the Menomonee Valley and at the mouth of the Kinnickinnic Creek expanded employment opportunities for new settlers and substantially increased the South Side's growth rate. Poles began to arrive in large numbers in the 1870s, and within a decade Milwaukee's South Side, particularly the southwest section, became a predominately Polish community.

By 1880, platted areas extended west to South Twenty-seventh Street and south to Lincoln Avenue, but except for Walker's Point, the South Side was still sparsely settled. Open land, farms, greenhouses, orchards, and private parks intermingled with new subdivided tracts, recently-graded city streets, and the cottages of newcomers. Several florists had greenhouses along Forest Home Avenue (formerly Janesville Plank Road) in the vicinity of Forest Home Cemetery, established in 1850. As far east as South Second and Mitchell Streets, Enos and Company conducted a large florist business, with twelve 100-foot long greenhouses on the site. Between 1891 and about 1925, Henry Comstock operated a celery farm on 250 acres of black peat bog, stretching from Orchard Street south to Forest Home Avenue, and from South Thirty-second to South Thirty-seventh Streets. The "celery fields" provided employment to recently-arrived Polish immigrants, mainly women, who made their homes on the South Side.[7]

Private parks and pleasure gardens, pre-dating the municipal park system, were a significant part of the developing South Side landscape. National Park, at the southwest corner of West National Avenue and Layton Boulevard, was the largest. Its fifty-two acres included a fishing lake, a horse racetrack, the city's first roller coaster, a deer enclosure, and a hotel. The park was popular between 1870 and 1900, after which the land was sold and subdivided for houses. Other private recreational retreats included Conrad's Grove, Melms Garden, South Side Park, and Weeks Garden.[8]

By the early twentieth century, however, housing construction and increased population densities had transformed the South Side. The demand for residential property chipped away remaining open space and agricultural land. Public parks (such as Humboldt, Kosciuszko, and Mitchell) replaced the older private picnic grounds and recreation sites. With the exception of a few tracts, platted areas reached south to Oklahoma Avenue and west to South Thirty-fifth Street, roughly the boundaries of the South Side defined herein.[9] Milwaukee's South Side had become a densely-settled area of urban neighborhoods.

Scandinavian Evangelical Lutheran Church, 202 W. Scott St., 1882. The congregation was organized in 1852, and the next year they built a frame church on the site of the present building. In 1882, this late Gothic Revival church, designed by Milwaukee architect Andrew Elleson, was erected. Services were held in Norwegian and English until the early 20th century. The congregation moved in 1923. Although the steeple has been removed and the Gothic windows replaced, the brick building retains its original doors with chamfered cross pieces.

Mitchell St. and Kinnickinnic Ave., looking west, 1876. This drawing, from the 1876 *Historical Atlas of Milwaukee County*, shows the pioneer residence of Horace Chase (now gone) surrounded by the developing South Side. In the horizon are the twin spires of St. Stanislaus Church (1872-73), which stands at the corner of S. Fifth and Mitchell Streets.

Walker's Point

The place where George Walker settled in 1834 was a narrow peninsula south of the Menomonee River, jutting northeasterly through swampy land to the Milwaukee River. Because this ridge was the only high ground immediately south of the rivers, the first South Side settlement began here. The original rectangular grid plat, in 1836, included the land bound by the rivers on the north and east, South Sixth Street on the west, and Washington Street on the south. By 1846, at the time Milwaukee was incorporated, Walker's Point was the city's Fifth Ward, with a population of 1,366. Platted areas extended west to South Twelfth Street and south to Greenfield Avenue by the "Walker's Point Addition" and other plats. "Walker's Point addition" was laid out with a central square, covering a city block between Mineral, Washington, South Ninth, and South Tenth Streets. Walker's Square, donated by George Walker, is now part of the county park system.[10]

Throughout the nineteenth century, Walker's Point developed into a thriving working-class community. In addition, wealthy merchants who owned businesses in the area built large Italianate homes along South Third Street (formerly Hanover Street). Several of these remain today in the 800 block of South Third Street. For a long time, South Second Street (formerly Reed Street) was the principal business thoroughfare. Milwaukee's main railway depot (Union Depot, built in 1866) stood in Walker's Point at the northwest corner of South Second and Seeboth Streets. The community was especially prosperous during the 1880s and 1890s, but growth leveled off about 1900. Although some Poles moved to Walker's Point in the early 1880s, the locus of Polish settlement soon moved south and west. A small group of Serbians settled in Walker's Point after 1910. Mexicans began to arrive in small numbers in the 1920s, and today Spanish-speaking people are the predominant ethnic group in Walker's Point.[11]

Walker's Point has distinct but overlapping residential, commercial, and industrial areas, and thus its character changes from street to street. National Avenue, South First, South Second, South Fifth, and South Sixth Streets are the major commercial corridors. Most of the industrial buildings are concentrated in the northwestern section. Churches, whose steeples are Walker's Point's most visible landmarks, and schools comprise the balance of neighborhood structures.

State Historical Society of Wisconsin

800 block of S. Third St. Hanover Street, now S. Third, was the South Side's showplace in the late nineteenth century. These Italianate houses, all similar in scale and style, were built between 1870 and 1875. They still stand at 803, 813, and 821 S. Third.

The majority of remaining buildings in Walker's Point were built between 1860 and 1910. The dominant building material is brick, either local cream or red. A substantial number of the residences, however, are wood-frame. Houses are generally modest, one to two stories in height, set back from the sidewalk, and almost always detached and clapboard-covered units. Residential architecture reflects the gradual process of development and infill in Walker's Point. The major residential styles are Greek Revival, Italianate, and Queen Anne. In addition, there is one brick Federal Style residence (built before 1858) presently standing at 605-609 West Virginia Street, and a few frame houses of Federal-Greek Revival derivation.[12]

Most of Walker's Point's houses date from the 1870s and 1880s; existing commercial buildings were constructed mainly between 1880 and 1910. Some are the second and third buildings to occupy each site, replacing houses as well as earlier stores and shops. There are many Italianate store buildings with bracketed cornices; Queen Anne, Romanesque, and Neoclassical features are also common in the commercial architecture. Substantial buildings with names like "Bahr" (801 South Second Street) and "Ritmeier" (438 West National Avenue) incised in stone tablets at gable ends attest to the economic success of Walker's Point German merchants. The three and four story business blocks built along West National Avenue in the 1880s and 1890s are indicative of its rise as the main commercial thoroughfare of the Fifth Ward.

800 block of W. Washington St.

Detail of Frederick Bahr Building, 801 S. Second St., 1887. An elaborate metal cornice crowns the highly-ornamented facade of this brick building, which originally housed Bahr's grocery business.

Alfred Hilton House, 1137 S. Fourth St., c. 1874. English-born Alfred Hilton, who was an engineer, built and lived in this wood-frame house. It has a stone foundation, and retains its original six-pane windows on the second floor. The bracketed porch may have been added a few years later.

Bay View

The village of Bay View had its beginnings in 1868, when the Milwaukee Iron Company (later the North Chicago Rolling Mills, and then the Illinois Steel Company) built a rolling mill on the Milwaukee Bay at the southern edge of the city. Milwaukee's first industrial suburb, Bay View was actually a company town, and it grew proportionately with the ironworks. The company erected cottages and boarding houses for the millhands, donated lots to several churches, and divided the rest of the initial tract into 50 by 150 foot lots which were sold to employees. The *Milwaukee Sentinel* described Bay View in 1868:

> The village of Bay View has sprung up within a year. There have already been twenty-five buildings erected, including a store and a large boarding house, and ten more are contracted for. They are mostly small cottages, costing about $500 each, but are exceedingly neat in appearance and very comfortably furnished.[13]

Most of the cottages were clustered south of the mill, which was located north of Conway Street on the lakeshore. Foremen and skilled workers were imported from Britain to construct and run the ironworks, and thus the majority of early Bay View settlers were English, Scottish, or Welsh. Germans and Irish were employed mainly as general laborers at the mill.[14]

At the time of village incorporation in 1879, Bay View had 2,592 inhabitants and included 892 acres. "To the original plat laid out by the Milwaukee Iron Company, now nearly all occupied and built over, have

Lithograph of the Bay View Rolling Mills (Milwaukee Works of the Illinois Steel Company) in the late nineteenth century.

State Historical Society of Wisconsin

Herman Wudtke Collection

Bay View "puddlers' cottages," Russell Ave. This twentieth century photograph shows a row of typical ironworkers' houses, built in the 1870s and 1880s, with clapboard siding and millwork ornament.

Puddlers' Hall, 2461-63 S. Clair St., 1873. Now serving as a tavern and much altered, this frame building was originally the Bay View lodge of the Amalgamated Iron and Steel Workers Association, the principal labor union representing Bay View millworkers.

been added several additions and subdivisions," reported Alfred Andreas in 1881.[15] The village had expanded south to what is now South Shore Park, and west of the railroad tracks. In 1887, Bay View was annexed to the City of Milwaukee.[16] Although its present "borders" are a matter of argument, Bay View is generally regarded as that area bound by the Kinnickinnic River on the north, Oklahoma Avenue on the south, and the Kinnickinnic River and Chase Avenue on the west.

Today, Bay View still reflects much of the scale and character of its nineteenth century village origins. The portion east of the railroad tracks, the section that was settled first and was nearest the mill, is most representative of the appearance of the former company town. The blocks north of East Pryor Avenue still contain numbers of company-built "puddlers' cottages" and former boarding houses. Below Russell Avenue, workers' houses mingle with the larger residences originally belonging to foremen and company executives. Most of the remaining structures were built between 1875 and 1915. The majority are small single-family dwellings one and a half or two stories high, with gable roofs and rectangular plans. Wood-frame, rather than masonry, buildings predominate. Simple renditions of the Greek Revival, Italianate, Queen Anne, and Georgian Revival Styles are represented in the millwork ornament and pattern-book plans of many houses.

The majority of structures in Bay View west of the railroad tracks were built between 1880 and 1910, with a few remaining early residences dating before that time. The street pattern combines a rectangular grid with diagonal streets formed by the northwest-southeast direction of Kinnickinnic Avenue. The major corridors, Kinnickinnic Avenue and Howell Avenue, are also the oldest roads in the area, dating from the 1830s. Most commercial buildings, as well as Bay View's finest churches, are located along these thoroughfares. Lot sizes and setbacks within west Bay View vary due to street layout, mixed land uses, and the gradual development of the area. Residential structures represent a composite of late nineteenth and early twentieth century styles, although few are high-style or designed by architects. Most dwellings are single-family or duplexes, seldom over two stories high, and are built on a variety of plans.

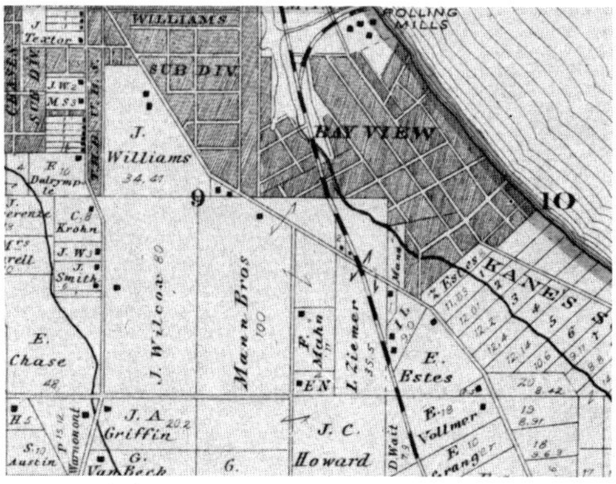

A part of the South Side below Lincoln Avenue in 1876, showing the village of Bay View. At this time the area lay outside the city limits, in the Town of Lake. From the 1876 *Historical Atlas of Milwaukee County*.

James Beddard House, 2731 S. Superior St., c. 1876. One of the best preserved Milwaukee Iron Company worker's cottages in Bay View.

Joseph Bearman House, 2593 S. Wentworth Ave., 1873. The houses of Bay View's skilled workers and foremen were frequently larger, with more stylistic variation, than the puddlers' cottages. Though considerably altered, this brick house still stands today.

Joseph A. Starkey House, 2582 S. Shore Drive, 1878-79. Starkey was the superintendent of the Bay View mill. His large Italianate house, which overlooks Lake Michigan, was added to in 1897 and has been well-conserved over the years.

John Engelhardt House, Windlake Ave. Late nineteenth century photograph of an early house, now gone, built on the 1500 block of Windlake Ave. prior to the development of the area. A promotional guidebook described Windlake Ave. at the time: "It runs along a high bank, overlooking a small thread of the Kinnickinnic River, the valley of which is wonderful in its rustic beauty."

Milwaukee Co. Historical Society

Near South Side

The Near South Side, for the purposes of this study, comprises all of the South Side west of Walker's Point and the North-South Freeway, north of Oklahoma Avenue, and east of South Thirty-fifth Street. Earliest development took place along the edge of the Menomonee Valley and along the plank roads: Mukwonago Road (West National Avenue), Muskego Road (Muskego Avenue), and Janesville Plank Road (Forest Home Avenue). Farms, speculative land holdings, and the cottages of Menomonee Valley laborers made up the Near South Side prior to the Civil War. "Clark's Addition" was one of the first platted sections west of Walker's Point, appearing on city maps as early as 1858. Clark Square, located in the center of the plat and designated simply as "public square" on old maps, is one of the city's oldest public squares. It was donated in 1837 by M. J. Brown and Norman and Lydia Clark.[17]

Yankees, Germans, and Scandinavians settled on the Near South Side in the mid-nineteenth century, primarily north of Greenfield Avenue. By the 1880s Polish immigrants began to populate the area. William George Bruce described the beginnings of the Polish community on the Near South Side:

> Usually a rickety express wagon took them to the southern limits of the city which up to this time had been only sparsely populated . . . The wooded lands south of Greenfield Avenue were soon transformed into a vast area of cottages with high basements accommodating two families, with gardens in the rear and some shrubbery and a rest bench in the front.[18]

The area south of Greenfield Avenue, where most Poles settled, developed as an ethnically and occupationally homogeneous neighborhood. Most residents were Polish (over eighty percent in one ward) and worked in unskilled and semi-skilled industrial jobs. The area's spatial uniformity and housing stock reflect this homogeneity. Land was platted and subdivided primarily between 1880 and 1900. With the exception of a few diagonal streets, subdividers left a legacy of long narrow blocks on a gridiron street pattern, and lots almost invariably measured 30 by 120 feet. Early subdivisions centered around the older diagonal routes, Forest Home Avenue and Windlake Avenue. In 1877 the Cream City Street Railway Company built a horsecar line along Forest Home Avenue. Although service was irregular at first, the route made the area accessible to the rest of the city.[19]

Polish immigrants, c. 1895.

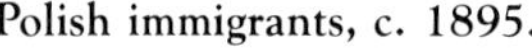

Milwaukee Co. Historical Society

2256 S. Eighteenth St., 1896. A frame worker's cottage typical of those built on the Near South Side during the 1880s and 1890s.

Despite the rapid urbanization of the Near South Side in the late nineteenth century, and the modest means of the immigrant settlers, the neighborhoods did not resemble the stereotypical crowded districts of America's largest cities, those built largely of tenement houses. Though densely populated, the Near South Side was and is comprised mainly of detached single-family cottages and duplexes. The cottages are generally wood-frame, one to two stories high, with gable roofs and square or rectangular plans. Duplexes, often with Queen Anne or Georgian Revival stylistic elements, and Bungalow Style houses occur with increasing frequency below Cleveland Avenue and west of Layton Boulevard, which is lined with some of the Near South Side's largest homes.

The Poles often built their dwellings with raised basements, in order to allow rental space to help pay off mortgages, and to provide inexpensive quarters for recently-arrived compatriots. In addition, they often erected alley-abutting cottages at the rear of the lots, further increasing the population density. Although both the raised cottage and the rear cottage are found in other sections of Milwaukee, both housing phenomena are most pronounced on the Near South Side. As in other Polish neighborhoods in Milwaukee, the Poles formed building and loan associations, called *skarbi*, to assist one another in home financing.

The Poles centered their South Side community around their Catholic parishes. Boreslaus Goral, a Polish Catholic priest in Milwaukee, wrote: "It has always been, and still continues to be, the ambition of the Poles to organize a parish and to have their own church and school whenever the numbers warrant it."[20] St. Stanislaus Church (1681 South Fifth Street), Milwaukee's first Polish parish formed in 1863, continually divided into offshoot South Side parishes. In addition to the rows of wood-framed cottages along the streets of the Near South Side, the numerous Catholic churches are familiar visual elements of the area.

Halls built by the Poles to house their societies and organizations, corner stores, and taverns further punctuate the residential neighborhoods of the Near South Side. Commercial streets, such as Lincoln Avenue and South Thirteenth Street, are lined with small commercial buildings originally belonging to Polish and German-established businesses such as meat markets, banks, building contracting firms, and Polish-language newspapers. Architecturally, they reflect the scale, materials, and styles represented on surrounding residential streets. Mitchell Street, which developed as the South Side's major commercial thoroughfare in the 1880s and 1890s, contains both neighborhood shops and the larger stores of citywide businesses.

Mitchell St. today.

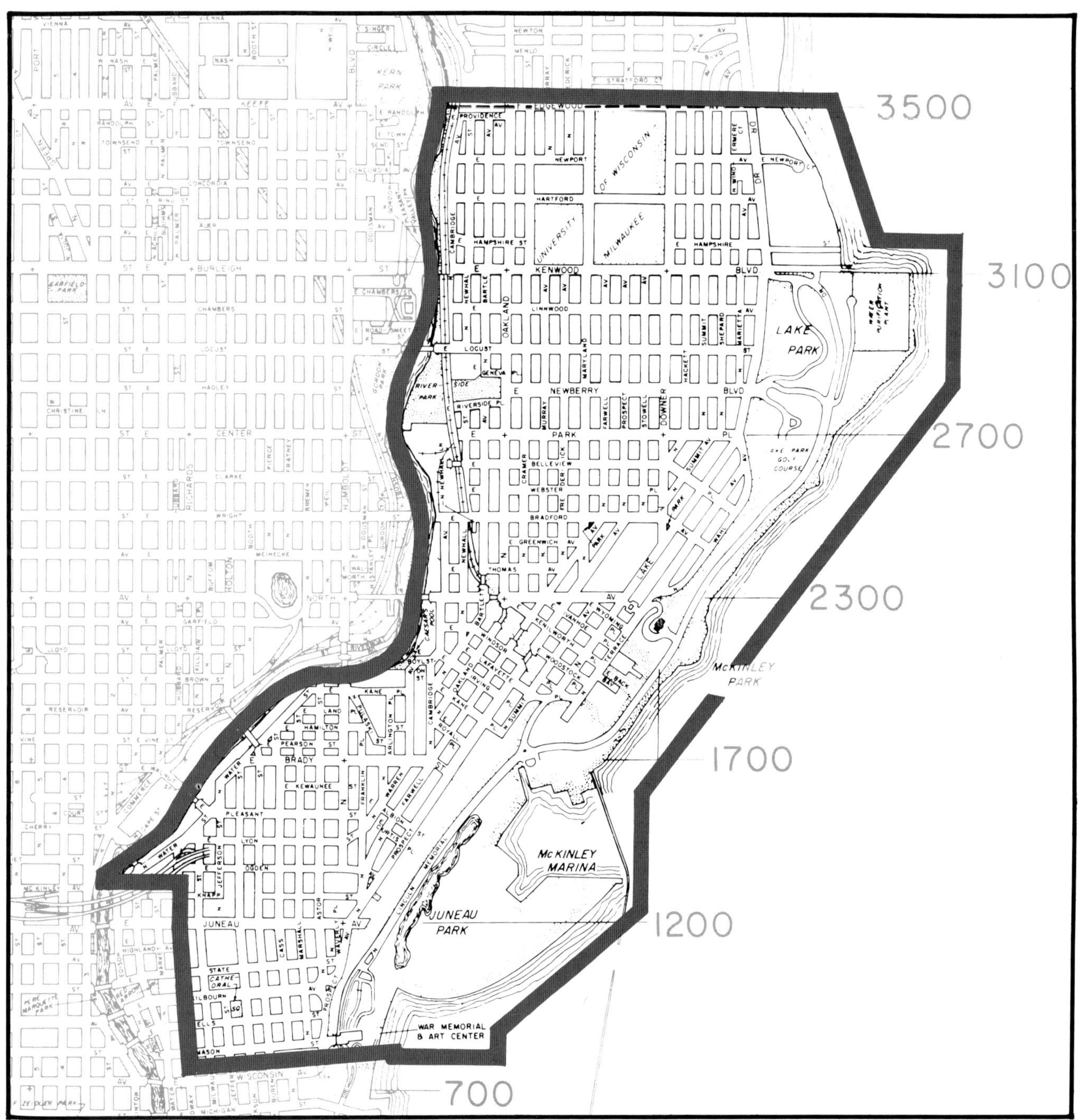
3500
3100
2700
2300
1700
1200
700
EDGEWOOD
NEWPORT
HARTFORD
HAMPSHIRE
KENWOOD
BLVD
LINNWOOD
LOCUST
NEWBERRY
BLVD
PARK
PL
BELLEVIEW
WEBSTER
BRADFORD
GREENWICH
THOMAS
UNIVERSITY OF WISCONSIN - MILWAUKEE
OAKLAND
DOWNER
LAKE PARK
LAKE PARK GOLF COURSE
RIVER SIDE PARK
LAKE
McKINLEY PARK
McKINLEY MARINA
JUNEAU PARK
WAR MEMORIAL & ART CENTER
BRADY
KEWAUNEE
PLEASANT
LYON
OGDEN
JUNEAU
STATE
CATHEDRAL
KILBOURN
WELLS
MASON
WISCONSIN
PROSPECT
FARWELL
WATER
JEFFERSON
CASS
MARSHALL
ASTOR
BURLEIGH
CHAMBERS
LOCUST
HADLEY
CENTER
CLARKE
WRIGHT
MEINECKE
NORTH
GARFIELD
BROWN
RESERVOIR
VINE
CHERRY
McKINLEY
MICHIGAN
GARFIELD PARK

East Side

East Side

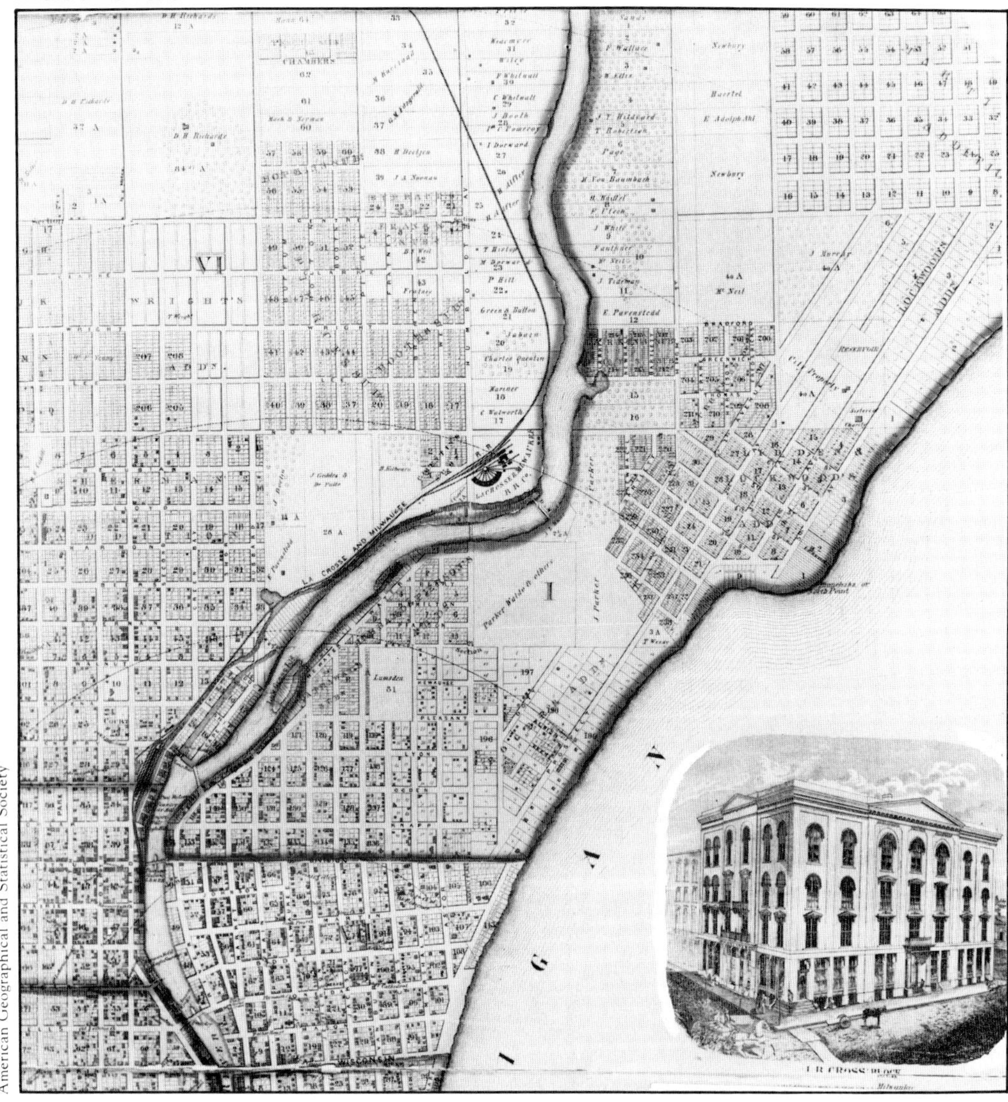

American Geographical and Statistical Society

The East Side in 1858. From H. F. Walling's "Illustrated Historical Atlas Map of Milwaukee and Environs."

The East Side is comprised of the neck of land between the Milwaukee River and Lake Michigan. Beginning in Yankee Hill at Mason Street, the area extends north to the city limits at Edgewood Avenue. Like much of Milwaukee, the East Side originally was covered with dense forest. The bluffs along the lake rose as high as seventy-five feet. Behind them lay low, rolling hills cut by ravines which descended to the Milwaukee River.

Early Development

The only pioneer route through the East Side was the Sauk Trail, as depicted on the 1836 Chase Map. Roughly following present day Prospect Avenue and Lake Drive, the route was not important in the settlement of this area, but did provide a guide for future transportation systems.[1] While other parts of the city were interconnected with plank roads and railroads in the 1840s and 1850s, the East Side did not experience such construction until after the Civil War.

In the mid-nineteenth century, there were few farms on the East Side. The 1858 Walling map shows that a few streets had been platted only as far north as Kenwood Boulevard. Above Brady Street were the large speculative land holdings of men such as attorney Donald A. J. Upham, civil engineer Peter Martineau, and real estate agent Charles Quentin.

Prospect Avenue was the "suburbs" in the 1860s. In an article in the September 21, 1861 *Milwaukee Sentinel,* a local writer made tongue-in-cheek comments:

> Prospect Street, like the banks of the Nile, depends on Heaven for irrigation. The waters come up and overflow it, and lay in broad pools upon it, coquetting with the sunshine and the incipient bull frogs. A long lake stretches down the east side of Prospect Street, beneath the windows of overhanging houses, it bears upon its calm surface the many boards that belong to the plank road, and to desolated fences, it entices suburban geese and ducks, and it is the oasis for stray pigs who wander that way . . . but the residents of that locality, being so near the greater lake, probably live in utter unappreciation of its beauties.

Twenty years later A. T. Andreas reported in the *History of Milwaukee:*

> Following Terrace Avenue, past St. Mary's Hospital . . . a smooth and hard gravel driveway, a hundred feet in width, stretches to the north into the distance. This is White Fish Bay road, one of the finest drives in the country. It has been improved at great expense by the turnpike company, of which Chas. Andrews is president, until it has become the thoroughfare, in pleasant weather, for the elite of the city who delight in pure air, beautiful scenery, and the exhilarating sport of a five-mile drive over such unrivalled road. On the way, in addition to natural attractions of lake and grove, are many elegant resorts . . . the end of the drive is White Fish Bay, a charming spot.

The first major road through the East Side, Whitefish Bay Toll Road was constructed in 1872. It began at the intersection of Kenwood and Downer Avenues and extended northward along the lake, on what is now Lake Drive. Unlike Milwaukee's plank roads built for commerce, the Whitefish Bay Toll Road was built to offer an improved route for the many patrons of the Whitefish Bay resorts, which were established in the early 1860s. Prior to the construction of the toll road, transportation to Whitefish Bay was provided by omnibus on a winding trail or by the schooner which sailed twice daily from the Grand Avenue (now Wisconsin Avenue) bridge.[2] By 1876, a few homes were built along the toll road, including those of Clarence Shepard, a wholesale hardware dealer, and merchant tailor Denis D. French.

Commercial rail lines were built on the East Side in the same year as the toll road. In 1872, the Milwaukee, Lake Shore and Western Line was constructed. Running north along the east bank of the upper Milwaukee River, the line turned east toward Lake Michigan at North Avenue, where it connected with the Chicago and Northwestern Railway.[3]

Below Brady Street along the Milwaukee River, the riverbanks were strategic sites for industrial development, and tanneries, lumber yards, and ice houses were built there before 1860. The tanneries dominated the east bank, and some of the city's largest firms located there after the Civil War. Their facilities sprawled along North Water Street from Lyon to Brady Streets, forming a significant tanning district, of which a considerable number of buildings still remain. Dating from the 1870s and 1880s, the architecture of the tanneries reflects the industrial functionalism of the period. Their multi-story, multi-bay blocks are embellished with arches, pilasters and corbelling.

From the 1850s through the 1880s the area south of Brady Street attracted Yankee, Irish and German residents, many of whom were employed in the riverfront tanneries. They built a variety of dwellings, including frame cottages, cream brick residences and a number of rowhouses. Al-

1661 N. Water St., Star Tannery, c. 1885. The Star Tannery was established by Albert Trostel and August Gallun in 1858. The firm moved to this site in 1861. They became the second largest tanning company in Milwaukee by the late nineteenth century.

though rowhouses were built in small numbers throughout the city, the largest number and those of greatest architectural significance are still to be found on the lower East Side.

The frame cottages in this area appear to have been constructed between 1860 and 1880. Intermixed with the cottages are an interesting group of residences located between Brady, Pleasant, Humboldt and Cass Streets. Architecturally, they are good examples of 1880s Italianate, Queen Anne and Romanesque Styles.

By 1876, extensive residential subdivision proceeded as far north as Bradford Avenue. The area south of North Avenue near the river was an extension of the Juneautown grid. The blocks were square, with lots measuring sixty by one hundred and twenty feet. The area east of Humboldt Avenue, near the Whitefish Bay Toll Road, was platted along a diagonal grid following the natural line of the lake bluffs. Jefferson Glidden and John Lockwood platted this area in 1854, which became known locally as "North Point".[4] Glidden and Lockwood were private contractors who came to the city from Ohio in the early 1850s to build a municipal gas and water works. The gas plant was completed in 1852, but the water works project was abandoned, and in 1853 the two men purchased the North Point property.[5] Then a considerable distance from the settled lower East Side, this area would not become a prime residential area until nearly fifty years later.

The area north of Bradford Avenue was platted during the 1880s and 1890s. Mitchell Heights (1884), Prospect Hill (1893) and Kenwood Park (1891) are representative of the subdivisions which later attracted middle and upper-middle income groups desiring homesites near fashionable North Point, Newberry Boulevard and Lake Park.[6]

During the late nineteenth and early twentieth centuries, East Side residential development was stratified according to the desirability of land sites and topography. Workers and immigrants lived nearest the Milwaukee River. Middle-income families built ample single family and two-family dwellings in the central blocks, roughly between Oakland and Downer Avenues. Prosperous Yankees and second and third generation German businessmen and professionals built their large homes near the lake.

E. Lyon St. cottages.

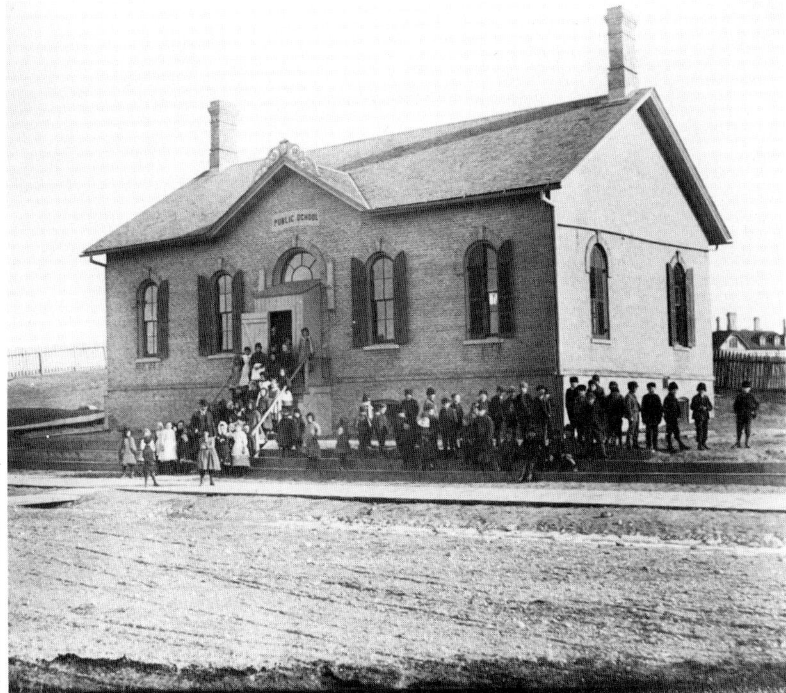

Milwaukee Co. Historical Society

First District Branch School, Prospect and Maryland Avenues. This view, probably taken about 1900, shows the small building which preceded the current Maryland Avenue School. The design of the building is a very simple rendering of the Italianate. In the background are buildings of an orphan asylum which no longer stands.

Public Transportation

The first public transit lines on the East Side were the omnibuses and horse cars of the 1860s. After the Civil War, new horse car routes were built by the Milwaukee City Company along Farwell Avenue to Lafayette Place, the southern edge of North Point. Because this was a sparsely settled area and ridership was low, the Milwaukee City Company was forced to abandon this line in 1874.[7]

East Siders were not solely dependent on streetcar service since many owned personal carriages. In 1874, however, the Cream City Railway Company petitioned the Common Council for a fifty year franchise to operate the abandoned Milwaukee City Company routes. A franchise was granted in the same year and the routes were extended to North Avenue. As development of the East Side spread farther from the city's commercial center in the 1880s and 1890s, streetcar lines became more profitable. In the early 1890s, an Oakland Avenue line was added by the Milwaukee Electric Railway and Light Company.[8]

Six streets converged at North Avenue where the streetcar line ended. Commonly referred to as "Six Points" this area developed as a neighborhood commercial center of small shops and service centers. The Cream City Car House and Mule and Horse Storage Plant dominated the crossroads. On this site is now an East Side landmark, the Oriental Theatre.

The Six Points area was also the transfer point between the Cream City Railway and the Whitefish Bay Railway. Whitefish Bay's popularity as a summer resort increased with the opening of Fred Isenring's Hotel in 1882 and the Pabst Hotel in 1888. The Whitefish Bay Railway, co-owned by Frederick Pabst, Guido Pfister, and Charles Vogel, opened its first car line in 1888. The Railway's terminal was three blocks from the Farwell Station at Murray and Bradford Avenues. Proceeding from this point, the line ran east along Bradford to Downer Avenue and then north along Downer to the Bay resorts. The streetcars were pulled by steam engines disguised as "steam dummies" so pedestrians and horses would not be frightened by their presence on the streets. As the Whitefish Bay Toll Road was built to make leisure spots more accessible, so too, the Bay Railway, which was operated from April to November, was constructed for the convenience of the resort patrons.[9]

Yankee Hill

On the high ground east of the Milwaukee River and north of downtown was the major settlement of New Yorkers, New Englanders, and English in Milwaukee. Referred to as Yankee Hill, or "Yankeeberg" by the German community, it was the choice residential district in the city during the nineteenth century. Street grading and house construction began in the early 1840s. Historically Yankee Hill comprised the area north of East Wisconsin Avenue to Ogden Avenue, and east of Milwaukee Street to the lake. Today vestiges of this neighborhood lie within the bounds of Mason Street, Van Buren Street, Ogden Avenue, and Lake Michigan.

Yankee Hill was home to many of Milwaukee's pioneer civic, financial, and business leaders. Its Yankee ancestry was reflected in street names like Cass, Astor, and Marshall. At the turn of the century the area began to decline, resulting from expansion of the business district as well as suburbanization. During this period prosperous Germans and Irish purchased some of the homes, thus maintaining Yankee Hill as a desirable residential neighborhood. In the early twentieth century, numerous residences were subdivided for rooming houses or were replaced by larger apartment buildings. By the 1950s the city targeted deteriorated portions of Yankee Hill for urban renewal, and large sections were demolished.

Thorsen House, Jefferson St. The first bathtub in the city, made of tin, was installed in this house on Yankee Hill, pictured here in 1904. The building is no longer standing.

State Historical Society of Wisconsin

Architecturally, Yankee Hill still contains an impressive collection of nineteenth century homes and churches. The oldest surviving residences date from the years 1850 through 1875. Many are two-story, three-bay Italianate houses constructed of cream brick. A significant concentration is found along Cass and Marshall Streets from the 800 to 1200 blocks. Examples are the Robert P. Fitzgerald House (1874) at 1119 North Marshall Street and the George Peckham House (1855) at 1029 North Marshall Street. A number of large Queen Anne and Richardsonian Romanesque houses also remain in Yankee Hill.

There are also excellent examples of religious and institutional architecture in Yankee Hill. Edward Townsend Mix of Milwaukee designed three churches in this area. The All Saints Episcopal Cathedral (1868-69) at 804 East Juneau Avenue, designed in the Gothic Revival, is one of the oldest churches in Milwaukee in continuous use. Immanuel Presbyterian Church (1873-75), at 1100 North Astor Street, is designed in the Victorian Gothic Style. It has walls of local cream limestone trimmed with red-orange and gray sandstone. Often regarded as Mix's greatest religious work is St. Paul's Episcopal Church at 904 East Knapp Street. Its design was modelled after two of Henry Hobson Richardson's Romanesque-inspired churches. Completed in 1890, the brownstone edifice features an intricately beamed nave and transept, and Tiffany stained glass windows.

John D. Inbusch House, 1135 N. Cass St., 1874. Fashionable Italianate houses once lined the streets of Yankee Hill. Leonard A. Schmidtner is listed as the architect of this cream brick house, described by the *Milwaukee Sentinel* in 1874 as a "brick residence, built in the modern Roman style, with all improvements, heated with steam." Of note are the heavy bracketed cornice and molded window hoods. The original owner, John Dietrich Inbusch, was a partner in Inbusch Brothers, wholesale grocers.

A portion of Yankee Hill in 1886. Nineteenth century publicists noted the elegance of Yankee Hill's stately homes, tree-lined streets, gardens, sloping lawns, and terraces. "Waverly Place, Astor Marshall, Cass, Van Buren, with the cross streets, present the appearance of continuous parks," wrote Andreas in 1881. Juneau Park, pictured in this lithograph published by Caspar and Zahn, was one of the city's early parks, praised for its plantings, statuary, rustic bridges, and its outstanding view of Lake Michigan.

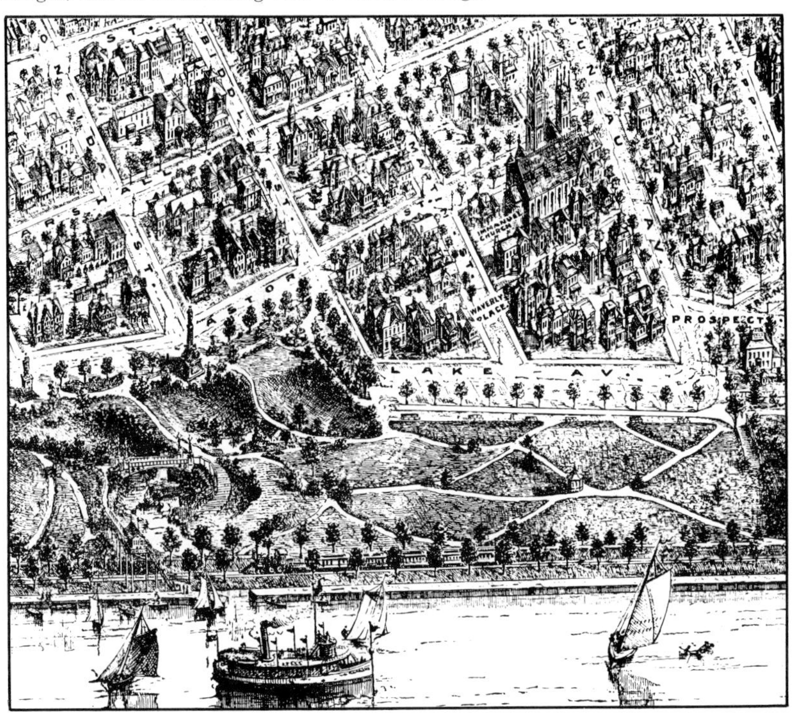

927-29 N. Marshall St., photograph 1979. A significant collection of nineteenth century multi-family dwellings remains on the lower East Side. Local architect H. Paul Schnetzky designed this Victorian Italianate four-flat building, constructed of cream brick, for James Clark.

1775 N. Marshall St. Frame clapboard-clad cottages such as these are typical of dwellings built during the 1870s and 1880s in the former Polish neighborhood north of Brady St.

Brady Street

Brady Street was the primary nineteenth century commercial district of the lower East Side. Development began in the early 1860s by the Germans and Irish who lived in the southern part of the neighborhood. Marshall Street bisected Brady, dividing it into a residential section to the west and a commercial section to the east. Both land uses, however, were generally mixed along Brady Street. Brady Street gained importance after the Milwaukee River was bridged at Humboldt Avenue in 1860 and at Pleasant Street in 1870.[10] The early commercial structures built between 1860 and 1875 of frame and cream brick construction operated as livery stables, grain and feed supply, dry goods, repair shops and groceries. Excellent extant examples from this period are the cream brick structures at 1200, 1214 and 1224 East Brady Street.

When the first large groups of Polish immigrants arrived in the 1880s, a large number settled north of Brady between the river and Sobieski (now Arlington) Street. Their neighborhood was developed with numerous raised flats similar to those also found in the North and South Side immigrant neighborhoods. By 1886, the new residents established St. Hedwig's Church at the northeast corner of Brady and Humboldt. It was the second parish organized by Poles in the city. City directories of the period give evidence that Brady Street had a distinct Polish character by the turn of the century.[11] Brady Street and its adjacent neighborhoods remained a strong center of the Polish community until after World War II. Italians who arrived in Milwaukee during the early 1900s gradually moved into the area from the Old Third Ward, and by 1950, the lower East Side had become predominantly Italian.[12] Brady Street continues to be a center of strong, ethnic culture, particularly Italian.

State Historical Society of Wisconsin

H. M. Benjamin House, Prospect Ave. Most of the Queen Anne and Romanesque mansions along Prospect Ave., such as this one pictured in the 1890s, have been replaced by large apartment buildings, but the avenue's lakefront setting and proximity to downtown continue to be its chief residential attractions.

Prospect Avenue

Among the upper income neighborhoods of the East Side, Prospect Avenue was the first to be developed as an enclave of expensive homes in the late nineteenth century. Known as Milwaukee's "Gold Coast" Prospect Avenue was rivaled by the West Side's Grand Avenue and Highland Boulevard as an address of high social standing. Residential development of the avenue did not occur until after the construction of the Milwaukee Water Works Plant at North Point in 1872. Prior to this, individual wells were impractical because of the necessary depth of their bore. A municipal system was needed to pump water from the lake up the steep grade of the bluffs for residential use.[13]

Some of the city's finest mansions were constructed from Juneau Avenue to North Avenue between 1875 and 1910. Prospect Avenue once displayed the work of local architects such as Edward Townsend Mix, James Douglas, and Henry C. Koch, who designed homes for Milwaukee's lumber barons, brewers, packers, tanners and merchants. Remaining on this once-fashionable avenue are a few mansions and several fine smaller residences. Beginning in the 1920s, many of the Prospect Avenue mansions were demolished because of the demand for central city housing and the end of the Victorian "lifestyle". These palatial residences were replaced with four to six story apartment buildings. The first apartment buildings, usually of brick construction with stone trim, were of simple square or rectangular form. Their facades were embellished with Classical and Georgian Revival details. Apartment building construction has continued to the present, with a number of apartment towers built after World War II.

North Point

North Point includes the area bounded by the lake shore, Prospect Avenue, Lafayette Place, and Park Place. The elongated rectangular grid pattern follows the shoreline, breaking the traditional north-south layout of the city. Within the North Point area, the principal Avenues — Lake, Terrace and Summit — were designated as boulevards and "pleasureways" by the Common Council in 1906. Wahl Avenue, the avenue closest to the lake between North Avenue and Park Avenue, was added in 1914.[14] Water Tower Park, situated midway, divides North Point into north and south districts. North Point South, listed in 1979 as a historic district on the National Register of Historic Places, was developed first. Carved out of the eastern half of Glidden and Lockwood's Addition (1854), the first residences were built by 1860. Houses sited along the lower reaches of Terrace Avenue and the former Woodland Court were usurped by the expansion of the lakefront park in the 1890s.[15] The primary building period in North Point South occurred between 1890 and 1910 with a brief spurt of building activity in the early 1920s. The architecture of North Point South reflects the popular revival styles of the period, which borrowed from English, Spanish, Italian, and American Colonial sources, and are well-crafted in stone, stucco, frame, and red or brown brick. Only one house in all of North Point was built of traditional Milwaukee cream brick, the Paine House at 2214 Terrace Avenue, built about 1860. Residences of the early 1890s stand out among the period revival houses because they vividly display the influence of the preceding generation of Victorian architecture.

North Point North was developed between 1900 and 1930. It was first platted as Gilman's Addition in 1876, but houses were not built until 1897. Like North Point South, the area attracted the families of business and professional men.[16] The residences were of similar period revival Style architecture as North Point South, but exhibited far less exterior ornamentation and were smaller in size. The houses of greatest architectural significance lie along Wahl and Terrace Avenues. Elaborate, individualized architectural design diminishes somewhat as one proceeds west, while housing density increases.

Bradford and Terrace Aves., North Point North.

North Point. North Point's large houses are stylistically eclectic, but similar in scale, materials, and setback.

Drive Out Newberry Boulevard

You will immediately decide the location of the home you are going to build.

When planning a home one should study location, elevation, environment, prospective neighbors, view and improvements already in existence. Search the town over and you cannot match Newberry Boulevard lots at anywhere near the price.

Aavertisement for Newberry Blvd. in the *Milwaukee Journal,* **1920s.**

Newberry Blvd., photograph 1981.

Newberry Boulevard

Newberry Boulevard, similar to the North Point area in both its architecture and income level of residents, was promoted by an extensive newspaper campaign which spanned several decades. The *Milwaukee Journal* ads described it as "unquestionably Milwaukee's distinctively select, yet inexpensive, street."[17] It extends from Lake Drive to Oakland Avenue, and was officially designated a boulevard by the Common Council in 1906.[18]

The building permits for Newberry Boulevard reveal that a large number of the residences were built speculatively by a few builders and architects like Louis Auer and Sons, Maynard and Picken, Julius Bachman and George Schley.

Prior to 1900, development of Newberry Boulevard was sporadic; the peak building period was from 1905 to 1915. After World War I, the mid-1920s experienced another rush of construction activity. East of Maryland Avenue the residences are larger and of more individualized design than west of Maryland, where there are more uniform examples of period revival duplexes and bungalows in greater densities.

Prospect Hill and Kenwood Park

Prospect Hill, between Park Place and Kenwood Boulevard and Downer and Lake Park, a subdivision platted in 1893, offered East Side homesites within the reach of middle and upper middle income residents. A considerable amount of Prospect Hill was built about 1900, and the architecture is heavily influenced by Victorian proportions and Queen Anne, Georgian and Colonial Revival millwork details.

North of Kenwood Boulevard, between Downer and Summit, Kenwood Park was developed primarily after 1910. The houses are of considerable size, and are situated on large, wider lots. Like Prospect Hill, architectural styles are period revival, with heavy emphasis on English Tudor and Italian Renaissance precedents.

2757 N. Shepard Ave., 1900. The unique Alpine facade of this well-crafted frame house harmonized well with its Queen Anne and period revival neighbors on the upper East Side.

3360 N. Hackett Ave., 1927. The influence of the Prairie School can be seen in the horizontal lines, window arrangement, entry and eaves of this brick residence designed by Hugo V. Miller.

University of Wisconsin-Milwaukee (UWM)

The campus of the University of Wisconsin-Milwaukee (UWM) is largely contained on three blocks bounded by Edgewood and Hartford Avenues on the north, Downer Avenue on the east, Kenwood Boulevard on the south, and Cramer Street and Maryland Avenue on the west. An institution originally founded for the training of teachers, UWM now serves the metropolitan area with a varied university curriculum.

Throughout the nineteenth century, the campus site remained an undeveloped tract, first as peripheral farm land and later as an open field, as the city limits moved north to Kenwood Boulevard in 1876 and to Edgewood Avenue in 1898. In 1895, the Milwaukee Female College, then located downtown on Milwaukee Street, merged with Downer College of Fox Lake, Wisconsin to form Milwaukee-Downer College. A new campus site was proposed, and in 1899 construction of the college began on the northwest corner of Downer and Hartford Avenues.

The Milwaukee-Downer College "Quad" is composed of Merrill Hall (1899); Holton Hall (1899); Johnston Hall (1901); and Greene Hall (1904). The first building, Merrill, was designed by Milwaukee architect Howland Russel. Alexander C. Eschweiler designed the other three halls in the same style, scale, and building materials in order to provide a harmonious campus setting. All four are constructed of red sandstone and red pressed brick with terra cotta trim. Their Collegiate Gothic designs employ Tudor elements such as steep gables, pointed arch openings, and crenellated turrets. Five other compatibly-designed buildings, constructed between 1910 and 1937, round out the former Milwaukee-Downer campus.[19]

In 1909, the Wisconsin State Normal School relocated its campus on the northwest corner of Downer Avenue and Kenwood Boulevard. The original school building, opened in 1885, stands on the 1800 block of West Wells Street (see Civic Structures). The Normal School's new building (now Mitchell Hall) was designed by architects Henry Van Ryn and Gerrit J. DeGelleke in the Neo-classical Style; its walls are red brick with contrasting limestone trim and colonnade.

During the next fifty years, the Normal School changed administration and expanded its curriculum and facilities. In 1951 it became the Wisconsin State Teachers College, and in 1956 the school was integrated into the University of Wisconsin. In expanding its facilities, UWM purchased the Milwaukee-Downer College campus in the early 1960s.[20]

Myron T. MacLaren House, 3230 E. Kenwood Blvd., 1920-23. The lakeshore above Lake Park became the twentieth century counterpart to earlier mansion-building along Prospect Ave. Designed by Milwaukee architects Fitzhugh Scott and Macdonald Mayer, the house is especially notable for the quality of materials and workmanship, evident in the Plymouth Stone walls, slate roof, ornamental leaded glass, carved stone trim, interior woodwork, and hand-wrought hardware. The total plan included a sunken garden, swimming pool, tennis courts, and landscaped terrace descending to a private beach. The State of Wisconsin purchased the MacLaren estate in 1949, and it is now used by the University of Wisconsin-Milwaukee as a conference center.

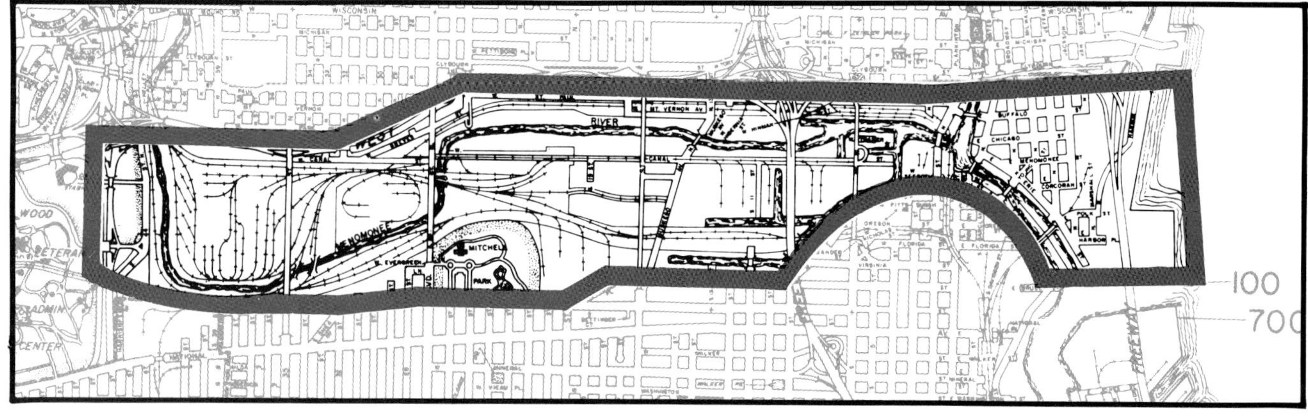

Menomonee Valley

As one approaches the South Side, he is impressed with the truth of what he has been told — that this is the manufacturing center. The docks of the transportation companies near West Water street bridge, the immense tobacco factory of Ed. Aschermann & Co., on South Water, with the railroad facilities of that great corporation, the St. Paul Company, are what first strike the eye as evidences of the fact. The two ship yards, one on Vogel's Island, Menomonee River, the other at the foot of Washington street, are both on this side. . . . The Menomonee Valley hums with industry. Pfister & Vogel's tannery, Burnham's brick yards, the immense slaughter houses, sash, door and blind factory of Sanger, Rockwell & Co., and at the western extremity the machine shops of the St. Paul road conspire to animate it from morning to night.

A. T. Andreas, *History of Milwaukee,* 1881.

The Menomonee Valley is the low, flat river basin of the Menomonee River. It extends west and southwest from the confluence of the Milwaukee and Menomonee Rivers. Varying in width from one-half to almost a mile, it divides the city into distinct north and south sides. The Menomonee Valley is defined here as the area between Interstate 94 (including an extension in the northwest corner) on the north; Pierce and Bruce Streets to the south; Highway 41 on the west; and Lake Michigan on the east.

Menomonee Valley

At the time of Milwaukee's first settlement, the valley was a wetland covered with marsh grass and wild rice fields. "Menomonee" is derived from the Indian Meno-o-mene, or wild rice. Steep bluffs along the river's edge were later taken down to fill the swamplands. Because it was a natural habitat for waterfowl, the Valley was a common destination for pioneer duck hunters.[1]

When development began, the Menomonee Valley was a natural marshland and tamarack swamp at the edge of downtown. Its proximity to the Milwaukee harbor attracted early land speculators who saw the area's potential as an industrial site. The construction of the railroad through the valley in 1851 and the construction of ship canals in the 1860s firmly established the industrial land use of the area. There were few barriers to the growth of industry since residential development within the boundaries of the Menomonee Valley has been minimal.

The Menomonee River originally ran southeast from present-day Muskego Avenue to Lake Michigan. This portion of the river was straightened to an easterly course during the major canal building period of the 1870s, and was then named the North Menomonee Canal.

Prior to the Civil War, the land east of what is now the Sixth Street Viaduct was part of the Kilbourntown and Walker's Point plats. Early maps show that a conventional grid street layout was planned for the valley, extending the grid of the present-day downtown area. West of Sixth Street, the land was in private ownership of community and business leaders such as James Martin, Samuel Marshall, Charles Ilsley and Alexander Mitchell. The far western portion, west of Twenty-seventh Street, was owned by Alexander Mitchell's Chicago, Milwaukee and St. Paul Railroad (Milwaukee Road).

The Harbor

Milwaukee's natural harbor was shallow and unprotected, and the Milwaukee River was partially obstructed by a sand bar. Development of the harbor was initiated by dredging and channeling. In 1857, a major channel was cut. Combined with the extension of the railroad from Milwaukee to the Mississippi in the same year, Milwaukee's inner harbor at the eastern edge of the Menomonee Valley became a center for the storage and transfer of goods, the first stage in its development as an industrial center of national importance.

First Improvements

While a swampland, the valley was a convenient and inexpensive site for storing coal and other raw materials. Railroads were the first to alter the pattern of swampland and storage areas. In 1851, the Milwaukee and Mississippi Railway (Milwaukee Road) was completed as far as Waukesha. The line ran along West St. Paul Avenue to the confluence of the Milwaukee and Menomonee Rivers. A second line was completed in 1868 by the Milwaukee, St. Paul and LaCrosse Division Railway (Milwaukee Road). It ran along the valley's southern edge of Florida Street, curving north with spurs at the base of both North Plankinton Avenue and North Third Street. This line was connected to the Milwaukee and Chicago Railway (Chicago and Northwestern) south to the Lake Shore line and west to the Beloit line.

Menomonee Valley, photograph c. 1875-1880. Remnants of the valley's pre-industrial landscape are visible in this early photograph. In the background are grain elevators, the first large industrial structures built in the valley.

Herman Wuhlke Collection

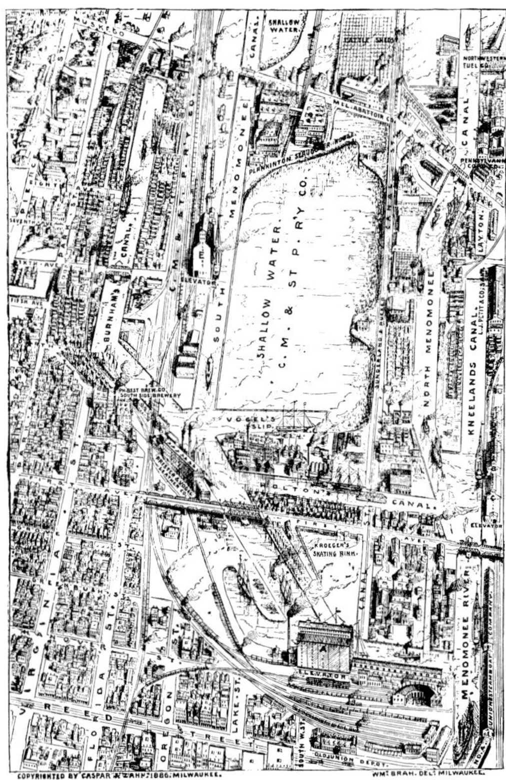

Menomonee Valley, between S. Second St. and Muskego Ave., 1886. Caspar and Zahn's detailed lithograph depicts the eastern side of the valley, the first section to be heavily developed for industrial use in the 1870s and 1880s.

Further Improvements

Prior to opening the valley for industrial development, an extensive amount of dredging and dock construction was necessary. The first activity of this kind occurred in 1857, when private investors drained the marshes immediately west of South Second Street for the construction of the valley's first small factories, warehouses, and foundries. James Kneeland, an official of the Chicago, Milwaukee and St. Paul Railroad (C.M. & St. P.R.R.) financed the first major ship canal in the early 1860s. In 1869, railroad agent-turned bank president, Edward Holton, financed a second canal. The marshes were drained as far as Twenty-seventh Street by 1875. West of this Line, the C.M. & St. P.R.R. continued to drain land into the late 1870s, in preparation for the construction of their car shops. Various schemes were considered by private businesses and government during the 1860s for the valley's development. In 1863, the City of Milwaukee recommended to the Federal War Department that the area be used as a site for a Naval Station. The Menomonee Valley Improvements Bill of 1864 recommended that a system of canals, bridges and viaducts be built.

A formal petition of the Major Improvements Bill was filed in 1869 with both the State Legislature and the Milwaukee Common Council, and dredging for the canals and draining of the swamps began in 1870. The major canals created by the Provisions Bill were the North Menomonee (which rerouted the main course of the river); the South Menomonee (extending just west of Sixteenth Street); and Burnham's Canal (extending just west of Muskego Avenue). A number of major industrialists, such as Frederick Pabst and Frederick Vogel, constructed their own slips. Throughout the 1870s and well into the 1880s, the canals were continually redredged and widened to accommodate the increasing volume of trade and larger sailing vessels. Of the original canals and slips, the North Menomonee and Burnham's remain intact. The South Menomonee and Holton Canals have been shortened significantly and the others have been filled.

The earliest industrial activities in the valley predate the extensive physical improvements, such as roads and bridges, of the 1870s. Brickyards and slaughterhouses were among the pre-Civil War establishments situated in the area. Benoi Finch established the first brickyard in the city at St. Paul Avenue and North Thirtieth Street. John and George Burnham, natives of New York, established a brickyard in 1844 at the foot of North Thirtieth Street. The operation moved to a site on Bruce Street on the clay bluffs south of the Menomonee River in 1848. George Burnham and Sons became the city's largest producer of "Cream City" brick, producing fifteen million bricks in 1880.

Pfister and Vogel Leather Co., 600-740 W. Oregon St. The tannery's main plant consisted of thirty-eight buildings one to seven stories tall, of brick mill construction. One of the company's first brick buildings, and the oldest remaining one, is the five-story Currier Shop, built about 1870. The large complex, still intact, is now owned by the Pfister and Vogel Atlas Corp.

Tanning and Food Processing

In addition to the soap and candle making industries which thrived in the valley, was tanning, an important off-shoot of the slaughtering and meat packing industries. Frederick Vogel opened his Sheep Skin Tannery in 1847 on what was then called Vogel's Island, north of the intersection of Sixth Street and the South Menomonee Canal. In 1857, Vogel merged his firm with Guido Pfister, a leather dealer and formed the Pfister and Vogel Leather Company. Between 1876 and 1910, they expanded the operation to a complex of thirty-eight buildings situated on fifteen acres. Located south of the old Sheep Skin Tannery, the Pfister and Vogel Tannery was one of the world's largest by World War I. Because of decreased demand for finished leather goods during the 1920s, the Pfister and Vogel Leather Company liquidated in 1931 and reorganized the same year as the Pfister and Vogel Atlas Corporation.

State Historical Society of Wisconsin

View south from Clybourn Ave. and N. Fifteenth St., photograph 1890s. Grain elevators, lumber yards, and meatpacking firms were among the early industries to locate in the Menomonee Valley.

The nineteenth century building products industries of the valley — including lumber, bricks, cement and finished stone — served a largely local market. The food processing industries, however, served a regional and national market.

The first slaughterhouses in the valley were north of the Burnham Brickyards, east of present-day Muskego Avenue and Canal Street. The Plankinton and Layton Packing Company built a large slaughterhouse on the Menomonee marsh in 1857. Construction here was probably the result of an 1849 city order prohibiting slaughterhouses within its municipal boundaries. John Plankinton, a butcher, became one of Milwaukee's leading industrialists, and assisted in developing other major meat-packing concerns, including the firms of Frederick Layton, Phillip Armour, and Patrick Cudahy. The meat-packing industries attracted great public comment about their smell, including Charles King's often quoted comment published in *Cosmopolitan* of 1891:

> Out in the broad Menomonee Valley are placed the slaughter-houses, the mammoth beef and pork packeries, the tanneries, soap and candle shops, and other malodorous trades; but no one is inconvenienced thereby except those south and west siders who dwell within sniffing range of the valley, and consequently have the profound commiseration and best advice of those of us who do not.

The city's first flour mills, like its sawmills, were built along the Milwaukee River. As wheat supplies moved through the city because of its rail and harbor facilities, Milwaukee became an important milling center and primary exporter of wheat to Europe and the eastern United States. By 1865, Milwaukee was the largest primary wheat exporter in the country, with shipments of 10.5 million bushels per year. To accommodate the tonnage received by the city, the Chicago, Milwaukee and St. Paul Railroad built a number of grain elevators between 1858 and 1877. Elevators B (1861) and C (1858), situated on Kneeland's Canal, had an average capacity of 500,000 bushels. Elevator A (1864), on the South Menomonee Canal at Canal Street, had a capacity of one million bushels. The largest elevator, Elevator E (1877) was situated on the South Menomonee Canal at Eleventh Street, with a capacity of 1.5 million bushels.

Milwaukee Co. Historical Society

Milwaukee-Western Malt Co., 300-350 S. Water St. In 1903, the Milwaukee-Western Malting Co. erected this malting plant, a group of three to six story cream brick buildings designed by Chicago architect Otto Lurbkert. Although minor additions were made in 1911 and 1913, the next major construction was not until 1932, when these 130 foot high concrete grain elevators were built. Kurth Malting Corp. is the present owner of the plant.

These elevators were among the more impressive structures in the valley, rising to a height of 80 to 100 feet. Their construction was of wood, with tin hurricane roofs. On the site of Elevator E is the last operating grain elevator in the valley, now operated by Cargill, Incorporated. Reinforced concrete tanks replaced the original structure, and the facility has a capacity of 2.5 million bushels.

Elevators in the Menomonee Valley also stored barley, the primary source for malt used in brewing. At the end of the nineteenth century, the center of malting activity was in the eastern valley near South Water, East Florida, and East Bruce Streets.

Prior to the improvement of the Menomonee Valley, Milwaukee's lumberyards were situated along the Milwaukee River. In the early 1870s, several large firms such as Sanger, Rockwell and Company relocated in the valley, and many of the city's lumberyards and millworks followed. Five of the city's major firms were concentrated between South Ninth and South Twelfth Streets and West National Avenue and West Bruce Street. These firms had a combined output of thousands of feet of moldings, sash, blinds, mantels, doors, and fancy scrollwork. The largest, Sanger, Rockwell and Company originated downtown in 1860 as Judd and Hiles. Their first plant in the valley was built at 1038 West Bruce Street in 1871.

The largest parcels of land in the valley were devoted to storage and transportation. Stockpiles of salt, sand, coal, and lumber were part of the industrial landscape. Commercial warehousing was developed in this area primarily after the Civil War, and was concentrated on South Second Street, and Plankinton Avenue between West St. Paul Street and West Florida Street. The major firms stored and distributed hardware, groceries and fruit, agricultural implements, seed and flour, drugs, liquor, soap and paper. The warehouse district of the valley was second in importance to the Old Third Ward warehouse district across the river.

Menomonee Valley, photograph c. 1900.

State Historical Society of Wisconsin

Breweries and Distilleries

Herman Teutelshofer opened a German lager brewery in the Menomonee Valley in 1841 near 748 West Virginia Street. This brewery was eventually acquired by the Best Brewing Company (later Pabst Brewing Company). The only remaining building within the complex is Best's South Side Bottling House, a well-preserved cream brick structure built in 1881. Along the upper valley, the Plank Road Brewery (later the Frederick Miller Brewery), was established in 1848, and followed by a number of others, including the Falk, Jung, and Borchert Brewery at 639 South Twenty-ninth Street, established in 1855.

The distilling and rectifying of liquor was also an early valley activity. The first distilleries were built along South First and South Second Streets during the 1850s and 1860s. The oldest known extant distillery is located at 131 South First Street. Built in 1855 for Emil Schneider, the distillery produced rye and bourbon whiskies. The major distillery in the valley was the Meadow Spring Distillery. Established in 1882 at 325 North Twenty-seventh Street, the company soon became a major supplier of yeast, a by-product of the distilling process. Prohibition significantly changed the production of consumable liquor to industrial and medicinal alcohol. The production of yeast marketed under the Red Star label established the company as a national firm. The company attained increased prominence in 1940 with the development of the first active dry yeast. Today, this company is owned by the Universal Foods Corporation and the Menomonee Valley plant is the second largest yeast producer in the country.

Change in Industrial Focus: Manufacturing

In the 1880s, Milwaukee's dominance in the upper Midwest as the center for grain shipments and processing was usurped by Minneapolis and St. Paul to the northwest. In the 1870s, rail lines connected the Twin Cities with direct routes to Chicago to the south and with the expansive wheat belt to the west. The packing industry also moved its locus to Chicago and the more accessible markets of Kansas City and Omaha. By 1880, Milwaukee's processed grain exports, such as flour, dropped to pre-Civil War production levels.

The establishment of Bay View Steel Rolling Mill in 1867 foreshadowed Milwaukee's shift to a center of the heavy metals industry. Several foundries had located in the valley prior to the Civil War, the first in 1842. Early metal work produced included locomotive parts, steam engines, holloware, stoves, and boilers. The development of the Bay View Rolling Mill, however, secured Milwaukee's position as the "machine shop of the world" as the plant grew to be the second largest rolling mill in the country. Subsequently, many small machine shops grew into heavy equipment companies. Among them were E. P. Allis and Company (founded 1860), Pawling and Harnischfeger (founded 1884), the Falk Corporation (founded 1895) and the Chain Belt Company (organized 1892), with the well known REX trademark. Sheet iron goods, concrete mixing equipment, elevators and pumps were among other industrial products manufactured in the valley.

Agricultural and automotive equipment, aircraft equipment, metal treating, tinware, rubber goods and chemicals, paper processing, and clothing and shoe industries all flourished in the valley prior to World War I. One of many huge industrial installations was the West Milwaukee Carshops, established by the Chicago, Milwaukee and St. Paul Railroad (now the Milwaukee Road). Originally situated on a sixty acre tract west

West Side Plant, Milwaukee Gas Light Co., 2463 W. St. Paul Ave. The West Side Gas Plant was constructed on the north side of the North Menomonee Canal at S. Twenty-fifth St. in 1902-03. The five Romanesque-influenced red brick structures were designed by Milwaukee architect Alexander C. Eschweiler, and are among the most architecturally significant group of buildings remaining in the valley. All of the buildings have iron or steel structural members, except the seven-story tower, which has a wood-truss roof. The complex is currently leased to Chicago Tube and Iron Co., dealers in tubing, valves, and fittings.

West Milwaukee Car Shops, Chicago, Milwaukee, and St. Paul Railroad, photograph c. 1885. The West Milwaukee Car Shops were designed to function as a self-contained servicing point, construction and repair facility for a railroad system that eventually included 11,000 route miles.

of the Thirty-fifth Street Viaduct, the carshop complex, begun in 1878, is the oldest, largest, and most intact industrial complex remaining in the valley. Between 1879 and 1937, the West Milwaukee Carshops produced 668 locomotives, 151 passenger cars, and 66,676 freight cars. "The Milwaukee Road's ability to forge and machine its own locomotive and freight car components made it unique among the nation's railroads."

A diverse collection of small general manufacturing plants were located along the valley's edges. Unlike their larger industrial counterparts, these small plants did not require expansive tracts of land. Long, narrow loft buildings, common in the late nineteenth century, housed textile mills, printing companies, and glove and shoe works.

After decades of growth and improvement of facilities, the industrial development of the valley peaked in the 1920s. Falk, Pfister and Vogel, International Harvester, Johns-Manville, Pawling and Harnischfeger, Rich-Vogel Shoes, and Red Star Yeast were among the major manufacturers of the decade, employing thousands of Milwaukeeans. After World War II, however, industries sought space in the suburbs which were accessible to truck traffic, and many of the facilities in the valley became obsolete. Today, however, the valley is again providing storage space for a variety of industrial goods and is a key site for industrial redevelopment.

Milwaukee Co. Historical Society

Looking west from Water Street, photograph c. 1950.

Menomonee Valley, photograph c. 1960. The view was taken from the southeasterly knoll in Mitchell Park.

Herman Wudtke Collection

Glossary

The following glossary is provided to assist readers in understanding terms used in the description of nineteenth and early twentieth century buildings. The glossary is adapted from the "Glossary of Old House Parts" published by the *Old House Journal,* and is used with permission.

Baluster
A spindle or post supporting the railing of a balustrade. Balusters can be turned or sawn.

Bargeboard
The decorative board attached to the projecting portion of a gable roof; the same as a vergeboard. During the late part of the 19th century, bargeboards were frequently extremely ornate.

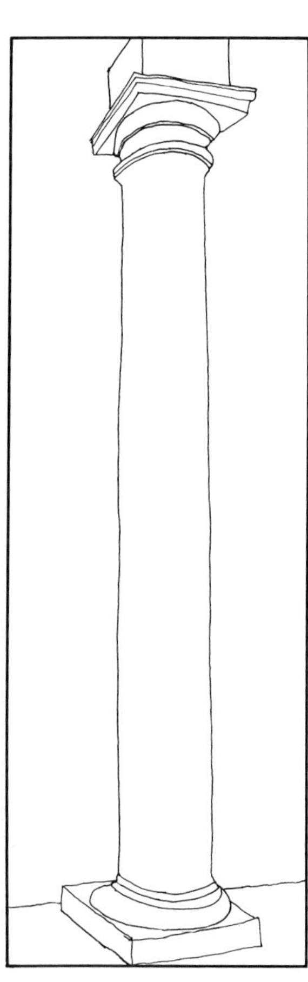

Bay
An element that protrudes from the facade, usually defined by windows. A bay window rises from the ground one or more stories.

Board and Batten
Vertical siding composed of wide boards that do not overlap, and narrow strips, or battens, nailed over the spaces between the boards.

Bracket
A projection from the face of the building to support a cornice or ornamental feature. Sawn wood brackets were an important decorative feature in many Victorian house styles.

Columns
Part of the Classical Order in the architecture of ancient Greece and Rome. Comprised of the base, column, capital and entablature. The proportion for each and every element was spelled out based on the diameter of the column.

Corbel
A bracket or block projection from the face of a wall that generally supports a cornice, beam or arch. "Corbelling out" refers to the building of one or more courses of masonry out from the face of a wall to support timbers or a chimney.

Cornice
In classical architecture the upper, projecting section of an entablature; also the projecting ornamental moulding along the top of a building or wall.

Cresting
A line of ornament finishing a roof. Victorian houses (especially the Second Empire and Eastlake styles) often feature a small cast iron railing with decorative points on roofs and balconies.

Cupola
A small dome or similar structure on a roof. In the 19th century Italian villa style house, a square-shaped, windowed cupola was used from which to enjoy the view and was called a belvedere. Also called a lantern.

Dormer
A vertically set window on a sloping roof; also, the roofed structure housing such a window.

Eaves
The projecting overhang at the lower edge of a roof.

Fanlight
Semi-circular window over a door or window with radiating bars or tracery in the form of an open fan.

Gable
The triangular part of an exterior wall created by the angle of a pitched roof.

Half-timbered
Descriptive of 16th and 17th century houses built with timber framing with the spaces filled in with plaster or masonry. This style of building was imitated in the 19th and early 20th centuries with the Tudor Revival.

Keystone
The central stone of an arch.

Lancet Window
A narrow window with a sharp, pointed arch; it was a feature of the Gothic Revival house.

Lattice
Open work produced by interlacing of laths or other thin strips used as screening, especially in the base of the porch.

Leaded Glass Window
A window composed of pieces of glass that are held in place with lead strips; the glass can be clear, colored or stained. Leaded glass windows are often called "stained glass windows."

Lintel
The piece of timber or stone that covers an opening and supports the weight above it.

Mansard
The classic mansard roof has steep sides broken by dormer windows. Named after the French architect, Francois Mansart, the mansard roof was a prominent feature of the Second Empire Style in the mid-19th century.

Modillion
An ornamental horizontal block or bracket placed under the overhang of the cornice.

Mullions
The strips inside the sash that divide a multi-paned window. Also called "muntins."

Oriel Window
A bay window that projects from the wall of an upper story and is carried on brackets, corbels, or a cantilever. The oriel window is often confused with the bay window. The difference is that a bay starts at the ground while the oriel begins above the first story.

Pediment
A wide, low-pitched gable surmounting the facade of a building in a classical style; also any similar triangular crowning element used over doors, windows and niches, usually triangular but may be curved.

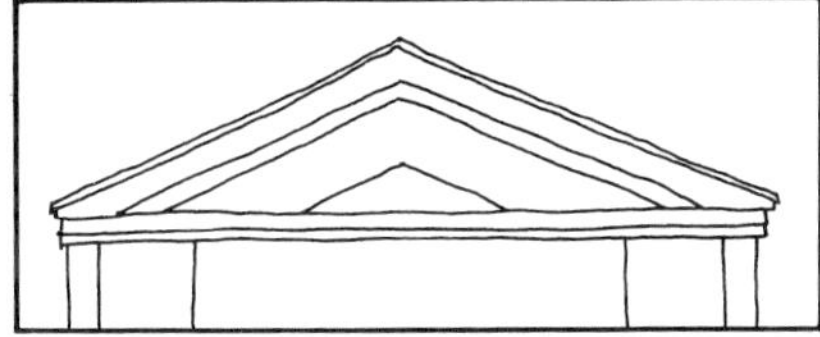

Pendant
A hanging ornament, on roofs and ceilings, used extensively as a decorative feature in Gothic Revival architecture.

Pilaster
A shallow pier attached to a wall; commonly used around doors and windows. Pilasters are often decorated to resemble classical columns and are generally fluted (with grooves and channels) or reeded (the opposite of fluted; a series of convexities like a bundle of reeds).

Portico
A porch, entrance way, or walk consisting of a roof supported by columns.

Quoin
The stones or bricks which form the corner of a building, often distinguished decoratively from the adjacent masonry.

Sawn Wood Ornament
Ornamental woodwork, popular in the Victorian era for trim on porches, eaves, fences. Often called gingerbread, scrollwork and fretwork.

Soffit
The underside of any subordinate member of a building, such as the under surface of an arch, cornice, eave, beam or stairway.

Stained Glass Window
A window with a painted scene or words on the glass that is then fired onto the glass. Windows with just colored glass are often called stained glass, but a true stained glass window is more the product of the art of the painter than the glazier.

Swag
A festive decoration of semi-loops with loose ends, similar to a swag of fabric. They are also called festoons, and when composed of flowers, called garlands. Swags in stone, wood or stamped metal were popular ornaments for the Queen Anne and Colonial Revival houses.

Tracery
Delicate ornamental work consisting of interlacing lines, the intersecting of ribs and bars, as in rose windows and the upper part of Gothic windows.

Transom Window
Any small window over a door or another window, often containing stained or leaded glass.

Victorian
Term used to cover all the various kinds of houses and public buildings built during the reign of Queen Victoria — 1837 to 1901. Although "Edwardian" is used in England to describe buildings in the first decades of the 20th century, here in America they are generally known as "turn-of-the-century." The styles popular in the latter part of the 19th century — Queen Anne, Colonial Revival, Stick and Shingle — continued to be built right up until the First World War.

Wheel Window
Round windows with mullions radiating from the center, as in the spokes of a wheel. Also called Catherine wheel. Those with tracery are generally known as Rose Windows, while the round window without tracery or mullions is known as an "oculus" or "oeil-de-boeuf" — Bull's Eye Window.

Footnotes: Chapter I

1. *Increase Lapham, The Antiquities of Wisconsin, as Surveyed and Described* (Madison, 1855; reprint ed., 1973), pp. 10-19.
   Alfred T. Andreas, *History of Milwaukee* (Chicago, 1881), p. 92.
2. Andreas, p. 92.
3. James Buck, *Pioneer History of Milwaukee* (Milwaukee, 1876), p. 10, map opposite p. 18.
   Bayrd Still, *Milwaukee: History of a City* (Madison, 1948).
4. Jack L. Hough, *Geology of the Great Lakes* (Urbana, 1958).
   Lawrence Martin, *The Physical Geography of Wisconsin* (Madison, 1916).
5. Buck, pp. 53-67.
6. Buck, pp. 53-67.
7. Kathleen Neils Conzen, *Immigrant Milwaukee* (Cambridge, Mass., 1976), p. 12. Still, pp. 13-15, 24-25, 37.
8. Still, 19, 36.
   John W. Reps, *The Making of Urban America: A History of City Planning in the United States* (Princeton, 1965), pp. 294, 364.
9. Still, p. 51.
   Buck, pp. 39-40, 46.
10. Increase Lapham, *Wisconsin: Its Geography and Topography* (Milwaukee, 1846; reprint ed., 1975), p. 113.
11. Still, pp. 23-24, 97.
12. Conzen, p. 138.
    Buck, pp. 22, 45, 47-48, 183, 280.
    Still, p. 66.
13. Buck, pp. 79, 281.
14. Conzen, pp. 15-21.
    Buck, pp. 34, 217.
15. Still, p. 107.
16. Still, p. 107.
    Roger Simon, "The Expansion of an Industrial City: Milwaukee 1880-1910" (Ph.D. Dissertation, History, University of Wisconsin, 1971), pp. 27-28, 29-33.
17. Simon, pp. 33, 34.
18. Still, pp. 50-51.
    Increase Lapham, "Map of the City of Milwaukee" (New York, 1855).
19. Still, pp. 44-47, 169-178, 201, 327.
20. Simon, pp. 35, 38, 41.
    Conzen, pp. 35, 69, 124-125.
    Still, pp. 112, 570.
21. Conzen, pp. 166-167.
    Simon, p. 41.
    Still, pp. 268-269.
    Milwaukee County Historical Society, *The Negro in Milwaukee, A Historical Survey* (Milwaukee, 1968), frontispiece.
22. Simon, p. 23.
    Milwaukee Dept. of Public Works, City Engineer, Annexation Map of Milwaukee (n.d.).
    Milwaukee Dept. of Public Works, City Engineer, Maps Showing City and Ward Boundaries, 1848-1958.
    H. Belden and Company, *Illustrated Historical Atlas of Milwaukee County* (Milwaukee, 1876).
    Wrights Directory Company, "Wrights Maps of Milwaukee and Suburbs" (1877).
23. Conzen, pp. 138, 140.
24. Moritz Wagner and Carl Scherzer, *Reisen in Noramerika in den Jahren 1852 und 1853* (Leipzig, 1854), II, p. 114; quoted in Conzen, p. 126.
25. Conzen, pp. 129, 135, 147.
26. Conzen, pp. 142-143.
    Simon, p. 41.
27. Frederika Bremer, *The Homes of the New World: Impressions of America* (New York 1854, I, pp. 615-17; quoted in Still, p. 112.
28. Still, p. 70.
29. Conzen, pp. 143-145.
    Increase Lapham, "Map of the City of Milwaukee" (New York, 1855).
    William Hogg, "Map of the City of Milwaukee" (Milwaukee, 1880).
30. Conzen, p. 146.
    Still, pp. 268-69.
31. Conzen, p. 146.
32. *The Negro in Milwaukee,* frontispiece.

33. Still, pp. 23-24, 37, 96, 107, 230.
    Milwaukee Sentinel (June 26, 1865); quoted in Still, p. 242.
34. Simon, pp. 47-52.
    Milwaukee Board of Public Works, *Annual Report, 1880* (Milwaukee, 1881) pp. 6, 7, 9, 13; quoted in Simon, pp. 49, 53.
    Still, pp. 238, 358-59, 517-18.
35. Clay McShane, *Technology and Reform: Street Railways and the Growth of Milwaukee, 1887-1900* (Madison, 1974), pp. 52-55, 58-59.
    Still, 368.
    U.S. Department of the Interior, *Tenth Census, Report on the Social Statistics of Cities,* Part II (Washington, 1887); in Simon, p. 58.
36. Conzen, pp. 142, 152.
    McShane, pp. 58-59.
    Simon, pp. 46-47.
37. Still, p. 476.
38. Simon, p. 62.
39. Still, pp. 477-78, 484-86, 494-95.
    Victor Clark, *History of Manufacturers in the U.S.* (New York, 1929), v. 3, p. 227.
40. Simon, pp. 65, 68.
    Still, pp. 329-331.
41. Still, pp. 492-93.
42. Simon, p. 68.
    Still, pp. 484, 496.
    First Wisconsin National Bank, *Industrial Milwaukee: A Trade Review, 1920* (Milwaukee, 1920), p. 24.
43. *Milwaukee Sentinel* (April 15, 1900).
44. Still, p. 487.
45. Simon, pp. 72, 75.
    Sanborn Fire Insurance Maps, 1888, 1894, 1910.
46. Simon, p. 123.
47. Still, p. 325.
    Simon, pp. 72, 74.
48. Simon, pp. 82, 83, 86.
49. Simon, p. 82.
50. Still, pp. 268-269.
    Jerome A. Watrous, "The Poles in Milwaukee," *Memoirs of Milwaukee County,* vol. 1 (Madison, 1909), pp. 612-33.
51. Still, pp. 273-78.
52. Milwaukee Commission on Community Relations, *The Negro in Milwaukee* (Milwaukee, 1963), n.p.
    Still, pp. 454, 471-72.
53. McShane, pp. 84, 133.
54. McShane, pp. 134-135.
55. Milwaukee Department of Public Works, City Engineer, Annexation Map of Milwaukee (n.d.).
    Milwaukee Department of Public Works, City Engineer, Map Showing City and Ward Boundaries.
    A. G. Wright, "Map of Milwaukee, 1930" (Milwaukee, 1930).
56. Simon, pp. 75-76.
57. Simon, pp. 298-301.
58. Simon, p. 298.
59. Still, p. 388.
60. Still, p. 544.
61. Writers' Program, Works Projects Administration, *Wisconsin: A Guide to the Badger State* (New York, 1941), pp. 240-42.

Footnotes: Chapter II

1. Andreas, p. 144.
2. *Milwaukee Sentinel,* August 17, 1842.
3. W. W. Coleman, *Milwaukee Illustrated* (Milwaukee, 1877), p. 106.
4. Andreas, p. 1509.
5. H. Russell Zimmerman, "Milwaukee's Cream City Brick," *Historical Messenger of the Milwaukee County Historical Society,* 26 (March, 1970).
6. Andreas, 1515.
7. Conzen, p. 100.

8. Carl M. Condit, American Building Art: The Nineteenth Century (New York, 1960), p. 44.
9. Leland Roth, A Concise History of American Architecture (New York, 1979), p. 122.
10. Roth, 65.
11. "Letters of the Right Reverend John Martin Henni and the Reverend Anthony Urbanek," *Wisconsin Magazine of History,* 10 (1926), p. 77.
12. *Wisconsin Magazine of History,* p. 79.
13. *Wisconsin Magazine of History,* p. 79.
14. Richard V. E. Perrin, *Historic Wisconsin Buildings, a Survey of Pioneer Architecture 1835-1870* (Milwaukee, 1962), p. 22.
15. *Milwaukee Sentinel,* May 31, 1849.
16. *Milwaukee Sentinel,* June 22, 1849.
17. Roth, p. 321.
18. *Milwaukee Sentinel,* May 2, 1880.
19. *Wisconsin Magazine of History,* 10, (1926), p. 78.
20. *Milwaukee Sentinel,* September 25, 1847.
21. Andreas, p. 1527.
22. W. W. Coleman, *Milwaukee Illustrated,* (Milwaukee, 1877), p. 25.
23. *Milwaukee Sentinel,* September 18, 1881.
24. Andreas, p. 421.
25. Marcus Whiffen, American Architecture Since 1780: A Guide to the Styles, (Cambridge, 1969), p. 11.
26. Roger Simon, "The Expansion of an Industrial City: Milwaukee 1880-1910" (Ph.D. dissertation, University of Wisconsin, 1971), p. 123.
27. Simon, p. 123.
28. Frank Lloyd Wright, *An Autobiography* (New York, 1943), p. 139.
29. Frank Lloyd Wright, *The Natural House* (New York, 1954), p. 17.
30. Bungalow Magazine, 3 (November, 1914), p. 675.
31. Craig Reisser, "Immigrants and House Form in Northeast Milwaukee", (M.A. Thesis, University of Wisconsin-Milwaukee, 1977), p. 64.
32. Reisser, p. 4.
33. Reisser, p. 53, 57.
34. Simon, p. 34.
35. Reisser, p. 35.
36. W. W. Coleman, p. 24.

Footnotes: Chapter III

1. Andreas, p. 421.
2. Andreas, p. 1460.
3. Andreas, pp. 1404-05.
4. Leland M. Roth, *A Concise History of American Architecture* (New York, 1979), p. 127.
5. Carl M. Condit, *American Building Art: The Nineteenth Century* (New York, 1960), pp. 30-36.
6. William J. Anderson, *Hotel Pfister Souvenir* (Milwaukee, 1893), p. 23.
7. Anderson, p. 57.
8. *Milwaukee Sentinel* (February 25, 1888), p. 4.
9. Peter B. Wight, "Milwaukee Revisited," *Architectural Record,* v. 40 (August, 1916), p. 144.
10. Historic American Buildings Survey, Report on Pabst Theater (1970), p. 2.
11. Roth, p. 173.
12. Condit, p. 115.
13. "Pabst Office Building," *Architectural Record,* v. 1, n. 4 (April-June, 1892), p. 472.
14. Perrin, p. 84.
15. Tirrell J. Ferrenz, "The Milwaukee Journal Building," *American Architect,* v. 128 (Nov. 20, 1925), p. 437.
16. Diane Turner, Milwaukee Landmarks Commission Nomination, Northwestern Hanna Fuel Company Building (1979).
17. "Building for Industrial Engineering Research," *Engineering News Record,* v. 105 (Dec. 4, 1930), pp. 881-84.
18. Still, p. 491.
19. Daniel I. Vieyra, *Fill 'er Up: An Architectural History of America's Gas Stations* (New York, 1979), introduction.
20. Wayne Attoe and Mark Latus, "Buildings as Signs: An Experiment in Milwaukee," *Popular Architecture* (1975), p. 84.

Footnotes: Chapter IV

1. Bayrd Still, *Milwaukee: The History of a City* (Madison, Wis., 1948), p. 356.
2. Richard W. E. Perrin, *Milwaukee Landmarks* (Milwaukee, 1979), p. 55.
3. Perrin, p. 54.
4. Mark A. Latus and Mary Ellen Young, *Downtown Milwaukee* (Milwaukee, 1978), p. 52.
5. Latus and Young describe the competition for the Library Building, as does Perrin. An illustration of the central pavilion of the Leipzig Library is contained in Waltrand Volk, *Leipzig* (Berlin, 1979), p. 40.
6. Information for this section is contained in Alfred T. Andreas, *History of Milwaukee* (Chicago, 1881) and William George Bruce, *History of Milwaukee, City and County* (Milwaukee, 1922). *Our Roots Grow Deep* is a recent historical account of the city's school system by William Lamers (Milwaukee, 1974).
7. Andreas, p. 524.
8. Bayrd Still, *Milwaukee: The History of a City* (Madison, 1948), p. 418.
9. R. L. Nailen and James S. Haight, *Beertown Blazes* (Milwaukee, 1971) contains important pictures of early fire facilities and information about Sebastian Brand. This source, combined with information from the files of the Bureau of Bridges and Buildings provided by James Boerner, constitutes the principal data for this section.
10. The principal source for information on Engine House No. 3 is the Wisconsin Inventory of Historic Places form prepared by Mark A. Latus in which a full bibliography appears.
11. Diane Turner, "Milwaukee's Public Natatoria", August 18, 1978 (typewritten paper), contains all the information summarized in this section.
12. Charles Harger, *Milwaukee Illustrated* (Milwaukee, 1877), p. 31.
13. Information on the movable bridges of Milwaukee presented in this section comes largely from *Bascule Bridges* and *Swing Bridges* prepared by the Works Progress Administration for the City of Milwaukee, Bureau of Bridges and Public Buildngs in 1941. A good general source is David Plowden, *Bridges: The Spans of North America* (New York, 1974). The bridges in the Menomonee River Valley are well documented in the Historic American Engineering Record survey of that area.
14. *Milwaukee Sentinel,* June 23, 1889.

Footnotes: Chapter V

1. W.P.A. Writers' Project, *Wisconsin: Guide to the Badger State* (New York, 1941), p. 241.
2. All of the public open spaces acquired by the city to 1910 are listed in the *Annual Report* of the Board of Park Commissioners for that year.
3. Kathleen Neils Conzen, *Immigrant Milwaukee* (Cambridge, Mass., 1976), p. 145.
4. Charles Harger, *Milwaukee Illustrated* (Milwaukee, 1877), p. 72.
5. Harger, p. 12.
6. Alfred T. Andreas, *History of Milwaukee* (Chicago, 1881), p. 430.
7. W. W. Coleman, *Milwaukee: das Deutsch-Athen America's* (Milwaukee, 1880), p. 63.
8. Most of the information on the commercial pleasure parks presented here derives from Andreas, pp. 431-434.
9. Frederick Law Olmsted, Jr. and Theodora Kimball, *Frederick Law Olmsted, Landscape Architect* (New York, 1922), discusses the history of Central Park in detail.
10. Published information on Horace William Shaler Cleveland is confined to his own short books and a reprint of his 1873 booklet *Landscape Architecture As Applied to the Wants of the West* (Pittsburgh, 1965) edited and with a biographic preface by Roy Lubove.
11. General sources for landscape design and city planning are Norman Newton, *Design on the Land* (Cambridge, 1970), and Mel Scott, *American City Planning Since 1890* (Berkeley, 1969).
12. Information on Forest Home Cemetery presented here is derived solely from Gail Hunton's National Register Nomination materials (unpub.) in which a complete bibliography is included.
13. Silas Chapman, "The Forest Home Cemetery, Milwaukee, Wisconsin With a Map of the Grounds," (Milwaukee, 1871).
14. Harger, p. 18.
15. Marvin Christian, "The Milwaukee Park Movement" (M.A. Thesis, UWM, 1967) provides valuable information on the political aspects of the park movement in the pre-commission era.
16. Edward O'Neill, *Proceedings of the Common Council, City of Milwaukee* (Milwaukee, 1869), (foreword, n.p.)
17. *Milwaukee Sentinel,* (October 19, 1870), p. 4.
18. Information on sanitary engineering may be found in Andreas, 412-417, and in William George Bruce, *History of Milwaukee, City and County* (Milwaukee, 1922).
19. *Milwaukee Sentinel,* (January 16, 1879), p. 8.
20. Howard L. Conard, ed. *History of Milwaukee* (Chicago, 1895), v. I, pp. 300-306, includes an essay by Christian Wahl.
21. *Annual Report of the Board of Park Commissioners,* (Milwaukee, 1892).

22. *Annual Report of the Board of Park Commissioners,* (Milwaukee, 1893).
23. Research on the Olmsted-designed Milwaukee parks included a visit to the Olmsted National Historic Site in Brookline, Mass., where there are over 150 items related to the three Milwaukee designs.
24. *Annual Report of the Board of Park Commissioners* (Milwaukee, 1902), p. 9.
25. Board of Public Land Commissioners "A Neighborhood Park Plan for Milwaukee," 1931 (typewritten report).
26. Florence Schulson, "History of City Planning Activity in Milwaukee, 1892-1952," 1952 (typewritten report), p. 4.
27. Charles Zueblin in a series of articles in the *Chautauquan* in 1903 and 1904 presented the arguments for democracy being associated with city planning and particularly the City Beautiful idea as represented by the White City and the Washington plan.
28. Eileen Eagan, "Parks, Planners, and People" (M.A. Thesis, UWM, 1970) deals with some of the political aspects of the park movement after the formation of the Board of Park Commissioners and with subsequent park and city planning activities. Excellent information on Hegemann is included.
29. John Holdridge, "Milwaukee's Civic Center: From Proposal to Execution, 1905-1930" (M.A. Thesis, UWM, 1967) gives a detailed account of the political and bureaucratic development of the civic center plan.
30. The Charles B. Whitnall Papers are collected at the Milwaukee County Historical Society. In them are notes related to lectures and essays which reveal his connections with Geddes.

Footnotes: North Side

1. Information for this section is contained in Alfred T. Andreas, *History of Milwaukee* (Chicago, 1881), Craig Reisser, "Immigrants and House Form in Northeast Milwaukee: (M.A. Thesis, Geography, University of Wisconsin—Milwaukee, 1977) and Roger Simon, "The Expansion of an Industrial City. Milwaukee 1880-1910" (Ph.D. Dissertation, History, University of Wisconsin, 1971).

Footnotes: Northwest Side

1. Roger D. Simon, "Expansion of an Industrial City: Milwaukee 1880-1910", (Ph.D. Dissertation, University of Wisconsin, 1971), pp. 164, 165.
2. Annexation Map of Milwaukee (n.d.).
   Maps showing city and ward boundaries, 1848-1958.
3. *Milwaukee Sentinel* (January 9, 1851), p. 2, col. 3.
   Milwaukee Sentinel (December 20, 1851), p. 2, col. 6.
   Lipman and Riddle, "Milwaukee City and Environs", (Milwaukee, 1858-59).
4. Charles Rascher, *Rascher's Fire Insurance Atlas of the City of Milwaukee* (Chicago, 1888), III, pl. 176, 189, 191, 197.
5. City of Milwaukee, *General Ordinances of 1914,* Chapter 4, pp. 138-39.
6. C. N. Caspar and H. H. Zahn, "Map of Milwaukee County" (Milwaukee, 1886).
7. *Milwaukee Sentinel* (February 3, 1849), p. 2, col. 5.
8. H. Belden and Company, *Illustrated Historical Atlas of Milwaukee County* (Chicago, 1876), p. 5.
9. H. Belden and Company, pp. 5, 8, 12, 13.
10. John G. Gregory, *History of Milwaukee Wisconsin* (Chicago, 1931), pp. 1, 296.
    William George Bruce, *History of Milwaukee City and County* (Chicago, 1922), pp. I, 212.
    Jerome A. Watrous, *Memories of Milwaukee County* (Madison, Wisconsin, 1909), pp. I, 104.
    Milwaukee Sentinel (May 1, 1846), p. 2, col. 4.
    Milwaukee Sentinel (October 18, 1848), p. 2, col. 3.
    Milwaukee Sentinel (October 17, 1899), p. 2, col. 4.
    Milwaukee Sentinel (March 13, 1854), p. 3, col. 1.
11. C. N. Caspar and H. H. Zahn, "Map of Milwaukee County" (Milwaukee, 1886).
12. Simon, pp. 163-168.
    William Knell, "Knell's Quarter-Sectional Maps of Milwaukee County," (Milwaukee, 1893).
    G. William Baist, "Baist's Property of the City of Milwaukee," (Philadelphia, 1898).
    C. N. Caspar, "Official Quarter-Sectional Atlas of the City of Milwaukee," (Milwaukee, 1906).
13. Simon, 169, 171, 211.
    "The Charter of the City of Milwaukee," (Milwaukee, 1889), Chapter 6, sec. 25, 74.
14. C. N. Caspar, *Map and Guide of the City of Milwaukee* (Milwaukee, 1888), p. 28.

15. Simon, pp. 42, 72, 75, 128, 129.
16. Clay McShane, *Technology and Reform* (Madison, State Historical Society of Wisconsin, 1974), pp. 54, 56-59.
    Simon, pp. 121, 162.
17. Simon, pp. 78-80, 136-145, 181, 183, 188.
18. Louis J. Swichkow, "A Dual Heritage: The Jewish Community of Milwaukee, 1900-1970" (Ph.D. Dissertation, Marquette University, 1973), pp. 49-50, 56, 59, 64, 65, 87, 97, 98, 100, 101, 290.
19. City of Milwaukee, "Annual Report of Inspector of Buildings" (1910-1918).
    Milwaukee Sentinel, "Annual Report on Building and Progress", January 1, 1895 - January 1, 1909.
20. *Milwaukee Journal* (March 28, 1926), p. 12, sec. 7.
21. City of Milwaukee, *General Ordinances of 1896,* Chapter 25, sec. 62-66, 734, 735.
22. City of Milwaukee, *General Ordinances of 1914,* Chapter 29, Article 3, sec. 1209, 504, 505.
    City of Milwaukee, *General Ordinances of 1914* (Amended to 1935) sec. 1209, 268a.
23. Milwaukee County Register of Deeds, Book 33, p. 2; Book 31, p. 49; Book 35, p. 14; Book 34, p. 53; Book 31, p. 15; Book 32, pp. 6, 41; Book 33, p. 16.
24. Helen Terry, "Garden Homes Housing Project" (Municipal Reference Library, 1934).
25. Milwaukee Writer's Project, *History of Milwaukee County* (Milwaukee Public Library, 1947), pp. 507-509.

Footnotes: West Side

1. H. H. Bailey, "Milwaukee, Wisconsin 1872" (Milwaukee Lithographing and Engraving Company, Holzapfel and Eskuche, publishers).
   Souvenir of Milwaukee Sangerfest: Guide Through The City (Milwaukee, 1886), pp. 31, 32.
   Milwaukee Sentinel (November 19, 1858), p. 1, col. 5.
2. Lipman and Riddle, "Map of Milwaukee, City and Environs" (Milwaukee, 1858-59).
   J. M. Van Syck, "Map of Milwaukee" (Milwaukee, 1854).
   C. H. Caspar and H. H. Zahn, "Map of Milwaukee County" (Milwaukee, 1886).
3. H. F. Walling, "Illustrated Historical Atlas Map of Milwaukee and Environs" (New York, 1858).
4. State Historical Society of Wisconsin/University of Wisconsin-Milwaukee, "Menomonee Valley Industrial Survey" (1980).
5. *Ibid.*, 4000 West State Street.
6. *Ibid.*, 4000 West State Street.
7. H. Belden and Company, *Illustrated Historical Atlas of Milwaukee County* (Chicago, 1876).
   William R. Knell, "Quarter-Sectional Map of Milwaukee County" (Milwaukee, 1893).
   C. H. Caspar and H. H. Zahn, "Map of Milwaukee County" (Milwaukee, 1886).
8. Kathleen Neils Conzen, *Immigrant Milwaukee* (Cambridge, 1976), pp. 128-29.
   Roger Simon, "Expansion of an Industrial City: Milwaukee 1880-1910" (Ph.D. Dissertation, University of Wisconsin, 1971), pp. 79, 86, 140, 150.
9. City of Milwaukee, General Ordinances of 1888, Section 43, 14 and Section 135, 53.
10. City of Milwaukee, General Ordinances of 1896, Chapter 3, Sections 157, 55.
11. City of Milwaukee, General Ordinances of 1896, Chapter 25, Sections 62-66, 734, 735.
12. Milwaukee Department of Public Works, City Engineer, Annexation Map of Milwaukee (n.d.).
    Milwaukee Department of Public Works, City Engineer, Maps showing City and Ward Boundaries, 1848-1958.
13. Milwaukee County Register of Deeds, "Dousman's Subdivision, 1848", plat book 1, no. 50.
14. Annexation Map of Milwaukee (n.d.).
    Maps showing City and Ward Boundaries, 1848-1958.
15. *Milwaukee Sentinel* (May 13, 1886), p. 8, col. 1.
    Milwaukee Sentinel (May 16, 1886), p. 3, col. 4.
16. *Milwaukee Sentinel,* p. 8, col. 1.
    Milwaukee Sentinel, p. 3, col. 4.
17. *Milwaukee Sentinel* (November 4, 1876), p. 8, col. 2.
    Milwaukee Sentinel (March 9 and 10, 1878), p. 8, col. 1.
18. *Milwaukee Sentinel* (March 11, 1854), p. 2, col. 5.
    Milwaukee Sentinel (April 10, 1871), p. 2, col. 1.
19. John Gurda, *West End* (University of Wisconsin System Board of Regents–Milwaukee Humanities Program, 1980), 10, 11.
20. Gurda, 10–14.
21. Gurda, 59–65.

Footnotes: South Side

1. Buck, pp. 107-108.
   Increase Lapham, *The Antiquities of Wisconsin* (Madison, 1855; reprint ed., 1973), p. 13.
2. Buck, pp. 107-108.
   Howard L. Conard, *History of Milwaukee County,* v. 1 (Chicago, 1895), p. 23.
3. Jerome A. Watrous, ed., *Memoirs of Milwaukee County,* v. 1 (Madison, 1909), pp. 187-188, 191-193.
4. Buck, pp. 140-141.
   Still, p. 36.
   Andreas, p. 468.
5. Conzen, pp. 128-129.
   Harry H. Anderson, "Early Scandinavian Settlement in Milwaukee County," *Historical Messenger* of the Milwaukee County Historical Society, v. 25 (March, 1969), pp. 2-19.
6. Andreas, pp. 1285-87, 1617.
   H. F. Walling, "Illustrated Historical Atlas Map of Milwaukee and Environs", (New York, 1858).
7. Hogg, Wright, and Co., "Map of the City of Milwaukee" (1881).
   Andreas, p. 1539.
   Edward Kerstein, My *South Side* (Milwaukee, 1976), n.p.
8. Andreas, pp. 433-34.
   Kerstein, n.p.
   John G. Gregory, *History of Milwaukee, Wisconsin* (Chicago, 1931), v. 2, p. 1064.
9. *Baist's Property Atlas of Milwaukee* (Milwaukee, 1898).
10. Increase Lapham, "Map of the City of Milwaukee" (1848).
    Julius P. Bolivar MacCabe, *Directory of the City of Milwaukee* (1847-48), p. 8.
    Gregory, v. 2, p. 598.
    Watrous, p. 254.
11. National Register of Historic Places, Nomination Form for Walker's Point Historic District, 1977.
    Gregory, v. 2, p. 675.
12. National Register of Historic Places, Nomination Form for Walker's Point Historic District, 1977.
13. *Milwaukee Sentinel* (March 13, 1868).
14. John Gurda, *Bay View, Wisconsin* (Univ. of Wisconsin, 1979), 15-16.
    Andreas, pp. 1616-18.
15. Andreas, p. 1630.
16. City of Milwaukee, Bureau of Engineers, Maps and Plats Section, "Map of the Village of Bay View" (1887).
    H. Belden and Co., *Historical Atlas of Milwaukee County* (Milwaukee, 1876).
17. H. F. Walling, "Map of Milwaukee" (New York, 1858).
    Lipman and Riddle, "Milwaukee City and Environs" (1858-59).
    Milwaukee County Parks Commission, Historical Files on Parks.
18. William George Bruce, *History of Milwaukee* (Chicago, 1922), v. 1, pp. 182-83.
19. Simon, p. 217.
    City of Milwaukee, Bureau of Engineers, Maps and Plats Section. Subdivision and plat maps.
20. Bruce, p. 185.

Footnotes: East Side

1. Casper and Zahn, pub., *The City of Milwaukee Guide - A Souvenir of the 24th Sangerfest,* (Milwaukee, 1886), p. 23.
2. *Milwaukee Sentinel,* July 18, 1872, p. 2, col. 4.
   Milwaukee Sentinel, July 17, 1862, p. 1, col. 5.
   Milwaukee City Directories, 1878.
3. *Milwaukee Sentinel,* November 22, 1872, p. 4, col. 2.
   C. N. Caspar and H. H. Zahn, "Map of the City of Milwaukee", (Milwaukee, 1886).
4. C. N. Casper Co., pub., *Official Quarter Section Atlas of the City of Milwaukee,* (Milwaukee, 1906), Vol. 1, plat no. 48.
   H. Belden and Company, *Illustrated Historical Atlas of Milwaukee County* (1876).
5. Shirley duFresne McArthur, *North Point South,* (Milwaukee, 1978), p. 11.
6. C. N. Caspar Co., pub., vol. 1, plat nos. 10, 11, 13.

7. Clay McShane. *Technology and Reform: Street Railways and the Growth of Milwaukee, 1887-1900,* (Madison, Wisconsin, 1974), p. 53.
8. McShane, p. 54.
   Simon, p. 267.
9. McShane, p. 61.
   Milwaukee Sentinel, (January 15, 1882), p. 4, col. 3.
   Milwaukee Sentinel, (February 6, 1888), p. 3, col. 2.
   Milwaukee Sentinel, (July 3, 1888), p. 5, col. 1.
   Milwaukee Sentinel, (December 2, 1889), p. 3, col. 3.
10. Board of Public Land Commissioners, "City of Milwaukee, 1870," (City Planning Division, 1958).
11. *Milwaukee City Directories,* 1885-1900.
12. *Milwaukee City Directories,* 1935-1950.
13. W. W. Colemann, pub., *Milwaukee Illustrated,* (Milwaukee, 1877), pp. 109, 110.
14. City of Milwaukee, *General Ordinances of 1906,* Chapter 25, Sec. 81-83.
    City of Milwaukee, *General Ordinances of 1914,* Chapter 29, article 3, pp. 504, 505.
15. McArthur, pp. 13, 14.
16. *Milwaukee Society Blue Books,* 1890-1915.
    Milwaukee City Directories, 1890-1915.
    C. N. Caspar Co., pub., vol., plat no. 12.
17. *Milwaukee Journal,* (May 2, 1920), p. 9, sec. 6.
18. *General Ordinances of 1906,* 230, 231.
19. "The Milwaukee-Downer Quad", National Register of Historic Places Inventory-Nomination Form, (State Historical Society of Wisconsin, 1973).
20. Douglas A. Woods, *UWM Buildings,* (University of Wisconsin-Milwaukee Library, 2nd edition, 1977), pp. 7, 11, 19, 30, 36.

Footnotes: Menomonee Valley

1. Sources for the Menomonee Valley research included standard works on the history of Milwaukee, and the Menomonee Valley Industrial Survey (1980). The Menomonee Valley Industrial Survey project, sponsored by the State Historical Society of Wisconsin and the University of Wisconsin-Milwaukee, inventoried industrial sites and compiled a detailed report of the development of the Menomonee Valley. We referred to an unpublished manuscript by Ramond H. Merritt and Carol L. Snook, "Milwaukee's Menomonee Valley, An Inventory of Historic Engineering and Industrial Sites," and Historic American Engineering Record Inventory Cards compiled by the project team.

XI Bibliography

Books, Articles, Theses

Anderson, Harry H., "Early Scandinavian Settlement in Milwaukee County, *Historical Messenger of the Milwaukee County Historical Society*, V. 25 (March, 1969).

Anderson, William J., *Hotel Pfister Souvenir* (Milwaukee, 1893).

Andreas, Alfred T., *History of Milwaukee* (Chicago, 1881).

Art Work of Milwaukee. Plates. (Chicago, 1895).

Association for the Advancement of Milwaukee, *Milwaukee's Great Industries* (Milwaukee, 1892).

Attoe, Wayne and Mark Latus, "Buildings as Signs: An Experiment in Milwaukee" *Popular Architecture* (1975).

Barton, Elmer, comp., *Industrial History of Milwaukee* (Milwaukee, 1886).

Beckman, Thomas, *Milwaukee Illustrated: Panoramic and Bird's-Eye Views of a Midwestern Metropolis, 1844-1908* (Milwaukee, 1978).

Borun, Thaddeus, *We, the Milwaukee Poles* (Milwaukee, 1946).

Bremer, Frederika, *Homes of the New World: Impressions of America* (New York, 1854).

Bruce, William George, "Old Milwaukee's Yankee Hill," *Wisconsin Magazine of History*, V. 30 (March, 1947).

Bruce, William George, *History of Milwaukee* (Chicago, 1922).

Buchanan, Thomas R., "Black Milwaukee, 1890-1915" (M.A. Thesis, University of Wisconsin-Milwaukee, 1974).

Buck, James, *Pioneer History of Milwaukee*, (Milwaukee, 1876).

"Building for Industrial Engineering Research," *Engineering News Record*, V. 105 (December 4, 1930).

Caspar and Zahn, *The City of Milwaukee Guide: A Souvenir of the 24th Sängerfest* (Milwaukee, 1886).

Chapman, Silas, "The Forest Home Cemetery, Milwaukee, Wisconsin, With a Map of the Grounds" (Milwaukee, 1871).

Christian, Marvin, "The Milwaukee Park Movement," (M.A. Thesis, University of Wisconsin-Milwaukee, 1967).

Clark, Victor, *History of Manufacturers in the U.S.* (New York, 1929).

Cleveland, Horace William Shafer, *Landscape Architecture as Applied to the Wants of the West* (Chicago, 1873).

Coleman, W. W., *Milwaukee: das Deutsch-Athen America's* (Milwaukee, 1880).

Conard, Howard L., *History of Milwaukee County* (Chicago, 1895).

Condit, Carl M., *American Building Art: The Nineteenth Century* (New York, 1960).

Conzen, Kathleen Neils, *Immigrant Milwaukee, 1836-1860: Accommodation and Community in a Frontier Community* (Cambridge, Mass., 1976).

Downing, Alexander Jackson, *Cottage Residences or a Series of Designs for Rural Cottages and Villas and Their Gardens and Grounds adapted to North America.* (New York, 1865).

Eagan, Eileen, "Parks, Planners, and People" (M.A. Thesis, University of Wisconsin-Milwaukee, 1970).

Ferrenz, Tirrell J., "The Milwaukee Journal Building," *American Architect*, V. 128 (November 20, 1925).

First Wisconsin National Bank, *Industrial Milwaukee: A Trade Review, 1920* (Milwaukee, 1920).

Gregory, John G., *History of Milwaukee, Wisconsin* (Chicago, 1931).

Gurda, John, *Bay View, Wisconsin.* (University of Wisconsin, 1979).

Gurda, John, *The West End* (University of Wisconsin, 1980).

Harger, Charles, *Milwaukee Illustrated* (Milwaukee, 1877).

Holdridge, John, "Milwaukee Civic Center: From Proposal to Execution, 1905-1930" (M.A. Thesis, University of Wisconsin-Milwaukee, 1967).

Hough, Jack L., *Geology of the Great Lakes* (Urbana, 1958).

Ilsey, Samuel, "The Work of Alexander C. Eschweiler," *Architectural Record* (March, 1905).

Kerstein, Edward, My *South Side* (Milwaukee, 1976).

Koss, Rudolph A., *Milwaukee* (Milwaukee, 1891).

Lamers, William, *Our Roots Grow Deep* (Milwaukee, 1974).

Lapham, Increase, *Wisconsin: Its Geography and Topography* (Milwaukee, 1846; reprint edition, 1975).

Lapham, Increase, *The Antiquities of Wisconsin* (Madison, 1855; reprint edition, 1973).

Latus, Mark A. and Mary Ellen Young, *Downtown Milwaukee* (Milwaukee, 1978).

Long, Elias, *Ornamental Gardening for Americans* (New York, 1884).

Lubove, Roy, *Contributions of the Regional Planning Association of America* (Pittsburgh, 1963).

McArthur, Shirley du Fresne, *North Point South* (Milwaukee, 1978).

McShane, Clay, *Technology and Reform: Street Railways and the Growth of Milwaukee, 1887-1900* (Madison, 1974).

Martin, Lawrence, *The Physical Geography of Wisconsin* (Madison, 1916).

Milwaukee County Historical Society, *The Negro in Milwaukee: A Historical Survey* (Milwaukee, 1968).

Milwaukee of Today: Cream City of the Lakes (Milwaukee, 1892).

Milwaukee Real Estate Board, *Milwaukee: 100 Photogravures* (Milwaukee, 1892).

Milwaukee Writer's Project, *History of Milwaukee County* (Milwaukee Public Library, 1947).
Nailen, R. L. and J. S. Haight, *Beertown Blazes* (Milwaukee, 1971).
Newton, Norman, *Design on the Land* (Cambridge, 1970).
Olmsted, Frederick Law, Jr. and Kimball, Theodore. *Frederick Law Olmsted, Landscape Architect* (New York, 1922).
"Pabst Office Building," *Architectural Record,* V. 1, N. 4 (April-June, 1892).
Palliser's Model Homes for the People. Palliser, Palliser and Company, Architects, (Bridgeport, Connecticut, 1876).
Perrin, Richard W. E., *Historic Wisconsin Buildings, a Survey of Pioneer Architecture, 1835-1870* (Milwaukee, 1962).
Perrin, Richard W. E., *Milwaukee Landmarks* (Milwaukee, Second Edition, 1979).
Reisser, Craig, "Immigrants and House Form in Northeast Milwaukee" (M.A. Thesis, Geography, University of Wisconsin-Milwaukee, 1977).
Reps, John W., *The Making of Urban America: A History of City Planning in the U.S.* (Princeton, 1965).
Roth, Leland M., *A Concise History of American Architecture* (New York, 1979).
Scott, Frank J., *The Art of Beautifying Suburban Home Grounds* (New York, 1881).
Scott, Mel, *American City Planning Since 1890* (Berkeley, Calif., 1969).
Simon, Roger, "The Expansion of an Industrial City: Milwaukee 1880-1910" (Ph.D. Dissertation, History, University of Wisconsin, 1971).
Stein, S. L., *Milwaukee* (Milwaukee, n.d.).
Stickley, Gustav, *Craftsman Homes* (New York, 1909).
Still, Bayrd, *Milwaukee: History of a City* (Madison, 1948).
Swichkow, Louis J., "A Dual Heritage: The Jewish Community of Milwaukee, 1900-1970" (Ph.D. Dissertation, History, Marquette University, 1973).
Swichkow, Louis, *History of the Jews in Milwaukee* (Phila., 1963).
Terry, Helen, *Garden Homes Housing Project* (Milwaukee, Municipal Reference Library, 1934).
Vieyra, Daniel I., *Fill'er Up: An Architectural History of America's Gas Stations* (New York, 1979).
Wagner, Moritz and Carl Scherzer, *Reisen in Noramerika in deu Jahreu 1852 und 1853* (Leipzig, 1854).
Watrous, Jerome A., *Memoirs of Milwaukee County* (Madison, 1909).
Wight, Peter B., "Milwaukee Revisited," *Architectural Record,* V. 40 (August, 1916).
Withey, Henry F. and Elsie Rathburn, *Biographical Dictionary of American Architects* (Los Angeles, 1956).
Woods, Douglas A., *UWM Buildings* (University of Wisconsin-Milwaukee Library, 1977).
Wright, Frank Lloyd, *An Autobiography* (New York, 1943).
Wright, Frank Lloyd, *The Natural House* (New York, 1954).
Wright's Directory Company, *Wright's City Directories of Milwaukee.*
Writer's Program, Works Projects Administration, *Wisconsin: A Guide to the Badger State* (New York, 1941).
Young, Mary Ellen and Wayne Attoe, *Places of Worship - Milwaukee* (Milwaukee, 1977).
Zueblin, Charles, Various Articles in Series on City Planning, *Chautauquan* (1903-04).

Maps, Atlases, Lithographic Views

Bailey, H. H., *Milwaukee, Wisconsin 1872.* Lithographic View. (Milwaukee Lithographing and Engraving Co., 1872).
Baist, G. W., *Baist's Property Atlas of the City of Milwaukee* (Philadelphia, 1898).
Beggs, John I., *Map of Electric Railway System. T.M.E.R. & L. Co.* Lithographic View (Milwaukee, 1898).
Belden, H. and Co., *Historical Atlas of Milwaukee County* (Milwaukee, 1876).
Caspar, C. N., *Official Quarter-Section Atlas of the City of Milwaukee* (Milwaukee, 1906).
Caspar, C. N. and H. H. Zahn, *Map of the City of Milwaukee* (Milwaukee, 1886).
Hogg, William, *Map of the City of Milwaukee* (Milwaukee, 1880).
Hogg, Wright, and Co., *Map of the City of Milwaukee* (1881).
Knell, William R., *Quarter-Sectional Map of Milwaukee County* (Milwaukee, 1893).
Lapham, Increase, *Map of the City of Milwaukee* (New York, 1855).
Lapham, Increase, *Maps of Milwaukee* (1836, 1845, 1848, 1856).
Lipman and Riddle, *Map of Milwaukee City and Environs* (Milwaukee, 1858-59).
Milwaukee, Dept. of Public Works, City Engineer, *Annexation Maps of Milwaukee* (n.d.).
Milwaukee, Dept. of Public Works, City Engineer, *Maps Showing City and Ward Boundaries, 1848-1958.*
Palmatary, James T., *View of the City of Milwaukee,* Wisconsin Lithographic View. (Cincinnati, 1856).
Pauli, C. J., *Milwaukee, Wisconsin from the Rolling Mills.* Lithographic View. (Milwaukee, 1876).
Rascher Fire Map Publishing Co., *Rascher's Fire Insurance Maps of the City of Milwaukee* (Chicago, 1876).

Robertson, George J., *Milwaukee, Wisconsin.* Lithographic View. (New York, 1854).
Sanborn and Perris Map Co., *Insurance Maps of Milwaukee* (1888, 1894, 1910).
Van Slyck, *Map of Milwaukee* (Milwaukee, 1854).
Walling, H. F., *Illustrated Historical Atlas Map of Milwaukee and Environs* (New York, 1858).
Wright, A. G., *Map of Milwaukee* (1900).
Wright's Directory Co., *Wright's Maps of Milwaukee and Suburbs* (1881, 1884, 1895, 1904, 1916, 1926, 1930).

Government Documents

Milwaukee, Board of Park Commissioners, *Annual Reports,* 1892-1920.
Milwaukee, Board of Public Land Commissioners, "A Neighborhood Park Plan for Milwaukee," Typewritten Report, 1931.
Milwaukee, Bureau of Engineers, Maps and Plats Section. Subdivision and Plat Maps.
Milwaukee County Parks Commission, Historical Files on Parks.
Milwaukee County Register of Deeds, Property Records.
Milwaukee, General Ordinances.
Milwaukee, Office of the Building Inspector, Building Permit Records.
O'Neill, Edward, Foreword-Untitled Typescript, *Proceedings of the Common Council, City of Milwaukee* (1869).
Works Progress Administration, *Bascule Bridges* and *Swing Bridges,* Reports to the Bureau of Bridges and Public Buildings (Milwaukee, 1941). Copy at the Legislative Reference Bureau, Milwaukee.
Schulson, Florence, "A History of City Planning Activity in Milwaukee" (Milwaukee, Board of Public Land Commissioners, 1952).

Archives and Manuscripts

American Institute of Architects, Wisconsin Chapter, Files on Architects.
Historic American Buildings Survey, Records.
Milwaukee Landmarks Commission, Records.
Illustrated Architectural Designs from the Office of Cornelius Leenhouts and Hugh W. Guthrie, Milwaukee, Undated (c. 1910).
Mt. Sinai Neighborhood Historic Buildings Survey (Milwaukee, Department of City Development, 1973).
National Register of Historic Places.
Olmsted, Frederick Law, "Collections," Olmsted National Historic Site, Brookline, Mass.
Sanger, Rockwell and Company, Milwaukee. Sash Doors and Blinds Price List (1891). Copy at Milwaukee County Historical Society.
State Historical Society of Wisconsin/University of Wisconsin-Milwaukee, Menomonee Valley Industrial Survey (1980). Copy at the State Historical Society of Wisconsin.
University of Wisconsin-Milwaukee, Dept. of Architecture, Milwaukee Places of Worship Survey (1975). Copy at Milwaukee County Historical Society.
Whitnall, Charles B., Papers, Milwaukee County Historical Society.
Wisconsin Architectural Archive, Milwaukee.

Newspapers

Milwaukee Journal.
Milwaukee Sentinel.

The National Register of Historic Places in Milwaukee

Property	Address
All Saints' Episcopal Cathedral Complex (1868-69)	804-828 E. Juneau Ave.
Allis, Charles, House (1909)	1630 E. Royall Pl.
Bogk, Frederick C., House (1916-17)	2420 N. Terrace Ave.
Central Library (1895-99)	814 W. Wisconsin Ave.
Federal Building (1892-99)	515-519 E. Wisconsin Ave.
First Unitarian Church (1891-92)	1009 E. Ogden Ave.
Forest Home Cemetery & Chapel	2405 Forest Home Ave.
German-English Academy (1890-91)	1020 N. Broadway
Graham Row (c. 1885)	1501-1507 N. Marshall St.
Holy Trinity-Our Lady of Guadalupe Roman Catholic Church (1849-50)	605 S. Fourth St.
Immanuel Presbyterian Church (1873-75)	1100 N. Astor St.
Iron Block (1860-61)	205 E. Wisconsin Ave.
Kalvelage, Joseph W., House (1896-98)	2432 W. Kilbourn Ave.
Knapp-Astor House (1891)	1301 N. Astor St.
Machek, Robert, House (1893-94)	1305 N. Nineteenth St.
Mackie Building (1879-80)	225 E. Michigan St.
Milwaukee City Hall (1893-98)	200 E. Wells St.
Milwaukee County Historical Center (1911-13)	910 N. Third St.
Milwaukee-Downer "Quad" (1897-1905)	Hartford & Downer Aves.
Milwaukee High Pressure Pumping Station (1911)	2011 S. First St.
Milwaukee News Bldg. (1879) & Milwaukee Abstract Assn. Building (1884)	222 E. Mason St.
Mitchell Building (1876-78)	207 E. Michigan St.
North Point South Historic District	(map available)
North Point Water Tower (1873-74)	E. North Ave.
Old St. Mary's Church (1846-47)	844 N. Broadway
Pabst, Frederick, House (1890-92)	2000 W. Wisconsin Ave.
Pabst Theater (1895)	144 E. Wells St.
Quarles, Charles, House (1891-92)	2531 N. Farwell Ave.
St. James Episcopal Church (1867-68)	833 W. Wisconsin Ave.
St. John's Roman Catholic Cathedral (1847-53)	812 N. Jackson St.
St. Josaphat Basilica (1896-1901)	601 W. Lincoln Ave.
St. Patrick's Roman Catholic Church (1893-95)	1105 S. Seventh St.
St. Paul's Episcopal Church (1882-90)	904 E. Knapp St.
Jos. Schlitz Brewing Co. Saloon (1897)	2414 S. St. Clair St.
Sixth Church of Christ, Scientist (1902)	1036 N. Van Buren St.
Smith, Lloyd R., House (1923-24)	2220 N. Terrace Ave.
611 North Broadway Building (1885-86)	605-623 N. Broadway
Trinity Evangelical Lutheran Church (1878-1880)	1046 N. Ninth St.
Turner Hall (1882-83)	1034 N. Fourth St.
Walker's Point Historic District	(map available)

INDEX

Adamesque (Georgian period,) 103
Advertiser, 147
Alberti, Leon Battista, 106
All Saints Episcopal Cathedral, 185
Alley House,
definition of, 69
examples of, 155, 159, 179
Allied Architects of Milwaukee, 161
Allis, Edward P., Reliance Iron Works, 173, 195
Alpine facade, 188
Ambrosia Chocolate Company, 100
American Colonial Style, 187
American Georgian Style, 55
Andreas, Alfred T., 27, 29, 31, 112, 139, 176-177, 182
Andree, F. W., 158
Apartment buildings, 62, 63, 161, 166, 167, 184, 186
Architectural Review, 127
The Architecture of Country Houses, 115
Arlington Street, 186
Armann, G. J., house, 54
Art Deco Style, 90, 91, 98, 103
example of, 90
The Art of Beautifying Suburban Home Grounds, 71
Ascension Chapel, 132
Astor Street, 184, 185
1100 N., 185
1663 N., 140
Atwood, Charles, 100
Auer, Louis, 124
Auer, Louis, & Sons, 66, 188
Beachman, Julius, 188
Backes and Pfaller, 57
Bahr, Frederick, Building, 175
Baist's Property Atlas, 23
Balloon frame construction, 32, 34, 68, 74
definition of, 31
Baptist Church, 101
Baroque detail, 80
Baroque Style, 98
motifs, example of, 68
Bartlett, 3029 N., 66
Bascule bridge,
definition of, 109
example of, 109
Baubletz, Albert, House, 168
Bay State Foundry, 173
Bay View, 171, 176-177
boundaries of, 177
Bay View High School, 103
Bay View Rolling Mill, 7, 13, 18, 176, 195
Bearman, Joseph, House, 177
Beaux Arts Classicism, 85, 98
definition of, 54
Becher Street, 1407-11 W., 81
Bechtel's, John, Mansion House, 5
Beddard, James, House, 177
Beecher, Catherine E., 10
"Bellanger Row", 62
Bellview Place, 2508 E., 130
Beman, Solon Spencer, 82, 88
Benjamin, Asher, 31
Benjamin, H. M., House, 186
Bennett House, 35
Bentley, John, 43
Bentley, Percy Dwight, 56
Bentley, Tom, House, 55
Berninger Garden, 114
Bethany Church of God and
Christ, 158
Bicknell, A. J., 41
Bigelow, Jacob, 115
Bird, Augustus, 109
Emil Blatz Temple of Music, 124
Blatz Park, 148
Board of Park Commissioners of Milwaukee, 121
Board of Public Land Commissioners, 128
Bogardus, James, 77
Bogk, F. C., House, 57
Booth, John, 167
Boulevard Park, 160
Bours, Dr. T. Robinson, house, 56
Boyington, William, 140
Boy's Technical School, 35
Bracketed Style, 36
examples of, 36
Bradford Avenue, 184
Bradford & Terrace Avenues, 187
Bradford, Maryland and Farwell Streets, intersection of, 112
Brady & Humboldt, 186
Brady Street, 181, 182, 183, 186
1200 E., 186
1214 E., 186
1224 E., 186
Brielmaier, Erhard and Sons, 136
Broadway and East State, 131
Broadway and Wells, 32, 62
Broadway,
317-339 N., 73
611 N., 82
844 N., 132
1020 N., 9
Broadway bridge, 109
Bruce Street, 190, 192
Brumder Building, 86
Brust, Peter, 161
Buck, James, 3, 5, 139
Buemming and Dick, 65
Buemming, H. W., 57
"Bungalow Man", 159
Bungalow motifs, examples of, 67
"Bungalow" fire stations,
definition of, 105
example of, 105
Bungalow Style, 53, 60, 65, 153, 179
definition of, 66-67, 160
examples of, 66, 67, 156, 159, 160, 188
Burdick, Morgan L., Farmhouse, 172
Burka, John F., House, 153
Burleigh near Third Street, 113
Burleigh Street, 3113 W., 90
Burnham Brothers Brickyard, 29, 173
Burnham, Daniel Hudson, 89, 127
George Burnham and Sons, 192
Burnham, John and George, 192
Burnham Street, 2720-22 W., 65
Burnham's Canal, 192
Button Block, 83
Button, Dr. Henry H., House, 41
Byzantine Style, example of, 136
Calvary Presbyterian Church, 168
Canal Street, 169
Capitol Drive, 148
742 W., 103
Carver Park, 114, 147
Cass and Knapp Streets, 101
Cass Street, 183, 184, 185
1135 N., 185
Caswell Building, 88, 89
Cathedral Square, 6, 112
Cedar Street, 165
Cedarburg Plank Road, 148
Center Street, 5001-03 W., 95
Central Public Library, 100
Chamber of Commerce Building, 140
Chapman, Silas, 117
Chase Avenue, 177
Chase, Frank D., 91
Chase's Point, 172
Chateauesque Style, definition of, 48
Cherry & Commerce Streets, 7
Cherry Street, 108
2033 W., 134
Chesborough, E. S., 120
Chicago and Northwestern Railroad, 150, 182
Chicago and Northwestern Railway Depot, 24, 83
Chicago, Milwaukee & St. Paul
Railroad (Milwaukee Road),
163, 164, 191, 192
Chicago, Milwaukee, & St. Paul
Railroad terminal, 18
Chicago Road, 5
Chicago Street, 311 W., 83
Chief Lippert Engine House No. 1, 104
Church, Benjamin, 34, 147
Church, Benjamin, House, 34
City Beautiful Era, 127, 128
City Code,
amended 1914, 155
amended 1935, 160
City Functional Era, 127
City Hall, 19, 99, 110, 112
City Hall Approach, Scheme for, 127
City Planning for Milwaukee:
What It Means and Why It Must Be Secured,
report, 128, 161
Civic Center Scheme,
First, 128
Revised, 128
Civic Improvement in Milwaukee, Wisconsin,
pamphlet, 127
Clair Street, 2461-63 South, 176
Clark and Rapuano, 99
Clarke Square, 112, 178
"Clark's Addition", 178
Clas, Alfred, C., 56, 83, 122, 123, 127, 128, 142
Classical, 104, 186
Cleveland Avenue, 179
Cleveland, Horace William Shaler, 112, 116, 118, 119
Clinton House, 75
Clybourn Avenue, 320 E., 79
Clybourn Street Bridge, 109
Clybourn Street, W., 169
Cobb, Oscar, 77
Coleman Park, 121
Coleman, W. W., 113
Collegiate Gothic Style, 98, 103
examples of, 189
Colonial Queen Ann Style, 55
Colonial Revival Style, 57, 188
example of, 95
Commercial Italianate Style,
definition of, 78-79
Commercial pleasure park,
definition of, 113
Commercial Style, 89
definition of, 88
examples of, 88
Commission Row, 73
Comstock Hill/Uihlein Hill, 150
Concordia College, 164, 167
Concordia neighborhood, 167-168
Congregation B'nai Jacob, 158
Conrad's Grove, 173
Conroy, James, Building, 81
Conway Street, 176
Conzen, Kathleen, 31, 111
Cook, Thomas D., Double House, 165
Cooperative housing, 161
Le Corbusier, 103
Cottage, 151, 153, 178, 179, 182, 183
definition of, 60
examples of 61, 150, 155, 164, 165, 168, 176, 177, 179, 183, 186
Cottage Residences, 36, 115
Country Life, 53
Country Park Commission, 129
Court House Square, 112, 150
Courthouse, 6
The Craftsman, 66, 67
Craftsman Homes, 67
Craftsman House, 65
Craftsman Style,
definition of, 67
examples of, 67
Cramer Street, 189
2451-53, 64
3267 N., 67
Crane, Charles, D., and Carl C. Barkhausen, 9, 65
Cream brick, 39, 155, 157, 163, 167, 172, 175, 182, 185, 186, 187
examples of, 39, 40, 131, 134, 135, 149
"Cream City" brick, 6, 29, 192
Cream City Car House and Mule and Horse Storage plant, 184
Cream City Mills, 75

Cream City Railway Company, 184
Cream City Street Railway Company, 178
Cross Keys Hotel, 76
Czaskos, Joseph, Store Building, 94
Davis, Alexander Jackson, 35
Dearborn, H. A. S., 115
de Gelleke, Gerrit J., 161, 189
Deutscher Markt (German Market), 15
Deutscher Werkbund, 103
Dictionary of Architecture, 64
Douglas, Alexander, 139
Douglas, J. A., Architects and Builders, 139
Douglas, James, 42, 49, 138, 139, 186
Douglas Style, definition of, 139
Dousman, 2914 N., 147
Dousman, Warehouse, 74
Dousman's Subdivision, 167
Downer Avenue, 183, 184, 189
Downer College, 102, 142
Downer College of Fox Lake, Wisconsin, 189
Downer, Judge Jason M., House, 42
Downing, Andrew Jackson, 35, 36, 46, 114, 115-116, 117
Duplex, 155, 158-159, 161, 168, 169, 177, 179, 188
  definition of, 64
  examples of, 23, 63, 64, 65, 152, 153
East Center Street Natatorium (No. 243), 106
East Indian Style, 32
East Side, 180-189
  boundaries of, 181, in 1858, 181
Eastlake, Charles Locke, 47
Eastlake ornament, description of, 47
Eastlake Style, examples of 47
Edbrooke, Willoughby J., 100
Edgewood Avenue, 181, 189
Eighth & Juneau Street, 40
Eighth, N., and West Michigan, 101
Eighth Street, 1215 S., 134
Eimermans Park, 114
Eleventh Street Bridge, 109
Eliot, Charles, 127
Elleson, Andrew, 134, 173
Elsa's on the Park, 83
Engelhardt, John, House, 178
Engine House No. 3, 105
Engine House, No. 35, 105
English Domestic Style, 55
English Garden City projects, 161
English Gothic Style, 130
  examples of, 117, 136, 173
English Gothic Revival Style, examples of, 133
English Medieval Style, 38
English Renaissance Style, 103
  example of, 142
English Style, 187
English Tudor Style, 55, 56, 63, 65, 160, 167, 188
  definition of, 55
  example of, 143
  motifs, 142
Enos & Company, 173
Erbach, Henry, Bakery, 94
Eschweiler, Alexander Chadbourne, 58, 93, 117, 137, 142, 143, 161, 189
Eschweiler, Alexander C., Jr., 142
Eschweiler & Eschweiler, 91, 142
Eschweiler, Theodore, 142
Esser, Herman J., 89, 135
Estabrook Park, 34, 147
Evangelical Lutheran Zions Kirche, 134
Everglades, 63
Exposition Hall, 19
Fachwerkbau, 68
Fahsel, Charles, General Store, 150
Falk, 196
Falk Brewery, 114
Farwell Avenue, 184
  1708, 1714 N., 42
  1741-43 N., 47
Federal Building, 100
Federal-Greek Revival Style, 175
Federal Style, 31, 32, 74
  definition of, 33
  examples of, 28, 33, 36, 54, 62, 139, 175
Feiler and Mylers, 67
Ferry, George Bowman, 56, 83, 132, 138, 141, 142
Ferry, George B., & Alfred C. Clas, 54, 85, 98, 100 102, 117, 122, 126, 142
A Few Hints on Landscape Gardening in the West, 116
Fifth Street, N., and Wisconsin Avenue, 93
Fifth Street
  2376 N., 151
  2576 N., 134
Fifth, S., and Mitchell Streets, 173
Fifth Street, S., 174
  1681 S., 135, 179
Fifth Ward Primary School, 102
Filtering styles, creative eclecticism, 38
Finch's Subdivision, 164
First Baptist Church, 131
First District Branch School, 183
First Independent Congregational Welsh Church, 132
First Street, 2816 N., 147
First Ward Triangle, 112
Fitzgerald, Robert P., House, 185
Flemish motifs, 86
Flemish Renaissance Style, 87
  examples of, 142
Florida Street, 191
Flushing Tunnel, 120
Flushing Tunnel Park, 118, 120
Fond du Lac Avenue, 158
Forest Home Avenue, 8, 113, 173, 178
  2504, 33, 139
Forest Home Avenue and Layton Boulevard, 117
Forest Home Cemetery, 117, 173
Fourteenth District School, 102
Fourth Street Public School, 103, 150
Fourth & Walker, 102
Fourth Street,
  1034 N., 9
  1542 N., 102, 103
  1553 N., 34
  2215 N., 102
  2576 N., 47
Fourth Street, South, & Pierce Street, 35
Fourth Street,
  1137 S., 175
  1646 S., 106
Fourth Ward Square, 112
Fowler, Orson Squire, 38
Frank and Mueller, 49
Franklin Street and Prospect Avenue, intersection of, 112
"Free classic" phase, 49
French Baroque Style, 38
French, Denis D., 182
French Gothic Style, 135
French Renaissance Style, 48, 85, 103
  examples of, 85
French Romanesque Style, 130
French Second Empire Style, 80, 81
  definition of, 43
  examples of, 43
Fribers, Fred, 167
Frost, Charles Sumner, 83
Galena Street, 235 W., 148
Galvanized Iron Works, 78
Garden Homes, 52
  definition of, 161
  example of, 161
Garden Homes Corporation, 161
Gardens, examples of, 69, 70, 71, 107
Garfield Avenue School, 102
Garfield, 418-420 E., 150
Garfield Avenue, 642 W., 94
Garfield Park, 113
Gas Light Building, 142
Geddes Patrick, 129
Georgian Revival Style, 63, 142, 155, 160, 168, 169, 177, 179, 186
Georgian Style, example of, 55
Gerdis, F. H., cottage, 61
German Baroque Revival Style, example of, 165
German Baroque Style, 48, 50, 86
  motif, 142
German beer hall & restaurant, 73
German-English Academy, 9
German Gothic Style, 130
German Renaissance Style, 86, 87, 88, 167
  details, 148
  example of, 86
  forms, 135, 167
German Stadt Theater, 86
Germania Building, 86
Germania Publishing Company, 86
Gesu Church, 141
Gettelman, A., Brewing Company, 163, 164
Gilman's Addition, 187
Gimbel Brothers Store, 88, 89, 90
Gipfel, Jacob, House, 68
Gipfel Union Brewery, 74
Glidden & Lockwood's Addition, 187
Glidden, Jefferson, 183
Globe Iron Works, 173
Golda Meir School, 102, 103
Gold's Perfect Heater, 41
Gombert, Charles A., 120
Gordon Place, 153
  2443 N., 38
Gothic details, 104
  forms, 135
Gothic Revival Style, 32, 35, 42, 76, 115
  definition of, 35
  examples of, 35, 76, 132, 134, 150, 173, 185
Gothic Style, 41, 44, 55, 63, 104
  motifs, 68
Grace Presbyterian Church, 136
Graham Row, 63
Grand Avenue, 19, 167-168, 186
Grand Avenue bridge, 182
Grand Avenue Congregational Church, 168
Grant Boulevard, 155, 158
Grant Street, 160
Granville, 157
Gray, Asa, 115
Grecian Style, 32
Greek Revival Style, 32, 33, 35, 36, 38, 39, 54, 74, 75, 85, 98, 112, 175, 177
  definition of, 34
  examples of, 31, 34, 62, 70, 74, 75, 98, 101, 112 131, 147
Green Bay & Green Tree Roads, 68
Green Bay Avenue, 5
Green Bay Plank Road, 148, 153
Green Bay Road, 5
Greendale, 52
Greene Hall, 189
Greenfield Avenue, 174, 178
Greenfield Avenue Natatorium (no. 1645W), 106
Green's, Schubert's and Conrad's establishments, 114
Grieb, Donald, Associates, 99, 100
The Grouping of Public Buildings, report, 128
Guthrie, Hugh W., 55
Hackett Avenue, 3360 N., 188
Half-timbered house, definition of, 68
Halfway House Tavern and Inn, 76
Hampshire, 2717 E., 137
Hanover Street, 174
The Harbor, 191
Harger, Charles, 118
Harnischfeger Corporation, 168
Harnischfeger, Henry, House, 168
Hartford Avenue, 189
Hawley Road, 407 N., 105
Haynes, Rowland, 126
Hegemann, Werner, 128, 161
Heilbrouncer, L., house, 55

Henni, Reverend Bishop Dr. Johann Martin, 32
Herbst and Kuenzli, 103
Hi Mount Street, 160
Hicks Heights, 152
Highland Avenue, 205 W., 82
Highland Boulevard, 165-167, 186
Hilton, Alfred, House, 175
Hints on Household Taste, 47
Historical Atlas of Milwaukee County, 156, 173, 177
History of Milwaukee, 182
Holabird and Roche, 89
Holabird and Root, 92
Holly, Henry Hudson, 41
Holly's Country Seats, 41
Holton Canal, 192
Holton Hall, 189
Holy Rosary Roman Catholic Church and
  Rectory, 135
Home for All, or the Gravel Wall and
  Octagon Mode of Building, A 38
A Home Building . . . . . at about 400 Places from
New York to San Francisco, 1876, 29
Home Show Winner, 1933, 58
Hope Avenue, between Sherman Boulevard and
  N. 47th Street, 161
Hopkins Avenue, 158
The Horticulturist, 35, 70, 115, 116
Hotel Pfister, 82, 141
Housing Authority of the City of Milwaukee, 161
How Much Playground Space Does a City Need?, 126
How the Kinnickinnic Should Look, 129
Howard, Ebenezer, 161
Howard, Needles, Tammen & Bergendorff, 99
Howard, William, House, 34
Howe Truss type (swing bridge), example of, 108, 109
Howell and Oklahoma, 126
Howell Avenue, 177
Howell Avenue Park, 121
Howell Avenue, 5905 S., 76
Humboldt, 148
Humboldt Avenue, 158, 183
Humboldt Avenue bridge, 186
Humboldt Boulevard, 148, 153
  2435-37 N., 153
Humboldt Park, 121, 126, 173
Humboldt School, 150
Hunholz, Frank, 65
Hunt, Richard Morris, 48
Hussey, E.C., 29
Illustrated Historical Atlas
  Map of Milwaukee and Environs, 163, 172, 181
Immanuel Presbyterian Church, 185
Immigrant Garden, 69
Immigrants and House Form in Northeast Milwaukee,
  68
Inbusch, John D., House, 185
Inland Architect & News Record, 142
Inner City Arts Council Facility, 194
International Harvester, 196
International Style, 53, 58, 90
  definition of, 58
  examples of, 58
Iron Block, 77
Irving Street, 1502-04 E., 62
Isenring's, Fred, Hotel, 184
Italian Renaissance Style, 38, 76, 78, 86, 160, 188
Italian Villa Style, examples of, 36, 37, 140, 157
Italianate Style, 32, 35, 36, 37, 39, 40, 41, 78, 98, 104,
  175, 177, 183, 185, 187
  definition of, 36-37
  examples of, 37, 39, 40, 76, 78, 94, 101, 104, 132
  150, 151, 153, 155, 157, 163, 174, 177, 183
Jackson Park, 160
Jackson Street, 112 812 N., 132
Jacobethan Style, 98, 103
  definition of, 103
  examples of 103
Jacobs, Colonel William, House, 70
Janesville Plank Road, 8, 173, 178
Janesville Plank Road and the Kilbourn Road,
  junction of, 117
Jefferson Heights, 160
Jefferson Street and St. Paul Avenue, 12
Jefferson Street, 184
  706 N., 81
  759-61 N., 90
  775-781 N., 140
  831-33 N., 83
Jenney, William Le Baron, 87, 89
Jensen, Jens, 126, 129
Johns-Manville, 196
Johnston Hall, 189
Jones, Alfred, house, 57
Jones, Inigo, 100
Jugendstil, 103
Juneau and Waverly Place, 140
Juneau Avenue, 164, 167, 186
  706-08 E., 62
  804 E., 185
  1060 E., 48
  423 W., 74
Juneau Park, 24, 118, 185
Juneau, Solomon, 2, 3, 4, 5, 6, 15, 27, 109, 111,
  112, 150
Juneau Square, 6
Juneau Street (Chestnut) Swing Bridge, 108
Juneautown, 5, 68, 147, 183
Jung, John S., house, 57
Kalvelage, Joseph B., House, 165
Kalvelage Schloss, 165
Kaminski, Frank, Grocery and Saloon, 94
Kane, Alonzo House, 49
Kane, Sanford House, 49
Keenan, Matthew, House, 140
Kenwood & Downer Avenues, 182
Kenwood Boulevard, 181, 189
  2419 E., 137
  3230 E., 189
Kenwood Park, 183, 188
Keyes, Joseph, House, 32
Keystone, 160
Kilbourn Avenue, 128, 165, 167, 168
  1327 W., 165
  2432 W., 165
  2825 W., 168
  3019 W., 168
  3033 W., 168
Kilbourn, Byron, 3, 4, 5, 15, 109, 111, 112, 119,
  147, 150
Kilbourn Park and Reservior, 118, 119
Kilbourntown, 5, 68, 109, 148, 164, 191
Kinnickinnic and Maple, 104
Kinnickinnic Avenue, 5, 177
  2900 S., 81
  3317 S., 35
Kinnickinnic Avenue Bridge, 109
Kirchoff, Charles, and Thomas L. Rose, 85
Kleczka, F., house, 55
Kleinschmidt, Herbert, house, 58
Kleinsteuber's Machine Shop, 75
Knapp Street,
  820 E., 103
  904 E., 185
  119 E., 50
Kneisler's Tavern, 81
Knurr's Greenfield Park, 114
Koch and Leopold, 168
Koch, Armand, 141
Koch, Henry C., 9, 40, 48, 86, 88, 103, 104, 138,
  141, 186
Koch, Henry C., and Co., 73, 82, 98, 99, 102, 125,
  135, 141
Kosciuszko Junior High, 103
Kosciuszko Park, 121, 126, 173
Kroening, W., Store, 149
Krug Brewery, 148
Kunckell, Carl, Residence, 36
LaCrosse and Milwaukee Railroad, 148
Lafayette Place, 184, 187
Lafever, Minard, 31, 139
Lake Avenue, 114, 187
Lake Dells, 114
Lake Drive, 181, 182, 188
Lake Park, 110, 121-122, 123, 125, 189
  General Plan of, 122
Lake Superior Sandstone, 112
Lake, Town of, 177
Lakeshore Railroad, 150
Landscape architecture, 115-116
Landscape Architecture as Applied to the Wants
  of the West, 116
Lannon stone veneer, 160
Lapham, Increase, 2, 5, 6, 11, 117
Lapham, Increase, House, 5
Lapham Park, 114
LaPoint and Pfenning, 28
Layton and Co. Beef and Pork Packers, 75
Layton Boulevard, 179
  938, 51
  1510, 57
  1516, 57
  1546, 54
Layton House, 33, 139
Leenhouts, Cornelius, 55
Leenhouts, Cornelius, and Hugh W. Guthrie, 55, 65
Leidersdorf House, 71
Leipold, Gustav H., 50
Lenox Street, 2571 S., 103
Lesser, Charles, 106
Liebert, Eugene R., 86, 168
Lilienteich, or lily pond, 126
Lincoln Avenue, 172, 173, 179
  1405-07 W., 94
  1629-31 W., 95
  1701-03 W., 94
Lincoln Avenue Park, 121
Lincoln between Sixth & Tenth, 126
Lincoln Junior High, 103
Lincoln Memorial Drive, 123
Lincoln Park or Lincoln Triangle, 112
Linwood Avenue, 2926 E., 143
Lisbon Avenue, 8, 156
  7707 W., 157
Lisbon Plank Road, 8, 148
Lloyd, Gordon William, 133
Lockwood, John, 183
Locust Street, 122
  1615 E., 103
Long, Elias, 71
Loudon, John Claudius, 125
Lueddemann Garden, 114
Luening, August and Frederick, 32
Luscombe, Samuel, House, 36, 157
Lyon Street, 182
Lyon Street, E., cottages, 183
MacArthur House, 43
Machek, Robert, House, 68
Maher, George, 56, 57
Malig, Charles E., 105
Manning, Warren H., 121, 124, 125, 126, 161
"Mansard" Style, 43
Mansart, Francois, 43
Marietta Avenue, 2951 N., 55
Market Square, 111-112
Marquette University, 164, 165
Marshall and Fox, 85
Marshall Avenue, 43, 184, 185
  1501-07 N., 63
Marshall Street, 186
  927-29 N., 185
  1029 N., 185
  1119 N., 185
  1535 N., 40
  1775 N., 186
Martin, Morgan L., 3, 112
Maryland Avenue, 188, 189
Maryland Avenue School, 183
Mason Street, 111, 181, 184
Matthews Building, 83
Mayer, Macdonald, 189
Maynard & Picken, 188
McFayden, Archibald, House, Sign and
  Ornamental Painter, 28
McKinley Avenue,
  325 W., 5
  1229 W., 45
  3112 W., 54

McKinley Marina Park, 120
McKinley Park, 118
Mechanicsville, 148
Mediterranean Style, 63
  example of, 63
Meinecke Street, 155
Melms Garden, 173
Memorial Drive, 24
Menge, John, Jr., 55
Menomonee River Valley bridge, 109
Menomonee Valley, 190-197
  between S. Second Street & Muskego Avenue, 1886, 192
  Brewery, 163, 173
  defined as, 190
  photograph of, c. 1875-1880, 191
  photograph c. 1960, 197
Mentkowski, Joseph Butcher Shop, 95
Mequanego (Mukwonago) Plank Road, 8
Merrill Hall, 189
Merrill Park, 165, 169
  boundaries of, 169
Merrill Park station of the Chicago, Milwaukee, & St. Paul Railway, 169
Merrill, Sherburn S., 168, 169
Messmer, H., and Son, 106
Messmer, Henry, 65, 138, 140
Messmer High, 103
Messmer, John, 140
Messmer, Robert A., 140, 161
Messmer, Robert and Henry, 137
Metropolitan Commission, 127-128, 129
Metropolitan Parks, 127
Michigan Avenue, W., 169
  231 W., 84
Miller Beer Gardens, 163, 168
Miller Brewery, hill garden, 114
Miller, Frederick, Brewing Co., 164
Miller's Frederick, Plank Rd. Brewery, 164
Miller, Hugo V., 66, 188
Milwaukee Academy Building, 101
Milwaukee & Chicago Railway (Chicago & Northwestern), 191
Milwaukee & Mississippi Railway (Milwaukee Road), 191
Milwaukee and Rock River Canal, 148
Milwaukee Art Center, 24
Milwaukee Auditorium, 19
Milwaukee Bridge Company, 109
Milwaukee Cement Works, 30
Milwaukee City Hall, 86, 87, 141
Milwaukee Club, 81
Milwaukee County Court House, 34, 98, 99
Milwaukee County Historical Society, 85
Milwaukee: das Deutsch-Athen Americas, 113
Milwaukee-Downer College, 10, 189
Milwaukee Downer Seminary, 142
Milwaukee Electric Railway and Light Co., 184
Milwaukee Female College, 10, 189
Milwaukee Female Seminary, 10
Milwaukee Garden, 114
Milwaukee Gas Light Co., 195
Milwaukee of Girls' Trade and Technical High School, 102
Milwaukee Illustrated: Its Trade, Commerce, Manufacturing Interests and Advantages as a Residence City, 40, 70, 118
Milwaukee Interurban Terminal, 84
Milwaukee Iron Co., 7, 13, 173, 176
Milwaukee Journal Building, 91, 92,
Milwaukee, Lake Shore & Western Line, 182
Milwaukee Railroad and Rock River Canal Co., 157
Milwaukee School of Engineering Bookstore, 132
Milwaukee, St. Paul and LaCrosse Division Railway (Milwaukee Road), 191
Milwaukee Street, 184, 189 and Juneau Avenue, 10
  727 N., 81
  1001 N., 132
Milwaukee — Western Malt Co., 194
Milwaukee Turner Society, 9
Milwaukee Water Works Plant, 186
Milwaukee Zoo, 124
Milwaukee's "Gold Coast", 186
Mineral Street, 174
Mitchell, Alexander, Estate, 168
Mitchell, Alexander, Garden, 70
Mitchell, Alexander, House, 43
Mitchell Block, 80
Mitchell Building, 140
Mitchell Hall, 189
Mitchell Heights, 183
Mitchell Park, 121, 125, 126, 173, 197
Mitchell Park Conservatory, 125
Mitchell Street, 179
  and Kinnickinnic Avenue, looking west, 1876, 173
  today, 179
Mix, Edward Towsend, 19, 41, 42, 43, 48, 52, 79, 80, 81, 101, 107, 112, 138, 140, 165, 185, 186
Mix, Edward Townsend, House, 37
Modern Architect, The 31
Modern Dwellings in Town and Country, 41
"Modern Movement", 90
Moderne Style, 40, 90, 91, 92, 103
  examples of, 40, 90
Moore, Fred, 109
Moorish Style, 90
Movable bridges, 108-109
Mt. Auburn Cemetery, 115, 117
Mt. Vernon Avenue, 6415, 103
Mt. Zion Assembly of the Apostolic Faith, 134
Mukwonago Road, 5, 178
Murray and Bradford Avenues, 184
Muskego Avenue, 5, 178, 191, 192
Muskego Road, 5, 178
Mygatt, George W., 141
National Avenue, 8, 71, 174
  West, 5, 178
  West and Layton Boulevard, 173
  438 W., 175
  2904 W., 54
National Park, 113, 173
National Register of Historic Places, 187
National Soldier's Home, 107
Near South Side, 178-179
  boundaries of, 178
Neo-Baroque Style, example of, 132
Neo-Classical Revival Style, 65, 85, 88, 98
  definition of, 54
  example of, 85
Neo-Classical Style, 130, 142, 175
  examples of, 95, 106, 137, 189
Neo-Classical vaults, 117
"New American Pointed Style", 42
New Fond du Lac Plank Road, 8, 155
Newberry Boulevard, 122, 125, 183, 188
  2430, 56
Nicolson's New Carpenter's Guide, 31
Ninth Street, 1046 N., 133, 138
Ninth Street, S., 174
  2977 S., 73
Nolen, John, 127, 128, 129
Normal School, 102
North Avenue, 151, 158, 182, 183, 184, 186, 187,
  540, 149
  2030 W., 134
North Avenue bridge, 149
North Found du Lac Plank Road, 148
North Menomonee Canal, 191, 192
North Point, 183, 184, 186, 187
  boundaries of, 187
  North, 187
  South, 187
North Presbyterian Church, 132
North Side, 147-153
  boundaries of, 147, 151
North-South Freeway, 178
Northwest Side, 155-161
  boundaries of, 155
Northwestern Hanna Fuel Company Building, 91, 92
Northwestern Mutual Insurance Company, 85
Northwestern Mutual Life Insurance Company, 82, 86
Northwestern National Insurance Company, 85, 142
Oakland Avenue, 183, 184, 188
  2003 N., 135
Oberhauser's Blacksmith Shop, 171
Obermann, Jacob, Brewing Co., 148
"Octagon House", 38, 153
Ogden Avenue, 184
Oklahoma Avenue, 173, 177, 178
  529 E., 55
  2500 W., 103
Old Engine House No. 7, 104
Old First Ward School House, 101
Old Fourth Ward Public School House, 101
Old Green Bay Trail, 153
Old Huron Avenue Bridge (Clybourn), 108
Olive Street, 1801, W., 103
Olmsted, Frederick Law, and Co., 121-122, 124, 125, 126
Olmsted, Frederick Law, Jr., 116, 127, 128, 129
Olmsted, John Charles, 116, 121
Olmsted, Olmsted and Eliot, 122, 124
Oneida Street bridge, 109
Orchard Street, 173
Oregon Street, 171
  600-740 W., 192
Oriental Style, 93
  elements, 160
  motifs, example of, 68
Oriental Theatre, 184
Ornamental Gardening for Americans, 71
Pabst Brewing Company, 163, 195
Pabst Building, 19, 87, 88
Pabst, Captain Frederick, 86, 87, 184, 192
Pabst, Frederick, House, 40, 141, 142
Pabst Hotel, 184
Pabst Park, 113
Pabst Theater, 86
Pabst Theater Cafe, 86
Paine House, 187
Palliser and Palliser, 41
Palliser, Charles, 41
Palliser, George, 41
Palliser's Model Homes for the People, 41
Park Avenue, 187
Park Hill Avenue, 169
  West, 169
Park Place, 187
Parklawn Public Housing Project, 52, 161
Parks, Private, 173
  examples of, 113-114, 136, 148, 173
Parks, Public, 118-120, 121-126
  examples of, 118, 120, 121, 122, 123, 124, 125 126, 173
Parks, Rufus, 109
Pawling & Harnischfeger, 195 196
Paxton, Sir Joseph, 125
Peckham, George, House, 185
Period Revival cottages, 160
Period Revival Style, 63, 65, 90, 93, 156, 187, 188
  definition of, 55
  example of, 55
Perkins, J. T., Planning Mill, 28
Perrigo Tract, 126
Pettibone, Sylvester, House, 163
Pfaller, Mark, 57
Pfister & Vogel, 196
Pfister & Vogel Atlas Corporation, 192
Pfister & Vogel Leather Co., 192
Pfister & Vogel Tannery, 173
Philadelphia Baptist Church, 134
"Philadelphia System", 158
Phillip Morris Company, 164
Phoenix Knitting Works, 83
Phoenix Mills, 7
Pierce Street, 190
  1008-18 W., 63
  2315, 2317A W., 60
  3118 W., 63
Pigsville, 169
  boundaries of 169

Pittsburgh Street, 171
Plank Road Brewery, 163 195
Plankinton Avenue,
bridge, 109
North, 75, 191
Plankinton Building, 88, 90
Plankinton Hotel, 142
Plankinton House, 52
Plankinton, John, Building, 89, 90
Pleasant Street, 183
bridge, 186
East, 108
"Pleasant Valley", 148
Plunkett, Henry Phillip, 58
Plymouth Congregationsl Church, 137
Plymouth stone, 189
Plymouth United Church of Christ, 137
Polish flat, 68
definition of, 68
Pope, John Russell, 103
"Post Office", 157
Prairie Avenue, 166
Prairie School Style, 53, 56, 90, 188
definition of, 56
examples of, 56, 57, 95, 160
Prairie, 2617, 64
Preliminary Reports of the City Planning Commission, 128
Prentiss, William A., 27
Pritzlaff, John Hardware Co., 79
Prospect Avenue, 19, 49, 167, 168, 181, 182, 186, 187, 189 and Maryland Avenue, 183
1201 N., 42
1260 N., 63
1363 N., 139
1425 N., 139
1672 N., 48
2150 N., 91, 92
Prospect Hill, 183, 188
Pryor Avenue, East, 177
Przybla, Frank, Flour and Seed store, 73
Public Library and Museum, 142
"Puddlers" cottages", 176, 177
Puddlers' Hall, 176
Pulaski High, 103
Pulaski Park, 126
Queen Anne Style, 38, 39, 47, 48, 62, 65, 81, 141, 155, 165, 167, 169, 175, 177, 179, 183, 185, 188
definition of, 49-50
examples of, 49, 50, 51, 63, 67, 81 94, 135, 168, 186
Quentin's Park, 114
Rague, John F., 28, 33, 139
Railway Exchange Building, 88, 89
Raised cottage, 179
Raised flat, 68, 151, 186
definition of, 68
Rear house, 68, 151
definition of, 69
A Recreation Survey, 126
Red Star Yeast, 195, 196
Reed Street, 174
Refectory Building, West Park, Design for, 124
Reich's, 114
Reisser, Craig, 68, 69
Renaissance Style, 88, 130
motifs, example of, 68
Republic House, 78
Residence Park, 160
Rich-Vogel Shoes, 196
Richards, 2602 N., 105
Richardson, Henry Hobson, 48, 49, 82, 100, 185
Richardsonian Romanesque Style, 48, 82, 83, 87, 185
definition of, 48
examples of, 48, 82, 83, 100, 185
Rische, Herny C., 134
"Ritmeier", 175
River Park, 121, 122, 124, 125
Riverside High School, 103
Riverside Park, 121
Rogers, James Gamble, 103, 112
Rogers, James, House, 40
Roman Catholic Church of the Gesu, 135
Roman Neo-Classic Style,
example of, 99
Roman Revival Style, example of, 98
Roman Style, 100
example of, 185
Romanesque Revival Style, 167
Romanesque Style, 55, 81, 88, 102, 141, 165, 167 175, 183,
examples of, 63, 77, 103, 166, 186
Ross, Albert Randolph, 99
Rossbach, Arwed, 100
Rowhouses, 62, 182-183
examples of, 63
Rufus King High School, 103
Ruskinian Victorian Gothic
chapel, 107
Russel, Howland, 125, 189
Russell Avenues, 176, 177
Saarinen, Eero, 123
Salem Evangelical Lutheran Church, 132
Salem Kircher Gemeinschaft, 133
Sanger, Rockwell and Company, 60, 71, 194
Sanne, Oscar, 122
Sarnow Street, 160
"Sauerkraut Boulevard", 167
Saveland Avenue,
125 W., 136
157 W., 50
Saylor, Henry, 64
Scandinavian Evangelical Lutheran Church, 173
Schley, George, 65, 188
Schlitz Brewing Company, 114, 148, 150
Schlitz Palm Garden, 73
Schlitz Park, 114, 147
the Observation Tower, 114
Schmidtner, Leonard A., 98, 135, 140, 185
Schneider, Emil, House, 37
Schnetzky and Liebert, 106
Schnetzky, H. Paul, 86, 185
Schuchardt, William, 55, 161
Schulte, Victor, 132, 138
"Schwartzburg Station", 157
Scott, Fitzhugh, 189
Scott, Frank, 71
Scott Street,
202 W., 173
1111, 1107, 1105, 1103, W., 61
Second Empire Style, 41
Second Street,
North, 77
1825 N., 36
South, 171, 174, 192
801, S., 175
807-809 S., 79
Second Ward Savings Bank, 85
Seeboth Street, 174
Seventh Street, 114, 128
1209 S., 33
Seventh Ward Park, 112, 118
Seventh Ward School House, 101
Shaver, Joseph Marble Company, 30
Shaw, Richard Norman, 49
Sheep Skin Tannery, 192
Shepard Avenue,
2732 N., 49
2757 N., 188
2924 N., 57
2959 N., 55
Sherman Boulevard, 158, 160
Sherman Park, 126
Sherman's Addition, 152
Shingle Style, example of, 168
Sholes, Christopher, 75
Shooting Park, 114
Sims, Albert G., 54
"Six Points", 184
Sixth Street, 40, 191 and Galena, 39
South, 174
Viaduct, 191
Smith, A. O., Corporation Research Building, 92
Sobieski Street, 186
Solomon Juneau High, 103
South East Side Natatorium, 106
South Menomonee canal, 192
South Park, 121
South Shore Drive,
2550, 61
2582, 177
South Shore Park, 126, 177
South Side, 170-179
below Lincoln Avenue, in 1876, showing Bay View, 177
boundaries of, 172, 173
in 1858, 172
South Side Park, 173
South Tenth Street Natatorium (No. 2361 S.), 106
Sozialer Turnverein Milwaukee, 9
Spanish Colonial Style, 55, 56, 90, 160
Spanish Style, 63, 187
example of, 63
Spring Street, 163, 164, 167
Spring Street Road, 168
Squares, examples of, 111, 112, 174, 178
St. George's Byzantine-Melkite Church, now Syrian Roman Catholic Church, 136
St. Hedwig's Church, 186
St. James Episcopal Church, 133, 168
St. John de Nepomuc Society Rectory, 150
St. John's Cathedral, 112, 132
St. John's Episcopal Church Parsonage, 35
St. Mary's Hospital, 182
St. Mary's Roman Catholic Church, 132
St. Paul Avenue, 169, 192
West, 191
143, 78
St. Paul's Episcopal Church, 117, 185
St. Peter's Evangelical Lutheran Church, 134
St. Stanislaus Catholic Church, 135, 173, 179
Stack house, 54
Stadt Theater, 86
Star Tannery, 182
Starke, Christopher H., — Charles and Matilda Baerwald House, 165
Starkey, Joseph A., House, 177
State Fair Park, 129
State Street, 8, 163, 165, 167, 168
1024 E., 41
West, 5
322 W., 75
333 W., 91, 92
1617 W., 136
1725 W., 48
2824 W., 50
400 W., 164
Steinmeyer Building, 82, 83
Stick Style,
definition of, 46
example of, 47
Stickley, Gustav, 66, 67
Still, Bayrd, 98, 101
Stoelting, Roland, 128
Strack, Otto, 86, 138, 165
"Streamlined Moderne" phase,
example of, 58
Strothman's Grove, 113
Subdivision, 155-156, 158, 160, 167, 169, 173, 178, 183, 188
Suburb, 176, 182
Suburban Garden, plan of a, 70
Suburban Life, 53
Sullivan, Louis, 56, 84, 88, 90
Summit Avenue, 187
Superior Street,
2731 S., 177
2739 S., 132
Swing bridge,
definition of, 108-109
examples of, 108, 109
Syrian Roman Catholic Church, 136
Tabor Kirche der Evangelische Gemeinschaft, 134

Temple Emanu-El, 131
Temple Emanu-El B'ne Jeshurun, 137
"Ten Milk House St Wattsville", 157
Tenth Street, S., 174
Terrace Avenue, 182, 187
2214, 187
Teutonia Avenues, 8, 148 and Atkinson Avenue,
intersection of, 161
and N. Twelfth Street, 155
Tharinger, Charles, 57
Third Street,
and Juneau Street, 6
N. and St. Paul Avenue, 76
N. and Wisconsin Avenue, 73
N. at Juneau Avenue, 5
N. near Burleigh, 150
North, 148, 153, 191
411 N., 104
910 N., 85
1948 N., 37
800 block of S., 174
803 S., 174
813 S., 37, 174
821 S., 174
910 S., 34
3765 S., 58
Thorsen House, 184
Tiffany, 133
Tippecanoe Amusement Hall, 136
Tippecanoe Lake, 136
Tippecanoe Presbyterian Church, 136
Treatise on the Theory and Practice of Landscape Gardening, A 115
Trimborn and Sons Lime, 30
Trinity Evangelical Lutheran Church, 133, 138
Truettner, Walter, 159
Tudor Revival Style, 57
Tudor Style, 90
elements, 189
example of, 126
Tullgren, Herbert W., 63, 92, 161
Tullgren, Martin, & Sons, 90, 91, 92
Uehling and Linde, 5, 83, 152
Uehling, Otto, 64
Uhrig, Franz Joseph, House, 157
Union Architectural Iron Works, 77
Union Depot, 8, 174
Union Station, 112
United States Veterans' Administration Center, 107
University of Wisconsin, 189
University of Wisconsin — Milwaukee, 10, 189
University of Wisconsin — MIlwaukee campus,
boundaries of, 189
Upjohn, Richard, 140
Van Buren Street, 184, 185
and Division Street, 100
1624 N., 42
Van Ryn and DeGelleke, 89, 103
Van Ryn, Henry, 189
Vaux, Calvert, 41, 116
Velguth, Frederick, 138
Venetian Style, 78
Victorian Gothic Style, 35, 47, 98, 167
definition of, 42
details, 134, 139
examples of, 42, 107, 120, 138, 167, 185
Victorian Italianate Style, 40, 43, 44, 105
definition of, 40-41, 78-79
examples of, 40, 41, 70, 165, 185
Victorian Style, 32, 104
Victorian Workers Houses, definition of, 44
Vieau School, 102
Vignola, Giacomo Barozzi, 106
"Villa Uhrig", 157
Villas and Cottages, 41
Vine Street, 325 W., 149
Virginia Street,
100 W., 105
605-609 W., 175
Vliet Street, 8, 148, 158
and 41st Street, 124
west of 35th Street, 163
Vogel's Island, 192
Wadham's Oil Company Filling Stations, 93
Wadsworth, Alexander, 115
Wahl Avenue, 123, 187
Wahl, Christian, 121, 125
Walker, George H., 3, 27, 112, 171, 172, 174
Walker Square, 112
Walker Street,
104 W., 93
928 W., 42
Walker's Point, 3, 5, 13, 34, 37, 105, 109, 147, 171, 172, 173, 174-175, 178, 191
"Addition", 174
boundaries of, 174
Bridge, 109, 172
Walker's Square, 174
Walks and Talks of an American Farmer in England, 116
Walber, Emil, House, 39
Walling, H. F., 163, 172, 181
Walling Map of Milwaukee, 1858, 147
Walnut Street, 148, 158 and Eighth Street, 147
War Memorial and Art Center Building, 123
Ware, William R., 100
Warnimont, 149 W., 58
Washington Avenue, 165, 167
Washington Boulevard, 124, 160
Washington, 5816 W., 67
Washington Park, 121, 124, 125
Washington Park, 121, 124, 125
Washington Park subdivisions, 160
Washington Street, 174
714 W., 45
800 block of W., 175
Water Street, 33, 75
East, Bridge, 109, 139
East, toward Market Square, 111
looking west from, 197
East, 111
North, 182
N. and Pulaski Street, 21
North, Bridge, 109
400-402 N., 76
500 N., 83
1661 N., 182
Water Tower, 123
Water Tower Park, 120, 187
Waterford Avenue, 473 E., 172
Watertown Plank Road, 8, 163, 165, 167, 169
Waterworks Park, 118
Watts Building, 90
Wauwatosa, 157
Wauwatosa Plank Roak, 8, 148, 163
Wauwatosa, Town of, 164
Wauwatosa Township in 1876, 156
Waverly Place, 185 and Juneau Street, 37
Weeks Garden, 173
Weil, 2700 block N., 152
Weiner, H. W., 57
Wells Building, 88, 141
Wells Street Junior High School 102
Wells Street, 46, 164, 165, 167, 168
144 E., 86
West, 189
152 W., 86
3119 W., 168
3130 W., 167
3209 W., 168
3413 W., 168
Welsh Congregational Church, 132
Wentworth Avenue, 2593 S., 177
West and Northwest Sides, 1858, 163
West Milwaukee Car Shops,
Chicago, Milwaukee, and St. Paul Railroad,
169, 195, 196
West North Avenue Natatorium
(No. 1609), 106
West Park, (Washington Park), 121, 122, 124, 125, 126
General Plan, 125
West Side, 163-169
boundaries of, 163
West Side Park, Preliminary
Plan (Washington Park), 124
Western Avenue, 167
(now N. 35th Street) and Lisbon Plank Road
(now Lisbon Avenue), 157
Western Road, 5
Westminster United Presbyterian Church, 130
Wheeler, Gervase, 31
White Fish Bay road, 182
Whitefish Bay, 114
Whitefish Bay Toll Road, 182, 183, 184
Whitefish Bay Railway, 184
Whitnall, Charles B., 128, 129, 147
Whitnall, Frank, House, 147
Whitnall, 4261 S., 34
"Whitnall's Knoll", 147
Whitnall's Study Map for a County Park
System, 129
Wight, Peter B., 86
Wiley, Guy E., 103
Wilhelmsburg or Williamsburg, 148, 150
Williamson, Russell Barr, 56, 57
Windlake Avenue, 178
971, 103
Wisconsin: A Gudie to the Badger State, 111
Wisconsin Avenue, 165, 168, 182
and Milwaukee Street, 131
at N. 27th Street, 93
bridge, 109
East, 83, 184
205 E., 78
233 E., 88
324 E., 88, 141
515 E., 100
526 E., 85
626 E., 90
720 E., 86
West, 163, 164, 167
101 W., 88, 90
152 W., 88
161 W., 88, 90
301 W., 83
814 W., 100
833 W., 133, 168
900 W., 70, 80, 168
935 W., 168
1145 W., 135
1500 block of W., 141
2000 W., 142
2051 W., 163
2133 W., 168
3424 W., 168
Wisconsin Gas Company, 90, 91
Wisconsin Leather Company, 97
Wisconsin Lutheran Synod, 167
Wisconsin State Normal School, 189
Wisconsin State Teachers College, 189
Wisconsin Telephone Buildings, 142
Wojciechowski, Frank, Grocer, 21
Wolf and Davidson's Shipyard, 172
Woodland Court, 187
Woodward, George E., 41
Wootsch's South Park, 114
Wright, Frank Lloyd, 56, 57, 65, 84, 90
Wright Street, 4503 W., 67
Wright's "Map of Milwaukee,
1900", 23
Wyman, Phelps, 161
Yankee Hill, 19, 62, 168, 181
184-185
a portion of, in 1886, 185
boundaries of, 184
Zagel, George and Bro., 63, 65, 66, 90, 95
Zarse, Alfred H., 58
Zeidler Park, 112
Zelickowski, K., store, 81
11th Street,
845 N. 39
1037 S., 133
12th Street,
North, 148, 165, 168
1647 N., 79
South, 174
2567 S., 95

13th Street,
North, 158
1930 N., 158
South, 172, 179
14th Street between State & Prairie
(now Juneau), 114
15th Place, 1329 S., 61
16th Street, 192
824-26 S., 95
2221 S., 36
17th, 853 N., 165
18th Street, 102
and Mineral, 112
2256 S., 179
19th Street,
1305 N., 68
1917 N., 155
1244-46 S., 65
21st Street,
1220-22 N., 65
1916 N., 68
22nd Street, 735 S., 57
23rd Street, 922 S., 51
24th Place, 1242-44 N., 65
24th Street, N., 165
26th Street, 169
27th Street, 164, 191, 192
North, 167, 168
3533 N., 92
South, 173
South and W. National Avenue, 70
28th Street,
2021 N., 23
2065-67 N., 158
1646 S., 45
29th, N., 168
30th, N., 169, 192
2901 N., 105
31st Street,
North, 155, 158
936 N., 168
32nd Street, South, 173
33rd Street,
North, 168, 169
1030 S., 45
34th Street,
North, 168
1727 N., 157
35th Street,
North, 158, 164, 167, 169
2501 N., 94
South, 173, 178
Viaduct, 196
37th Street,
2442 N., 55
South, 173
39th Street, 169
North, 169
40th Street, 2813-15 N., 67
41st Street, North, 126
44th Street, North, 169
46th Street,
2357 N., 159
2922 N., 66
47th Street, 160
51st Street, 160
1929 N., 67
55th Street, 3840 N., 58
60th Street, 160
107th Street, 6814 N., 132